JUST MEMORIES

SERIES ON TRANSITIONAL JUSTICE

The Series on *Transitional Justice* offers a platform for high-quality research within the rapidly growing field of transitional justice. The research is, of necessity inter-disciplinary in nature, drawing from disciplines such as law, political science, history, sociology, criminology, anthropology and psychology, as well as from various specialised fields of study such as human rights, victimology and peace studies. Furthermore, the research is international in outlook, drawing on the knowledge and experience of academics and other specialists in many different regions of the world.

The series is aimed at a variety of audiences who are either working or interested in fields such as crime and justice; human rights; humanitarian law and human security; conflict resolution and peace building. These audiences include academics, researchers, students, policy makers, practitioners, non-governmental organisations and the media.

All books published within the series are subject to a double-blind peer review by recognised authorities in the field.

Published titles within this Series:

10. Bas van Stokkom, Neelke Doorn and Paul van Tongeren (eds.), *Public Forgiveness in Post-Conflict Contexts* (2012), 978-1-78068-044-6
11. Ilse Derluyn, Cindy Mels, Stephan Parmentier and Wouter Vandenhole (eds.), *Re-Member. Rehabilitation, Reintegration and Reconciliation of War-Affected Children* (2012), 97894-000-0027-4
12. Anne-Marie de Brouwer, Charlotte Ku, Renée Römkens and Larissa van den Herik (eds.), *Sexual Violence as an International Crime: Interdisciplinary Approaches* (2012), 978-1-78068-002-6
13. Estelle Zinsstag and Martha Albertson Fineman (eds.), *Feminist Perspectives on Transitional Justice: From International and Criminal to Alternative Forms of Justice* (2013), 978-1-78068-142-9
14. Josep M. Tamarit Sumalla, *Historical Memory and Criminal Justice in Spain. A Case of Late Transitional Justice* (2013), 978-1-78068-143-6
15. Catherine Jenkins (ed.), Max du Plessis (ed.), *Law, Nation building and Transformation The South African experience in perspective* (2014), 978-1-78068-184-9
16. Susanne Buckley-Zistel and Stefanie Schäfer (eds.), *Memorials in Times of Transition* (2014), 978-1-78068-211-2
17. Nico Wouters (ed.), *Transitional Justice and Memory in Europe (1945–2013), 978-1-78068-214-3*
18. Agata Fijalkowski and Raluca Grosescu (eds.), *Transitional Criminal Justice in Post-Dictatorial and Post-Conflict Societies*, 978-1-78068-260-0
19. S. Elizabeth Bird and Fraser M. Ottanelli (eds.), *The Performance of Memory as Transitional Justice* 978-1-78068-262-4
20. Bo Viktor Nylund, *Child Soldiers and Transitional Justice*, 978-1-78068-394-2
21. Peter Malcontent (ed.), *Facing the Past: Amending Historical Injustices through Instruments of Transitional Justice*, 978-1-78068-403-1
22. Francesca Capone, *Reparations for Child Victims of Armed Conflict: State of the Field and Current Challenges*, 978-1-78068-438-3
23. Cheryl S. White, *Bridging Divides in Transitional Justice: The Extraordinary Chambers in the Courts of Cambodia*, 978-1-78068-440-6
24. Jeremy Sarkin (ed.), *The Global Impact and Legacy of Truth Commissions*, 978-1-78068-794-0

For previous volumes in the series, please visit http://tj.intersentia.com

SERIES ON TRANSITIONAL JUSTICE, Volume 25

JUST MEMORIES

Remembrance and Restoration in the Aftermath of Political Violence

Edited by

Camila de Gamboa Tapias
Bert van Roermund

INTERSENTIA
Cambridge – Antwerp – Chicago

Intersentia Ltd
8 Wellington Mews
Wellington Street | Cambridge
CB1 1HW | United Kingdom
Tel: +44 1223 736 170
Email: mail@intersentia.co.uk
www.intersentia.com | www.intersentia.co.uk

Distribution for the UK and
Rest of the World (incl. Eastern Europe)
NBN International
1 Deltic Avenue, Rooksley
Milton Keynes MK13 8LD
United Kingdom
Tel: +44 1752 202 301 | Fax: +44 1752 202 331
Email: orders@nbninternational.com

Distribution for Europe
Intersentia Publishing nv
Groenstraat 31
2640 Mortsel
Belgium
Tel: +32 3 680 15 50
Email: mail@intersentia.be

Distribution for the USA and Canada
Independent Publishers Group
Order Department
814 North Franklin Street
Chicago, IL 60610
USA
Tel: +1 800 888 4741 (toll free) | Fax: +1 312 337 5985
Email: orders@ipgbook.com

Just Memories. Remembrance and Restoration in the Aftermath of Political Violence

Artwork on cover: Author Jan Jordaan, title 'Hurt', medium Linocut, 1999. From the Universal Declaration of Human Rights – International Print Portfolio, Article 5, published by Art for Humanity, South Africa, 1999.

ISBN 978-1-78068-908-1
D/2020/7849/59
NUR 828

GPRC
Guaranteed
Peer Reviewed
Content

British Library Cataloguing in Publication Data. A catalogue record for this book is available from the British Library.

ACKNOWLEDGEMENTS

This volume originates from a seminar of the same name convened by the editors at Tilburg University Law School in March 2014. The financial and organizational support, in particular from the Department of European and International Public Law and its staff, is gratefully acknowledged. Special thanks go to Michael C. Leach for copy-editing the various chapters of the present volume.

The editors would also like to thank SAGE Publications for their permission to republish Stewart Motha's text with minor changes, and Taylor & Francis Group for their permission to publish a rewritten text by Eldad Ben Aharon.

Camila de Gamboa Tapias and
Bert van Roermund
June 2020

CONTENTS

PART III. RESTORING LAND

PART IV. RESTORING LAW

LIST OF CONTRIBUTORS

Beira Aguilar Rubiano is an assistant professor at the Escuela de Ciencias Humanas, Universidad del Rosario, Bogotá, Colombia.

Eldad Ben Aharon is a university lecturer at the Leiden University Institute for Area Studies; the Netherlands; he obtained his PhD at the Holocaust Research Institute, Department of History, Royal Holloway, University of London, United Kingdom.

Lina M. Céspedes Báez is a titular professor at the Facultad de Jurisprudencia, Universidad del Rosario, Bogotá, Colombia.

Camila de Gamboa Tapias is an associate professor at the Centro de Estudios sobre Paz y Conflictos, Universidad del Rosario, Bogotá, Colombia.

Antonio Gómez Ramos is an associate professor of philosophy at the University Carlos III, Madrid, Spain.

Wilson Herrera Romero is an associate professor at the Escuela Ciencias Humanas and director of the Center for Teaching Ethics and Citizenship – Phronimos, Universidad del Rosario, Bogotá, Colombia.

Fatma Kassem holds a PhD from the Department of Behavioral Sciences at Ben-Gurion University of the Negev in Beer Sheva, Israel.

Anél Marais is a lecturer at the School of Law and Criminology of Aberystwyth University, Wales, United Kingdom.

Stewart Motha is professor of law at Birkbeck School of Law, University of London, United Kingdom.

Felix Mukwiza Ndahinda is the director of Research, Policy and Higher Education (RPHE) at the Aegis Trust; an honorary associate professor at the University of Rwanda Law School; and a research fellow at Tilburg University, the Netherlands.

Juan Francisco Soto Hoyos is a professor at the Facultad de Jurisprudencia, Universidad del Rosario, Bogotá, Colombia, and a consultant at the Comisión Colombiana de Juristas.

Carlos Thiebaut is a professor of philosophy, focusing on contemporary moral and political philosophy in particular, at Universidad Carlos III, Madrid, Spain.

Bert van Roermund is professor of philosophy (em) in the Department of Public Law and Governance at Tilburg Law School, the Netherlands.

CHAPTER 1
INTRODUCTION

Camila de Gamboa Tapias and Bert van Roermund

In the aftermath of the Second World War, with memories of the Holocaust growing to horrifying dimensions, a new humanitarian consciousness began to emerge that was grounded in the discourse of human rights. At the same moment in time, a new field of what is now called "transitional justice" began to develop. Transitional justice is the contemporary term used to refer to tools that societies adopt to bring about the rule of law following massive and systematic criminality, perpetrated by oppressive regimes.[1] Deploying such tools is a complex task involving the design of various mechanisms, such as: criminal investigations and trials, procedural frameworks for seeking out the truth, official and social acknowledgments of what occurred in the past, reparation measures, and institutional reforms. More often than not such mechanisms have to be introduced under irregular and even chaotic conditions, at moments when private actors, both inside and outside the country, exploit opportunities to acquire power and property. Even establishing the most basic of legal infrastructure, like reliable real estate registries, fair tax systems, or systems to monitor and sanction public procurement, frequently meet with

1 The Secretary General of the United Nations defined transitional justice as "the full range of processes and mechanisms associated with a society's attempts to come to terms with a legacy of large-scale past abuses, in order to ensure accountability, serve justice and achieve reconciliation. These may include both judicial and non-judicial mechanisms, with differing levels of international involvement (or none at all), and individual prosecutions, reparations, truth-seeking, institutional reform, vetting and dismissals, or a combination thereof". United Nations (2004) 4.

obstruction and sabotage by such actors. As such, establishing the rule of law and curbing corruption often have to go hand in hand. Unsurprisingly, this is easier said than done. To curb corruption effectively, one has to deploy a robust set of policies that do not always sit happily with the demands of political self-restraint that are enshrined in rule of law principles. At the same time, however, one cannot afford to curb them and diminish their effectiveness, as this will surely frustrate rule of law principles they are trying to establish.

Under such conditions, it is far from obvious how transitional justice can be conceived as being "restorative" justice. What is clear, however, is that doing so speaks to a broad spectrum of ideas, some practical and others reflective.

1. At the practical end, one can design relatively simple instruments, like the application forms issued by the International Center for Transitional Justice that are used for identifying, verifying, and registering people who are entitled to reparations.[2] These forms are designed based on best practices research, and are crucial for providing "adequate, effective and prompt reparation for harm suffered", as articulated in the 2005 UN Basic Guidelines on the Right to a Remedy and Reparations for Victims of Gross Violations of Human Rights and Serious Violations of Humanitarian Law.[3] By alleviating the administrative burden of victims seeking access to reparations, their significance goes far beyond their instrumental usefulness. They are part and parcel of processes that acknowledge the dignity of those who have suffered from oppressive violence in the past.
2. In the middle range one can find standard transitional justice mechanisms that are amply argued for in the public proposals and policies of the designers of transition. In any given context, the designers of transition can include the state itself and its institutions and bureaucracy, as well as victims' organizations, academics, NGOs and international organizations, among others. Such institutions include, for instance: accountability mechanisms aimed at reducing impunity; national, international and mixed models of judicial and non-judicial decision-making in post-conflict justice; and various strategies of peacekeeping and policing.[4] In a broad sense, all these measures are restorative since they share the overall aim to respond comprehensively to an unjust past.
3. At the other end of the spectrum, one finds ideas that prompt deeper reflection, such as reconciliation, forgiveness, remembrance, restitution and the rule of law. Such concepts go beyond the specific, multifarious

2 Caranza, Correa et al. (2017).

3 UN General Assembly, Basic Principles on Reparation.

4 A far from outdated overview offers Bassiouni (2002).

> and diverging features of past conflicts and present political constellations, even though they are inspired by specific case studies. It is at this latter end of the spectrum that this volume should be positioned as a philosophical contribution to the realm of transitional justice studies, informed by empirical observations in various countries (Israel, South Africa, Rwanda, Colombia, among others), written by authors who are personally and intensely acquainted with the difficulties of overcoming violent conflict.

While concepts like these are often called "abstract", this does not necessarily make them vague, let alone irrelevant. In political thought, no less than in, for instance, mathematics or physics, abstractness comes with pertinence, pervasiveness and precision. Abstraction allows us to see structure rather than mass, to discern the core from the fringe, and to compare and choose on the basis of reason. However, these concepts are also problematic in how they oscillate between different meanings and perspectives. In other words, the trouble with these concepts is that they are not only abstract, but they are also ambiguous in the sense of "essentially contested" by the very agents who put them at work. One example that will be explored in greater depth later is the concept of "restorative justice". One state-of-the-art handbook on restorative justice[5] distinguishes three different conceptualizations of the term:

(a) as an encounter concept that refers "to programmes that bring affected parties together to agree on how to respond to crime";
(b) as a reparative concept that refers "to a theory of reparation and prevention that would influence all criminal justice";
(c) as a transformative concept that refers to "a belief that the preferred response to all conflict – indeed to all life – is peace building through dialogue and agreement of the parties".

Useful as these distinctions may be in their own right, they are also illustrative of the problem at hand. For instance, the procedural features of (a) do not warrant the material outcomes pursued under (b). The primarily moral belief of (c) seems to ignore that the "affected parties" of (a) often are, or were, parties in civil conflict if not war. Furthermore, the reparative intentions pursued under (b) cannot possibly aim to restore a distribution of rights at the root of a conflict in the first place, since reparation (b) often requires transformation (c). In short, these conceptions are distinct and are not easily joined in pursuit of the same ends. If they are proposed as "mechanisms" of transitional justice,

---

5 Johnstone and Van Ness (2007) 636.

i.e., as instruments to achieve transitional justice goals, one risks fostering new antagonisms while trying to overcome the old. A deeper understanding of such concepts, therefore, is needed.[6] Indeed, there is a demand for greater philosophical inquiry in transitional justice studies, and this volume aims to respond to this need by exploring the role that memory plays in restoring the rule of law in transitional contexts.

The first thing this Introduction should do, therefore, is offer a conceptual framework to structure this co-authored endeavour. This framework was not imposed on the contributors *ex ante*, and we do not expect them to subscribe to it *ex post*. Rather, challenging and exploring the framework from different angles was the very point of this project. This framework is also helpful for mapping out in advance how to best understand the relationship between the individual chapters. This is what we will do in the remainder of this Introduction. First, we will relate the notion of memory to the general conceptual matrix of restorative justice and transitional justice. This will usher in some working definitions against the backdrop of some contemporary discussions in the field. We then point out some important lines of convergence between the chapters, not only within but also across the four Parts of the volume. Ultimately, it will become clear how philosophical contemplations are dependent on topical and empirical research, and vice versa.

1. TRANSITIONAL JUSTICE, RESTORATIVE JUSTICE AND MEMORY: A CONCEPTUAL FRAMEWORK

We already pointed to the understanding of "transitional justice" that is at the core of this book, with its focus on legal orders in transition from pasts wrought by oppressive violence to futures under the rule of law. Unpacking this definition, though, requires a number qualifications and caveats. The first and perhaps simplest is that "justice" here does not mean some moral virtue, ideal or obligation, but rather a positive legal order. This is a matter of idiom, certainly, and other languages use different wording to distinguish between them. However, English phrases like "access to justice", "obstruction of justice" or "the administration of justice" importantly speak to the law of a country rather than the world view of a particular group. By implication, what such language regards as being in transition from the rule of violence to the rule of law is a legal order. Law is not solely the *terminus ad quem*, the goal which a political process of transition has to arrive at. It can also be part and

6 Johnstone and Van Ness's handbook abundantly provides this deeper understanding. In their own contribution to the handbook they offer an incisive explanation of why restorative justice as a concept is so "profoundly contested". Johnstone and Van Ness (2007): 6ff.

parcel of the *terminus a quo*, i.e., also part of past systematic oppression and the violence that undergirded it. Thus, notwithstanding regime change, in the eyes of those with memories of suffering from oppression, the legal order in transition can be as suspect as its new administrators. A transitional legal order, therefore, has to regain trust while simultaneously dealing with the past and building the future of a particular society. While doing so, as a legal order it cannot abstain from what is characteristic of law in the first place: it is imposed coercively, if need be by applying violence. It must reconcile its transformative goals with the claim that in specific circumstances, under conditions specified beforehand, violent coercion is permitted or obligated under norms that are publicly set and found valid. Whatever substance is given to the rule of law, it is supposed to be the touchstone of such public procedures; yet, given the definition of transitional justice, the situations it refers to are those where this touchstone is yet to be achieved. Thus, the question arises how a legal order that is transitioning to the rule of law can legitimately impose itself, with binding force, while its authority is still suspect due to widespread memories of its violent past? This dilemma, we think, is the key problem of transitional justice.

Given this dilemma, we concur with those who advocate greater precision in how we articulate the relationship between transitional justice and restorative justice.[7] The conceptual pedigree of restorative justice is, after all, quite different from that of transitional justice. From a philosophical point of view, which is admittedly as limited as any other point of view, "restorative justice" is merely the contemporary version of what has been traditionally known as "commutative justice", in a long-standing Aristotelian tradition to be distinguished from "distributive justice". Rather than justice as distributed in equal parts among equal agents, commutative justice is a matter of equal payment. It responds to agents in ways that are considered "equal" to the value of their actions. Thus, in the name of commutative justice we require prices for deliveries, salaries for a month of labour, protections for who obey authority, or penalties for crimes. Although it is only in the latter type of cases that we use the predicate "retributive" justice, all commutative justice is fundamentally re-tributive rather than dis-tributive. However, we should refrain from scholastic discussion at this point and simply note instead that restorative justice proposes responding to crime with more than just penalties imposed by public authorities representing the citizens. Restorative justice should also encourage criminals to "pay back" in other ways than just serving their sentences. It should also look to the involvement of victims in the trials, both in procedure and in sentencing,[8] as well as to the re-integration of convicts back into their societies notwithstanding

---

7 For solid argumentation see e.g., Clamp and Doak (2012); Clamp (2016).

8 See Duff, Farmer et al. (2004), the other volumes under the catching title *The Trial on Trial*, and H. Zehr (2015).

their obligation to make amends. Where possible, it should even seek to restore a viable social relationship between victims and perpetrators in order to bring closure to the past. All of these proposals aim to effectively redress "real" harms done to victims and to society at large, rather just than retributing the evil of past crimes by running a criminal law "if – then" algorithm.

The stakes of restorative justice are usually set "against the backdrop of advanced democratic societies and focused at criminal justice processes."[9] In other words, restorative justice initiatives are typically imagined with a full-blown rule of law regime in the background, something that is largely absent from transitional settings by the very definition of transitional justice proposed above. Coming from a situation of violent conflict, oppression, and resistance, with allegations of human rights violations from both sides of a conflict, advocates of restorative justice face a number of huge difficulties. Summarising a host of literature we point to the following as the most prominent:

- How to distinguish between who is victim and who is perpetrator? In many situations people are both, in different respects.
- What to do with perpetrators who were juveniles at the time of the conflict?[10] They cannot be held to account.
- What does re-integration mean in situations where a community is torn apart? The community should be broader than family and friends, but its boundaries are vague.
- What to do when a transitional state does not or cannot hold a monopoly on violence? Restoration by war lords seems to be self-contradictory.
- What to do with unspeakable harms for which reparation or compensation are not possible, or where repairing harms would simply recreate the injustices at the root of the conflict?
- Should perpetrators be excused if their past acts were done in accordance with valid state law? Law does not have to be morally "good" law in order to count as law.

One approach to coping with these and other challenges is the TARR-model proposed by Parmentier[11] and others,[12] which focuses on four issues that should be addressed by restorative justice initiatives in post-conflict settings: Truth, Accountability, Reparation and Reconciliation. Although it is explicitly presented as an *heuristic* model, it prompts investigation into how these four issues are intertwined and interdependent. In this way, it is not only a felicitous

9 Clamp and Doak (2012) 345.
10 A problem Ann Skelton has tirelessly pointed to. See e.g. Skelton (2015).
11 Parmentier (2003).
12 Parmentier, Vanspauwen et al. (2008); Parmentier, Aciru et al. (2017).

but also a pervasive device. It entails, for instance, that the order between the issues is not sequential, with truth coming first and reconciliation last with remorse, amendment and forgiveness somewhere in between.[13] In some cases before community courts victims point already to the possibility of forgiving and being forgiven before any facts are reported, as if this is a necessary ground for truth to be revealed. By doing so, they imply that they trust the addressees, their former oppressors as people one could imagine living with (again). Indeed, what else is reconciliation after political oppression than a mutual commitment to the joint labour of creating and sustaining "life opportunities", as one of the contributors to this volume aptly calls it?[14] Building trust and truth-telling are parallel, but interdependent courses of action. Similar two-way streets run between accountability and reparation. It is all well and good to hold perpetrators to account before the law, but in order for legal authority to really *hold* offenders to account, it first has to develop a firm grip so that they can be *brought* to justice (as the law is supposed to do) and reparations can be (seen to be) done. Whatever form that restitution may take is largely a matter of political priority. Prominent among them, however, are forms of restitution that deal with land. The reason for their importance is as simple as it is basic: no life opportunities are often possible without land, and in most transitional justice settings, it is the restitution of land as a redistributive goal often turns out to be the most difficult part of the transitional process. It is at the core of the Israel–Palestine conflict; it has greatly frustrated reconciliation in South Africa; it was the hardest nut to crack in the Colombian peace negotiations; and it is a central and fascinating aspect of governmental policy in Rwanda. One should not, however, forget or underestimate what the land issue stands for. It is more than just a dream of a lost land, let alone a preoccupation with rural concerns. Given issues of land and water scarcity around the world today, one should bear in mind that water is the essence of life; that minerals are crucial for technology; that even things like computer servers have to be put *somewhere*; and that "the environment", for many, is just another word for land. "Land", understood in this way, is the metonymy of life opportunities, a part that stands for the whole, and is deeply interdependent with law.

In this volume the contributors use the heuristic potential of the TARR-model to focus on the poles of two interdependent relationships: one between *truth* (as the hallmark of all narratives of suffering) and *trust* (covering the core of reconciliation and forgiveness); the other between *law* (as the main institution of accountability) and *land* (as the paradigm of human life opportunities). This is

13 This sequential ordering used to be advertised on the website of the International Center for Transitional Justice, but it was withdrawn. It may well be rooted in traditional Christian orthodoxy around the sacrament of confession.

14 See Céspedes-Báez's Chapter 9 in this volume.

why there are four Parts in this volume, each related to restorative justice by the keywords: Trust, Truth, Land and Law. They are scrutinised from one angle running through all chapters: the angle of *memory*. We submit that each of these four issues correlates to a specific mode of remembering, which may be briefly characterised in the following way:

1. Restoring trust engages memory in the sense of *retrospection and regeneration*. It aims to bring new life to social relationships through a shared commitment to look back on past experiences as a history of suffering. Although it is far from guaranteed that this will achieve forgiveness and reconciliation, getting perpetrators and victims to jointly look back notwithstanding accountability procedures is in itself a mode of reconciliation.
2. Restoring truth deploys memory as the exercise of narrating this history of the past and recalls the past through procedures of *retrieval and recollection*. Here memory strikes at least two overtones: on the one hand, improving the span and power of a society's memory; on the other, to apply sincere and concentrated thought to the facts. Both converge on the assumption that the facts of the past will remain "worth telling" if the narrative will ultimately steer away from a myriad of singular stories as well as from sacrosanct collective versions of the past. Re-collection is an iterative process. It seeks to gather facts together *again*.
3. Restoring land in the sense of life opportunities calls on memory as *reclamation* and *reform*. Memory in general has a ring of reclaiming the past by recalling salient bits of the past to the present, mostly for the sake of the future. With regard to land, reclaiming in this sense pertains both to a reform of the evil and erroneous practices that dominated the distribution of life resources in the past, and to the demand of sustainable cultivation of life resources in the future.
4. Finally, the restoration of law interrogates memory in the mode of *retention and revision*. Law retains and stores best practices of social ordering probed in the past so that they can be re-applied in the future. In this sense, the binary of "law in action" versus "law in the books", celebrated by legal realism, is a false one, since law in the books is law in action retained. Moreover, and in the technical sense of retention, a legal order should retain the capacity to engage the services of public authority in case the redistribution of life opportunities is thwarted. However, such power should be subject to fair trial requirements, a ban on corruption, the abolition of privileges, etc.

Under these four captions, therefore, this volume presents an inquiry into the restorative aspects of memory.

2. JUSTICE, REMEMBRANCE AND A POLITICS OF CLOSURE

The overall structure of the book that emerges from its composite chapters did not necessarily frame the ways in which their authors thematised their topics, nor did it prescribe the vocabulary they should use. It is worthwhile, therefore, to trace a few salient lines between the specific topics they address and the questions they discuss. This will allow the interdependencies of the four issues presented above to be shown. In doing so this Introduction will criss-cross the whole of the volume, referring summaries of the various chapters to their respective introductions.

One such salient line is that of remembrance as closure. The reason why transitional justice *qua* process should be entrusted with an incremental awareness of the rule of law (some may say: why *any* practice of justice should be trusted with such awareness) is that it presupposes not only the denunciation of violence as a matter of principle, but also the closure of violence as an individual and collective experience. Arguably, closure is an important parameter for the restoration of trust and is a precondition for all truth-telling and holding to account. No restorative policy can be proposed, therefore, let alone be implemented, without some previously articulated stance of former victims that reflects their basic attitude towards their own suffering in the past and transforms it into a critical one. Thiebaut and Gómez Ramos, writing on "difficult forgiveness" (in Chapters 3 and 4 respectively), find a common philosophical take on restoration and closure in Ricoeur's seminal work on memory, history and oblivion.[15] Acknowledging throughout that, in most cases, a stance on the possibility of forgiveness will take on different forms over time, it should be noted that these gradual changes will deeply affect the *terminus ad quem* of transitional justice, i.e., the idea of the rule of law. Chapter 2 by De Gamboa Tapias and Herrera on critical remembrance explores the possibility of becoming and remaining critical towards one's individual and collective memory of suffering.

The factual character of closure does not reduce it to a matter of mere (social) psychology. There are philosophical questions to be asked here, and the editors of this volume have chosen to put them up front. Among the most vexing are those about reconciling former victims and perpetrators. While most readers will be familiar with reconciliation's ambiguous relationship to truth-telling, since the truth can simultaneously be a requirement as well as an impediment for reconciliation, relatively few will see reconciliation as not being necessarily tantamount to forgiveness. Carving out the concept of "civic" reconciliation in

15 Ricoeur (2000), translated into English as Ricoeur (2004).

contrast to forgiveness on the one hand, and retributive justice on the other, Thiebaut (in Chapter 3) points to the importance of a third "voice" – that of the moral community – as striking some sort of balance between them. Closely related to this line of argument is the question posed by Gómez Ramos (in Chapter 4) about how a model of political (or in Thiebaut's terms "civic") reconciliation can (or cannot) accommodate closure over and against deliberate resentment, such as in the case of Jean Améry's determined attitude towards his experience of the Nazi concentration camps. Resentment amounts to the refusal of reconciliation and, *a fortiori*, forgiveness, and should not be reduced to the mere incapability to forgive or to reconcile. The dissociation of a resentful individual from the temporal mechanisms of the polity that is always working towards its continuity marks a moment of "counter-closure", that acquires a certain positive moral quality in itself as a stubborn fidelity to the truth of the suffering experienced. As Gómez Ramos says, it casts doubt upon the exemplary use of memory for future purposes, laudable as they may be in their own right, and possibly also on the very idea of a politics of memory.[16]

At least these two dimensions, the principled denunciation of violence for the future and the wholehearted closure of violence from the past, are captured in the nuclear phrase "never again" that is the focus of Van Roermund's Chapter 5. Inspired once more by Ricoeur, as in the case of Thiebaut's and Gómez Ramos' contributions, "never again" expresses the hope for a future that will leave the past behind as if it did not happen *and* will remember it forever precisely because it should not return. The two processes are linked but distinct. While the practice of principle may be regarded, ultimately, as a normative issue, the practice of closure is first and foremost a factual matter that develops over time. Victims are different in how they come to terms with their pasts, and groups are often heterogeneous, with each going through various, often unpredictable stages of grief and reconciliation at different times. Just as it makes little sense to propose general rules for mourning lost love, it makes little sense to establish rules for coping with violent past oppression.

3. JUST MEMORIES AND A POLITICS OF DISCLOSURE

A second salient line is the political character of memory borne out by the express ambivalence of the title of this section. In what account of memory can memories of past human rights violations become and remain more than

16 This is why Nalani Malani's painting *All We Imagine as Light* (2017) uses the lines of the poet Agha Shahid Ali: "My memory keeps getting in the way of your history". Malani had to flee war-torn Kashmir as a child.

"just memories", i.e., retrievals of information stored in the seemingly neutral warehouses of an archive, a library, a museum? Marais (in Chapter 6) elaborates on this question, arguing that "the archive", as a proxy for a politics of memory, can never be sealed in the sense of coming to definite closure. It has to be re-opened again and again as an enduring legacy that challenges new political agendas and alliances by incessant efforts to return to the dramatic events of the past. How do societies bear such memories in mind so that they become, and remain, dignifying of those who suffered and restorative for those who survived? How do memories become and remain part and parcel of restorative justice, as *just* memories in the sense of memories that enable former victims and former perpetrators, as well as new citizens and new authorities to be a part of a society in which justice inspires the transition to the rule of law? These are not simple questions by any standard. Some will be quick to point out that an archive, a library, a museum – or even, for that matter, a calendar, a list of deceased persons, a war cemetery, a necropolis – are all far from being neutral containers of information. On the contrary, by defining entries, selecting names and dates, and allowing cross-references, each tells a story and arranges information in such a way that the story becomes worth telling. It is precisely because any such story should be "worth" telling, that narrative arrangements are rooted in values that are somehow shared by the story-tellers and their audiences.

However, such values do not amount to an "*acquis communautaire*" based on lived experiences alone. They are also contingent on a language that is supposedly shared. This presupposition is frequently a "pre-" supposition in the temporal sense, meaning that it comes too early or that it is pre-mature. Even those pieces of language that we call "proper names" are often "proper" only to some participants in the process of memory and not to others. Take, for example, the name "South Africa". From what northern vantage point is it "south"? Or, more intriguingly, by what right has the name "Africa" spread from the coasts of the Mediterranean Sea all the way to the "Cape of Good Hope"? Whose hopes are remembered through the daily use of that name? By what colonial might would several contributors to this volume feel necessitated to call themselves Colombians after Christopher Columbus? All such names are "baptismal" names, as one African philosopher[17] aptly called them; i.e., names given at ritual occasions by virtue of a performative act,[18] and backed up by a specific arrangement of power(s) beyond the reach of those who

---

17 See Mogobe Ramose, for instance, in his incisive conversation with Boaventura de Sousa Santos in Part 1 of the latter's *Conversations of the World*, held on 5 March 2014 at Freedom Park in Pretoria, South Africa. See https://www.youtube.com/watch?-v=UEDNoZg3G4Y.

18 Note that the original definition of 'performative language' Austin (1946 [1970]) contained reference to the ritual character of the occasion.

are "baptised".[19] If restorative justice does not return to the question of by what name the subjects of this baptismal language would call, or would have called, themselves – if it does not inquire into the way in which they would understand, or would have understood, their world as "their own" – one has reason to ask how it can pretend to be "restorative" and why it can pose as "doing justice". The chapter by Stewart Motha (Chapter 7) presents an in-depth discussion of this topic, confronting Antjie Krog's *Begging to Be Black* (2009) with the radical position taken by Mogobe Ramose. Both provide us with tools to grapple with the relationship between past, present and future, tools derived, on the one hand, from epistemology ("how to know what it means to be black?"), and, on the other hand, from ontology ("what are the conditions for becoming if one is black?"). But there are important differences between the two thinkers, succinctly described by Motha as the difference between anti-colonial longing (Ramose's project) and postcolonial becoming (Krog's project).

If this matter of proper names already affects the sense in which memories may be called "just" or not, then how much more would this be the case with regard to the grand ideas that purport to mark "the way forward" for societies coping with the remembrance of violent and ruthless oppression? Take, for instance, the idea of "the rule of law" that is so prominent in the very definition of transitional justice, including its restorative overtones. How can we be certain that it conveys a specific direction, or a sense of direction at least, that would guide people to leave the past behind and head towards a future that deserves to be called "just"? The phrase "rule of law" suggests a normative threshold calibrated against social values that try to define a common wealth. It promises, indeed it imposes, a practice of measuring, determining whether this threshold has been fully, partially, or not met at all somewhere. The suggestion goes even one step further, namely that this phrase is little more than an English idiom that is equivalent to other idioms that capture or refer to the same meaning. This is not to suggest that there is a common concept that is expressed in these various idioms. Rather, the variety of idioms is accompanied by a conceptual variety that is not easily accommodated and replete with incompatibilities. Even within Western Europe, lawyers from different legal cultures find it almost impossible to reconcile the anchor points of, for instance, the French idea of *légalité*, the

[19] Critically, this emerged even as early as Rousseau: "When Nuñez Balboa, standing on the sea-shore, took possession of the South Seas and the whole of South America in the name of the crown of Castille, was that enough to dispossess all their actual inhabitants, and to shut out from them all the princes of the world? On such a showing, these ceremonies are idly multiplied, and the Catholic King need only take possession all at once, from his apartment, of the whole universe, merely making a subsequent reservation about what was already in the possession of other princes." Rousseau (1762 [1964]), as translated by G.D.H. Dole in the edition of the *Social Contract* in the Everyman's Library (1920).

German touchstone of *Rechtsstaatlichkeit*, and the English "rule of law". The idea that morality pervades the tiniest capillaries of the legal order, so crucial to the German concept, is not only absent from the French emphasis on the autonomous doctrinal logic of the legal order, it is also a persistent critique of the latter. Similarly, the "value-driven" judicial decision-making (*Wertjudikatur*) that is inherent to the former is clearly at odds with the idea of legal certainty that is central to the common law conception of the rule of law, to wit, that legal norms should be predictable by virtue of their being enacted by "the King in Parliament". If there is already such a deep dissent on the *terminus ad quem* of transitional justice among neighbouring legal cultures in a small part of the globe (Western Europe), then what should one expect when this phrase is imposed as a peremptory norm for the administration of justice in other and bigger parts?

Similar issues may be raised with regard to the specifically restorative character of transitional justice. Chapter 11 by Soto Hoyos amply illustrates the complexity of the very idea of the rule of law in transitional contexts, in particular the question of if (and when) it should undergird judicial decision-making. He argues that under transitional conditions a teleological interpretation of the law is inescapable in light of human rights and in spite of the obvious risks that this entails, namely the exposure of a still vulnerable legal order to political pressure and the undermining of values that are inherent to the rule of law. Soto Hoyos translates this teleology into the consequential model of legal reasoning of the late Neil MacCormick. He puts the model to the test with Colombia's Land Restitution Process, and thereby also to the approaches chosen by Céspedes-Báez (in Chapter 9) and Aguilar (in Chapter 8).

Arguably, "restorative justice", as part and parcel of a transition from oppressive violence to the rule of law, received legislative recognition with the Promotion of National Unity and Reconciliation Act 34 of 1995 in South Africa, which, in turn, followed up on the epilogue of the "National Unity and Reconciliation" Interim Constitution of 1993. The legislation that established the Truth and Reconciliation Commission in South Africa considered – among other things, like keeping the nation together and granting amnesty for certain forms of violent political action – "the taking of measures aimed at the granting of *reparation* to, and the *rehabilitation* and the *restoration* of the human and civil dignity of, victims of violations of human rights (emphasis added)." Such wording clearly indicates that restorative justice was regarded as going beyond the "mere" reparation of loss and harm (caused by "political actions"), and that, first and foremost, it has to do with treating people as human beings worthy of respect and protection, and recognising their voices as those of full-blooded citizens in pursuit of common freedom and well-being.

The prefix "re-" in words such as reparation, rehabilitation and restoration suggests an orientation to the past; a time when powers and possessions were distributed in accordance with more acceptable principles. However, more often than not, these suggestions can be understood only if the "past" is taken to mean, paradoxically, "a time to look forward to", i.e., a promising future. A future can only be promising in a certain polity if there are robust guarantees in the present that a normative core of human well-being will be preserved. Casting this hope for the future in the mould of a *promise* is a figure of speech that deploys a necessary conceptual logic imposed by political agents the moment such promise is made. Retrojecting into the past is a matter of obeying a logic of promising rather than of deriving a blueprint for a just society from history. Ndahinda's (Chapter 12) contribution on the Rwandan government's efforts to cope with the 1994 genocide on the Tutsis by reaching beyond criminal law is an impressive illustration of how "practised principles" of the past may carry a hope for the future, in the face of odds that a new violent conflict might emerge. It emphasises, in particular, how important it is that such principles become viable as everyday practices rather than ideological beliefs. Furthermore, it stresses how they have to pervade major aspects of socio-political life if "justice", in the narrow sense of a system of laws administered by designated agents, is to take hold. Keeping the past "open", rather than storing it in boxes labelled by the powerful of the present, is also a central tenet in Marais' Chapter 6 on the archive, as well as in Van Roermund's Chapter 5 reflection on *anamnesis*.

However, restoring a polity's orientation towards the normative poles of human dignity, citizen freedom and shared well-being requires one to conceptualise remembrance as a sustained critical attitude towards *one's own* past. Such a conceptualisation must deal with the moral ambiguities of "a plural self" over time that is to be regarded as "common". This challenge is taken up in Chapter 2 by De Gamboa Tapias and Herrera, who ask whether remembrance should be understood to be a moral obligation to past generations, an obligation to distinguish harmful from inspiring choices on a timeline recognised as "one's own"? Is it possible to tell them apart, not only in the sense of passing critical judgement from above, but also by narrating them in such compelling ways that harmful aspects of this common identity can be contested and inspiring aspects recommended? Only such narratives will allow people to see why some principles are more acceptable than others.

However, the same parlance of restorative justice may also amplify quite different overtones, as if rehabilitation and the restoration of human and civil dignity could be practised apart from reparation. As is well-known, in South Africa the restitution of land became a separate issue, regulated under a different body of legislation and before a different Commission.[20] Up to the present day "the consensus of opinion is indeed that, while remarkable in many respects,

20 "Restitution of dispossessed land ... was addressed in a subsection of the right to equality contained in the chapter on fundamental rights [Interim Constitution, s. 8) and in several sections towards the end of the interim Constitution laying down the basic criteria and procedures for the right to restitution [Interim Constitution, ss. 121–123]." Du Bois (2008).

the land restitution process in South Africa has largely failed to address the moral harm done to victims of apartheid forced removals."[21] Once more, such ambiguous parsing of the predicate "restorative", by no means unique to South Africa, underlines a need to profoundly reflect on the conceptual framework that is ultimately adopted once the call for "transitional justice" is heard and responded to. It would be naïve to believe that the conceptual frames that an oppressive regime used to impose its will would simply evaporate into thin air when the regime ends. On the contrary, they may linger on for decades, until alternative, often more indigenous formats, are rediscovered, i.e. remembered.

The clearest example of this is precisely the concept of "land", which explains why land takes centre stage in several otherwise divergent chapters, such as those by Aguilar, Soto Hoyos, Kassem, and Céspedes-Báez. What is commonly called "the land issue" is not merely a matter of redistributing real estate. As demonstrated by Aguilar (in Chapter 8), it also crucially involves tapping into a different conceptual register that sometimes is succinctly expressed by inverting the terms that usually accompany the predicate "belong"; thus, "we belong to the land" rather than "the land belongs to us". Remembering older and more genuine layers of concepts in restorative discourse may be important for revealing to both officials and citizens how regained access to justice can avoid adherence to the conceptual constraints of the old regime by just reversing the charges. It is precisely in this conceptual domain, though, where the going of transitional justice processes gets tough, and this volume features two chapters that lend more than sufficient ground to this thesis, both written from feminist perspectives. In the first, on the basis of extensive case studies in Colombia, Céspedes-Báez's Chapter 9 shows what can go wrong when these constraints are taken for granted or expressly put up front. In spite of a recognition of gendered harm to women during the years of conflict, in particular sexual violence, the legal order nevertheless appears unable to deploy the categories that would ensure gender equal reparation when it comes to land. In the second, Kassem analyses (in Chapter 10) how the sexualised discourse by which Palestinian women depict the 1948 occupation of their towns and villages acquired a subversive potential with regard to both the Zionist and Palestinian masculine nationalist narratives, and how it may well sow the seeds of freedom in dignity for all involved in a seemingly irresolvable conflict.

---

21 Roux (2008) 145. However, the question is to what extent this consensus is based on facts. Land Centre of Excellence (2017): "The Reconstruction and Development Programme (RDP) document for example set a target of 30% of land to be transferred to PDIs [i.e. Previously Disadvantaged Individuals, authors' translation] by 2014. The National Development Plan (NDP) set a target of 20% of commercial agricultural land per district to be transferred by 2030. The setting of targets has created expectations. At the same time, there was no way to measure whether these targets were being achieved as no comprehensive land audit was done."

Ben Aharon's Chapter 13 reveals the reverse and dark side of the same thesis. From a political science perspective, he analyses over three decades of denial of the Armenian genocide by the State of Israel. Remembrance of the Holocaust in the restorative sense, as a vow to offer robust protection to Jewish people worldwide, had to be realised in the specific international context with states like Turkey and Azerbaijan. It was precisely because that remembrance was so central to the very existence of Israel as a state that successive Israeli governments have been compelled to collude in the denial of the Armenian genocide. The chapter therefore tables the question under what preconditions a state with a monopoly on violence can be the driver of restorative justice within itself. While this chapter mainly targets a long-term parliamentary exercise in "restoring law", one can contrast it to Ndahinda's Chapter 12 focus on a single set of government policies or to Soto Hoyos' Chapter 11 study on the efforts of the judiciary. Taken together, thus, Ben Aharon, Ndahinda and Soto Hoyos cover the three branches of public authority.

Overarching the chapters in this volume is the awareness that remembrance of suffering is inexhaustible. Both in terms of a politics of closure and in those of a politics of disclosure, remembrance should preserve an openness towards memories of suffering that even the most widely shared narrative would betray in the end; towards memories of harm that even the most advanced scheme of redistribution could not repair; towards memories of loss that continue to paralyse communities in spite of initial commitments to ban oppressive violence into the future; and towards memories of victimhood that risk becoming petrified as political privilege under new regimes. Let us end, therefore, on the predicate of "victimhood" as a final note. Victims should be remembered as victims, no doubt, but this qualification of "victim" comes with overtones that need not be logically implied or colloquially implicated. Even though "passion" is derived from the Latin word for "suffering", victims do not have to be remembered necessarily as being "passive". Kassem's chapter beautifully demonstrates how the women she interviewed gave voice to this self-awareness. The philosophical reflections by Van Roermund as well as by De Gamboa Tapias and Herrera also undergird Kassem's point. This self-awareness of victims does not trickle down into any form of political self-legitimation. It is their protest, their resistance, their refusal and their sacrifice that are the qualities for which they are to be remembered. They do not have to be remembered as being "on the right side of history" by virtue of their victimhood, as if anyone could oversee the whole of history and speak on its behalf. They do not have to be remembered as heroes or saints. Firstly, they would be the first to admit that their lives were much more ordinary and ambivalent than any such canonisations would demand. Furthermore, canonisation on the basis of victimhood alone can be a way by which a current regime purchases the basis of its legitimacy. Minding such pitfalls is part and parcel of a worthy, though critical, politics of remembrance, and is of the utmost importance in situations where the line between victims and perpetrators is blurred and remains blurred in hindsight. When massive violence is perpetrated on all sides of a conflict, when people are coerced or lured into violent acts, when despair rather than dominance drives opposite camps against one another, in these and similar cases there is reason to apply the predicate of victimhood from a politico-moral point of view to agents with a certain quality rather than to human individuals of a certain type.

References

Austin, J.L. (1970 [1946]) "Other Minds" in J.O. Urmson and G.J. Warnock (eds.), *Philosophical Papers*, 2nd edn. London/Oxford/New York: Oxford University Press, 76–116.

Bassiouni, M.C. (ed.), (2002) *Post-Conflict Justice*. Ardsley N.Y.: Transnational Publishers.

Caranza, R., Correa, C. et al. (2017) *Forms of Justice. A Guide to Designing Reparations Application Forms and Registration Processes for Victims of Human Rights Violations*. New York: International Centre for Transitional Justice.

Clamp, K. (2016) *Restorative justice in transitional settings*. London: Routledge.

Clamp, K. and Doak, J. (2012) "More than Words: Restorative Justice Concepts in Transitional Justice Settings" in *International Criminal Law Review*, **12**, no. 3: 339–360.

Du Bois, F. (2008) "Reparation and the Forms of Justice" in F. Du Bois and A. Du Bois-Pedain (eds.), *Justice and Reconciliation in Post-Apartheid South Africa*. Cambridge: Cambridge University Press, 116–143.

Duff, R.A., Farmer, L. et al. (eds.), (2004) *The Trial on Trial*, vol I. Oxford: Hart Publishing.

Johnstone, G. and Van Ness, D.W. (eds.), (2007) *Handbook of Restorative Justice*. Portland O.R.: Willan Publishing.

Land Centre of Excellence (2017) *Land Audit: A Transactions Approach*. South Africa: Agri SA, Weekblad Landbou, ADS.

Parmentier, S. (2003) "Global Justice in the Aftermath of Mass Violence. The Role of the International Criminal Court in Dealing with Political Crimes" in *International Annals of Criminology*, **41**, no. 1–2: 203–224.

Parmentier, S., Aciru, M. et al. (2017) "Human Rights in Situations of Transitional Justice" in L. Weber, E. Fishwick and M. Marmo (eds.), *Routledge international handbook of criminology and human rights*. London: Routledge, 235–246.

Parmentier, S., Vanspauwen, K. et al. (2008) "Dealing with the Legacy of Mass Violence: Changing Lenses to Restorative Justice" in A. Smeulers and R. Haveman (eds.), *Supranational criminology: towards a criminology of international crimes*. Antwerpen/Portland O.R.: Intersentia, 335–356.

Ricoeur, P. (2000) *La mémoire, l'histoire, l'oubli*. Paris: Du Seuil.

—— (2004) *Memory, History, Forgetting*. Chicago I.L./London: The University of Chicago Press.

Rousseau, J.-J. (1964 [1762]) *Du contract social; ou principes du droit politique*. Paris: Gallimard.

Roux, T. (2008) "Land Restitution and Reconciliation in South Africa" in F. Du Bois and A. Du Bois-Pedain (eds.), *Justice and Reconciliation in Post-Apartheid South Africa*. Cambridge: Cambridge University Press, 144–171.

Skelton, A. (2015) "Rights and restoration within youth justice" in *Restorative Justice*, 3, no. 1: 135–138.
United Nations Security Council (2004) *Report of the Secretary-General The rule of law and transitional justice in conflict and post-conflict societies*, S/2004/616, at https://www.un.org/ruleoflaw/files/2004%20report.pdf.
Zehr, H. (2015). *The Big Book of Restorative Justice*. New York: Good Books.

PART I

RESTORING TRUST

CHAPTER 2

THE DUTY TO REMEMBER A VIOLENT PAST

A Restorative (Re)Construction of Our Identity

Camila de Gamboa Tapias and Wilson Herrera Romero

1. INTRODUCTION

This chapter offers a reflection on the role that the duty to remember could play as a restorative measure against large-scale past abuses and as a mechanism to transform harmful identities. A true knowledge of the past is the first step of a critical reflection on the institutions, traditions and identities that have contributed to violence and the degradation of relations between members of a given political community. As was advanced in the Introduction to this volume, our critical remembrance proposal explores the possibility of becoming and staying critical toward our memory of suffering. However, this action of remembering, as we will discuss in this chapter, could not be guaranteed without a perspective of justice from which the value of the human dignity of all its members is established or restored in terms of inclusion and equality.

To that effect, Section 2 involves a philosophical discussion of the ideas of identity and tradition and the way that these notions are intertwined. Section 3 develops the notion of the duty to remember, particularly in the case of a troublesome past. It raises the common objections to a moral obligation with respect to past generations, and the importance of traditions and promises among generations in understanding this duty. Section 4 addresses the perils derived from the duty of remembering a difficult past, and the final section describes certain historical narratives that are able to contest and eventually transform harmful identities that are constructed in situations of political violence.

2. THE CONSTRUCTION OF IDENTITY AND TRADITION

A basic condition for being an active member of a political community is being recognized by the rest of the members as a moral agent, i.e. as a person who is able and has the right to make his or her own decisions, and in regard to others as being responsible for his or her own actions. However, moral agency is not a capacity that one possesses from birth. Rather, it is a capacity that one acquires through a process of socialization. At the same time, as moral psychologists have shown, the development of moral agency depends on the way that the social identity of the individual is constructed.[1] From a hermeneutic viewpoint, personal and social identity is not based on some essence, but is constructed by traditions.

Tradition may be harmful in two senses: the first is when its account of peoples with other traditions or cultural backgrounds distorts the history, customs and character of these peoples with the aim of destroying their identity. We take this notion from Amos Funkenstein, who introduces in his analysis what he calls "counter-history", a genre of history that distorts the past with "[the aim of depriving] the adversary of his positive identity, of his self-image, and substitute for it a pejorative counter image."[2] According to Funkenstein's principle, two examples of harmful traditions are anti-Semitism and that of the extreme right in Israel in regard to Palestine. Secondly, a tradition is harmful if it denies moral agency to some members of society who can otherwise share such a tradition, on the basis of natural and social features like sex, race, class or religion. In this case, it is probable that a tradition may have a respectful account of another's traditions and yet nevertheless justify an arbitrary and hierarchical distribution of rights and burdens between people who consider themselves to be part of it. Accordingly, the principle of agency in this second sense assesses how a tradition treats people who belong to it. Taking into account these two senses, a tradition is morally wrong if, in its account, it diminishes the self-image of other people and rejects the moral agency of some of its members.

1 See Gilligan (1982); also Thomas (1993) on the construction of identity of Afro-Americans in the age of slavery.

2 Funkenstein (1992) 80.

Iris Marion Young, in *Justice and the Politics of Difference*, uses the principle of inclusion in her defense of a deliberative democracy. Perhaps the best way to understand this notion is through its opposite, namely exclusion. According to Young, there are two forms of exclusion: oppression and domination. The first involves

> systematic institutional processes which prevent some people from learning and using satisfying and expansive skills in socially organized settings, or institutionalized social processes which inhibit people's ability to play and communicate with others or to express their feelings and perspective on social life in contexts where others can listen.[3]

The most patent examples of oppression for her are poverty, slavery, violence, sexual exploitation and discrimination. In all these cases, individuals do not have the chance to freely develop their most precious abilities like creativity, reasoning, and affection. Domination involves the "institutional conditions which inhibit or prevent some people from participating in determining their actions or the conditions of their actions."[4] Perhaps the simplest way to explain what domination means would be to say that one suffers domination when one is coerced by others (institutions or individuals), that is, when others decide what one has to be (identity) and what one ought to do (action). In the political sphere, clear situations of exclusions are restrictions upon citizens from participating in elections, voicing their opinions and accessing public offices.

For Young, the principle of inclusion entails the idea of political freedom and equality, in which all citizens, regardless of their conditions, have the right to participate equally in decision-making processes as well as to express their opinions and to listen to others. Indeed, in *Inclusion and Democracy*, Young, following Habermas, affirms that a political institution, and more specifically a democratic decision, can be considered just "only if all those affected by it are included in the process of discussion and decision making."[5] Given these conditions, we could rightly claim that they are so stringent that it is hard to find a real institutional arrangement that fulfills the principle of inclusion. In response to this critique, we could argue that the principle of inclusion must be seen as a normative principle that expresses better than any the central tenets of Enlightenment, namely freedom and equality. In this sense, a society in which at least one person or a group is arbitrarily excluded from the process of decision-making, or is entitled to fewer rights and burdened with more obligations than other citizens, is a society whose political regime and system of

---

3 Young (1990) 38.
4 Young (1990) 38.
5 Young (2000) 23.

law are not legitimate in a normative sense for those who still consider these two tenets of Enlightenment to be valid.

So far, it has been shown how the principle of inclusion can be applied to political institutions. The question now is how this principle can be used to evaluate traditions. According to Gadamer, a hermeneutic approach that tries to correct the excesses of the Enlightenment must see traditions as partners in a dialogue whose final end is to open our horizons. Likewise, for Young, democracy must be taken as an extended dialogue among the members of a polity with the aim of reaching just and inclusive solutions to problems of living in the context of a pluralistic society. It is not far-fetched to affirm that the extent to which a society is inclusive depends on the way citizens regard one another. This idea of inclusion requires that each citizen be open to others, which means that one must be ready to listen to others, but also to change one's own opinions if, after a serious examination, one judges that others' arguments are better than one's own. The extent to which one is capable of doing this, however, depends again on the traditions in which one has grown up. Assuming the validity of the principle of inclusion, a tradition is harmful and wrong if, instead of opening one's horizons, the tradition closes them and blinds us to other people's claims. A tradition that, for instance, forswears free discussion and the progress of science is therefore wrong because it impedes the development of our capacity for reasoning, creativity and listening to others' opinions. Similar things can be said about traditions that are against the incorporation of the idea of human rights or that accept oppression and exploitation.

Furthermore, traditions play an important role in the origination and reproduction of political violence. In many cases, political violence is directed against groups that in ordinary situations suffer oppression or domination. Such vulnerable groups suffer violence perpetrated by actors in armed conflicts, as the academic literature has shown to have happened with women and poor social classes of patriarchal and hierarchical societies.[6] Conversely, social groups that are oppressed or exploited and, therefore, unable to participate in the public sphere often tend to think that violence is a political strategy to fight for their rights.[7]

The field of transitional justice that is currently used to respond to violent political situations[8] encompasses various mechanisms to achieve justice by

---

6 For an analysis of the exacerbation of violence against women in political conflicts, see Walker (2009) 18–62. See also Grupo de Memoria Histórica (2013). This final report of the Centro Nacional de Memoria Histórica, in Colombia shows that a high number of victims came from minority groups: Afro-Colombian groups, poor rural areas, women, and children.

7 See Grupo de Memoria Histórica (2013) 112–135. In Colombia, the National Front, an alliance between the conservative and liberal parties to share political power to the exclusion of any other party, is considered by many academics as one of the factors leading to the appearance of guerrilla groups.

8 See United Nations Secretary-General (2010).

taking the past seriously and contesting traditions that played a role in the origination and perpetuation of political violence. Transitional justice is the contemporary term used to refer to measures that societies must adopt in order to achieve a transition to democratic peace after massive and systematic crimes perpetrated by oppressive regimes, civil wars, internal armed conflicts, and even international conflicts. Such measures have two clearly defined and essentially intertwined objectives: on the one hand, to respond seriously to a past marked by serious violations of human rights, and, on the other, to build new political institutions or to reform and transform existing ones in order to guarantee that atrocities committed in contexts of violence never repeat themselves. This very complex task involves the design of mechanisms such as criminal investigations and trials, processes that aim to uncover the truth, official and social acknowledgment of what occurred in the past, reparation measures, and institutional reforms that respond to the serious violations committed in the past and make a lasting peace possible.[9] The following section, we will analyze the role that the duty to remember could play as a restorative measure against large-scale past abuses and as a mechanism to transform harmful identities.

3. AGENCY, IDENTITY, AND THE DUTY TO REMEMBER

As will be explain later in this chapter, to say that one is responsible for the past, at least in a Kantian sense, entails that one has some sort of duty or obligation. But what kind of duty is this? It is first of all a duty to remember, and secondly a duty to critically assess our past. In both cases, the duty to the past is a special duty. It refers not to actions in a physical sense but to beliefs. Two problems are involved here. On the one hand, a moral duty involves avoiding actions whose execution or omission by a moral agent can harm other moral agents. In the case of the duty to the past, however, it is obscure how the act of forgetting can harm someone. On the other hand, a central value of the Enlightenment, which most people in Western societies would not accept putting limits on, is "freedom of thought". Yet the duty to the past imposes some restrictions on the beliefs we can have today. Given this, on what grounds can one morally impose such limits?

It is hard to answer the first objection, because if the duty to the past is a duty to past generations, then to what extent is the act of forgetting today

9 The Secretary General of the United Nations defined transitional justice as "the full range of processes and mechanisms associated with a society's attempts to come to terms with a legacy of large-scale past abuses, in order to ensure accountability, serve justice and achieve reconciliation. These may include both judicial and non-judicial mechanisms with differing levels of international involvement (or none at all) and individual prosecutions, reparations, truth-seeking, institutional reform, vetting and dismissals, or a combination thereof". United Nations Secretary-General (2004) 4.

harming someone who is already dead?[10] To overcome this objection, one could assume some kind of religious belief in an afterlife; but in a secularized society this sort of argument would not have any public appeal, unless, of course, one lives in a homogeneous religious community, which is not the case in modern Western societies. Another way to face the problem would be to say that the act of forgetting can harm those who were directly affected by the forgotten events and are still alive.

Following a liberal tradition, Pablo de Greiff has criticized all attempts to justify a duty to remember based on the claims of the victims of the past. The core of his argument is that by definition a moral duty involves avoiding a moral harm, and only living people can be harmed. de Greiff also argues that those who defend the duty to remember based on the idea of a debt that present generations have toward the past, are employing merely a form of speech, a metaphor.[11] Nevertheless, this liberal perspective of duty in the view of the present authors is too restrictive. Paraphrasing Raul Bellah, individuals are not islands; they form a web in time and in space. In time, I see myself as being an heir to some property and to debts left by my predecessors, but also as one who has to be grateful for or critical of what they did for me. As part of a chain, I may choose to break with it or to continue with it. To harm, *prima facie*, means to produce some suffering. In the case of moral harm, the suffering goes along with the break-up of a moral relationship between the culprit and the victim.

Margaret Urban Walker considers a moral relationship to be "a certain disposition of people toward each other and the standards they trust, or at least hope, are shared."[12] As such, moral relationships are based on trust and create certain expectations of one another "that require us to take responsibility for what we do or fail to do, and that allow us to call others to account for what they do or fail to do."[13] In contrast to harm produced by physical phenomena, a moral harm consists of something other than pain suffered by our bodies. Rather, it is suffering that is caused by the breakdown of the relationship itself. When someone willingly hurts us, she or he is sending a sign that for her or him we are not worthy of respect. It is the humiliation and the lack of consideration and recognition that the victim suffers the most from. However, this is valid not only for relations between people who are alive. Indeed, the idea that one is part of a web in time implies that present generations have moral relations with past and future generations. One can validly break off one's relations with the past when one finds that prior generations perpetrated atrocities and humiliations.

---

10 See de Greiff (2002) 160–174. In his otherwise illuminating essay, de Greiff set forth this critique and has defended the idea that the only way to defend a duty toward the past is by appealing to what a present generation reasonably would accept as worthy of remembering.

11 de Greiff (2002) 164.

12 Walker (2006) 23.

13 Walker (2006) 23.

Perhaps, instead of asking the general question of whether or not there is a duty to remember, one must ask a more concrete question: under what conditions must one continue or break with the past?[14]

In order to address this question, one might consider another way of extending the notion of moral harm. As is well known, the paradigmatic example of a moral duty is the contract. When two people agree to make a contract they both promise, willingly and mutually, to do something. Through the contract, the actors create a set of expectations that they both wish to be fulfilled. The arbitrary breaking of the promise by one of the parties produces a harm by not fulfilling expectations. From this one can infer that harm is also done in cases where one of the parties arbitrarily breaks the expectations of those affected by the act of promising something. Understood in this sense, the notion of harm can be extended in such a way that one can say that our actions today can harm past generations that no longer exist. In every present, besides creating new expectations and trying to satisfy old ones, people can either break or fulfill the hopes and dreams of past generations. Thus, drawing on what earlier was said about promises, one may also say that breaking the hopes of past generations without justification must also be wrong. Someone may argue against this conclusion by saying that there is a crucial difference between a promise made to other living persons and the dreams that past generations had in regard to their futures. In the former case, both the promisee and the promisor agree voluntarily to be bound by the promise, whereas in the latter case such mutual agreement seems to be absent. In other words, unlike a contract between two living people, it is hard to see how past generations could reach a voluntary agreement with us in the present. We think, however, that there is a way to escape this problem.

Every person and every generation have hopes and dreams that they expect future generations will fulfill. Through acts of remembrances and through dialogue with traditions, these expectations are enacted and can be seen as a kind of claim that "here is our offer, we worked so much for you, we built all these institutions, so that you can live better and can satisfy both your dreams and our dreams." It is up to the present generation to accept or to refuse such an offer. If they accept it, if they accept incorporating past dreams as part of their own dreams and hopes, then they have acquired a duty toward the past. However, not all contracts and promises that are offered to us are feasible and morally permissible. Just as it is morally wrong to enter into a contract with someone with the aim of killing people, likewise there are dreams and hopes from the past that would be morally wrong to fulfill today, for instance the tendency in peace negotiations in Latin America to hide the responsibilities of the perpetrators of

---

14 As we will show later, this does not mean that breaking with the past entails some sort of forgetting. On the contrary, it requires a judgement about the past.

gross human rights violations in the 1980s.[15] Thus, it is obvious that not all of the duties that one voluntarily accepts from the past are morally valid. The fact that, for example, I promise my grandfather that I will kill the sons of his enemies does not mean that I have a moral obligation to do it. On the contrary, so long as the promise commands one to do something evil, then it is morally wrong to fulfill it. This reflection sheds light on what breaking or continuing with the past means, leaving aside expectations raised in the past or promises made then to satisfy them. The question remains, though, how to morally assess claims of the past; that is, under which criteria can one judge the expectations of the past? As we will show, this cannot be made out *a priori*, but only after engaging in critical dialogue with past traditions.

As for the second objection, limits to what one must believe about the past can be justified by principles of agency and inclusion. This way of grounding the duty to the past is different from de Greiff's attempt. According to de Greiff, there are three kinds of arguments for defending a duty to remember. One, oriented toward the future, is a utilitarian argument, and its best expression is Santayana's dictum: "those who do not learn from the past are condemned to repeat it."[16] Another argument is past-oriented in a Kantian-Benjaminian way based on the idea of debt. The last argument is present-oriented and follows the tenets of discourse ethics. It is grounded on the need to construct trustful relationships between the heirs of victims and the heirs of culprits. de Greiff defends the last argument and rejects both the utilitarian and the Kantian approaches. The former, according to de Greiff, is problematic not only because it instrumentalizes the victims but also because, as a matter of fact, it is impossible for the past to be repeated in the future. With regards to the Benjaminian-Kantian argument, as was said before, for de Greiff the argument assumes a non-standard conception of responsibility, according to which, "present generations should be burdened with the moral debts of their parents."[17] We have already shown one way to defend the argument for such a debt that can overcome de Greiff's objection. We can also argue that through the principles of agency and inclusion it is possible to justify a duty to remember that takes into account the claims of present generations, which is the focus of de Greiff's thesis, but also the claims of past and future generations that he seems to disregard.

First of all, the duty to remember, and generally a duty toward the past, can be grounded in the relation between agency and identity. In the history of philosophy there have been two approaches to the question of identity. One is the essentialist view, according to which a moral agent is constituted by some kind

15 The authors understand gross human rights violations as wrongful actions, such as genocide, crimes against humanity, and grave breaches of International Humanitarian Law.

16 de Greiff (2002) 164.

17 de Greiff (2002) 166.

of essential attributes that are invariable in time, such as Kant's transcendental subject, for instance. The other approach corresponds to what we would call the empiricist view, first set forth by Locke and later by Hume. In this view, identity is constituted by memory, where who I am, and what I am, is determined by my recollections, that is, by the past that in one way or another I am aware of. For the sake of the argument, in the next section we will follow a subtler version of this second approach developed by Paul Ricoeur.[18] The advantage of this approach is that it may include historical narrations in the constitution of personal identity.

According to Ricoeur, in the formation of moral agency two processes intertwine: one relates to the formation of the agent's moral character, and the other to what Ricoeur calls "self-constancy" or "the endeavor of keeping one's word", which corresponds to the capacity of making and keeping promises. Following Aristotle, Ricoeur conceives of the agent's moral character as "the set of lasting dispositions by which a person is recognized."[19] In general, one recognizes a person as such for the way he or she faces a set of situations. In other words, one may perceive in a person a set of behaviors from which one attributes a disposition, an attitude that the observed person expresses in his actions. For Ricoeur, the character's formation involves two components, namely: the learning of a set of practices and habits, and the acquisition of a set of "values, norms, ideals, models and heroes".[20] For the child and the newcomer, social practices and social beliefs (norms, values, ideals, models, and heroes) appear as something new and alien. The processes of formation, socialization and adaptation can be characterized as processes of appropriation in which such practices and beliefs are interiorized by the child or the new members of the community. At the end of these processes, the child regards himself or herself as a full member of the society and the newcomer no longer feels like a foreigner, but as part of a "we" that is constituted by the members of his or her new society.

All these practices and beliefs are not only embedded in historical traditions *but are learned in dialogue with them*. For instance, to become an active citizen of a political community one must learn to act in accordance with a set of practices and beliefs that is shared by citizens and is embedded in tradition. It is in politics and morality where narratives turn out to be crucial in this process. In the political sphere, stories tell us how nations emerged with their cultures as well as their social and political institutions. They also tell us the history of economic, social and political transformations, and of periods of internal conflicts, wars and stability. In this sense, the formation of the moral character of

18 Ricoeur (1992). Ricoeur starts his reflection on identity with a strong criticism of Hume's and Locke's views. Nevertheless, in his further analyses he holds the thesis that our personal identity is determined by our historical consciousness.

19 Ricoeur (1992) 121.

20 Ricoeur (1992) 121.

a citizen is a process through which she or he internalizes the shared traditions of the community, its social and political practices and its beliefs. Hence, one can conclude that the construction of identity, a central part of the formation of character, is determined by the ways that traditions are handed down and learned.

The other element that mediates the construction of the identity of moral agents is the agents' endeavors to preserve their own world. The allegiance that we feel towards our parents, friends, social and religious groups, and political movements all form part of our identity. To keep a promise, to be faithful is another way in which moral agents have some permanence in time. Hence, regardless of circumstances or of any profound changes in our character, we can still be identified as the one who has kept a promise or has not. Keeping my word to someone is like saying "here, I stand for you". In general, the bond of close relations between friends, lovers, spouses, parents and children relies on mutual trust, in the singular endeavor to fulfill their promises. These promises are about the future as well as about the past. But how is it possible to make promises with regard to the past? A way to answer this is by analyzing the tension that usually exists between the moral character of an agent and the obligations imposed by his promises.

There are situations in which the traditions one firmly believes in are put into doubt or are in conflict with others. In this kind of experience, one must choose between being faithful to one's traditions and therefore not to change one's character, or breaking with them and to change as a result. Of course, these are extreme situations. Normally one tries to make some trade-off by promising to change part of what one is, and by demanding others' acceptance of parts of one's traditions. The point we want to make here is that when one chooses not to break totally or partially with traditions, then one is engaging in a sort of promise to those traditions, in the sense that one has chosen to be faithful to what one has been, up to that moment. In these situations, the agent's role in the constitution of his/her identity can become more active. The agent can examine to what extent it is worthwhile to keep his or her faith in his or her traditions. If, after this questioning, the agent chooses not to change his or her habits and beliefs, s/he can assert in a stronger sense than before that the examined traditions are his or her own traditions.

4. THE PERILS OF THE DUTY TO REMEMBER A TROUBLESOME PAST

So far, we have established a necessary connection between moral agency and the formation of identity and tradition. From this premise, together with the idea of debt, we may develop a justification for a duty to remember. Such a justification does not imply, however, that this obligation would be valid in all circumstances.

As we are going to show, to be valid this duty must be accompanied with the obligation to know the past. In general, the acts of forgetting and remembrance are involuntary acts. Now, since a duty cannot demand actions that are beyond one's control, the fact that one's strivings to remember or to forget something do not guarantee that one can or will remember or forget means that it does not make sense to say that someone has the obligation or the duty to perform this kind of action. Nevertheless, this objection fails because *not all* acts of remembrance are involuntary. Thus, history and acts of commemoration are vital examples of voluntary memory. In the case of traumatic events, such as gross human rights violations in the context of political violence, remembering and forgetting are the result of restorative and collective processes, as we will explain soon, rather than of mere individual decisions. From this observation one can derive a key clarification about the realm of application of the duty to remember. Such a duty is not about involuntary memory or forgetting, but rather demands a conscious effort to remember. This demand can be invoked through different means: therapeutic processes, acts of commemoration and historical reconstructions of a troublesome past.

A second objection could claim that the argument is ambiguous because it assumes that the duty to not forget is the same as the duty to remember. As was said before, the duty to the past includes two sorts of duty: to remember, and to know the past. Both are similar in their opposition to the duty to forget, and yet they are different. Todorov and de Greiff in their criticisms of the duty to remember seem to restrict their argumentation to a specific kind of recollection, that of public commemoration. In this kind of voluntary memory, a person or a group tries to revisit past situations that are accompanied by attitudes of recognition and sympathy toward certain people of the past, especially victims and heroes. In the act of commemoration, people in the present pay tribute to someone in the past. In general, most of these sorts of recollection are acts of reverence that involve some form of *sacralization*. The duty to know the past, in contrast, does not necessarily have these connotations. As Todorov rightly points out, the knowledge of the past refers to two processes: establishing of the facts and understanding the meaning of what happened.[21] This duty is part of the historian's task of knowing the truth about the past. For today's historian, reconstructing the past does not aim at awakening identification with the past. The promises that one makes to fulfill past wishes and the debt that one accepts to owe to the past involve a sympathetic attitude towards some people and events from the past, and not seeing our predecessors as strangers. Therefore, what these notions of promise and debt ground is a duty to remember and not the historian's duty to know the past. Despite this, there is a way to interpret this duty to know the past that can be taken as a necessary complement to the duty to remember.

---

21 Todorov (2000).

The duty to know the past is not only incumbent on the historian; it can also be a citizen's duty. As was discussed above, the promises a person makes to his or her ancestors and traditions are an important part of his or her identity. There are many motives that can lead someone to make such promises. Some can be non-reflective motives, like blind faith in one's ancestors, sudden impulses, or loyalty and trust toward close friends. Alternatively, they can be reflective where we examine and consider the set of values that our traditions and our ancestors defended as well as their accounts of past events. If we assume that in modern democratic societies it is the duty of citizens to responsibly form their own identities reflectively, then this must include a critical examination of their own traditions and ancestors. This clearly requires true knowledge of the past.

The idea that the duty to remember is not a historian's duty but a citizen's duty can be explained especially when the members of a political community deal with a troublesome past by using a model of transitional justice.[22] As we have stated in the Section 2 of this chapter, transitional justice has two intertwined objectives: on the one hand, to respond to a past marked by serious violations of human rights, and, on the other, to build new political institutions or to reform and transform existing ones in order to guarantee that the atrocities committed in contexts of violence never repeat themselves. In these situations, the duty to reflectively examine our own traditions and the identities that we have constructed based on them makes it essential for us to act as responsible members of a society that must confront gross human rights violations. These situations show the relevance of the concrete question of the duty to remember that we proposed in Section 3: *under what conditions must one continue or break with the past?* Here, a true knowledge of the past constitutes the first step towards reflecting critically on our own institutions, traditions and identities that are the foundations of the political regimes, moral values, legal norms, and institutions that have contributed to past violence and the degradation of our relationships as human beings and citizens.[23] Although this is the first and necessary step, the

---

22 Although there are certain mechanisms that belong to transitional justice, in real cases not all governments leading transitions implement all mechanisms; nor do they do so in the same ways. Currently, there is a certain unanimity among scholars and in international jurisprudence about a comprehensive approach of the mechanisms. In a comprehensive approach, transitional justice mechanisms are complementary, in the sense that all efforts to protect the rights of the victims to justice, truth, reparation, and the guarantee of non-repetition are interrelated.

23 See McCarthy (2002) 623–648 and Spinner-Halev (2012). Transitional justice deals with violence committed in the recent past and should be distinguished from other contexts in which violence took place in the remote past, as in the case of slavery in the United States. In such cases, transition is a question of historical injustice in which transitional justice mechanisms are not adequate, because, among other reasons, direct victims and perpetrators of past injustices are long gone. In those cases, the duty to remember has other instruments to achieve its purposes.

process of moral and political transformation requires more drastic measures, since breaking with the past in many cases means: eliminating a political regime; creating a new constitution; lustrating former public officials of the old regime; designing criminal investigations, trials, reparations programs and truth commissions; acknowledging officially what occurred in the past; carrying out institutional reforms that respond to violence; and creating or transforming many public and social institutions that recognize, guarantee, and protect all persons and citizens.

However, in order to really achieve all these transformations, there must be a set of values that serves as a standard for the members of a community to set up or to morally and politically restore their society. In other words, a political community must ask which identities are permitted and which are prohibited. In modern liberal democracies, the central values that any identity must respect are freedom, equality, and fraternity. Should one adopt a critical perspective, like Young's and Habermas's, such criteria would be inclusion and universal solidarity. Liberal democratic values have inspired the basic values of transitional justice, as evidenced by the literature dedicated to this field.[24] Therefore, in the context of transitional justice, inclusion and universal solidarity are the kinds of values that serve as normative ideals to respond to past violence and to transform the existing institutions, traditions and identities that must be contested. In this particular context, the duty to remember can contribute to setting up or restoring morally and politically the members of these societies. In order to explain more deeply the idea of moral and political restoration, we will follow the notion of moral repair that is developed by Walker, for whom "moral repair is the process of moving from the situation of loss and damage to a situation where some degree of stability in moral relations is regained."[25] As Walker states, this process of restoration or recreation is particularly difficult in cases of serious wrongs, since, if repair is possible to a certain degree, it frequently comes with a price:

> for the victim the cost of absorbing some irreparable loss, pain and anger; for the wrongdoer, the cost of some shame, vulnerability, and compensating action; for the communities, the cost of providing acknowledgment and vindication for victims, placing responsibility and its demands on wrongdoers, and showing that standards are affirmed and enforced.[26]

Although Walker believes it is essential that "[t]hose responsible for wrong and harm must remain at all times clearly in the frame",[27] moral repair is so vital

24 See de Greiff (2002) 160–174, and United Nations Secretary-General (2004).

25 Walker (2006) 6.

26 Walker (2006) 6.

27 Walker (2006) 8.

to human lives that a society cannot entrust the acts of reparation entirely to wrongdoers, given that there is a risk that wrongdoers will deny their actions or refuse to respond to victims.

In situations of generalized violence, gaining or regaining stability in moral relations is not the exclusive task of victims and perpetrators, given that violence has typically distorted all human relations, and therefore the process of restoration concerns the majority of social groups and individuals. In these cases, as Walker points out, repair cannot mean a mere return to the status quo, but rather has to bring about a real change in social patterns of disregard, subjugation or violation.[28] Clearly, implementing remedies in these conditions constitutes a long-term process, as we already explained. In addition, this long-term process of restoration is a collective effort that occurs in the public sphere and involves the past, present and future. Hence it is an intergenerational dialogue.

The quest for the past goes beyond the historical concern about how to reach a truthful account of an historical event or an age, as people use the past to justify present and future actions. But as Todorov points out, the problem is that "not all uses of the past are good."[29] The way in which the past is linked with the present and with future actions is that it contributes to the construction of identity of both individuals and groups. In this direction, three kinds of perils can be identified.

A first peril is the distortion of the past. Personal and collective identities are partly constructed on historical narratives. Unlike critical and scientific explanations, however, in these narratives the account of the past is not politically and morally neutral and the facts are presented as parts of a story, containing a plot with a beginning and an end. According to Todorov, historical narratives can promote four kinds of roles: heroes and villains, and benefactors and victims. Present generations, like the readers of fairy tales, tend to identify themselves and their ancestors with those protagonists who either perform good actions (heroes) or who suffer evil (victims). From this, Todorov rightly concludes that the two main forms of historical narrative that build both personal and collective identities are: "heroic narratives, which lead the triumph of 'our side' and the victim narrative, which relates its sufferings."[30] Hence, it is not unusual to find that two persons or communities, or even historians may have different versions of the same events and protagonists. Todorov offers an interesting example of this: the commemoration of the fiftieth anniversary of the Hiroshima atomic bomb. For the Japanese, the episode represents the most terrible suffering ever inflicted upon any nation. In the Hiroshima Peace Memorial Museum the Japanese are depicted as victims and not as culprits. Meanwhile, Americans see

---

28 Walker (2006) 23.

29 Todorov (2000) 134.

30 Todorov (2000) 142.

the atomic bomb as the only way of putting an end to "an aggressive fanatical and savage enemy";[31] as the last battle against the forces of evil. Todorov points out that both of these accounts hide important facts. Americans downplay the fact that the bomb was not necessary to defeat Japan and that it caused terrible and unjustified harm to civilians. On the other hand, in the Hiroshima museum, "there is not the slightest mention of the Japanese government's possible responsibility for starting and pursuing the war, for the inhuman treatment of POWs [prisoners of war] and civilians by Japanese soldiers."[32] These two versions clearly show how the duty to remember can lead to the distortion of the past. Real history is not black and white. Those whom a tradition depicts as heroes could actually have been murderers, rapists and robbers, and those seen as victims could perhaps have also been culprits. In Colombia, paramilitaries and guerrillas have presented themselves as heroes forced to take up arms and kill to fight for a just order.[33] It is for this reason that it is no accident that the respect of a person or a community for their ancestors goes hand in hand with efforts to clean up history in order to present a positive image of them. Apart from those few who actually want to embody evil characters, most of us would prefer not to be the heirs of villains. A major expression of this phenomenon is people's tendency to sacralize the past. When this happens, the past becomes untouchable and sanctified. This is precisely the case for nationalist discourses and religious narratives, which contain partial versions of historical facts, facts which followers may sometimes be forbidden to examine critically. In sum, the duty to remember is grounded on narratives of identity and public expressions like commemorations, museums, political speeches and textbooks, which are usually accompanied by partial and manipulated versions of the past. One can object that this is an assumption that history as a discipline is always true and complete. However, as matter of fact, history is a contested field. An answer to this objection, therefore, is that when historical controversies are taken seriously, participants can be led to believe that there are no absolute truths, and therefore that past events and heroes should not be sacralized.

A second peril of the duty to remember is that it may foment violence. This can be the case for those who either were victims or have close relations with them. As Primo Levi writes, "an oppressed person can become an oppressor, and often does."[34] Today, there is no war or internal conflict in which the past is not one of the motivations (or excuses) of at least one of the parties. Thus, for instance, in Rwanda, the Hutus, who had been oppressed by Belgians and Tutsis,

---

31 Todorov (2000) 146.

32 Todorov (2000) 146.

33 See Pecaut (1997). Also Grupo de Memoria Histórica (2013).

34 Primo Levi, *Conversazioni e intreviste, 1967–1987* (Turin: Einaudi, 1997) 247, quoted in Todorov (2000) 166.

killed hundreds of thousands of Tutsis in the 1990s. The rhetoric used by the Hutus invoked the humiliation inflicted upon them by the Tutsis during Belgian colonial rule. Similarly, Serbian leaders justified going to war against Croatia on the basis of Croatia's collaboration with the Nazis during WWII. In Colombia, *Tirofijo*, the founder and well-known chief of FARC, the largest guerrilla group in this country, declared that he was fighting because he and his family had been displaced by the government.[35] Meanwhile, Carlos Castaño, one of the founders of the paramilitary group AUC, affirmed in a biography that he was fighting because guerillas had kidnapped and murdered his father.[36] In all these cases, it seems that political leaders and people in general do not learn from the past. Indeed, if the past teaches anything, it is that terrible and unjust violence and oppression inflicted upon innocent people ultimately generates more violence in the future, and, importantly, that in such situations, people can be encouraged by their leaders to commit atrocities in the name of their ancestors. For those who are possessed by this feeling of revenge, the desire for retribution becomes an essential part of their personal identity. As was said earlier, to keep a promise contributes significantly to who I am. So, one can see exacting revenge as fulfilling a promise that one has made to one's ancestors. In other words, revenge is one manifestation of the duty to remember.

A third peril of the duty to remember is victimization. The problem here is not the condition of being a victim, but the relationship between this condition and compassion. As Todorov points out, being a victim sometimes is accompanied with certain privileges and benefits, "[it] gives you grounds to complain, to protest, and to make demands."[37] When the victim is recognized as such by society, her opinions, her mere appearance before others and her complaints are listened to with some sense of reverence. But, we may ask, why is it wrong to ground these privileges in compassion?

Suffering harm, especially moral harm, such as slavery, racial and gender discrimination and oppression of any kind, is something no reasonable person would wish to experience. In moral suffering, the worth and respect of the victim have been seriously undermined and damaged. In that sense, it is fair for victims to demand some sort of alleviation of their suffering. It would be a sign of an unjust society that those who have not suffered do not feel compassion for victims. If that is so, then one may wonder how victimization could be perilous. Following Lawrence Blum's analysis of compassion, one may say that it is a complex altruistic emotion that involves at least two aspects: the imaginative

35 See Álape (2004) 64–77. FARC is the *Fuerzas Armadas Revolucionarias de Colombia* (Revolutionary Armed Forces of Colombia).

36 See Aranguren (2001) 53–74. AUC is the *Autodefensas Unidas de Colombia* (United Self-Defense Forces of Colombia).

37 Todorov (2000) 143.

reconstruction of negative conditions that another person or group has experienced and a "serious concern for the victim's good."[38] Recent discussions about the moral value of compassion focus on the connection that may exist between this sentiment and the duty to aid others. For its critics, the problem of compassion is that it is accompanied by a sense of humiliation toward the victim.[39] Its defenders answer this objection by saying that it is necessary to distinguish between compassion and pity. They argue that in the case of compassion, the person who has this feeling sees the other person as "a fellow human being" whose suffering is "the kind of thing that could happen to anyone."[40] In other words, compassion includes a sense of shared humanity and therefore of equality that by definition is alien to humiliation. Meanwhile, with pity, the person who pities the other not only sees himself as immune to the other's suffering but also judges the other as having less moral value. This may lead that person to help the victim in a humiliating way. The whole argument in favor of compassion is focused on the kind of attitude that a person must have in the face of the suffering of others. For Blum, the problem of Kantian morality is its demand for some sort of coldness in our endeavors to fulfill the duty to help others. Following a Humean approach, Blum instead argues that the motivation to help others must not merely come from our sense of duty but from our compassion and general sympathy toward the others' plight. Although Blum may be right, the problem nevertheless arises concerning the attitude of the person or the group who is the object of that compassion or pity.

In his defense of compassion, Blum points out that this emotion must be accompanied with acts of beneficence towards those who suffer. This assertion is not far from Kant's view of compassion. For Kant, compassion seen merely as an emotion is worthless. It acquires worth only if it is accompanied by benevolent actions guided by moral principles. In this sense, Kant writes, "we not only must find satisfaction in the well-being and happiness in others, but also that such satisfaction ought to produce effective actions that contribute to the other's welfare."[41] The moral connection between compassion and benevolent actions is the key justification for victims having certain material and symbolic privileges. They convey society's true concern for the plight of

---

38 Blum (1980) 509. In addition to these two aspects, Blum mentions another two: "a view of the victim as a fellow human being" and "emotive responses of a certain degree of intensity" (509). In his article, Blum defends Schopenhauer's thesis according to which it is compassion and not the categorical imperative that must occupy the center of morality. See Schopenhauer (1969), Book IV, §§66–67, 366–378.

39 See Margalit (1996). For an interesting version of this critique see esp. Chapter 14, "Justifying Respect".

40 Blum (1980) 509.

41 Kant (1980) 143. For an insightful analysis of Kant's view of compassion, see Sherman (1997) 141–158.

victims. Since the imaginative reconstruction of what happened to victims is a part of compassion, the role of the duty to remember with its accompanying narratives and commemorations would be to revive this feeling of compassion in the members of the community and to remind them of the duty to alleviate the situation of victims. Insofar as compassion is a morally valid motive, the duty to remember is not a peril. However, there are two kinds of situations in which both victims and non-victims may abuse the benevolent acts that accompany compassion. One was foreseen by Kant and consists of a loss of autonomy; the other was foreseen by Nietzsche and consists of a threat against an authentic life.

A possible consequence of suffering a moral harm is a loss of moral independence. According to Kant, truly helping others is not about merely alleviating their situation, it also requires restoring their moral independence if that is possible. Part of the problem of acts of benevolence done for the sake of compassion is that they often fall short of this demand of restoring moral independence. One can truly help poor people, for instance, not by donating money that one does not need, but by providing poor people with means such as education, employment and so on that allow them to have independent lives. A dramatic example of this is the welfare state policies in Europe that sought to solve the problem of unemployment. Unfortunately, most people who live in poverty in developed countries belong to minorities who, in the past, have suffered many forms of discrimination and oppression. This is the case, for instance, for African Americans, Puerto Ricans, Chicanos and Latinos in the United States. There, the duty to remember may increase the dependence of people in need. If one follows Kant's assertion that true aid must try to restore moral independence, then narratives that go hand in hand with the duty to remember ought to aim at restoring the moral agency and self-respect of victims.

Another abuse is related to the heirs of past victims. As was said earlier, in a democratic and pluralistic society, being a victim entails certain symbolic and material privileges. This may lead present generations for many reasons to identify with past victims to "appropriate" their suffering.[42] This is the case for some relatives of victims, who derive material and symbolic benefit from being regarded by society as representatives of past victims. In *Hope and Memory*, Todorov discusses the case of Louis Farrakhan, the leader of the "Nation of Islam", who not only has made outrageous remarks comparing the plight of slavery with the Holocaust, but has also has exploited the suffering of African Americans to gain power and privilege.[43] In his critique of Christian morality, Nietzsche considers compassion and resentment to be the axes of

---

42 See Spelman (1997) 117–189. We take the term "appropriate" from Spelman who uses it to analyze the tensions between black women slaves and white women who fought to abolish slavery and to improve women's conditions.

43 See Todorov (2000) 143.

what he calls "herd morality", a morality that is based on the rejection of an active life. The constant recalling of Jesus, with his sufferings and miracles, has led later generations of Christians to adopt moral and political values that for Nietzsche were life-denying. In general, Nietzsche's point is that to live for the sake of others' values is a sign of an inauthentic life. This is partly what happens with the heirs of victims. Many are chained to the past, unable to build new and meaningful lives.

To sum up, victimization and compassion are not in themselves wrong. Rather, they become troublesome when they lead victims and their heirs to heteronomous and inauthentic lives. To fail in this kind of life depends partly on how victims and society remember and deal with the past. A narrative that, for instance, depicts victims and their heirs as totally lacking in agency and unable to overcome their circumstances is not helpful for building an autonomous and authentic life. It is not far-fetched to say that in modern Western societies, public discussion has been dominated by historical narratives that concentrate on either the greatness of the nation or the suffering of victims. As already discussed, the problem of these narratives is that they generate a misleading view of the past that instills in public opinion sentiments of revenge and victimization. A defense of the duty to remember must indicate how such perils can be overcome. As we explained before, from a hermeneutic perspective a reflective moral community has the duty to critically appraise any historical narrative before assuming it as part of its own identity, a necessary process for transforming the narratives that are oppressive or excusatory, that justify violence, or treat victims as less than moral and political agents. With this objective in mind, we introduced Funkenstein's notion of counter-history. In Section 5, we will show how this notion is also useful to counteract the mentioned perils.

5. TRANSFORMING NEGATIVE IDENTITIES

We have argued that the identity of a person or of a group is constituted by historical narratives that, besides historical facts, include ways in which members must treat and recognize others, as well as some version of how others treat and recognize one's own group and others. In other words, the ways we and our fellow community-members recognize others and the ways that others recognize us and our community form part of our identity. According to Funkenstein, a counter-history is a type of historical narrative that uses "the adversary's most trusted sources against their grain … [in endeavoring to distort] … the adversary's self-image of his identity".[44] When the identity of a people is based on

[44] Funkenstein (1992) 69. Funkenstein derives this notion of counter-history from Luckman and Berger's conception of "counter-identity". See Luckman and Berger (1966) 166–177.

a counter-history they see themselves as mirror images of a twisted view of the other, the other being a dangerous enemy who must be destroyed or dominated. In Colombia, civil society groups have been stigmatized by different parties in the conflict as groups that support their enemies. As Funkenstein notes, the peril of constructing one's identity in a counter-history is that the attempt to distort and destroy the other's image may also lead to a distortion of one's own identity. In other words, what happens with counter-history is that identity is built in a negative way. This is what leads to revenge and victimization. If the narratives that constitute my identity portray the others as corrupters of our culture or usurpers of our territory, and if those narratives demand that we take revenge, then one of the meanings of our lives, perhaps even the central one, may become the destruction of the enemies. Likewise, those narratives that focus on the singularity and the sacredness of the suffering of our people in the past and depict others as the only cause of this suffering may demand total reverence of the past and revenge, both of which lead to victimization. However, as was said earlier, the person or group whose only aim in life is to revere the past cannot be said to be living their own life.

From Funkenstein's notion of counter-history, we can derive an important normative principle: any historical narrative used for the restoration or instauration of a liberal democratic identity based on inclusion and solidarity must be grounded in a careful examination of historical facts. Since the truth of history consists of not only facts but also interpretations, historical narratives must avoid those interpretations that distort and destroy identities based on discourses of hatred, exclusion or domination. Of course the fact that one interpretation differs from another does not mean that the former distorts the latter. Confrontation between different versions is an integral part of history. In contrast to what happens with commemoration, those who study the past critically must take into account different versions of the events. Funkenstein's principle can be used to critically appraise traditions, such that one must distance oneself from and even change those traditions that are constitutive of one's identity but that misrepresent either one's own identity or that of another. The reason for this demand is that when historical narratives do not fulfill Funkenstein's principle, they suffer the perils of distorting the past and justifying vengeance and victimization. Thus, in the case of victim narratives that are prone to generate a sentiment of revenge, culprits are seen as diabolical beings who act for the sake of evil. A telling example of this is the anti-Semitic view of Jews that sees them as the embodiment of the devil and thereby as powerful enemies that must be expelled and destroyed. Moreover, in the case of victimization, the historical narrative depicts agents and their ancestors only as victims and not as a group of people who can build a new life, a new culture, a new society. Funkenstein's principle plays a central role in the avoidance of excesses that are inherent to victim narratives. If, in the case of revenge, we refuse to regard culprits as diabolical, but instead view them as finite human beings who have been determined by social and political institutions, we would not see them as objects of revenge but as a part of a social machinery that contributes to the generation of injustice and oppression. If, in the case of victimization, we do not see people as mere passive victims, but as agents able to rebuild their life, we will be less likely to fall into the trap of pity.

From another perspective, one may see Funkenstein's principle as a command to build a positive image of ourselves and others. In negative constructions of identity, one is in opposition to whatever one is not. Thus, a negative construction of our identity would regard any deed of ours as a mere reaction to others' behavior and not as an action expressing what we must be. Given this, a positive image must be understood as us seeing ourselves as a moral community with the capability of autonomously building our own form of life. In the end, what Funkenstein's principle establishes is that anyone must try to adopt historical narratives that allow one to recognize oneself and others as active agents; that is, with the capacity to build lives without distorting and destroying the identities of others.

According to Todorov, a good way to neutralize the perils of victim narratives is to take a critical view of history. This kind of history shows us that the past of any people is not black and white but grey. History teaches us that sometimes our ancestors were victims and sometimes they were culprits. Adopting such a view of history may allow us to modify our attitudes towards our own pasts and become less dogmatic in regard to the legacy of our ancestors. For this reason, we think that a duty to remember the past can claim validity only if it is based on a critical view of history, and by taking this seriously, moral and political communities that are transitioning from a violent to a democratic society can avoid falling into the traps of victimization and revenge.

6. CONCLUSION

To conclude, the duty to the past is grounded in a promise that we, present generations, make to fulfill the wishes of our ancestors. However, this promise has a limit. In the same way that one cannot promise to kill innocent people, one also cannot promise to our ancestors that we will satisfy their wishes for revenge. Also, a promise to the past does not entail that one may not have one's own life. The fact that we make a promise to our ancestors does not mean that we must embrace their principles if those principles were oppressive, either with respect to other communities or toward different groups of the same community. If, as moral agents emerging from civil war, a repressive regime, or an internal armed conflict, we accept justice as a moral principle and if we agree not to distort and destroy the identities of others, then we cannot make promises to versions of the past that are not consistent with such principles. Some may argue that what we as a moral community understand by justice is always relative and subjective, that each society has a different notion of justice, and even that for many nations justice is synonymous with revenge. As was said before, at least in modern Western societies the best way to conceive of justice is in terms of inclusion and equality. A society is more just if it is more inclusive and equal. And a society is more inclusive and equal if it allows the free and equal development of different groups of people with diverse cultural, political and social backgrounds. The aim of an inclusive society is to fight against any kind of oppression and domination. Accordingly, the duty to the past is valid only when it is grounded in a version of the past that is inclusive; that is, one that does not justify oppression, but on the contrary, places demands on present generations to oppose it. This way of expressing the principle of inclusion is very close to Funkenstein's principle of not distorting and destroying others' identity. A shared feature of all forms of oppression is the sense of humiliation and contempt toward the victim, which involves some form of misrecognition.

References

Álape, A. (2004) *Las vidas de Pedro Antonio Marín. Manuel Marulanda Vélez, Tirofijo.* Bogotá: Planeta.

Aranguren, M. (2001) *Mi confesión: Carlos Castaño revela sus secretos.* Bogotá: Editorial Oveja Negra.

Blum, L. (1980) "Compassion" in A. Oksenberg Rorty (ed.), *Explaining Emotions.* Los Angeles C.A.: California University Press, 507–517.

de Greiff, P. (2002) "La obligación moral de recordar" in A. Chaparro (ed.), *Cultura política y perdón.* Bogotá: Editorial Universidad del Rosario, 160–174.

Funkenstein, A. (1992) "History, Counter-History, and Memory" in S. Friedlander (ed.), *Probing the Limits of Representation.* Cambridge M.A.: Harvard University Press, 66–81.

Gilligan, C. (1982) *In a Different Voice: Psychological Theory and Woman Development.* Cambridge M.A.: Harvard University Press.

Grupo de Memoria Histórica (2013) *¡Basta ya! Colombia: memorias de guerra y dignidad.* Bogotá: Imprenta Nacional.

Kant, I. (1980) *Lectures on Ethics. (1775–1780)*, transl. L. Infeld. Indianapolis I.N.: Hackett Publishing.

Luckman, P. and Berger, Th. (1966) *The Social Construction of Reality.* New York: Anchor Books.

McCarthy, Th. (2002) "*Vergangenheitsbewältigung* in the USA: On the Politics of the Memory of Slavery". *Political Theory*, **30**, no. 5: 623–648.

Margalit, A. (1996) *The Decent Society*, transl. N. Goldblum. Cambridge: Cambridge University Press.

Pecaut, D. (1997) "Presente, pasado y futuro de la violencia". *Análisis Político*, no. 30: 3–36.

Ricoeur, P. (1992) *Oneself as Another*, transl. K. Blamey. Chicago I.L.: Chicago University Press.

Schopenhauer A. (1969) *The World as Will and Representation*, Vol. 1, trans. E.F.J. Payne. New York: Dover.

Sherman, N. (1997) *Making a Necessity of Virtue: Aristotle and Kant on Virtue*. Cambridge: Cambridge University Press.

Spelman, E. (1997) *Fruits of Sorrow*. Boston M.A.: Beacon Press.

Spinner-Halev, J. (2012) *Enduring Injustice*. Cambridge: Cambridge University Press.

Thomas, L. (1993) *The Vessels of Evil*. Philadelphia P.A.: Temple University Press.

Todorov, Tz. (2000) *Hope and Memory. Lessons from the Twentieth Century*, transl. D. Bellos. Princeton N.J.: Princeton University Press.

United Nations Secretary-General (2010) *Guidance Note of the Secretary General, United Nations Approach to Transitional Justice*. New York: United Nations.

—— (2004) *The Rule of Law and Transitional Justice in Conflict and post-Conflict Societies*, UN Doc. (S/2004/616). New York: United Nations.

Walker, M.U. (2009) "Gender and Violence in Focus: A Background for Gender Justice in Reparations" in R. Rubio-Marin (ed.), *The Gender on Reparations. Unsettling Sexual Hierarchies while Redressing Human Rights Violations*. Cambridge: Cambridge University Press, 18–62.

—— (2006) *Moral Repair. Reconstructing Moral Relations after Wrongdoing*. Cambridge: Cambridge University Press.

Young, I.M. (2000) *Inclusion and Democracy*. Oxford: Oxford University Press.

—— (1990) *Justice and the Politics of Difference*. Princeton N.J.: Princeton University Press.

CHAPTER 3

FORGIVENESS, RECONCILIATION AND JUSTICE

Carlos THIEBAUT

1. INTRODUCTION

This chapter explores the differences and intertwining of three structures and processes in which harm experiences are worked through and achieve resolution or closure, namely: forgiveness, civic reconciliation and justice in its different forms and institutional guises. As was advanced in this volume's Introduction, such resolution or closure can be understood as the achievement and restoration of trust. More specifically, by resolution and closure the text refers to three articulated demands and commitments that are present in the working through of such experiences: first, the demand that the infliction of harm be stopped; second, the demand for, and possibility of, a new beginning in a broken personal life or in a shattered social community; and third, the normative undertaking of repairing that harm and committing to it never being repeated or reiterated in the future. These three normative demands, and especially the third, underlie and intertwine in the revision of the TARR-model that this volume is developing. We normally convey the goal of ending harm in the imperative form of "Never again!", which has frequently gone hand in hand with historical experiences of harm. It was thus phrased, for example, in Adorno's formulation of the new categorical imperative that Auschwitz should not happen again or, in the ever-expanding wake of the Holocaust, in Sábato's presentation of the

CONADEPT report of human rights violations in Argentina under the military Junta. This chapter will outline the problematic role of forgiveness, as well as parallel, but distinct roles of civic reconciliation and justice in these processes of the closure of harm. Methodologically, these three different forms of closure can be mapped as being at the crossroads of the relations and ties that the three decisive figures of the drama of harm hold: the victim, the victimiser and the "we"-perspective of the moral and political community, that is, as will be elaborated below, the subject of justice.

2. THE ROLE OF FORGIVENESS, JUSTICE AND RECONCILIATION IN HARM EXPERIENCES

Forgiveness has a paradoxical structure in terms of what motivates it and how it is realised that makes its immediate, everyday understanding sometimes problematic and puzzling. We can map this puzzlement in three different dimensions. In the first place, *forgiveness appears as an intersection and confluence of the expectations, demands and normative actions of the three central figures in the experiences of harm*, namely the victim, her victimiser or wrongdoer, and a third party that is primarily understood as the moral and political community. The perplexity and fascination that forgiveness produces, such as how it is granted in some circumstances and justifiably denied in others, have typically been analysed as a dyadic relationship between the victim and her victimiser.[1] This dyadic structure seems initially appropriate because forgiveness is both the victim's privilege and her burden. As this argument will be insisting, just as we cannot substitute the victim in her harm, we as a concerned third party attending to her experience similarly cannot replace her in her forgiveness. Forgiveness, thus, has a certain personal and even individualistic dimension. However, as this chapter will be elaborating later on, along with this apparently dyadic predicament in the understanding of forgiveness, a third figure or party needs also to be brought into the picture somehow in the form of the moral and political community that assumes the different tasks of pursuing justice for the harm suffered, charging those responsible for its infliction, and attending to the victims and repairing their condition.[2] Forgiving is intertwined with these pursuits of justice. It is not infrequent that justice, in the form of imputations, reparations and compensations, is thought of as a condition and prerequisite

---

1 This dyadic structure appears clearly in standard analyses of forgiveness. See, for example, Griswold (2007).

2 Arendt already outlined the problem this way of speaking in the voice of the first person plural, as she does in her analysis in *The Human Condition*. More recently, Walker (2006) has discussed moral and political repair in terms of what here is called the "three figures".

for forgiveness and that the forgiveness that is asked for by a wrongdoer or a victimiser is suspended until justice is served. However, it is also true that in other cases those two forms of resolution – closing the past and starting a new future, forgiveness and justice – take different paths. Due to the more personal nature of forgiveness, it can even appear, surprisingly and beyond any due retribution, when some aspect of justice is suspended, such as when the victimisers cannot be indicted for their crimes or when the victims cannot be compensated for their loss, for example.[3] Nevertheless, even when justice is belated, or when the work of the third figure, the "we"-perspective of the community is postponed, the public dimension of begging forgiveness and forgiving becomes apparent. We can frequently attest to its symbolic force and public effects that go beyond the strictly personal relationship between the victim and the victimiser.[4] Forgiveness, then, seems unsettling and paradoxical. It is a private communicative action that sometimes acquires a public dimension and that elicits and changes the character of the public space. This unsettling nature of forgiveness, in the sense of how it sometimes requires normative public conditions of justice while in other moments or circumstances it may foment a need for such conditions, arguably stems from the differentiated moral authority of its actors (begging forgiveness if they are the victimisers, granting it if they are the victims, pursuing justice if they are the third figure) and from their relationships in specific contexts and cases. Furthermore, these different authorities are asymmetrical. They neither have the same powers nor articulate the same demands, in spite of the fact that they are mutually dependent, since forgiveness is given *because* it is asked for by a wrongdoer, or when achieving some form of justice may be a necessary – though perhaps not sufficient – condition for granting that forgiveness.

It is not only the intersection of these different perspectives that makes forgiveness problematic or even paradoxical. One must also recognise that *there is a central historical dimension to forgiveness in our era* that seems to press for it, on the one hand, but make it impossible, on the other. The very need for closure seems to increase when confronted with the terrible evil experiences that the past century had to face. A certain pressure of negativity, as it were, pushes forward demands not to leave behind these experiences unsolved, not dealt with, as if nothing had happened. Forgiveness, as an initial cultural

---

3 It is important to note that this gratuitous quality of forgiveness, in contrast with other processes of resolving harm, like civic reconciliation, asks for further elaboration. For example, the term "victim" refers to a collection of diverse persons or groups: the victim herself, the closest circle (like families) and, more extensively, her community (See Grovier (2002)).

4 There are forms of regret and asking for forgiveness that, being personal, have a powerful effect on the public sphere. For example, I am thinking of former ETA terrorists in Spain requesting to be pardoned (see Pascual Rodríguez (2013) and Madina et al. (2008) or the intense Argentine debate over former ERP guerrillas: Del Barco et al. (2007)).

response to wrongdoing that allows the world to restart anew, would seem a natural way to deal with such a demand not to leave evil without closure. But this naturalness of forgiveness – frequently reinforced by religious interpretations – has been radically questioned. Starting with the experiences of the Holocaust, whose shadow has extended over diverse harm experiences all over the world, the very possibility of forgiveness today confronts actions, behaviours and practices that today we view as unforgivable, like genocide, crimes against humanity and other human rights violations. That forgiveness might not be the adequate response to such crimes was already present in the case that Simon Wiesenthal (Wiesenthal 1998) presented and the extended public discussion that it provoked. Forgiveness, it was said, is a personal privilege of victims, and the dimension, the quality, the absolute negativity of such crimes would require a radically different approach if those crimes are to be faced. When considering great crimes against humanity, we are inclined to think that the magnitude and the quality of the harm inflicted in such cases exceed the limits of what is human and thus, of what can be dealt in interpersonal terms, such as forgiveness. They are evils, and in an interpretation inspired by Kant, they have even been thought of as "radical evils" (Arendt 1998; Derrida 2003), for which even the task of achieving justice through reparations, punishment and prevention seems wanting or incomplete. Faced with such crimes, forgiveness seems almost a meta-human, quasi-divine action that would require a transcendent motivation or an immense moral generosity on the part of the victims that neither rationally nor emotionally can be expected of them. Not only does the idea of forgiveness encounter problems when faced with such overwhelming cases; they frequently also reveal the inadequacies of human justice, which neither sutures nor cures the moral abyss that these cases create in us. As Arendt once said, we can only forgive what we can punish, and those crimes overwhelm us both in forgiving as much as in punishment. This chapter will periodically revisit her idea in an attempt to understand it. For Arendt it would seem that the limits of forgiveness are like the limits of an action, a performative action, it seems, that would confront what it could never encompass. But is that really the case? Would the great harms in history, the almost absolute evils, remain outside the realm of negative experiences of harm, pain and suffering that seek resolution?

On the opposite side of such impossible forgiveness we might find a third dimension that problematises the exercising of forgiveness. *Forgiveness is frequently under suspicion because it is easy to pervert and to instrumentalise in diverse ways, often for political ends.* One typical form that this suspicion takes is political pardons that, while seeming to be necessary in many circumstances as a precondition for transitional processes from war to peace or from dictatorships to democracy, in many other cases and processes they have had the opposite effect of prolonging harm, blocking justice and preventing such processes from being able to right the wrong. Indeed, many of the suspicions surrounding forgiveness and its public impact seem to stem from these distortions. Rhetorical appeals for forgiveness that, over time, appear more like acts of political correctness or acts of interested political prudence – like the one made by the Catholic Church regarding Galileo, or by the Spanish monarchy for the colonisation of the Americas, or by the United States for slavery – seem like symbolic but useless measures to whitewash the past. In such circumstances, we tend to think that something more than a mere verbal act would be required; rather, some form of active reparation is needed in order to really acknowledge harms of such magnitude. Also, hasty pardons for victimisers, like the Argentine Act of Due Obedience (*Ley de Obedienca Debida*) and Clean State Act (*Ley de Punto Final*) in transitional processes, or amnesties for crimes committed in dictatorships, even although they might be motivated by immediate political necessity, are generally perceived to be acts of concealment and amnesia. These are not the only distorted forms of forgiveness that may make it suspect, however. Indeed, when considering a specific crime – a terrorist act, an instance of torture, or an unjust imprisonment, for instance – any claim for *justice* usually tends to speak louder than whatever significance *forgiveness* might have. It would be too onerous, we think, to appeal to the victim's forgiveness if she has not received beforehand the benefits of justice, whatever these might be. In the public sphere and in consideration of specific actions, it would seem that forgiveness, such as these peculiar types of pardon referred to earlier, interrupts, delays or distorts justice. It is from these and other similar sources that suspicions can arise about forgiveness in its distorted forms, which can quickly lead us to declare it to be either useless or impossible; useless because seemingly what could be gained from it can surely be achieved through justice, and impossible because its demands can be too burdensome, almost inhuman.

It is quite unsatisfactory to try to resolve or clarify conceptually what experienced reality presents as being intermingled, mixed, problematic or even aporetic. However, conceptual clarifications can perhaps fulfil a lesser role of establishing conceptual maps that can help us try to understand the problems that we encounter. Thus, it may be advisable to establish some distinctions that could save forgiveness from some of the strongest suspicions that are cast upon it. We can differentiate forgiveness from civic and political reconciliation,[5] and we can contrast it with justice. These represent three ways of resolving and closing harm, but each seems to look in a different direction. They are three dimensions in which we can dissect the meaning and effects of broken human relationships when they are tainted with negativity, or of relationships that are themselves the origin of such negativity and harm. Though the "we" of the moral and political community may be especially relevant, as will be argued

---

5 See Digeser (2001) Verdeja (2009).

here, forgiveness is a form of communicative action, in some sense anomalously so,[6] between the victim and the victimiser. As a communicative action, it is specifically focused on the victim who carries the moral authority of the action of forgiving. The victim, therefore, is the subject of forgiving, she who grants it, and sometimes demands the power to exercise it. Civic reconciliation, on the other hand, focuses on the community and its "we"-perspective. Evidently, it overlaps with forgiveness in the sense that those who are reconciled are, after all, persons with their own histories and emotions, their reasons and their motives, although they may not identify with them as such. Reconciliation is a task of the community, civic or moral, and it is the community that must assume the chore of reconstructing or repairing the broken fabric of normative relations that harm has caused, such as the injury of rights, the breakdown of civic trust, and the destruction of the dignity of persons. This task of reconciliation is often made difficult and burdensome when serious harm has been perpetrated, like with crimes against humanity as referred to above. If that poses serious problems for personal forgiveness (Wiesenthal 1998; Del Barco 2007), then these great harms can hinder civic reconciliation by frequently making it dependent on prior justice, and they demand work that is never easy for both personal and collective memories. If *forgiveness* has a problematic relationship with the justice that is due to a victim because of her being a subject or agent, then *reconciliation* can be said to also have a complex relationship with justice. "Justice" refers here to the legal dimensions of liability of wrongdoers and due compensation for victims. It is part of the authority of the "we" of the community in its legal form or, more generally, in its attitude and normative practices. This chapter will return further on to the idea that justice might be a necessary but never a sufficient condition for forgiveness and also that justice is a necessary but insufficient condition for the reconciliation of a moral and political community. If the victim values forgiveness over justice, it means that it cannot be required, even if granting it is encouraged. At the same time, though, reconciliation similarly cannot be reduced to the serving of justice that is owed to the victims by compensating them or palliating the effects of harm they suffered, nor by merely making perpetrators responsible for their actions. Reconciliation also has to do with the moral tone or identity of the community, similarly to personal forgiveness that focuses on the character, qualities and circumstances of the victim. Civic reconciliation refers to the normative web of interactions of trust, mutual respect and shared cultural meanings, at least in the sense of the cultural meanings attached to the negative experience that the community has suffered. Thus, it can be thought of as an *achievement* of that community when it has done the *Trauerarbeit*, the working through harm, when justice has

6 It is anomalous because, as Grovier (2002) notes, forgiving is not a purely performative act: the granting of forgiveness is always open to reconsideration and revision.

been served, but also when the community has articulated the shared meaning and significance of its particular harm experience. Such an accomplishment is precisely what constitutes that social group as a repaired or rebuilt community. However, the contingencies that hamper this possible achievement are not small. Asymmetries, power relations and institutional complexities overdetermine the identity of a moral and political community. It is common for such conditions to cause the collective voice of that "we" to be overshadowed or altered. Beyond purely symbolic or metaphorical language, perhaps it is obvious that it has to be that way. As will be further elaborated later in analysing its normative, legal dimensions, "we" does not speak. Rather, institutional positions, authorities, and factual powers are the ones who speak. Like the diverse forms of hegemonic public discourse that assume a common voice, these differentiated positions of the "we" operate with their own particular rhetoric and jargon. In emergencies, in specific contexts, they underscore certain descriptions and assessments with their diverse, particular appreciations of circumstances and of what is relevant in each case. In a structurally pluralist society, like all complex contemporary societies, it is almost impossible that these diffracted voices that embody the meaning of the "we" will not be disputed, and it is almost impossible that agreements in the realm of shared meanings will be able to avoid any negotiation, disagreement or imposition and enforcement. Thus, any claim of reconciliation can also be misunderstood or, in the worst cases, perverted somehow. Due to these difficulties, the task of articulating a commonly assumed narrative of the experiences of harm of the past appears to be the most obvious and immediate task facing the construction of a "we"-perspective. As anticipated above, when such a narrative – fragile, revisable and provisional though it may be – is not distorted and is successfully accomplished it can turn into a signal or an emblem of the moral and political community's achievement as a community. Civic reconciliation, then, has a special temporal character. What initially might have seemed impossible can subsequently be achieved, but equally what in a particular historical moment may have been attained can in later moments be questioned due to particular circumstances and political pressures. The time vector, or the history vector, is especially relevant here. For example, the Spanish democratic transition of the 1970s proposed different tasks and meanings of reconciliation that afterwards proved to be insufficient because some voices in the political community demanded that justice be served and remembrance be undertaken. Reconciliation, as an accomplishment of a community identified as the subject of political and cultural action, is constrained by these ulterior conditions of legitimacy and common consent extended through time, in addition to the necessary constraints of justice. It is in these conditions that we can find the underlying normative core of civic reconciliation. The "we"-perspective of a moral and political community is articulated in the shared understanding of civic trust, of mutual respect and in the solidarity that emerges from a shared, common experience.

However, in spite of these differences between forgiveness, justice and reconciliation, and even in spite of the difficulties that reconciliation poses, it is not clear that we could or should dismiss forgiveness, as problematic as it may be, by attributing to it the risks of the always necessary, always pending, and always falsifiable reconciliation, or the burdens of justice that is always belated. Forgiveness is different, more radical, and perhaps more difficult. With the name "forgiveness", we name a specific way of giving closure to harm in daily relationships between people. It is the waiver of a debt, the desire to disassociate ourselves from something that in the past caused us harm, whether we are the ones asking for forgiveness or the ones granting it. If the past cannot be undone, as Amery's resentment reminds us, it nevertheless asks for a type of erasure or bracketing of past harms, at least in the sense of relinquishing the right or the proneness to recover past wounds when facing new difficulties. As will be further elaborated here, forgiveness seems to forgo and foreclose resentment. With forgiveness, we aspire to not repeat or prolong the chain of harm inflicted and suffered, and we hope that its echo will not reverberate heavily upon us. In some way, the term "forgiveness" prompts the very possibility of allowing life to go on, and for both victims and victimisers to not remain anchored to the harm done in the past. Perhaps, as mentioned, there cannot be forgiveness without justice, but *forgiveness* speaks specifically of our interpersonal ties with a colour and a unique force that are not present and need not be present in the more anonymous relations in the sphere of *justice* or in the mutual respect of the also anonymous public realm of *civic trust*. When forgiveness is granted, we can sometimes discover surprising dimensions of human life that we cannot explain, as Derrida noted, with a solely economic consideration of justice: as if it were a transaction, or a balance of interests in the accounting for the harm (Derrida 2003). However, in spite of the fact that this understanding of human relationships in economic terms impregnates our moral and political languages, and is even made explicit in legal language, justice need not be considered in those terms. Justice contains qualitative dimensions of evaluation and appraisal and forgiveness despite its distortions and difficulties, and it points to a further qualitative personal dimension that, when it appears, is frequently surprising and unsettling. When it does appear, it does so as a gift, sometimes an overwhelming donation.

3. THE DEMAND FOR A NEW BEGINNING: FORGIVENESS AND JUSTICE

What is the force that drives forgiveness and that can explain its peculiar character? To address this question, this chapter will need to mention some further features of what is a theory of harm that can help us to understand the problematic character of forgiveness. Such a theory can be articulated in two moments: in the first place, by noting the conceptual mechanisms that are present when we conceive of something as harm; secondly, by analysing the dynamic of the voices and perspectives that intervene in the experiences of harm. In discussing these two moments, the problematic role of forgiveness will be brought in.

Though this author has primarily in mind the great historical experiences of harm that have so powerfully marked with horror our epochal conscience, this section will focus instead on what is arguably a broader and deeper conceptual structure of more generalised harm experiences. In these more general terms, we should understand the conceptual framework of the experiences of harm by starting with the idea that these experiences are those that we manage to understand in different terms, in a different modality of judgement and conceptualisation, those actions and behaviours, institutions and practices that were, and frequently still are, considered as belonging to the realm of the inevitable, the necessary or the unavoidable. Those who suffer them bear them as part of their condition or, as something in the presence of which they can only, uselessly, raise protests, laments and curses. However, slavery, feminine subjugation, the repression of freedom of conscience, social and economic dispossession and political oppression, war, genocide and torture are some of these institutions and practices that, in spite of their obviously different causes and processes, and even in spite of differences in their experiential dimensions, have been wrenched out of what is considered inevitable and necessary in complex historical and conceptual processes. Here harm is conceptually distinguished from evil, where evil is something that we take as overwhelming, unexplainable and unavoidable, as beyond our control and dependent on a will that prevails over human beings, be it the divinities, Nature or the blind force of history. In contrast, when we designate something as harm we tend to understand it as something that is avertable, as something that could have been otherwise, and as something that should have been avoided and, above all, should be avoided. Designating something as harm is to bring it from the realm of necessary events into the realm of contingent human actions, by judging it and rejecting it, heeding its effects, preventing it. This contrast between inevitable evil and evitable harm, which we believe we can and should avoid, is what opens a space for the task that we may call practical reason or justice. Looking towards the past, justice claims that that harm might not have occurred and therefore heeds the claim of the person who suffered it. That demand wants this contingent condition of harm – that it could have been otherwise – to be acknowledged and thereby allows for responsibility to be attributed to whoever caused it. Looking towards the future, justice articulates a commitment to ensuring that that harm is repaired and never repeated. This dimension of the work of justice has a conceptual link to what forgiveness also wants to achieve.

In *The Human Condition*, Hannah Arendt proposed an idea of forgiveness parallel to the communicative power that, in her analysis of human action, would be capable of breaking the repetitive and chaining irreversibility of mechanised and institutionalised human practices in industrial societies. We can read Arendt as already stressing what has just been pointed out as harm, to conceive it not by the modality of necessity and inevitability, but instead by the category of what it is possible to suspend, detain, and make reversible. Her analysis focuses on "the *possible* redemption of the condition of irreversibility, the impossibility of undoing what one did even if one did not know, and could not have known, what she was doing" (emphasis added).[7] Indeed, Arendt seems to be thinking of the normal meaning of the term "forgiveness", such as when we excuse ourselves for something of which we were not fully conscious. If in these circumstances there was no forgiveness in the form of a communicative address by one who harms to her who suffers it and the forgiving on her part, we then would be permanently tied to what was done, repeating the wound or yoked to it. Even in the economic language by which we so often understand interactions and their normative meanings, we say that we have a "debt owed" or that there are "accounts to be settled" in that regard. Contrariwise, in this first approximation, forgiveness instead seems equivalent to justice in the experiences of harm. It is the cancellation of a debt, the disconnection from it, and the promise that it will not happen again. In Arendt's analysis, forgiveness severs us from something we were shackled to but that seems to be connected to a lack of consciousness or explicit intentionality. Certainly, we excuse ourselves and ask forgiveness in daily life for things that we were not aware of, and the very act of asking for it is a sign that we are already aware that it could have been avoided, and we commit ourselves somehow to seeing that it does not happen again.[8] Asking for forgiveness, then, is similar to the idea that it is indeed harm, rather than an inevitable evil, and once conceived as such we can start a new course of action. However, although she does not express it explicitly, Arendt also seems to suppose that the harm caused is, in some way, equivalent to something lesser, of a non-absolute dimension. Her analysis seems perfectly adequate for daily pardons, with which we excuse our mistakes, our lack of attention and our misunderstandings. But would this analysis be equally valid for great harms, those harms that previously were considered inevitable conditions but that we have since re-conceptualised, like slavery, subjugation, and exploitation? When Arendt wrote *The Human Condition* in 1958, she was already aware of the "speechless horror" of Auschwitz, which she considered, with some doubts,

---

7 Arendt (1998) 237.

8 That lack of consciousness of the act that harms has parallels with the reasons that can suspend reactive emotions, like resentment and indignation, in Strawson's classic analysis (Strawson 1978).

to be "radical evil", using a Kantian term though modifying its literal meaning. However, it would not seem that such immense and emblematic experiences of harm could fall within what she considered the object of forgiveness. Indeed, radical evil cannot be forgiven or punished, argued Arendt, because it transcends the realm of human actions and what is within reach of their power.[9] Forgiveness, Arendt thought, is the alternative to punishment and you can only pardon what you could punish. However, that possibility, she seems to suggest, is excluded from those evils that overwhelm the very sphere of human action. The great experiences of evil, those that we still try to re-conceptualise as harm, seem to escape being objects of forgiveness because of their magnitude and because of their quality of radically negating humanity. We can forgive that which we did not quite know that we were doing, because of our inertia, unawareness or clumsiness, but we cannot forgive something that harms in a systematic or absolute manner. We can forgive mistakes, but not massive, repeated, systematic wrongdoings. These elude the category of the mistake. Radical evil, like Auschwitz, Hiroshima, the Gulag, genocides and crimes against humanity, is not a mistake or a collection of mistakes; nor does it seem that it can be forgiven as such.

However, there is something paradoxical in this course of thought followed by Arendt. As stated a moment ago, she should be interpreted, in this author's view, as proposing that forgiveness is possible as a new beginning to overcome the irreversibility of actions that, due to their sheer mechanical nature were not known and could not have been known to be harmful. But can we say that such unawareness can exist among victimisers of their crimes against humanity? In the 1960s, Arendt faced that problem in the trial of Adolf Eichmann, the great bureaucratic organiser of the Nazi extermination campaigns.[10] Eichmann knew perfectly well what he was doing with the detailed and thorough organisation of the transport and the carefully planned economy of the Final Solution, but in a different sense, it also seems that he did not know what he was doing. Arendt suggests that he seemed incapable of seeing the harm that he had caused, utterly unable to put himself in the place of those he harmed – to have, as Kant would say, extended thought. The banality of evil, as Arendt then called it, is an extended unawareness and inability to see, as harm would require, the effects of our actions or the fact that they harm at all, or how, in Eichmann's case, these actions functioned within an incommensurable economy of evil. To see something as harmful is precisely to conceive of it from the perspectives of those who were harmed and of the concerned third party or community that seeks justice for them. Such a decentred awareness is what Eichmann lacked. This consideration can be given an ulterior twist. Referring to the Allied bombings of the German

9 Arendt (1998) 241. See a detailed analysis in Bernstein (2002) 205–224.
10 Arendt (2006).

civilian population at the end of the Second World War, the German writer W.G. Sebald in his *Natural History of Destruction*[11] analysed how the war machine acquired a natural momentum that seemed to move by itself, destroying without any awareness of its effects. Perhaps it may be thought that the very mechanical naturalness of evil might excuse its actors, as anyone who says they were "simply obeying orders" might think. They did not know what they were doing, so goes the defence, and they might even ask for forgiveness if they eventually came to regard their actions as needing forgiveness – an improbable predicament from the victors' perspective.[12] But is this really the case? Is unawareness a sufficient cause for granting forgiveness? Certainly in many cases great evils have gone unpunished; the cases of Hiroshima and the Gulag are paramount examples, as are generally the still on-going bombings of civilian populations in times of war. However, these have not gone unpunished because their agents were unaware of what they were doing. Rather, another mechanism of concealment was decisively at play in them: the blinding power of victory and complicity with it. When such a concealing omnipotence does not play its distorting role, we refuse and we have refused, to allow other equally mechanical or naturalised evils at least as evil as that exemplified by Eichmann, to go unpunished. The idea that the intended mechanised evils of genocides could be forgiven because they are endowed with the peculiar natural power of being unconscious phenomena sounds really scandalous to our everyday ordinary moral consciousness. Opposed to such exoneration is the moral awareness that such acts should be punished, that they should be divested of their mechanical naturalness, and because they should not have happened when it was possible for them not to occur. That is, in opposition to the idea that human actions can, in the realm of evil, be unconsciously necessary, the idea of harm brings forth the consideration that they were not necessary and that they could be a basis for the attribution of responsibility to their actors, even in spite of their avowed unconsciousness. If they did not know what they were doing, we argue, they *should* have known. Unawareness, we maintain, is not a sufficient condition for the exoneration of responsibility because implicitly actors are also recursively responsible for the "mistaken" beliefs they might have or for their lack of explicit understanding about what it is that they do. With these types of arguments, the task of justice to attribute responsibility seems to come before the possibility of forgiveness, and thus, justice takes precedence over forgiveness, appearing as a necessary condition for it.

However, such precedence of justice makes forgiveness itself problematic. Why would forgiveness be a necessary component in the closure of harm if

11 Sebald (2004). This text is discussed and analysed in Thiebaut (2014).

12 See Anders and Eatherly (1962).

justice could be enough to undo the supposed naturalness of harmful actions? With what does forgiveness contribute to such closure and how can justice and forgiveness unite in their forward-looking promises that the harm in question must never be repeated? Perhaps it is adequate to return to the triadic model previously introduced above to continue this query on the specific role of forgiveness. In the conjunction of the perspectives of the victim, the victimiser and the moral and political community we can discover a more hidden force behind the rejection of harm, and this force can shed new light on its closure and the problematic idea of forgiveness.

4. THE VOICES OF FORGIVENESS

Seeing something that was previously considered natural as now being harmful is a kind of achievement that arises from long and complex social and historical learning processes of advances and setbacks, and frequently producing uncertain results. In the elaboration of harm experiences, such an achievement requires the cooperation of different voices and perspectives. It requires the first-person voice of victims who show that what they are suffering is an experience of negativity, a non-acceptable negation of life and its dignity. The voice of victims therefore seems to be endowed with peculiar power – that of epistemic privilege and of moral authority that stems from its non-substitutability. This involves more than just the correlation of the act of being harmed and the experience of victims, with the inverted mirror image of the perspective and the acts of victimisers. The experience of victims also seeks and demands a wider space of meaning, understanding and closure. It demands acknowledgement, an answer or a reaction. The immediate normative content of any such request is the ending and suspension of the harm that was or is being suffered. We can suggest that this idea of the cessation of harm and its non-repetition is parallel to the idea that we have seen in Arendt about suspending the chain of the irreversible. In the first place, it adds urgency and immediacy to the breaking of that chain of necessity and, secondly, it is a demand to the victimiser to halt his action. A cry of pain can be one form of such a request, although it is frequently unheeded, such as when the cry of pain in torture is proof of the effect sought by the victimiser. It can also be a demand addressed to anyone who can intervene to stop the harm being suffered. In this way, therefore, it asks for the perspective of those who we can call the third party, of the person or persons who perceive and attend to that suffering as something that also concerns them and as something that requires and elicits some action on their part. The difference between the victimiser and this concerned third party, appearing here as the moral and political community mentioned earlier, is that whilst for the victimiser harm is something that is instrumental to his ends, and thus is agent-related, for the concerned third party the attention that the harm suffered requires is directed to whomever suffers it. The concerned third party therefore is focused on the victim, not on herself. This chapter's "concerned third party" is, then, a third figure in the experience of harm, as pointed out above. It is the centre or the emblem of the communal perspective, the first person plural of the "we"-perspective that, responding to the victims' suffering, takes upon itself the negativity that victims suffer and carries out the tasks of justice. This "we"-perspective is the normative subject of justice but, as has already been suggested, in order to perform its role it has to be materialised and enacted in differentiated tasks and institutions that may, at the same time, be coloured by different appropriate emotions and attitudes that modulate them. It attends and cares for the victim; it tries to heal and repair the harm that has been endured; it attributes responsibilities, judges the victimiser, punishes them and demands compensation from them; but it also encompasses and assumes the burden of negativity that the victim suffered. In this latter sense, it shapes the ultimate normative demand of "never-again", and provides the means for this imperative and commitment to achieve its institutional form. The "we"-perspective strives to be inclusive even with conflicts and tensions. That is, after all, why it is expressed in the first-person plural, even though it is diffracted into different roles, practices and guises. On the one hand, the institutional differentiation of this third figure, for example, in its legal dimensions and its political roles, requires that its concerns be discursively articulated. On the other hand, it also aspires to integrate the negativity of the victim and the negativity of the victimiser: the former as healing and compensation, and the latter as the attribution of responsibility. The concerned "we" does not assume these negativities as if it itself were the one who has been harmed. It is no substitute for the victim's predicament. Hegel thought that it is the law as an objective manifestation of the spirit that is hurt by every punishable act. If we conflate the law with the "we"-perspective as the subject who articulates the law and applies it, we could be tempted, as Hegel does, to consider law also as the subject of harm itself. However, just as the particular victim cannot be substituted in the harm that she endured, in her hardship or in the tasks she undertakes when claiming justice, she also cannot be substituted in the sphere of justice, or as a citizen in social life, nor in her personal relationships which endowed her with the moral capacity to forgive or to abstain from forgiving. It is not necessary to think that one must stand in the victim's shoes, or even take her place, to perceive the harm experienced for what it is and to understand how to respond to its demands. This answer is also projected as a perspective of a new beginning that does not nullify the past but receives it as a petition in the present and as a self-imposed obligation towards the future. When saying "Never again!" the "we"-perspective embodied in the moral and political community establishes a commitment that does not suture the past. What was harmed does not cease to be so, and an extinguished life cannot be compensated for. Instead, the "we"-perspective opens its wound of negativity towards the future. The work of justice, because it receives its power from a past riven by negativity, starts a new round of action in the world, or aspires to do so. On this, the work of justice and forgiveness coincide, at least in the interpretation that we have begun to draft with Arendt.

Earlier, in analysing that first moment of a theory of harm that emphasises its conceptual structure, it was suggested that, given the incommensurable harm of experiences of radical evil, justice takes precedence over forgiveness. Now we have just seen that, nonetheless, the work of justice and forgiveness coincide in that both try to establish a cessation and a new beginning; something that is also involved in Arendt's idea that forgiveness breaks with the irreversibility of human actions. But why introduce forgiveness here? Why is forgiveness important and to what extent does it question or problematise the way the theory of harm has been presented here? Indeed, the term "forgiveness" introduces other dimensions to that theory. Specifically, it suggests different ways of relating the three figures – the victim, the victimiser and the third party – that can now be understood as the "we"-perspective, as the subjects of justice. What is stressed with the term forgiveness is a double dimension: on the one hand, the personal relationship of the victim with the person who harmed her and, on the other, the relationship of the victimiser with the community. In spite of being intertwined, each of these two dimensions has its own proper logic. Thus, we usually tend to say that only the victim can (personally) forgive, and that only the community can (socially) carry out justice and (culturally) elaborate meanings and interpretations. However, is this differential assignment of tasks – that of possible forgiveness to the victim, justice to the "we" – so clear? Does not forgiveness imply other things than only justice? Is the fact that we can forgive not more unsettling than the demand that justice should be attained? Would it not be unsettling that sometimes, due to circumstances and limits, we could not carry out justice even though we could forgive? And is it not sometimes this possibility of forgiveness-without-justice, of forgiveness in incomplete or impossible justice, that surprises us and leaves us speechless because it is precisely then that an unexpected and unwarranted, foreclosure erupts? On the one hand, as this section has been saying, forgiveness and justice are linked, but on the other, paradoxically, they seem to follow different paths. Arendt underscored their relationship but also observed that forgiveness moves beyond justice. Justice, in the sense of what we can punish, is the threshold at which forgiveness might begin to appear, if at all. That relationship is not the same as what Derrida[13] argued when he claimed that justice is tied to an economic conception in which we speak in terms of debts and their cancellation, and what is conditioned in social interchanges of values and costs. Forgiveness, in contrast, has an unconditional character. If forgiveness were possible it would be

13 Derrida (2003).

as an absolute gratuity; it would confront and vanquish the unforgivable. On this account, justice is only understood in terms of an economy of reciprocity; the balance of what each person is owed and what they owe, the debits and credits of relationships between human beings, something that, we recall, seems to be taken for granted when we say that forgiveness cancels our debts, and as Arendt noted, that is even explicit in Christian prayer. Forgiveness, on the contrary, seems to have an immeasurable quality or value. Derrida argues, thus, that it escapes the economy of exchange with this absolute demand.

But this would not be the way in which a theory of harm needs to conceive of justice. Rather than as sheer interchange, justice owed to the victim attends to repairing what was damaged in her world and her life, attributes responsibility to the person who caused it, and is formulated as a normative promise or a practical restriction that will prevent it from happening again. It is an endeavour to remake the world that does not need to resort to the language of an economy of exchange in order to be expressed. Even when justice is phrased in that language, it is something that nevertheless underlies and can go beyond it. If the quest for forgiveness is different from the pursuit of justice, it is certainly not opposed to it. Any proposed theory of harm that ties justice to the idea of a new beginning will have to differentiate them in another way.

5. THE FORMS AND PROCESSES OF FORGIVING

To understand those differences, it is necessary to make the analysis even more complex and investigate, as proposed above, what relationships are established between the figures of harm in order to see how forgiveness can appear in them. Up to now, this chapter has only considered, statically as it were, the characters of the relationship of harming and forgiving. A more complex story now needs to be told that pays attention to the processes or the narrative in which these figures or characters develop their experience. None of these figures is to be thought of as a static portrait or a still photograph. Victims are more than just passively suffering human beings. They also interpret and speak out their experiences with voices and testimonies that seek a place in the narratives and the actions of the "we" that is concerned about their experience. As suggested at the beginning, that will take the form of them trying to discursively elaborate an interpretation of what happened. However, interwoven in the victims' voices are also beliefs and interpretations, emotions, feelings and attitudes that shape their identities. Their voices are furthermore directed at the victimiser, who they accuse, expressing resentment or demanding recognition that what she did to them was harm, and repeatedly expressing that justice starts with this bare acknowledgment of the truth of what happened. When the victim or the "we" third party charges and blames the victimiser, they highlight the normative contents that sustain and support their accusation and, in so doing, aim at the normatively public dimension of justice.[14] At other times, however, victims may not demand justice but revenge, its opposite. Revenge and retaliation are the opposite of justice because the victim herself assumes the role of the moral and political community and turns herself into an avenger who claims the exclusive right to remake her world according to her standards for retribution. In such cases, which popular culture identifies with the failure or the weakness of the institutions of justice, the victim or her vicarious substitute takes justice into their own hands. Likewise, the victim can also feel resentment towards the person who harmed her. Bishop Butler, and after him much of the Anglo-Saxon literature about forgiveness, claimed that forgiveness is precisely the forgoing of resentment[15] – something that seemed desirable or valuable because the harmed individual can be liberated from the burden that resentment imposes on her. Indeed, in this analysis, resentment ties the person to her wound and does not seem to allow her to liberate herself and follow her own path. As in Arendt's analysis, she is tied to the recurrent nature of her harm. Forgiveness, when it is possible, will again have the liberating power of severing her from her condition, but it may also be possible that the victim's voice instead addresses the "we" in a demand for justice, as mentioned above. A theory of harm in which the negativity experienced by the victim is transferred, as it were, to the "we"-perspective would normatively conceive it this way. In this way, the problem of forgiveness is more clearly outlined, but it begs the question of whether the victim's demand for justice, which involves the third person "we" of the political and legal community, is compatible with still retaining for herself the possible privilege of granting forgiveness, and if so, how? Before trying to advance with this problem, it will be helpful to continue sketching the other figures with a more detailed pencil.

The victimiser, for her part, can persist in her blind and self-centred perspective and she can continue to deny that what she did was harmful because, she may argue, it was a necessary action, perhaps resorting to arguments about obeying orders or the need to keep her community clean, that did not allow her to act differently from the way she did. In her stubbornness, the victimiser may think of the harm as evil, but perhaps a lesser or necessary evil, or a side-effect, if not – appallingly – as a benefit of having eliminated a greater evil. So, in her self-centeredness, she may continue to deny what is here called the experience of harm. She does not seem to have access to its negativity except as a sheer instrument of her own goals. However, the victimiser or the wrongdoer can also come to recognise that she could have acted otherwise, that she could have avoided harm, that her action caused harm, and it is possible that she

14 Sher (2006); Scanlon (2008).

15 Butler (1829). See Griswold (2007).

may regret what she did and repent.[16] Repentance – one of the more complex structures in human behaviour – establishes a continuity between the victimiser with her past deeds, in the sense that she acknowledges what she did, but also opens a discontinuity in her moral identity, in the sense that she no longer identifies with those deeds. Repentance, in this author's opinion, decentres the wrongdoer's identity. It drives her away from her self-centred predicament in the act of harming mentioned before. In so doing, repentance seems to be the gateway condition for the perspective of justice and the entrance into the "we"-perspective. If the victimiser was previously centred on herself and her goals and not on the victim's suffering, the recognition that repentance brings of the evil deed decentres the victimiser, refocuses her towards the community and binds her to the victim in a peculiar new symmetry. Certainly, on the one hand, the victimiser cannot undo her deed and, thus, remains in a situation of asymmetry with respect to the victim. On the other, however, when she aspires to belong to the moral and political community to which she and the victim both belong, the victimiser also strives to orient herself as a partner in the tasks of justice. In this way, repentance seems to open a new understanding for the victimisers themselves, as the cases of repentant terrorists who ask for forgiveness show (Pascual Rodríguez 2003; Del Barco 2013). The path may be directed towards a strict personal pardon, but also it endows forgiveness with a public dimension or a step forward in the reconstitution of the moral and political community – an element of its achieving the repair of the civic trust and solidarity that it relies on.

Is it possible, then, to forgive the victimiser, and if so, how? It would seem that disentangling the victimiser from her past alone is not enough. It appears that two ulterior conditions should also be met: one, she should actively collaborate in the reparation of harm, in compensating the victim and accepting her own responsibility for what she did and what she should do; and two, she should feel regret, although regret does not seem to be a sufficient condition for the victimiser to become part of the "we"-perspective that is the normative core of justice. Again, the economic terms that some retributionist theories yield come to mind in trying to elucidate what the victimiser might still have pending. "They must pay their debt to the community", it is said, and with these words it is suggested that in addition to becoming an active participant in the "we" community of justice that compensates and repairs, in the justice that will make them responsible, in the justice that will try to ensure it is not repeated in the future, victimisers will also have to show effective signs of their repentance, and of that peculiar discontinuity with their identity mentioned in the preceding paragraph. In these retributionist terms, even wrongdoers themselves may

---

16 Tavuchis (1991), Smith (2008).

demand forms of punishment or penalties to show their new predicament. An expressive theory of punishment – one that understands punishment as the expression of the community's repudiation of a wrongful action – might rather understand that the victimiser may ask for a chance to publicly express that she already meets the conditions to enter into the "we" of the moral community (De Greiff 2002). This expression can probably be considered functionally equivalent to a request for forgiveness, at least for public forgiveness. However, even meeting these conditions would not be equivalent to undertaking the precise, specific communicative action of appealing to the victim for her forgiveness. Such a communicative action is born of a demand for forgiveness and is answered (or not) with its granting. This action, which has the effect of putting the decision to forgive into the victim's hands, and that thereby acknowledges the wrongdoer's dependence on the victim with regard to that decision, can only be thought of as a personal demand that can only be responded to at a personal level also. The communicative action of forgiving is of a different quality than accepting that the conditions that will make justice possible have been met. Again, it seems that forgiveness and justice, while sharing the goal of bringing closure to the harm, have different tonalities. Forgiveness, as has been suggested here, is a communicative and performative action. It involves an appeal for forgiveness, which presupposes and expresses regret on the part of the person who harmed. Forgiving is also a performative answer on the part of the person who was harmed, an answer that may be delayed or remain pending, even beyond the verbal act of granting a pardon. This communicative action ties two persons or makes an institutional or structural relationship personal. Again, forgiveness differentiates itself from justice in that forgiveness retains the participating perspectives of the first and second person, and is produced in them, while justice transforms those perspectives into a normative "we"-perspective that comes to the foreground. The two dimensions are not in opposition, but may rather be thought of instead as orthogonal, at right-angles to one another. The perplexities that the relationships between forgiveness and justice produce come precisely from this intersection of their different dimensions: the personal and the normatively collective.

The story told here thus far – the movement and the narrative of the figures of the experience of harm – is still too abstract and continues to raise doubts. Neither the articulation of the victim's voice, nor her demands for justice, her resentment, or her vengeance are always clear-cut reactions and attitudes. They sometimes intertwine and blend, and each particular experience of harm and forgiveness displays a different, non-generalisable portrait. The victim can aspire to the recognition of her condition, but also to some form of retribution. Retribution need not be thought of only as a material or symbolic restitution of something that has been taken away; it can be the clear demand for a public acknowledgement and reminder of what happened. Retribution could even adopt the form of the adequate restoration of a damaged identity. Thus, retribution may be thought of as the victim's claim that something be met or given so that, from her perspective, the victimiser could in some way come to be part of the "we", to be able to live with her under a common legal and moral understanding. The victim can then demand conditions, to forgive without forgetting. When, in certain basically religious traditions, forgiveness operates as if it were a demand of total forgetting, or as if it were a waiver that temporarily sets aside the tasks of remembering, at least for the time being, there is an oft-repeated claim on the part of the victims of political violence that "we may forgive, but never forget". The cautionary role of memory that is displayed here, a "Never-forget imperative" running parallel to a "Never-again imperative", becomes a central tenet of a reconciled public sphere. Alternatively, the victims can refuse that possibility and suggest that what happened is simply unforgivable – that it would be necessary to think about their negative predicament differently and that the justice they demand as well as forgiving follow different, sometimes parting paths. What the victim may mean by such a refusal to forgive – setting conditions for forgiveness or suggesting, in other cases, that nothing about forgiveness can be subject to negotiable conditions – is problematic both for the victim as well as for the "we"-perspective that the victim is part of. The victim's perspective and the perspective of justice are not identical, regardless of the extent to which the "we" of justice incorporates the acknowledgement of harm that the victim suffered and its normative demands. The victim's demands can go beyond the path that justice can or must follow, but even the demands of justice, for their part, can be too heavy a burden for victims, such as when they are asked in a judicial deposition to provide testimony that may make them relive the harm that they suffered – something that they may reasonably consider unbearable. Therefore, the victims' relationships with the "we" of justice do not necessarily travel along a single path; nor do they travel in a single direction. Because neither the victim nor the community can ever replace one another, they can adopt different temporal rhythms and the asymmetry that always exists between them makes the working through harm a non-linear achievement.

The victimiser, for her part, also cannot be described in the neatly polar attitudes of denial and repentance I outlined before. The victimiser might have paid the penalty that society demanded of her; she might have served the time that a condemnatory sentence imposed, but she might still refuse to repent. On having paid her debt, nothing further can be demanded socially of her, as justice and law cannot intervene in the subjective realm of consciousness and moral attitudes. As far as legal relations go, when a victimiser is found guilty and when she has served her sentence, her reconciliation with society appears complete. That is why it is at once shocking and understandable that many terrorists or victimisers, having served their time do not seek forgiveness because they do not regret their acts. In terms of the moral and political community, it seems that harm does not achieve closure in such circumstances. Likewise, it may also happen that the moral and political community is divided and that part of it still demands further retribution, for example by trying to minimise the impact of a regulation that reduces sentences and, thus, that some type of closure is belated. The forms in which the penal dimension of the wrongdoer or victimiser returns to the "we"-perspective are, thus, contingent on social and normative contexts; but then, this highlights precisely the normative character that the "we"-perspective adopts when facing the resolution of harm.

6. CONCLUSION

This chapter began by suggesting that there was a difference between forgiveness and reconciliation. The first is focused on the victim and pays attention to the personal dimension and her moral authority. The second has to do with the moral and political reconstitution of the moral and political community. Both aspects, however, are interwoven. To the particular difficulties of reconciling a moral and political community – whose shared standards or values and meanings, if they existed, may have been shattered in a historical experience of harm – we now have to add the particular difficulties of a community that heeds the victims' demands for justice, the problems that have been described in the last paragraphs. Indeed, it is difficult for the concerned "we"-perspective to establish its own task of reconciliation if it does not know how to meet these demands.

If victims and victimisers seem to defer from their different positions towards the "we" upon whom the task of justice falls, their different attitudes and reactions determine how the concerned "we"-perspective can and should act. However, as I have been saying, the moral and political community diffracts and differentiates itself in diverse institutions, practices, organisations and policies. The "we"-perspective of justice operates with different instruments and procedures and also implements its attitudes and answers by way of different institutions and practices. In a constitutional democratic society, the "we"-perspective judges and punishes through the justice and legal system; it repairs and compensates the wrongs through executive powers (De Greiff 2008); and it sets the guidelines for what must not be repeated by way of legal proscriptions and active political measures. Experience shows that these different mechanisms do not always achieve their ends, nor do they always act in agreement. The tasks of the moral and political community, in their differences and contrasts, make one wonder about its very nature. Even the generic term used here, that of the moral *and* political community, subsumes under a single concept a series of different tasks and, in so doing, seems to refer to a single entity that is perhaps only an imagined community. One can think of that community as a generic term that accumulates different tasks of increasing complexity, from the nation state to diverse institutions of a cosmopolitan community which, for example, must face and deal with crimes against humanity. As stated above, the "we"-perspective of the moral and political community is differentiated in institutions, practices and policies and unifies them in the exercise of responsibility in reaction to harm. It must be constituted, albeit discriminatingly, as responsible for the working through harm, as an authority deferred to by victims, victimisers and third figures in diverse guises of imputation and compensation, but also guises of understanding and concern.

The political character of this communal and institutional perspective is, then, also an achievement insofar as its responsibility goes, but it is always a pending achievement, while the working through harm in its elaboration and resolution remains unfinished, even in the limited sense of a moment or a specific geography in which a particular harm occurred. In these terms, the moral and political community must still shape itself as a just community that establishes structural conditions that make it possible to attribute responsibility for harm, to compensate victims and reconstruct civic and public life. The social bases of self-respect mentioned by Rawls (Rawls 1998) as one of the primary goods of his egalitarian liberalism point in that direction of the establishment of structural conditions for the development of unharmed lives. But the experiences of harm are probably more demanding that what has been analysed here. Although the moral and political community can never be thought of as a person and, as such, cannot be assigned the tasks or the authority that forgiveness requires, it nevertheless has an effect on the forms and possibilities of forgiveness. In positive terms, it sets the institutional conditions for justice that make forgiveness possible. In negative terms, as pointed out above as one of the suspicions that forgiveness has to overcome, through public pardons the community sometimes assumes that it can substitute for tasks that really only correspond to persons. After what has been analysed, the risks of perverting the forms of forgiveness, for example, in the forms of closure to collective memories of harm, are not as much the risks of forgiveness itself, but rather the risks and responsibilities of the moral community and, specifically, of the political community that is expressed by the state.

The responsibility of the community *vis à vis* experiences of harm has other dimensions that lie not only in the state or in the civic community but also elsewhere. Earlier, when in sketching what this author understands to be a theory of harm, this chapter suggested that the experience of harm, and its work, is a long learning process and that when it attains its closure, even if only partially, it is an achievement. It is a process that de-transcendentalises and brings down to earth that what was presented as evil and endowed with meta-human power in earlier historical moments, whether they were considered in the transcendent terms of God, Nature or History. The working through harm suggests that there is no inevitability in what happened once it is conceived of as harm. However, this conceptual perspective collides precisely with processes and deeds that we are still loath to think of as being merely harmful. They are still being given to us through experience as overwhelming our concepts and comprehension. It can be said that they are still presented to us as forms of radical evil against which we still have no resources, comprehension or action. This is what happens when we perceive harm not only in its local, specific dimension, but also in its echoes and its effects – in the global dimension of its meanings. Some forms of harm – we think, obviously, of crimes against humanity and specifically of genocide – shape a cosmopolitan geography of evil. If we emphasise the evolving character of the working through harm, we might think of those radical evils as places in which the working through harm is still pending or ongoing, and as places where justice is still pending. It is pending, it can be thought, because the shaping of the moral community, the "we"-perspective on whose shoulders falls the burden of carrying out justice, is still pending. It is not easy to foresee its result or, even less so, its rhythms.

But if the closure of harm, or the achievement of the working through harm, are still pending, then forgiveness would not be itself something that is impossible but rather something that is also pending, as justice is. Forgiveness may have a personal, puzzling character, but when it does happen, it relates to a moral horizon in the victim's experience that may overflow and be surpassed in the expanded topography of yet unapproachable evils for which we do not yet have clear normative understandings. In spite of their different logics and courses, it would seem that the possibility of forgiveness will be pending while the task of justice remains unfinished. And, in crucial, absolute cases of not-yet-fully-elaborated harms, forgiveness might only be envisaged when justice can be carried out. Again, this amounts to Arendt's dictum that we could only forgive that which we can punish. We can, therefore, hypothetically, ask ourselves: if justice were carried out in those cases of radical evil, would forgiveness only then be possible? Or, can the personal power to forgive anticipate the pending tasks of justice? I do not think we have an answer to such questions. The closures of harm follow diverse and different paths and logics, and they intertwine precisely because of their differences. We can be shattered and fragmented not only according to our contrasting positions as victims, victimisers or concerned third parties, and each of these figures, as suggested here, is internally fraught with tensions. As subjects, we are crossed by these differences and it is not infrequent that we are divided within ourselves. Arendt suggested that this predicament is, precisely, the occasion that asks for thought.

References

Anders, G. and Eatherly C. (1962) *The case of the Hiroshima pilot Claude Eatherly told in his letters to Günther Anders*. New York: Monthly Review Press.

Arendt, H. (1998) *The Human Condition*. Chicago: The University of Chicago Press.

—— (2006) *Eichmann in Jerusalem*. New York: Penguin.

Del Barco, O. et al. (2014) *No matar: sobre la responsabilidad*, P.R. Belzagui (ed.). Córdoba: Del Cíclope, Universidad Nacional de Córdoba.

Bernstein, R. (2002) *Radical Evil. A Philosophical Interrogation*, Cambridge: Polity Press.
Butler, J. (1829) *Sermons*. Cambridge M.A.: Hilliard and Brown.
Corbí, J. (2012) *Morality, Self-knowledge and Human Suffering*. London: Routledge.
Derrida, J. (2003) *On Cosmopolitanism and Forgiveness*. London: Routledge.
Digeser, P.E. (2001) *Political Forgiveness*, Ithaca N.Y.: Cornell University Press.
De Greiff, P. (2002) "Deliberative Democracy and Punishment" in *Buffalo Criminal Law Review* **5**, no. 2: 371–403.
—— (2008) "Justice and Reparations" in P. de Greiff (ed.), *The Handbook of Reparation*. Oxford: Oxford University Press, 451–477.
Griswold, C.L. (2007) *Forgiveness. A Philosophical Exploration*. Cambridge: Cambridge University Press.
Grovier, T. and Verwoerd W. (2002) "Forgiveness: The Victim's Prerogative" in *South African Journal of Philosophy* **21**, no. 2: 97–111.
Madina, E. et al. (2008) *El perdón, virtud política*. Barcelona: Anthropos.
Pascual Rodríguez, E. (2013) *Los ojos del otro. Encuentros restaurativos entre víctimas y exmiembros de ETA*, Santander: Sal Terrae.
Rawls, J. (1998) *A Theory of Justice*. Cambridge M.A.: Harvard University Press.
Strawson, P.F. (1978) *Freedom and Resentment and Other Essays*. London: Routledge.
Scanlon, T. (2008) *Moral Dimensions. Permissibility, Meaning, Blame*. Oxford: Oxford University Press.
Sebald, G.W. (2004) *On the Natural History of Destruction*. New York: Random House.
Sher, G. (2006) *In Praise of Blame*. Oxford: Oxford University Press.
Smith, N. (2008) *I Was Wrong. The meanings of Apology*. Cambridge: Cambridge University Press.
Tavuchis, N. (1991) *Mea Culpa. A sociology of Apology and Reconciliation*, Stanford C.A.: Stanford University Press.
Thiebaut, C. (2014) "El relato del daño como historia natural: el caso de G.W. Sebald" in *Boletín de Estética* **11**, no. 29: 5–91.
Verdeja, E. (2009) *Unchopping a Tree. Reconciliation in the Aftermath of Political Violence*. Philadelphia P.A.: Temple University Press.
Walker, M.U. (2006) *Moral Repair. Reconstructing Moral Relations after Wrongdoing*. Cambridge: Cambridge University Press.
Wiesenthal, S. (1998) *The Sunflower: On the Possibilities and Limits of Forgiveness*. New York: Schocken Books.

CHAPTER 4

RESENTMENT AND THE LIMITS OF A POLITICS OF MEMORY

Justice vs. Time

Antonio Gómez Ramos

1. INTRODUCTION

This chapter explores how a politics of memory can be affected by the resentment of former victims. Drawing on Paul Ricoeur, first a model is sketched explaining how historical memory and political reconciliation can be conceived. Then, such a model is confronted with the moral plea for resentment by Jean Améry. It is suggested that the political elaboration of traumatic collective experiences from the past is unable to comprehend the subjectivity of resentment and the lost trust in the world that it implies. Any account of the political structure of memory must cope with the particular emotions of the individuals, and especially with resentment, which, as Améry argues, remains as the last connection between accomplished memory and the reality of the past. This incompatibility of political memory and resentment shows the limits of reconciliation and forgiveness, but also the condition for their possibility. Finally, the chapter discusses whether the public manifestation of resentment can have any real, even positive, effect on the actual process of political memory.

2. TIME AND THE DUTY OF MEMORY

Why ought we to remember? Why should the imperative of memory be the new categorical imperative, as Theodor Adorno once put it? (Adorno 1970, 358) Many persons would promptly answer that the moral reason to remember the atrocities of the past is for them not to happen again. This seems a most natural response, as it is connected with the ancient topos of *historia magistra vitae*: the idea of learning from history in order to avoid past mistakes and crimes in the future. To be sure, there is nothing wrong in preventing past misdeeds from being repeated, but there is something utilitarian in this argument, which makes it lose its moral force. If we feel that we are obliged to remember for the sake of our children and grandchildren, then the victims of past atrocities become mere instruments for shaping a better, more just future, and one might wonder whether they really get any moral retribution from it at all. From a moral point of view, it is to them that we owe retribution, whether they are dead or still alive and suffering, and not to future beings. Surely, we are responsible for the kind of society we leave to coming generations, but the victims of the past cannot be a mere means to that end.

One might argue that we are committed to remembering because any pluralistic, democratic political community in the present must take into consideration demands from all of its members. Since many former victims or their descendants have put forward such demands for remembrance, this would make memory a current issue that must be attended to. However, this would also mean that the political covenant is allowed to forget victims without descendants, or victims who, for any reason whatsoever, never come forward with their demand. To remember for the sake of the present, may actually involve neglecting the past.

Finally, one might appeal to some sort of anamnetic solidarity – a notion that we inherited from Walter Benjamin. One might say that we always owe something to the generations of the past, especially to those that have been oppressed, and one can thus assert that we are obliged to the past for the sake of the past itself. No doubt there is a large amount of rhetorical as well as moral force behind this argument, and this force surely sustains efforts to understand and promote memory and transitional justice, including this volume. However, being grounded on itself, it is a circular argument that does not really answer the question of why ought we to remember.

Now, the reader might ask: what is the point of demanding a moral reason to remember if there is no coherent answer, and if any discussion about it will end up in some sort of sophistry? The starting point for this chapter will be that we cannot find any moral reason to remember, because memory as such is not subjected to moral reason as if it were up to us whether we remember or not. Rather, memory is a fact of human life. Human beings cannot help remembering in whatever ways they do. As Nietzsche put it (Nietzsche 1980, 9), we humans always hang on to the past. Human temporality is such that the past always returns, and we can hardly decide the time for that return, nor the content of what is returning. Nevertheless, it is our responsibility to deal with it. It is not a matter of whether we ought to remember or not, but rather of how are we to remember in such a way that we do so justly and righteously.

To put it in Paul Ricoeur's terms, the question is: how are we to accomplish a *juste mémoire*, a just memory (Ricoeur 2000, 80)? We are talking then about justice *and* time – perhaps even about justice *in* time. That is, any possible accomplishment of a just memory takes place in two dimensions. Firstly, as a matter of justice, a just memory is the result of intersubjective work that society and political institutions must bring about in order for people to have trust in them. Secondly, memory is "a matter of time", so to speak, as it is in the course of time that remembrances of the past, especially of a traumatic past, can be saved and elaborated, or, alternatively, can be obliterated and forgotten. The first dimension is a political and a moral one, as it concerns human responsibility for the past time and for what others have suffered before us. The second dimension is, so to speak, ontological. However, since that ontological dimension suggests that time is somehow identical with the doing or undoing of justice, both dimensions are intimately connected. Time, historical time, human time, are not different from the work of memory. This is the reason why time is political. This connection, however, raises some questions about whether politics as time, or politics as justice in time, will be able to account for the sufferings and pain of concrete individuals. To what extent can the particular emotions of individuals be taken into account by a politics of memory trying to achieve a just memory? Or, in the words of van Roermund and De Gamboa Tapias in the Introduction to this volume, how can the reflection of former victims about their own suffering in the past produce a critical attitude towards it and contribute to the implementation of a restorative policy, while, at the same time, limiting such policy?

In addressing this question, this chapter will sketch an ideal model for the functioning of a politics of memory as *justice in time*, drawing strongly on Paul Ricoeur. It will then question that model by considering the personal experience and reflections on resentment by Jean Améry demanding *justice against time*, and finally it will offer some conclusions about the notions of *natural and reflective time* in politics and the possibility of *forgiveness*.

3. JUSTICE IN TIME: A MODEL FOR A POLITICS OF MEMORY

When dealing with memory, it is necessary to consider both personal and collective memory. Both levels are parallel in many respects, but they diverge in some crucial points that will simultaneously prove to be as problematic as they are illuminating.

In an individual life, behaviour can point symptomatically to unconscious traces of traumatic experiences from the past, especially from childhood. Traumatic experiences from the past may also return in social life. Just think of a big military defeat, a time of political repression, a civil war, a long-term exploitation such as African slavery in the Americas. Such collective experiences leave traces in the group that suffered through them. They can be followed by a time of forgetfulness and *Verdrängung* (displacement), but the traumatic experience can return, reappearing in public consciousness, usually as a claim by former victims. As with an individual life, where a long-repressed past can return to disturb mental stability in the present, such claims require some sort of answer and elaboration by the society to which they are directed. Psychologists call this elaboration mourning work. When society fails to do this mourning work properly, there comes what Tvetzan Todorov calls a *literal use of memory*, where the past is sacralized and society becomes obsessed with it – very often violently obsessed – and the traumatic experience is vindicated through compulsive repetition and collective madness. According to Todorov, many instances of ethnic nationalism follow this pattern (Todorov 2001, 11–39).

Sigmund Freud's essay on mourning and melancholy is usually interpreted as saying that in individual lives we can find cases in which mourning work has been properly accomplished. A person learns to accept the loss of a beloved object. Such a loss was surely traumatic, but she manages to live without that object, to admit the void in her new life, and may eventually redirect her libido towards a new object. This process of mourning can be seen as a process of maturation and self-liberation. The result would be what Todorov calls an *exemplary memory*, and what Ricoeur associates with a *happy memory*,[1] where the subject, having reflected on the trauma, can incorporate it in her own life and transform it into an example or a lesson for the future. To be sure, this elaboration of the past is psychically hard work that can absorb a long and painful period of a person's personal life. During this period, the memory of the traumatic experience can fully occupy the mind of the subject. Ultimately, though, when the mourning work succeeds, the painful memory can be put aside to the "fringes of consciousness". It can be forgotten, but it is an active forgetting, different from the passive forgetting – associated with ongoing violence – that aims to obliterate what happened in the past. The traumatic past experience, the experience of loss, no longer weighs disturbingly upon the present mind, but is part of life-knowledge and maturity.

1 "Happy memory" is the translation proposed for the *mémoire heureuse* by the English translators of Paul Ricoeur (Ricoeur 2001, 494).

In principle, it does make sense to apply this model, ideal as it is, to social life, in order to understand the process of historical memory in a similar way. An exemplary use of memory would be a kind of collective reflection and elaboration on determinate traumata that some members of society, or even the whole of society, have suffered in the past. Such a process would require, first, that painful memories of concrete individuals be made public; that they find some sort of public expression in the media, or through narrative in film and literature, in the arts, and also in historiography and academia. Those memories should then attain some kind of institutional recognition by the State, which might imply punishment for wrongdoers and reparations for victims. Above all, such painful memories held by a part of a society should be recognized as part of a shared past, and find expression in monuments, public signs and commemorations. You can only share a future if you have a shared past, and for the past to be shared – especially a conflictual past – it must be worked through collectively. Again, when that work is done, the past is not forgotten, but is relegated to the fringes of public life and need not be present in the public discussions of the day. This would be a form of active forgetting, different from evasive forgetting, which does not want to know, but also different from passive forgetting, which is associated with the compulsion to violence and repetition. Active forgetting does not really forget what happened, but rather re-signifies it and changes its meaning, opening up a possible common path into the future. Whether that eventually leads to forgiveness is an open question that this chapter will come to later on. In any case, active oblivion does not imply a recovered harmony or the restoration of something broken by the conflict. Divisions may continue to exist; the only difference is that the bigger offences of the past no longer shape present concerns.

Certainly, this is an ideal model. No mourning work can be fully successful. We all know this from individual life. When we lose someone who we really love, some kind of grief will stay with us for the rest of our life. One beloved person is not just substituted for another; rather the void after the loss is accepted and we learn that what is lost will never be recovered. This is probably the reason why some sort of melancholy is always associated to wisdom. Collective mourning is even more unlikely to be fully achieved. To be sure, nations, states, smaller communities do mourn and have rites for that. As we know, it is more than often that they justify their very existence and base their foundation on some experience of collective loss that they mourn institutionally.[2] But mourning here is mixed up with power interests and the hypocrisy that is inherent to politics. Even the sincerest of political ceremonies, necessary as they are for a collective

2 Anderson (1991) for instance, argues in *Imagined Communities. Reflections on the Origins and Spread of Nationalism* that this collective mourning is the real reason of modern nationalism.

catharsis, can fail to address the pain of memory that actually takes place in individual minds and hearts.

We can also conceive of a collective mourning wherein the polity takes charge of the past traumata of all of its members – not only that of the victors – as part of a common history. Such a polity implies a mature society, a society that is able to reflect on and deliberate about itself, very much like a mature, reflective individual who can go through her own mourning work. Hannah Arendt quoted more than once "Funeral Oration" by Pericles at the end of the first year of the Peloponnesian War. Democracy, said Pericles, is better than any other political regime because it is only democracy that remembers *every* citizen who dies for the polis, whereas other regimes only make funerals for the kings and the generals. Democracy might so be defined as an "organized remembrance" (Arendt 1958, 197), a political regime that is ready to mourn for all of its citizens, not just the few. That is, it is only democracy that can produce Ricoeur's just memory, while tyrannical regimes, in contrast, are unable to mourn sanely, and degenerate into violence and compulsive repetition through propaganda and repression.

This is certainly a very beautiful characterization of democracy and free society, and it speaks to the foundations of transitional justice by equating freedom and democracy with justice to the past. Nevertheless, it prompts at least two important issues to which we should attend. The first concerns the subject of remembering. Who is supposed to mourn for the harm that was inflicted upon victims? Must every citizen do so inwardly? Or is it more a task for officials, politicians and civil servants? Is it the job of some special type of civil servants who conduct services for the civic religion of memory? Or is it enough if citizens are given the proper education to read history books critically and to be conscious of the wrongs of their own society? The second issue concerns, so to speak, the space of remembering. At least for individuals, mourning work is supposed to be done in quietness, in retreat from the rush of everyday life. Mourning requires restraint. On the other hand, democracy is always, and has to be, a bit noisy. The public space cannot tolerate silence, and even where the most responsible of media are leading the discussion, new waves of testimonies, opinions, complaints, hasty judgements and the like will pour into the public discussion. Furthermore, since hypocrisy is inherent to social life, all ritualized forms of mourning – whether anniversaries, commemorations, funerals, or parades etc. – have a theatrical character that is hardly sensitive to the pain that was suffered. More often than not, solemn declarations that someone died for a sublime cause, for her country or liberty and so on, serve to attribute an ideological meaning to the suffering of an individual.

Forgiveness is the touchstone for these questions. In the ideal model sketched above, forgiveness would be the highest form of a successful memory. Only when the wrongs of the past have been acknowledged by both victims and wrongdoers – when they are made part of a shared history, and when the wrongdoer shows repentance for what she did – only then is forgiveness thinkable. It is nevertheless an exceptional act, as it implies a suspension of law and of punishment and depends on the gracious generosity of the victim towards her tormentor, such that it cannot be integrated into any legal system (Derrida 1999). Forgiveness is not, and cannot be, a necessary part of a politics of memory. At the same time, however, a politics of memory that does not pave a clear way to the possibility of forgiveness is a failed one.

In any case, who can forgive? Surely, if anyone, it is the victim who is entitled to forgive. She is and must be free to forgive or to refuse forgiveness. Yet, one must wonder, is this forgiveness supposed to be granted in the private sphere of the victim – he or she alone with her repentant wrongdoer? Or rather, should it be performed in public, maybe even within some institutionalized framework? Such was the case with the South African Truth and Reconciliation Commission, whose work and results were praised as much as they were criticized. In post-ETA Spain,[3] where the question of repentance by terrorists and forgiveness by victims is now part of the political bargain, it has never been clear how forgiveness should work or be performed; nor whether forgiveness should be asked for by every terrorist or by the nationalist parties that supported or tolerated their violence.[4] In any case, why should public institutions of a politics of memory be necessary for forgiveness if forgiveness is an individual matter? On the other hand, are institutions even authorized to forgive, or to play with forgiveness and repentance? In the last few years, we have been seeing how some politicians and public personalities expressed repentance for the misdeeds of their nations and asked for pardon.[5] Such acts rightly prompted questions of whether it was legitimate for them to make such petitions, and whether the manner of their doing so was correct, since usually they simply asked for forgiveness and did not await any reaction. On the other hand, one can ask: who, then, can legitimately forgive offences that were suffered collectively in the past? Is it possible to forgive in the name of another?

Surely, every single case demands and offers different answers. There is not, and there cannot be, any general solution to these final questions on the politics of memory, but they point to something that goes beyond the transactions and interchanges that sustain the legal system and the formal structure of the polity. This has to do with individuals and their subjective experiences, their sufferings, their grievances and how they cope with what was inflicted on them and on their fellow human beings. No doubt, emotions play an important role in these processes. In relation to memory, there is a particular emotion that is

---

3 *Euskadi Ta Askatasuna*: the main organization in the Basque separatist movement, formed in Spain in 1959 and active until 2010.

4 Rodríguez (2013). I thank Carlos Thiebaut for this reference.

5 Just think of Juan Carlos, the former King of Spain, apologizing for the excesses of the Spanish colonization in America, or Pope John Paul on Galileo's condemnation.

intrinsically associated with the past and directly challenges the model of a happy memory. *Resentment* is the particular feeling of someone who suffered damage and refuses to enter the social process of mourning work and reconciliation as it has been sketched here.

4. JUSTICE vs. TIME: RESENTMENT

Resentment is a reactive emotion with a bad reputation. According to Richard Solomon, it is the "villain of passions" (Solomon 1993, 291). This bad reputation goes back at least to Nietzsche, who identified *Ressentiment* as the source of Christianity and morality in general, and in so doing deliberately challenged the whole of Western moral philosophy (Nietzsche 1988). Max Scheler's book on *ressentiment* tried to overtake Nietzsche with a phenomenological analysis that ended up locating the "man of ressentiment" in practically every figure of modern life, depicting a man (or a woman, too) as the slave of an emotion that renders life impossible to live (Scheler 2014). When dealing with the question of memory, it is not unusual for a victim who refuses to participate in a process of political reconciliation to be disqualified as "resentful". For that reason, it is all the more interesting how the issue of resentment has been raised again, to the point of its rehabilitation, by an author who, as a victim, was familiar with the problem of memory and the Holocaust, and who was able to write from his own personal experience a plea for resentment that has dismantled the old condemnation by Nietzsche and draws our attention to the value – even the moral and political value – of resentment.

The son of a Jewish father and a Catholic mother, Jean Améry was born Hans Mayer in Austria in 1912. After the *Anschluss* in 1938 he had to flee to Belgium, where he later joined the Belgian Resistance against the German Occupation. In 1943 he was arrested and tortured, and spent two years in concentration camps, including Auschwitz-Birkenau and Bergen-Belsen. After the war, he settled in Brussels and changed his name to Jean Améry – a French-sounding acronym of Mayer – and made his living as a writer and a journalist, whose writing was always marked by the traumatic experience of exclusion, torture and prison.

As he himself wrote in the essay that this section will focus on (Améry 1980, 61–81), he travelled frequently to Germany during the 1960s and '70s, taking part in meetings, debates and radio programmes on the topic of the Holocaust. He conceded that the Federal Republic was totally different from Nazi Germany, and that the new Germans he now met were well-educated, peace-loving, and tolerant persons. Many among them were dramatically conscious of recent German history and felt responsible for what had happened in the 1930s and '40s. They felt responsible and showed understanding for his bitterness when he interacted with people from Germany. Améry also conceded, to some extent, that with Nuremberg and the post-War reparation payments, justice had been done in Germany. In spite of this, though, he said his resentment did not disappear: "I have preserved my resentments", he said. Those are resentments that did not start immediately after the War. They started later and increased in parallel with historical and personal circumstances, as he observed how punishment was meted out in a relatively limited fashion, and how Germans were conquering world markets with their industrial products, while forgetting the past at home. Some would object, saying that Améry's feelings were a personal matter – his own private business – and that you can find a lot of former victims who do not feel the same resentment that he did. But that is precisely the point: "what matters to me is the description of the subjective state of the victim", he said (Améry 1980, 64). In preserving his resentments, he did not want to get rid of them, but had "to live with them". Somehow, they became an integral part of his personality. For the moralist, resentment might be tainted, while for the psychologist it might be a sickness, but nevertheless, that taint or sickness was a part of him, and he was "obliged to clarify them for those against whom they are directed", speaking not only against his torturers, but to the world as a whole.

The Mind's Limits, Contemplations by a Survivor on Auschwitz and its Realities[6] was first published in 1966, after 20 years of silence by the author about his personal ordeal in the Holocaust. It was reissued in 1977, only a few months before he killed himself in Salzburg. It is not unimportant to note that, although Améry did not lack for recognition as a writer during his lifetime, it was only in the late 1990s and in the first decade of the twenty-first century that his reflections on resentment attracted the interest of many scholars of moral philosophy and became a central issue in the rediscovery of the emotion of resentment beyond, and sometimes contrary to, Nietzsche's negative judgement. Apart from Sebald, a rare post-WWII German writer who was sensitive to the real issue of the *Shoah* and wrote some insightful essays on Améry,[7] the Italian Guia Risari also commented on the moral value of Améry's resentment (Risari 2002). More recently, Thomas Brumhold has extensively used Améry's argument to question the rhetoric of forgiveness, closure and reconciliation that, according to him, pervades global discourses today. Focusing on the case of the South African TRC, he places the moral value of Améry's resentment in opposition to Desmond Tutu's discourse of reconciliation and harmony that, to his mind, *forced* victims to grant forgiveness. Furthermore, Jay Bernstein has

6 The original German title was *Jenseits von Schuld und Sühne*, which literally is rendered as "Beyond Guilt and Atonement". "Schuld und Sühne" was the traditional German translation for Dostoyevski's *Crime and Punishment.* The English translators preferred to ignore the Dostoyevskian flavour of the original book's title in German and choose the title of the first essay for the whole book.

7 See, among other essays, Sebald (2003).

reconstructed the puzzling vindication of such a negative emotion as resentment by arguing that Améry's personal devastation, expressed in resentment, actually plays a functional role in the reconstitution of the community or, in other words, in what we have seen as being the work of political memory.[8] If the present Federal Republic and its citizens have generated a collective memory that gives a moral meaning to their terrible history, he suggests, it is in part because of the intransigent attitudes of resentment like Améry's.[9]

All of these authors stress the moral importance of resentment, or, if you will, how individual resentment plays a decisive role in social morality. It might well be that the English language is more receptive than German or French to an ethical vindication of *resentment*. The word as such does not necessarily have to have a negative connotation in English. Indeed, there is a long tradition in English moral philosophy – from Bishop Butler and Adam Smith to P.F. Strawson and John Rawls – that has illuminated the positive sides of resentment as a justified bitterness and indignation at having been treated unfairly. *Ressentiment*, on the contrary, as a German word of French origin that came to English via Nietzsche, is directly connoted as a self-abasement that is connected to hatred and envy. Both words have co-existed in English, and moral philosophers like Steven Darwall (Darwall, 2013) could more or less establish that Nietzsche was right about *Ressentiment*, but not about resentment, seeing resentment as a positive moral value, as Butler or Strawson saw it. Améry, writing in German with Nietzsche in mind, used *Ressentiment* in the original, although his English translators chose to use the word *resentment* instead. The question of whether the feeling Améry was pleading for lay somewhere between Strawsonian resentment and Nietzschean *Ressentiment*, or whether it was both at the same time, as Brumhold contends (Brumhold 2008), could lead to a long discussion. To Améry, his feeling of *Ressentiment* was exactly as Nietzsche had described it, only he also felt entitled to proclaim and explain it, even if this was somewhat contradictory when its aim was to enlighten "those who wish to live together as fellow human beings" (Améry 1980, xiv). In reference to this last goal, Améry proclaimed that his resentment, or *Ressentiment*, might have some function in the moral reconstitution of German society. However, the function of the moralist as well as the historian to objectively acknowledge is somewhat

---

8 Brumhold (2008), Bernstein (2014). I thank Wouter Veraart for drawing my attention to Brumhold's book, and Hans K. Lindahl for doing the same with Bernstein's article.

9 To be sure, no one will ever be able to say the last word on the German *Aufarbeitung* of the atrocities committed by the Germans during the Nazi period. Nevertheless, in spite of many justified criticisms, it can be said that, throughout the last decades, the German public sphere has faced openly the past crimes and taken responsibility for them to a higher degree than any other society has done with its own wrongs.

different from the subjective emotion and suffering that the individual called Jean Améry – previously Hans Mayer – is actually experiencing within the uncertain and always unjust process of memory and forgetting.

It is this strong subjective aspect that Améry claims when he raises the question, which is worth dwelling on when reflecting on transitional justice. His own singularity as a human being is made of resentment. He knows it by introspection, and he is aware of how unnatural it is. It is more than unnatural:

> [I]t is illogical – resentment nails one of us onto the cross of his ruined past. Absurdly, it demands that the irreversible be turned around, that the event be undone. Resentment blocks the exit to the genuine human dimension, the future. ... The time sense of the person trapped in resentment is twisted around, disordered, if you wish, for it desires two impossible things: regression into the past and nullification of what happened. (Améry 1980, 64)

To be nailed onto the past, that is the sickness of the resentful, but it is also very human. Nietzsche, the great critic of *Ressentiment*, also wrote that to always be hanging on to the past is a distinctively human thing to do. It is what makes humans different from animals: where humans are animals who remember and cannot help remembering because the chain of the past is always with them. They are nailed to it, like Améry is to his resentment. Memory is the unnaturalness of humans, because the natural thing is to live in the present and to forgive. Memory sets an impossible task to human life, says Nietzsche. Living can be considered, as it were, the art of handling the past and creating something new. It is difficult to say whether Améry is actually the norm among Holocaust survivors. We know a few of them who were able to overcome resentment and who dealt more peacefully with their own past, like Primo Levi, or were even able to talk about reconciliation, like Martin Buber. However, we can also imagine that many silent victims also reserved and preserved their resentment. We also must accept that resentment must also be felt by other people who have suffered in conflicts where our sympathies may not be as clear as they are when we talk of the Holocaust and Nazism. It is not always easy to decide whether they are just resentful or their resentment has a moral dimension like Améry's. In any case, it is this unnatural and mostly subjective reaction of the resentful person what Améry is vindicating. A reading of his essay suggests that there are two different features to his resentment.

1. First, resentment is an integrating part of subjectivity. The resentful person is made from her resentment. That is also the reason why, for Améry, the victim has an epistemic privilege over what happened in the past. Through her own lived experience, says Améry, the victim knows much better than the torturer or any impartial observer what really happened.

This is arguable, but for Améry it is decisive. The historian can search and tell the objective truth of what happened, but she can never share the victim's experience, and she cannot know as much as the victim does. This is true, and not only in the sense that no one can have access to how others experience what they experience. That is a platitude. The epistemic privilege of the victim means that her lived experience separates her from the rest of the world. Her experience of persecution and being tortured is one of "extreme loneliness", a feeling of "abandonment that has persisted until today", because every trust in the world is lost after torture and will not be regained. The tortured person, the victim, can only speak from her isolated subjectivity.

2. Second, resentment goes against the natural course of time. The course of natural time is to forget, and the course of social time is to forget and forgive. The reason to do so might solely reside in efficiency or a need to recover normality. Societies, however, tend to look forward into the future, to try and move on and even re-integrate criminals at some later date. For society, punishment is not a matter of justice, but rather of re-adjusting, of re-establishing balance once again, and for people to live together in harmony. We all know how political transitions from dictatorships to democracies tend to be rather lenient with policemen and officials who worked for the previous regime. They are still necessary in the new administration for everyday life to keep functioning. This can be shocking when it is performed explicitly, as in the case of the *Leyes de obediencia debida* in Argentina, and many would rightly argue that, in the end, by refusing to do justice, it impedes any real confrontation with the past and allows the problem of the nation to persist. For many, though, such automatism of forgetting is in the nature of things.

The most important point in Améry's argument is the disconnect between the particular subjectivity of the resentful person and the temporality of the social body. Unlike the torturer, and unlike the people that judge him,

> only I possessed, and still possess, the moral truth of the blows that even today roar in my skull, and for that reason I am more entitled to judge, not only more than the culprit, but also more than society – who thinks only of its continued existence. The social body is occupied merely with safeguarding itself and could not care less about a life that has been damaged. At the very best, it looks forward, so that such things don't happen again. (Améry 1980, 70)

Such a passage portrays the abandonment experienced by the person tortured, the loss of any kind of trust in the world and the disconnect from all fellow human beings. Notably, he refers to *all* fellow human beings, not only the culprit, but also bystanders, and even concerned citizens who are engaged in the continuation of a common life. That is the reason why no trust can be fully restored and no reconciliation is possible for Améry.

> Whoever submerges his individuality in society and is able to comprehend himself only as a function of the social, that is, the insensitive and indifferent person, really does forgive. He calmly allows what happened to remain. (Améry 1980, 71)

For us, there remains also the question of how far this social, customary forgiveness that Améry denounces can be from (or how close to) the kind of exceptional forgiveness we have been discussing above with Derrida and Ricoeur. Where the former is unreflected and prompted by the demands of life and economy, the latter is the only possible result of a painful elaboration that aims to know and do justice to the past, as much as to a reflective and morally higher form of political life. It might well be that the difference between both is a matter of degree, and also that a measure of Ricoeurian pardon is always present in the automatic forgiveness that Améry denounces. Regardless, in any case, the latter is more down to earth and, for many people, is much easier to understand and to practise.

Améry's claim for resentment is directed against the de-individualized and interchangeable part of the social mechanism; that is, the person who simply forgives by letting herself be guided by natural healing through time. In this regard, his criticism parallels the Frankfurt School's apocalyptic vision of an administrated society that is blindly ruled by instrumental reason where there is no place for human responsibility or for the kind of consciousness and reflection that is proper for a humankind on its way to emancipation. It would take a longer chapter to analyse how the administered society, the impersonalized and de-individualized *verwaltete Gesellschaft*, returns to a "natural history" and achieves a "natural oblivion". Nevertheless, Améry is much more concrete than Adorno, for instance, who also claimed a real *Vergangenheitsaufarbeitung* and was forging a new ethics of memory, but who, in contrast to Améry, was able to find his place in post-War Germany and, though radically critical and pessimistic, was far from showing resentment. Améry does not appeal to great, thick notions, as the philosopher Adorno does. Instead, he remains concrete: "Whoever lazily and cheaply forgives, subjugates himself to the social and biological time-sense, which is also called the natural one." For those who yield to natural oblivion, to the efficiency of things and to on-going time, it is the particularity of emotion that aims to affect the state of things. In fact, "resentments are there in order that the crime become a moral reality for the criminal, in order that he be swept into the truth of his atrocity" (Améry 1980, 71). This is, in fact, the moral truth of resentment; a moral truth that denies and denounces physical reality, the reality of things moving on and functioning as if nothing had happened. Any person has the right, and the privilege, to protest against every natural process, and also against the biological healing properties of time. You cannot undo what has happened, but there is a moral faculty that nevertheless resists this natural reality. Oblivion might be healthier, but the moral faculty that resists oblivion is superior and has its groundings in that biased particularity of resentment. It is the particularity of resentment that is the point, not the general ethical notions of a duty of memory. The historical function of resentment is to keep alive the unresolvable conflict between victims and wrongdoers, even if the claim of resentment cannot be satisfied. Améry's point is that you cannot rewind history, and only through resentment is such injustice made evident.

5. NATURAL TIME, REFLECTIVE TIME AND FORGIVENESS

We can now confront Améry's argument for resentment with the ideal model of memory sketched earlier, in the first section. Whether there is compatibility between the two is an open question and should be decided in every historical case. Brumhold has tried to prove that, in the South African case, the conciliatory stance of Desmond Tutu appealing to an abstract *Ubuntu*[10] was incompatible with a resentment like Améry's or the resentment of those other victims of Apartheid who were reluctant to forgive. He also argues that this resentful reluctance has a higher moral value than many Christian conciliatory discourses that call for forgiveness. Be that as it may, the South African story is, regarding its social, historical and political conditions, very different from the Ricoeurian model that was presented in the first section of this chapter. Nevertheless, the question remains whether there is any place in our ideal model for Améry's grudging tone. Some recent interpretations of Améry, especially Brumhold and Bernstein, argue that his tone belongs to the process of mourning, collective memory and the reconstitution of the community, and that it can even trigger and drive the process forward. This might appear so from a third-person perspective, such as that of the historian who reconstructs the process afterwards. However, it is irrelevant for the resentful person, for someone like Jean Améry who certainly is not against mourning work and just memory, but is against natural time that naturally forgets. For the morally sensitive historian, this natural time is by no means the same as the time of memory and mourning that was under consideration in our first model. However, it is not certain that Améry, or any person submerged in resentment, would be able to appreciate the difference.

It would be very easy to conclude that Améry simply failed to do his mourning work. Of course he failed, and the failure expressed as resentment

10 Ubuntu is a Nguni Bantu term meaning "humanity". It is often translated as "I am because we are", or "humanity towards others".

was part of the collective process of memory that can eventually accomplish society's mourning work. His resentment nurtures the mourning as much as it makes it impossible that it will be accomplished. However, its impossibility is different from the impossibility of a fully just memory that ends in forgiveness. In fact, Améry does not even consider the possibility of such a happy memory or such forgiveness. What he envisages in claiming and arguing for resentment is not an elaboration of time, but rather its reversion. His is a protest against the irreversible, and that demand can only be met if others, not only the torturer, not only the bystander, but also their descendants, are really able to forever share in Améry's remembrances of the past – and even in his resentment if they are able to accept that Himmler is as much a part of their legacy as Goethe. The latter certainly might be the case in today's Germany, whose streets are studded with *Stolpersteine* and where memorials of the Nazi Terror appear to display more responsibility for the gruesome side of German tradition than was the case during Améry's lifetime. This shared memory of terror is part of the wisdom of happy memory that is achieved in collective mourning work. Even so, it is impossible, and Améry knows it, that the whole of the German people, and perhaps even the whole world from now on, share his demand for reversion, and his wish that what happened had not happened at all. He only expects that the impossibility of his demand actualizes the conflict and keeps it alive.[11]

He does not hope or conceive of a fortunate memory that is eventually accompanied by forgiveness. Instead, he reckons forgiveness and oblivion are natural processes that are imbedded in the efficiency of modern societies. As the popular saying goes, "Time heals all wounds". No doubt, in real life this is more often the case than the active forgetting of the just memory. As time goes by, wounds are covered and scars become almost unnoticeable. Society cannot eternally be angry at itself, and amnesties are no exception to this. Ricoeur himself complains that most cases of amnesty that we know of are not the result of the exceptionality of forgiveness, but rather are proclaimed for utilitarian, somehow therapeutic reasons (Ricoeur 2000, 582).

Clearly, here there are two notions of historical time at stake. One is the natural and blind passage of time, and does not require any special reflection on the part of human beings. In the long term, it destroys and erases all human achievements – good and bad – but it is also the condition on which the social mechanism can exist. The other, which Améry does not seem to consider, is the time of exemplary memory that is reflective and conscious, the historical time that is full of content resulting from the work of mourning and public

11 The fact that he wrote in the '60s, long before Ricoeur and all the theoretical work on memory that was produced in the '90s, is not irrelevant. How does this affect the comparison? He could not read Ricoeur, but Ricoeur, who has read him and quotes him, ignores the issue of resentment.

deliberations on the wrongs of the past, and on the harm and guilt of a shared history. It is a kind of consciousness, whether individual or collective, that rewrites and re-signifies the past. It is meaningful time and meaningful history.

Both notions of time are associated with two different kinds of forgiveness. Anyone would consider the forgiveness of the exemplary memory to be morally superior to the easy, utilitarian forgiveness of natural time. The former is fully conscious and requires a big amount of energy and generosity from the forgiver. It is rare, and political reconciliation might even happen without it. The latter, however, is really difficult to conceive of, unless one is forced by circumstance to do so. When things go the way Améry describes, it is not so much an issue of real forgiveness as it is of people, including many survivors, simply ceasing to talk about the past and instead plunging ahead into the demands, perhaps into the attractions, of a new life. This happens not infrequently when economic prosperity, for one reason or other, follows the transition to a new regime. This amounts to forgiveness by those whom Améry labels "indifferent and insensitive".

Certainly, there is a moral superiority in the former kind of forgiveness. Such forgiveness is not necessarily marvellous, as religious perspectives may want to have it; nor is Desmond Tutu's miracle, that leaves us with no response other than to "take off our shoes, because we are standing on holy ground" (Tutu 2002, xii). Rather, there is something sublime in it, a sublimity that one can find in an individual, not in a collective. This sublimity of the forgiveness of exemplary memory brings us back to reality. The second, instrumental forgiveness is not to be disdained, much as it is closer to earth.

Certainly, Hannah Arendt in 1958 was able to give a powerful characterization of the faculty of forgiving as a remedy for the fatal irreversibility of human affairs. The power "to begin again from anew," was for her the condition of plurality and the possibility of political life. It would require another chapter on its own for Arendt to locate "beginning again from anew" as lying between natural and reflective forgiveness. Certainly, forgiveness is action and not merely reaction, insofar as it is freeing. It frees "both the one who forgives and the one who is forgiven" (Arendt 1958, 241). This was not meant as the forgiveness that results from exemplary memory; such a notion would be alien to Arendt. A resentful person like Améry, who precisely wants to reverse the irreversible, not to escape from it, would be prompted to understand this "beginning again from anew" as the natural time of the insensitive and indifferent who just want to look forwards. This usual forgiveness is the result of natural time. Mostly, we forgive each other for the sake of the future because we have to continue living our lives together. Exemplary memory, on the other hand, is easily faked when displayed with a kind of solemnity that can degenerate into a rhetorical declaration, especially if it is proclaimed by politicians or in the theatrical context of political ceremonies. To this extent, Améry is not wrong when he criticizes the forgiveness of natural time. The point of his claim for resentment, this chapter suggests, is that the irreducible individuality of the resentful person, her stubborn subjectivity, points to the problems of natural time and also to the possible vacuity of exemplary political reconciliation.[12]

6. CONCLUSION

This exploration should come to a conclusion. Imagine a triangle with three vertexes: political rationality, historiography and the duties of memory. You can never find a balance between them. Power, or the institutions of social functioning, produce a natural forgetfulness, or, if necessary, may ritually simulate that they care for the claims of memory. History, in as much as it is a science that strives for impartial, objective knowledge, might conflict with power, but it also tends to play down the value of personal testimonies and the claims of subjective memory. In any case, both political rationality and academic history try to close time. Both seek continuity between the past and the present, even though they do so for different reasons. What about memory, the third vertex? To be sure, the claims of memory always challenge both politics and history at the same time. When confronted with this question, Ricoeur leaves the task of solving it to the reader of history, provided he is also a conscious citizen, who "listens to the voice of the unforgetting memory, excluded from the arena of power by the forgetful memory bound to the prosaic refounding of the political" (Ricoeur 2000, 501). However, the reader of history and the conscious citizen who reads history at home in privacy, and the polity remain divided. It cannot be any other way if you are to have an open society. Yet, this division in the polity cannot really be based on the responsible reader of history and the conscious, judgemental citizen. That is a very intellectual division. Arendt taught that judgement, as a political faculty, is the condition for a common space and presupposes plurality, but division, which is the other side of plurality, does not come from judgement, but rather results from the particular experiences and worldviews of citizens. Thus, when it comes to issues concerning memory, individual resentment expresses experiences that keep this division open. As Améry put it, his resentment is above all a protest against the natural course of time and its social functioning. As has been suggested here, he casts doubt on the possibility of an exemplary use of memory. Does it make any sense at all, in as much as such memory is intended to reconcile with time?

An individual's resentment is associated with the inalienable personal experience of the individual suffering and bearing it. In some cases, it could be the source of a literal use of memory, but in any case, it is constitutive for that individual's subjectivity. Can there really be any critical stance in a free society

---

12 This point has been developed in "Con o sin cicatrices. Sobre perdón y reconciliación" in Gomez-Ramos (2017).

without the personal lived experience that resentment expresses? To be sure, the individual resentments of particular citizens are highly susceptible to being manipulated. That is a real danger, and a collective resentment is likely to end in collective madness. It is not always easy to determine the divide between legitimate individual resentment and the political abuse of a group of resentful individuals. To determine such a divide is, no doubt, the most difficult task for a politics of memory that strives to achieve a happy memory, even forgiveness, and to attend, at the same time, to the demands of individuals who have suffered injustice. It is also a task for the resentful person – who must decide whether she merely resents in a particular way that seeks revenge and satisfaction, or whether hers is a resentment from which the others can learn – to reassure "that the moral standards are still in place" (Brumhold 2008, 40) and that it has a universalistic vocation. This is what Brumhold calls "resentment's virtue", and renders what we might label an *exemplary resentment*, referring to Améry. It is not for everyone to decide whether resentment is particularistic and revengeful or exemplary, but resentment strikes a discordant, necessary note in an open society by pointing to the necessity and impossibility of a happy memory that can heal the wounds of time.

References

Adorno, Th.W. (1970) *Negative Dialektik* (Gesammelte Schriften, Band 6). Frankfurt: Suhrkamp.

Améry, J. (1980) *At the Mind's Limits*. Indiana I.L.: Indiana University Press.

Anderson, B. (1991) *Imagined Communities. Reflections on the Origins and Spread of Nationalism*. London: Verso.

Arendt, H. (1958) *The Human Condition*. Chicago I.L.: Chicago University Press.

Bernstein, J. (2014) "Améry's Devastation and Resentment. An Ethnographic Deduction" in *Tijdschrift voor Filosofie* 76: 5–30.

Brumhold, Th. (2008) *Resentment's Virtue, Jean Améry and the Refusal to Forgive*. Philadelphia P.A.: Temple University Press.

Darwall, S. (2013) *Honor, History & Relationship. Essays in Second-Personal Ethics II*. Oxford: Oxford University Press.

Derrida, J. (1999) "Le siècle et le pardon" in *Le Monde des débats*, décembre 1999, http://hydra.humanities.uci.edu/derrida/siecle.html.

Gómez Ramos, A. and Sanchez Muñoz, Cr. (2017) *Confrontando el mal. Ensayos sobre violencia, memoria y democracia*. Madrid: Plaza y Valdés.

Nietzsche, Fr. (1980) [1874] *On the Advantage and Disadvantage of History for Life*. Indianapolis I.N.: Hackett Publishing Co.

—— (1988) [1875–79] *Jenseits von Gut und Bose. Zur Genealogie der Moral* (Kritische Studienausgabe, Band 5). München: De Gruyter.

Pascual Rodríguez, E. (ed.) (2013) *Los ojos del otro. Encuentros restaurativos entre víctimas y ex miembros de ETA*. Santander: Sal Terrae.

Ricoeur, P. (2000) *La memoire, l'histoire, l'oubli*. Paris: Seuil.
—— (2001) *Memory, History, Forgetting*. Chicago I.L.: The University of Chicago Press.
Risari, G. (2002) *Jean Améry. Il risentimento come morale*. Milan: Franco Angeli.
Scheler, M. (2014) *Das Ressentiment im Aufbau der Moralen*. Frankfurt: Klostermann.
Sebald, W.G. (2003) "Against the irreversible" in *The Natural History of Destruction*. New York/London: Random House.
Solomon, R. (1993) *The Passions, Emotions and the Meaning of Life*. Indianapolis I.N.: Hackett Publishing Co.
Todorov Tz. (2001) "The Uses and Abuses of Memory" in Howard Marchitello (ed.), *What Happens to History: The Renewal of Ethics in Contemporary Thought*. Cambridge: Routledge.
Tutu, D. (2002) "Foreword" to R. Helmick and R. Petersen, *Forgiveness and Reconciliation*. Philadelphia P.A.: Templeton Foundation Press.

PART II
RESTORING TRUTH

CHAPTER 5

ANAMNESIS

Or Reparation as Responsive Remembrance

Bert van Roermund

Phronesis, as distinct from a purely rational faculty, cannot be affected by Lethe.

Aristotle *Nic. Eth.* VI, 5, 1140b[1]

Fidelity to the past is a vow rather than a given.

Ricoeur, *La mémoire, l'histoire et l'oubli*, p. 643.[2]

---

1 I am indebted to Waldenfels (1994) 388 for this felicitous Aristotelian link between the present chapter and my contribution to Christodoulidis and Veitch (2001). The slightly twisted translation is mine. In the remainder of the argument it will become clear that I owe much more to Waldenfels's book than this quote, not to mention what I owe to his encouraging communications since December 2002. I also owe an awful lot to my co-convenors of the seminar "Law, Time and Reconciliation" (University of Glasgow, 17–18 May 2004, funded by the Leverhulme Trust (UK)): Emilios Christodoulidis (Glasgow), Scott Veitch (Hong Kong), and Johan van der Walt (Luxemburg). I also thank Andrew Schaap (Exeter) for sharing his thoughts on so many occasions.

2 Translations from this book in the text below are the author's own.

1. INTRODUCTION

In many polities, the transition from a rule of oppression to a rule of law[3] requires that various forms of "restorative justice" be done, as well as be seen to be done. Often enough, therefore, transitional justice entails not just a robust policy geared towards the rule of law, but also a policy that is mindful of a wrongful past. But then, not all forms of political mindfulness about a past of oppression, violence and suffering will work towards a future under the rule of law. This chapter argues that transitional justice, if and when it should usher in restoration somewhere, has to engage a specific kind of responsive remembrance that is here called *anamnesis*. The chapter will try and carve out the time structures involved in anamnesis and show that these are a good deal more complex than the links between past and future as they are usually distinguished in reflections on transitional justice. In particular, it will unravel these structures through an analysis of the nuclear formula "never again" that seems to capture the very core of various efforts to come to terms with political oppression in the past. The first part (Section 2) deals with three simplistic readings of the formula; Section 3 explores a more profound reading of "remembrance", while Section 4 ties this reading in with restorative action. Thus, "anamnesis" becomes a lodestar on the thin line between liberating and enslaving remembrance.

2. "NEVER AGAIN": THREE OVERLY SIMPLE STRATEGIES

How to live together with one's former oppressors? Both the attempt to fence oneself off from them and the effort to offer them a *modus vivendi* will use the same firm device: *never again* (*nunca mas*; *nie wieder*, etc.).[4] These two words neatly express a speech act. In its elaborated form it is a vow and its content is clearly structured by a specific time frame: here and *now* we pledge that what happened in the *past* should not (*never*) happen (*again*) in the *future*. Note that this vow is governed by the first-person indexical "we", so that it refers

---

3 Which is one (indeed my) definition of "transitional justice".

4 Desmond Tutu, Truth and Reconciliation Commission Final Report, I. 1, Chairperson's Foreword, para. 28: "In our case, dealing with the past means knowing what happened. Who ordered that this person should be killed? Why did this gross violation of human rights take place? We also need to know about the past so that we can renew our resolve and commitment that never again will such violations take place. We need to know about the past in order to establish a culture of respect for human rights. It is only by accounting for the past that we can become accountable for the future."

to "our" past and "our" future.[5] Thus, the frame points to time lived through in (shared) experience rather than set out on a calendar.

Intuitively, we can distinguish between different strategies to prevent the oppression of the past from returning at some point in the future. These differences are connected to equally different emphases on the various temporal dimensions inherent to "never again". Each strategy can try to take account of all three, but can only lend predominance to one. They all run into difficulties with their respective accounts of time.

1. The *legal* strategy. Here the emphasis is on facts that occurred at some point or other in *the past*: who did what to whom? When and where? Thus, the main question is: *what past* should never happen again in the future? In the background there is the assumption that without the truth about the past being revealed and established, there can be no common future, since there can be no ascription of guilt. This assumption is bound to encounter certain limits. To the extent that the truth about the past is conceived of as a historical matter of fact, the fact-finding process may turn into an endless battle. In a society biased by the legal approach, bringing more arms to such a battle is often the only point of historiography, archaeology, folk culture and, indeed, even tourism. For it is the *present* estimation of the future, as made by this society at a specific point in time, which determines, at the end of the day, its account of the past.[6]
2. The *political* strategy mainly turns towards *the future* by asking: which picture of the future is to be avoided at all costs? As such, this strategy is oriented towards "never" rather than towards "again", so to speak. The political approach is not particularly interested in the exact truth about the past. It is pragmatic in the sense that it purports to build a manageable, well-ordered society within as limited a period of time as possible. Thus, it takes into account what is instrumental to this purpose and ignores the rest of the past. If it can effectively deal with the troubles of the past through a general amnesty, it will be inclined to do so. It may even

5 For an extensive analysis of this pronoun in the politico-legal context, see my contribution "El *demos* como un yo plural, o más notas al pie a Rousseau" in Chaparro Amaya, van Roermund et al. (2015).

6 This is why the legal strategy in these contexts is so costly (see TRC final report) and, when pursued, often fails. Cf. On 7 October 2003, the South-African Ministry of Justice announced that the five policemen who were suspected of murdering Steve Biko in 1977 would not be prosecuted since, with no eye witnesses, there was insufficient evidence of the murder. Other charges like manslaughter and violent assault are barred by statutes of limitations. The TRC refused to give these men amnesty because they pleaded that they had no political motive and because they had not given full disclosure of their deeds. (*De Volkskrant*, 8 October 2003).

welcome amnesty as a form of amnesia.[7] If, alternatively, a population can only be satisfied by the ample administration of corrective justice, it will be glad to do so as well. Generally, though, this approach invests its energy in the new order that it wants to establish and tends to forget about the past, and thus about victims. It takes an interest in the past only to the extent that it can teach a lesson, at a sufficiently general level, about "the bad society" that is to be avoided. Thus, it runs the risk of seeing the past return without recognising it.

3. The *moral* approach, finally, celebrates the present. It emphasises the point in time at which "never again" is uttered, rather than the time frames of that at which it aims or that from which it turns away. This here and now is the space-time slot where a new beginning can be made by the mere performative decision to do so. This approach attaches to the promissory intention hiding in the nucleus "never again": "we *hereby* promise that we'll do whatever it takes to never let this happen again." It turns this into a volition of "people of good will". Often the claim is grounded in the truism that "we are all humans". Being human – a piece of work indeed! – is an ontological canopy that overarches (or should overarch) any historical antagonism, even between oppressors and oppressed. The present is not the hinge between the dark past of violence and the bright future of peace, but a moment that we just have to prolong in order to be rescued from our pre-occupation with either the past or the future. Typically, the arguments from this perspective favour the view that human dignity should be ascribed to every human individual, "even Hitler".

Obviously, when these ideal-typical approaches are characterised with the adjectives "legal", "political" and "moral", it does not mean that they are typified by actual legal orders, political regimes, or moral communities. What is meant is that there is a temporal perspective predominant in each of these approaches that makes it both possible and problematic. Existing legal, political and moral orders will therefore show signs of compensating for these problems. In actual practice, the respective accounts both need and distort one another's perspectives. For instance, an actually existing legal order may take a predominantly political perspective on transitional justice, but then it will probably also bring in moral and juridical aspects that are auxiliary to, indeed often corrective of, this perspective. It will try and reconstruct, to a certain

7 Alex Boraine warns against this danger in the case of South Africa, as he is quoted in Wittenberg (2004): "Blank amnesty is amnesia. Only remembrance can bring redemption. A nation that does not come to terms with its past, will be hunted down by it." (author's translation).

extent, the legal and moral perspectives within its own scope: *both* the ideology of a history that justifies reaching for the future *and* the ideology of a new beginning (a new era or order) are helpful in realising a political programme. For instance, the way in which Indonesia since the Suharto administration has largely ignored the 1965 violence perpetrated against, among others, alleged members of the (then legal) Communist party, is a case in point.[8] Likewise, a primarily legal conception of transitional justice, which conceives of it as largely a matter of rights and duties, attributed by rules, protocols and procedures will try and accommodate, albeit to a limited extent, a future-oriented political view of the common good as well as an ideal-oriented pre-occupation with values. However, the constraints of these accommodation strategies will be set by the predominance of the legal perspective.[9] Thus, these strategies, and their respective pre-occupations with time, do not seem to exclude each other in either the conceptual or the practical sense, but each will reconstruct, to a certain extent, the others within its own framework.[10]

As a consequence, then, these strategies will have to face the biases of their respective scopes in answering the main question: How to live with one's former oppressors in what somehow should be seen as a jointly travelable road towards the rule of law? The legal strategy will eventuate a kind of *Historikerstreit* between the formerly oppressed and the former oppressors by asking: Who did what?[11] The political strategy will obliterate the memory of suffering, so precious to survivors and the children of victims. The moral approach will evaporate into Arcadian air, as it recognises only "the past behind the past", a golden age when, as Ovid had it, "everyone did his due freely, without any judge or law".[12] All three of these approaches, therefore, run the risk of alienating a society from its past in pursuit of the firm intentions expressed in the phrase "never again". The obvious worry, then, is how people in such a society should prevent the evil of the past from returning at some future point in time if they risk alienating themselves from their past in the first place? If people trust that

8 See Kolimon, Wetangterah et al. (2015).

9 For an example in a slightly different, though related, context of violence against women, see Herman (2005), who argues that survivors' views of justice do not fit well into either retributive or distributive models of legal orders.

10 This chapter refrains from theorising the nature of these intertwinements. It should be stated, however, that it is not compulsory to see them as Luhmannian rationalities. A more liberal view is, for instance, Radbruch's (cf. Radbruch (1973 [1932])).

11 Liebenberg (1997); Liebenberg (1998). The original *Historikerstreit* (historians' dispute) was a debate in 1980s Germany over the how to incorporate Nazi Germany and the Holocaust into German historiography and the post-War generation's view of itself.

12 Ovid, *Metamorphoses*, Book I, *Quattuor Aetates, Gigantes*, line 89ff. "*Aurea prima sata est aetas, quae vindice nullo / sponte sua, sine lege, fidem rectumque colebat. / Poena metusque aberant; nec verba minantia fixo / aere ligabantur, nec supplex turba timebat / iudicis ora sui, sed erant sine vindice tuti.*"

"the past" will continue to be self-evident for everyone involved in building a better future, they will usually be disappointed to learn that five years after liberation many remnants of the past, reminiscent of the vow that it should not return, have either disappeared or have become objects of dispute and abuse. Indeed, *what* should never happen again? What *part* of it will have to be forgotten in order for the rest to be remembered? *Who* will be the guardians of that memory? In what sense, and indeed at what costs, can such memory be and remain "*acquis communautaire*"? And on top of all this, what is the "should" in "should never happen" supposed to express? Norm enactment? Shared hope? Joint intentionality? The contention of this chapter is that these and similar questions of restorative justice cannot even begin to be answered if the time problems of the core phrase "never again" are not articulated at a deeper level.[13]

3. REMEMBRANCE, HISTORY AND TIME

Applying Ricoeur's[14] conceptual framework with minor adaptations, one may structure the problem in the following way.

3.1. TIME AND MEMORY

There is, first and foremost, a problem of *time and memory*. In order to keep the violent oppression of the past at bay in the future, the past has to be remembered. Far from being the mere retrieval of information pure and simple, memory has to deal with a paradox: it involves the *present* representation of something *absent* under the hallmark of its being *anterior to the present*. It is this intentional hallmark that distinguishes memory from other forms of "representing something absent", notably things that are characterised as imagination or fiction. However, this specific pursuit by which memories are processed and tested does not, of course, guarantee that the distance between the present and the absent is overcome. In principle, the representation is always one step ahead of the represented, however strongly the anterior character of the represented is emphasised. Such distance allows for the use and abuse of memories, in particular for political purposes. One sad example of this is the phenomenon of organised groups with specific political agendas touring around the *gacaca* genocide court meetings in Rwanda,

---

13 Cf. this volume, Chapter 1, by De Gamboa Tapias and Herrera.

14 Ricoeur (2000).

trying to systematically monopolise the specific version of the past that is to be remembered.[15] It is only by mapping out and taking account of the various efforts that purport to deal with this distance that we will be able to grasp the structure of memory and remembrance. This account, in turn, is a necessary condition for answering the question of who is the subject of memory, i.e. the subject to whom the past is returned, as so many languages indicate by the reflexive modes governing the verbs of memory.[16] This subject, whether singular or plural, should be able to enter this reflexive mode; i.e., to regard herself, precisely *qua* subject, as an object. In still other words, she should have sufficient reason to see herself as an agent who is able to *turn* to the past instead of remaining one of its remnants. "Never again" is bound up with this paradox of memory.

3.2. TIME AND HISTORY

The second problem is the problem of *time and history*, which brings remembrance and representation into a new key. A personal memory seems relevant here. When I was giving a talk on one of the campuses of the (then) Vista University in the township of Sebokeng (South Africa) back in 1996, one of the students caught me out by making the following joke. Having learned that I was from Holland, he nodded and said: "Holland – I see. I remember a guy from Holland. You may well know him." I naively replied that that would be a coincidence, upon which he asked: "Jan van Riebeeck?" In an unexpected way he linked our meeting in the most hospitable but deplorable environments of the township campus with the commencement of Dutch colonialism in 1652 by playing with the ambiguity of "remembering". Memory, as it is committed to fidelity and reliability with regard to the past, cannot exist without history. However, history itself cannot be conceived of without historiography, i.e. the writing of history in the threefold temporal sequence of (i) identifying and gathering documentary data, (ii) understanding and explaining their connections and (iii) representing them by bringing them into the literary form of a narrative. As an epistemic process, then, history is about rewriting the written, about lending form to materials that are invariably already formatted as so many inscriptions and entries, such as in archives.

15 Communication of 11 November 2004 by my daughter Geertje van Roermund, who at the time was finishing her LLM thesis on the Rwanda tribunal (ICTR).

16 Cf. *se souvenir* (French), *ricordarsi di* (Italian), *acordarse de* (Spanish), *sich erinnern* (German), *zich herinneren* (Dutch).

3.3. COMMENCEMENT AND ORIGIN

This sequence itself, in turn, anticipates a matter that will be recognised as pertinent to "form" by the audience one is writing for.[17] One of the most salient conclusions that Ricoeur infers from this concerns the *aporia* in which the phrase "the birth of historical knowledge" may involve us if one does not appreciate that "birth" in this context hovers between the "commencement" and the "origin" of historiography. An audience may construe, in retrospect, the beginnings of a historical narrative as a constellation of dates and data, but it cannot ignore the ultimately mythical origin of the writings thus appropriated by the historian. This also applies to particular pieces of historical narratives, as the story of the Sebokeng student suggests. Letting a history of oppression begin at the date of a certain event ("Van Riebeeck setting foot on the shores of South Africa on 6 April 1652") is not tantamount to narrating the origin of violent colonialist oppression, not even in that part of the world. Colonialism had already spread over the globe when Van Riebeeck "negotiated" a stronghold for the Dutch East India Company on the Cape. At the end of the day, the roots of the oppression and violence that came in the wake of that first stage reach far back and vanish into a prehistory of both Europe and Africa, an area that cannot be retrieved and marked as a "beginning". Even so, the history of colonialism is reaffirmed, and its effects reinforced, every time that *we*, the inheritors and beneficiaries of colonialism, use the names given by the colonisers to refer to what they set foot on: the shores of *Tafelbaai*, the *Cape*, *South Africa*.

3.4. THE TEMPORAL NATURE OF THE HUMAN CONDITION

The fourth problem, as far as again Ricoeur is concerned, has to do with *the human condition* that is itself characterised by temporality. This "temporal" character of human existence is something to be restored in remembering. One should steer away, first and foremost, from a speculative *hubris* that would hypostatise History as an all-embracing object *and* subject of knowledge and truth. If history is truly the writing of history, it does not support the naïve thesis that history is merely at the side of the written object and not at all at the side of the writing subject. However, this cross-over is precisely the reason why neither of these poles can be all-embracing. History is always a partial history, since it develops from the vantage point of the subject writing it. This process of writing, however, can never be philosophically recaptured

17 The last part of this sentence is perhaps not entirely Ricoeur's in Ricoeur (2000), but it is certainly part of his thesis in Ricoeur (1983–85). See also Van Roermund (1997).

in toto as an act of reason, since it is thoroughly dependent on what appears to have been "already written", as well as on the physical modes of writing ("carving") available at a specific time and place. One cannot, for instance, mark the distinction between an oral and a literate culture without introducing one's own preferred idea of writing in the most physical sense of the word. There is, therefore, no point of view from which history can appear as reason itself.

Instead, we should acknowledge the historical condition of human existence in the Heideggerian sense. Not only is human existence always situated in the sense of "already confined", but humans also find themselves situated in the sense of *time and again* opening themselves up to *the future*, thus seeing their polity in the light of new opportunities for action, as well as new possibilities for coping with their memories. This is neither to say that this is necessarily a more promising light, nor to deny that the more promising light is the preferred one. What is important, however, is that "facticity" is not a mere constraint; it is also where we tie in with the world and realise "*le fait d'agir de soi-même*".[18] Even when the past is remembered in the same way time and again in spite of the constant flux of changes in the political circumstances of the day (for instance, when the same people continuously reject any communication with their former oppressors), one should not jump to the conclusion that theirs is the factual constraint of a trauma that stands in the way of judgement. On the contrary, if the past is remembered in the same way as before, in spite of changing circumstances, that is in itself a new light on the past and *prima facie* evidence that one has underestimated the invasiveness of its recognition. Victims of oppression never exhaust the right to express that their wounds have not healed. What they can exhaust, though, is the right to dictate how those wounds should be healed, but that is a different matter. The historicity of human existence entails that, in the case of remembered oppression in particular, the past remains "uncanny" for both victims and perpetrators. There is too much burial ground there, and the future may bring nothing but more and more exhumations. More generally, however, the historicity of human existence, pervasive as it may be, is so all-embracing that it cannot acquire concrete form and substance on the level of individual existence without mediation by socio-political institutions. Rather than trimming authentic self-expression to manageable proportions of "normality", these institutions provide the very possibility of being expressive in the first place. Elsewhere,[19] I compared the social institution of an "official" historiography of an oppressive past with the "cloud" under the Grand Arche de la Défense in Paris: the cloud allows us to surmise the incredible proportions of what we are looking

---

18 Cf. Descombes (2004).

19 Van Roermund (2001).

at and to find ways of expressing them that at least share a point of reference with the scale that our daily dealings with reality are used to. Both the cloud and social institutions do this precisely by partially hiding these very proportions. Similarly, in order to reach to the full dimensions of the sufferings in the past, one needs a memorial that covers them up to a certain extent.

3.5. FORGETTING AS PART OF REMEMBERING

By consequence, and this is the fifth problem, *forgetting* has to be part and parcel of remembering. *A priori* one should give up the intention of remembering everything; *a posteriori* one should consider putting to rest anything that appears to get in the way of a promising future. True enough, every memorial of oppression, whether in Johannesburg or Jerusalem, in Kigali or Berlin, bears the epitaph "to not forget". It bears testimony to the irrefutable risk that comes with maintaining a gulf between the present and the past in memory: the risk of losing the past to the present. However, by distinguishing between various strategies for evading this risk, the crucial point is whether or not this exhortation "to not forget" is subservient to the exclusive self-legitimation of a polity, or whether it is part of what Ricoeur calls its "*mémoire heureuse*" ("joyful memory").[20] The former is painfully illustrated, in my view, by Eyal Sivan's 1990 documentary film *Izkor, Slaves of Memory*, on the four different days of remembrance celebrated each spring in the State of Israel.[21] The state ideology underlying this annual practice of remembrance is severely criticised in the film by Yeshayahu Leibowitz.[22] Though it is fair to add that probably no state manages to escape entirely from such instrumental use of memory, the Israeli overkill transforms the *shoah* into an irrefutable "being-in-the-right" of the powers that be. Its mirror-image, "*mémoire heureuse*", therefore, can only be found in scattered and piecemeal efforts to come to terms with the past in processes where forgetting is linked to forgiving for the sake of a peaceful future, to which this section will turn in a moment.

3.6. THE CONSEQUENCES OF REMEMBRANCE

The sixth problem, then, deflects from the core issue governing the questions raised thus far with regard to remembrance, which was the representation of

20 Which Ricoeur calls "in retrospect, the lodestar of the whole [i.e. his] phenomenology of memory". Cf. Ricoeur (2000) 643.

21 Namely: Pesach, Commemoration of the Shoa, Commemoration of the Fallen Soldiers, and Independence Day, all within the space of a few weeks.

22 Leibowitz's criticism is also published in Leibowitz (1992).

the past in the present as anterior. This further problem concerns the follow-up of *remembrance* in terms of action rather than representation. The question thus arises, what is to be done (What can be done? What should be done?) by virtue of some particular memory? For instance, what if recognition of the past threatens to paralyse any capability to live a human life in hope of a promising future? What if the remorse one feels as a perpetrator is too great to bear or the sorrow one feels as a witness[23] transforms into a guilt that is too much to live with? This is what can happen when the past is remembered as a form of evil "beyond the will to make suffer or to eliminate", namely "the will to humiliate, to relinquish the other to dereliction and the loss of self-esteem".[24] Thus, the question arises how remembrance can work in the opposite direction by contributing to open up a range of action that restores and/or sustains some form of self-respect. Underlying this is the presupposition of the imputability of our acts to ourselves. Let us briefly contemplate what this means on the part of the perpetrator from a first-person perspective. By reflexively closing the gap between a certain act and myself – i.e. by confessing that "I" did it – I recognise that I may, or indeed should, be held to account. If this concerns an act that is forbidden by a rule, this recognition amounts to a confession of guilt, although this sense of guilt cannot embrace more than the scope that is determined by the rule. On a much deeper level than the moral quality of my act vis-à-vis a rule, I also become aware of the moral quality of the causal pattern that brought the act about in the first place. As my acting responded to a pattern that *preceded it*, I cannot but confess that I yielded to its workings and that, apparently, I am susceptible to that which disrupts my own desire for integrity, possibly in all my actions. To the extent that this pattern is evil, I became part of that evil. To the extent that it precedes my actions, it burst the empirical banks of my memory (and I can say that I am not responsible for all the evil in the world), but in confessing my guilt I cannot deny that I entered its history. "Apparently the bond between fault and self, between guilt and ipseity remains indissoluble."[25] Hence, Ricoeur concludes, forgiveness can only be conceived of as coming "from above".

Here Ricoeur points to "the common horizon of memory, history and oblivion", which is forgiveness.[26] He proposes an *epitheton ornans* to go with it: "*difficult* forgiveness", which is neither easy nor impossible, and both attractive and impracticable. The spatial metaphor of the horizon, though, only points to a new time-frame that renders the parameters for reconciliation "difficult". In "an epilogue to the epilogue",[27] Ricoeur speaks of "an eschatology of

23 Agamben (1999).
24 Ricoeur (2000) 601. Cf. Christodoulidis (2001).
25 Ibid., 604.
26 Ibid., 593.
27 Ibid., 642.

representing the past",[28] to underline the dimension of hope that is inherent in forgiveness. The proper grammatical mode for hope is the optative, in particular as distinct from the indicative of fact description and the imperative of norm prescription. It adds a distinctive overtone to the preferred mode of mimesis in contemporary philosophy, which is the "future anterior". Fidelity to the past, says Ricoeur, is a vow rather than a given.[29]

4. ANAMNESIS

Is it possible to grasp the disparities and ambivalences of remembrance in the context of restorative justice in the aftermath of political oppression and suffering? For a positive answer this section turns to a short essay by Lyotard in which he makes a link between remembrance and the key Freudian concept of "working through" (*Durcharbeitung*; *perlaboration*) under the heading of *anamnesis*.[30] Interestingly, Lyotard introduces the idea of anamnesis to point to similar patterns of restoration that take place in clinical, aesthetic and even biotic contexts. In a specific sense, restoring a patient's potential to get on with her life, creating a work of art, and giving birth, are all on a par. In what sense then? Here is Lyotard's answer:

> Above all, the painter, like the woman or the analysand, has to labour to keep open the passage through which may come what has not yet come: the child, the past, the phrasing of colour in the present case, and which is nevertheless already potential life, possible memory or eventual chromatism.[31]

Anamnesis is different from historical research and historical writing in that it does not comply with an established set of constraints on the "genre" of "truth-seeking". Rather, it works with a determined freedom to associate the most diverse memories, or feelings under the guise of memories, and to "be fearless of the incongruous, the absurd and the scandalous". "It is a matter of working to reach the disposition one already has, of labouring to prepare oneself for the labour in process."[32] The chain of associations (rather than argumentations) is not framed beforehand, least of all by an event in the past. It takes cues from all sorts of signifiers and depth clues. Thus, its origin remains "immemorial" in spite of the strong persistence of a source of energy that

---

28 Ibid., 643ff.; cf. 593.
29 Ricoeur (2000) 643. See Carlos Thiebaut's Chapter 2 in this volume.
30 Cf. Lyotard (2004).
31 Ibid., 107.
32 Ibid., 108. Note the parallel with Van Roermund (2001).

keeps driving the process that suggests a past pushing forward. Nevertheless, the chain owes its presence to it remaining unpresentable.

Lyotard speaks of the labour of anamnesis as belonging to a "talmudic" rather than an historical order. It is not about processes of recovering or retrieving a "lost object" that terminate with the finding of the thing. Rather, it consists in trying to listen, time and again, to a voice that speaks through what is "borne in mind". Part of this is memory in the historical sense, obviously, but then history itself ultimately feeds on anamnesis if it purports to evoke a response from a community and its representatives, rather than just to tell the truth. Anamnesis, I submit, is responsive remembrance, which, because of its interminable nature, always remains in debt to that which it tries to respond. The debt of suffering to be paid by this working-through is certainly not discharged; it is reduced. "Reason's" claim on this set of signified meanings is deferred to some extent: "you will 'suffer' still, but in a different way."[33]

The response elicited by responsive remembrance is not determined by the voice one hears, or by some rule beyond the anamnestic relationship. The response is a matter of virtue rather than compliance or correctness. It is about making your own judgement rather than following a path of judgement already laid out for you.[34] Nevertheless, this response is given in obedience, as an obligation one owes to … Indeed, to what or to whom? Let us leave Lyotard's exposition here, as it more and more veers towards the artist's agony in painting and writing instead of the patient's agony in coping with suffering. There will be reason to revisit it for the last stage of my argument, but for now the above suffices to show why the ground pattern of remembrance matches that of 'labour' in the pervasive sense of the word.

The overtones of sections 3.1–3.6 above provide so many reasons why the present section recurs to the term 'anamnesis'. It purports to express, as it does in some biblical contexts,[35] a form of remembrance that is committed to the anteriority of the past by vowing to actively pay tribute to it and rework its pertinence, again and again, into the yet unknown future. This comes to the fore, in particular, with exhortations "to remember". For instance, when the fourth of the Ten Commandments from Mount Sinai exhorts: "Remember the Sabbath day, to keep it holy" (Exodus 20:8), this is an appeal that is different from the instruction distributed by a municipality: "Remember Tuesday to

---

33 Lyotard (2004), 110.

34 "To be responsible means: you must be answerable to the Law and you must be unable to answer." Ibid., 111.

35 Ginn (1989) describes at numerous places (starting at p. 4) how "remembrance" in the Old Testament (various tenses of the verb root "*zkr*") does not just refer to "belief in God" but "belief in the *presence* of God" and acting accordingly. In this sense, remembrance is re-presentation *in actu*. For a critical discussion of the notion in biblical contexts, see also Arnesen (2002).

take the garbage bin out". Similarly, when Jahweh is petitioned to "remember" his covenant (Genesis 9:15–16; Exodus 2:24; 6:5; Leviticus 26:42, 45; Psalms 105:8, 42; 106:45; Ezekiel 16:60), this is not on a par with my gentle reminder to the Dean of the faculty that we set a date for a meeting. In such phrases, the addressees are exhorted, not just to live up to their promises as a practical conclusion arising from a rule or an agreement made in the past, but rather to bring the past to bear on the future by making it a touchstone of worthy action and renewing its possibilities to a range uncontemplated before. This is why in anamnesis the past is not only represented as anterior to the present, but also as posterior to the present, in the sense that it drives what Arendt called our "natality".[36]

Far from being restricted to a religious context, the core of all this is a deeply human mode of remembrance that we recognise also in the deeper layers of law. Take contract law, for instance. Parties to a contract are "bound" by their anterior agreement. However, the nature of the contract is hugely relevant to the sense in which it is binding. In a (long-term) sales contract it often boils down to the iterative application of the same rule that parties once agreed upon. However, this is precisely why this logic does not sit happily with other kinds of long-term contracts, such as a labour contract. Here, the parties' commitment entails, first and foremost, a kind of reciprocity in realising what the contract *is* (rather than *was*) about in the first place, and remaining committed to it under constantly changing circumstances, precisely insofar as it will have to be revised time and again.[37] The same goes for contracts that undergird loving relationships, which may explain why some find it so difficult to conceive of marriage as a "contract". In such cases, the contract shapes the future on the condition that the parties will remain committed to jointly deciding how the future will shape the contract; and *vice versa*: the future shapes the contract on condition that the parties will continue to jointly return to their commitment made in the past, over and over again.

At least one question remains if the concept of anamnesis is intended to capture the core of what is at stake in a *politics* of restorative remembrance. Neither the artistic, nor the biotic, nor the clinical context allow articulation of how Lyotard's notion of "labouring" or "working through" can be understood as a collective, "joint", or indeed "public" process, in the sense of a process in which "the people" or "the polity" are involved. Even a modest answer to this question would exceed the limits of the present chapter.[38] Nevertheless,

---

36 That natality, at least in the political context, is driven by anamnesis, birth as re-birth, like how Rome conceives of its foundation "*ab urbe condita*" in terms of "the new Troy". This is something that Arendt stresses only once, to my knowledge, namely in Arendt (1981 [1978]) vol II, 212–213.

37 Note that re-affirmation under new circumstances is also renewal.

38 This is part of the author's current research on the broader question: "What is bodily about the body politic?".

I owe the reader some indication of the direction that I would like to explore. The first tenet is a negative one. At the risk of sounding pedantic, this author believes that contemporary theories of "plural (intentional) agency" or "joint (intentional) action" will not set us on the right track.[39] The reason is as simple as it is pertinent. As the semantics of "labouring" and "working through" suggest, and as every woman in labour and every artist in action will confirm, these processes are not primarily a matter of intentional action, let alone of collective, corporate, plural or joint intentional action. Intentional action may be necessary in the preparatory stages of a process, not unlike the intentional action of cleaning the house might be preparatory to giving birth; or it may come in its wake, like cleaning the atelier after finishing a painting. Yet, neither giving birth nor, for that matter, creating a work of art are actions that are typically "intentional" in the sense of being "performed according to a plan". This is not to say that they are performed unintentionally or inadvertently. They obviously are more than just "behaviour", like stumbling or choking. These are the kind of things one does simply by "going with the flow", often experienced as movement of the body (the woman, the artist) in both the subjective and the objective sense of the genitive. What is at play here is the "body-subject", as Merleau-Ponty would call it in his early writings.[40]

This leads to the second tenet: a politics of memory in the sense of anamnesis will have to pervade the body politic (the polity) in the sense of a body-subject. Obviously, what is of interest here is not so much the organisation of the polity as allegedly analogous to the composition of the human body by brains, muscles, blood, etc. Rather, one needs to return to whatever constitutes the cutting edge between a polity and its habitat. Some would call this "economy" in the most basic sense of the word: locating the "metabolism" (as Marx put it) between man and environment in labour.[41] Others would extract the same from the original sense of "culture", where the first thing we learn about justice (i.e., what we owe to each other) we learn from our

39 Cf. in particular work by Bratman, Gilbert and Pettit respectively: Bratman (1999); Bratman (2007), Gilbert (1996); Gilbert (2000); Gilbert (2006) and List and Pettit (2011).

40 To return to Lyotard one more time: "We do not refer here to the body in time and space which is claimed by the doctor, the legislator, the recruiting sergeant, the manager and the sexologist. It is neither the sensory motor body of the psychologist nor the culturally normed body of the anthropologist, but the monster inhabited by the Thing and, because of this, endowed with spatiality, temporality and materiality other than that known by the experts or even our own bodily consciousness. *The bodily multiplicity encrypted on the body constitutes the indeterminate concealment and dimensionless place of the faceless Thing* (emphasis added)." Lyotard (2004), It is taken for granted that with respect to language the condition of writing is analogous to how painting or making music relates to space-time of colours and tonality. Singer and conductor Barbara Hannigan once described herself as "feeling like an animal" when making music.

41 Cf. Polanyi (1977) 19ff.; cf. Marx (1844 [1971]) 566.

laborious investments in the earth.[42] Still others, like Merleau-Ponty himself, refer to "the flesh" where world and body are intertwined; an intertwinement that is paradigmatically encountered in the structure of language.[43] In my view, Montesquieu had a similar intuition when he sensed "a primitive reason; and the laws are the relations between this reason and the different beings, as well as the relations of these various beings to each other."[44]

5. CONCLUSION: RE-READING "NEVER AGAIN"

So, taking the cue from these sketchy directions, let us ask what token of justice is restored in the language of *anamnesis* as a restorative mode of remembrance? In particular, does it provide a better understanding of what is at stake in the nuclear formula "never again"? The next sub-sections will explore what there is to gain from *anamnesis*, under two headings capturing a new reading of this nuclear formula.[45]

5.1. AGAIN AND AGAIN

The vow expresses a hope to give the victimised survivors of former oppression a *history* in the pregnant sense of a dignifying past, *a past to look forward to.* "What happened" is not necessarily the same as the past in the sense of history. History is the past that is believed to be "worth telling" in the future.[46] Indeed, it should be believed to be worth telling again and again. What should remembered, then, about the victims' suffering is "how they lived", rather than "how they died".

It is important to bear this in mind, as there are several reasons and causes that may get in the way of a past that is "worth telling" for the survivors of oppression.

1. Oppression tries to eradicate deviating collective categories that allow individual memories to store undesirable facts from the past. Individuals

---

42 Virgil in the *Georgics*, Book 2 (458–460) praises farmers for having the opportunity to learn about justice from "the abundantly righteous earth" rather than from "armed disagreement": "*quibus ipsa procul discordibus armis / fundit humo facilem uictum iustissima tellus.*" [author's translation].

43 See, e.g., Merleau-Ponty (1964) 182.

44 Montesquieu (1979 [1748]) Tome I, 1; 123 [author's translation].

45 Both aspects (again and against) may be expressed by the ancient Greek "ana" as a prefix to verbs, the latter in various modes like "backward" and "upward", i.e., against the flow of time or the pressure of mass. Thanks are owed to Tasoula Tseliou for references to modern Greek.

46 This is why, unjustifiably, history is so often "*Siegergeschichte*" (victors' history).

should only remember officially authorised, hence authoritarian, versions of what happened. After liberation, survivors therefore have to re-invent a language that can capture their history as a more or less collective one.

2. For the surviving victims, the suffering in the past is often one of absolute singularity. The mere demand that the past should be "worth telling", if only to prevent it from happening again in the future, means that it can be brought under some general idea of suffering in terms of its forms, its content, its means, its sense, its cause. This demand of subsumption may itself be perceived as a form of subordination and may well contradict the singular experiences of survivors, who then may decide that there is "no point" in telling their stories.
3. By the same token (singularity), the oppressive past is "*hors catégorie*" (beyond categorisation) in the sense that no narration will ever exhaust it. Whoever wants to try and make a start should know that there is no end to it. One can go on and on describing and re-describing it, in a never-ending memorial. The past of oppression is an imperfect past that lingers in the present in an incessant process of recapturing.
4. Sometimes former victims of oppression who try to recall the past find themselves under the spell of its ultimate forms, means, sense and cause, and themselves become fascinated with its violence. Instead of telling the past they feel compelled to undo it by reversing the charges and stepping into the role of the perpetrator.
5. Survivors find themselves to be unworthy narrators.[47] Apart from the past having to be "worth telling", it also has to be told by those who are entitled to tell it. That entitlement has to come from one's community, but survivors often feel ashamed of their survival. Feeling like traitors to the victims who died under oppression, they feel alone and without their past community, but also ignored or betrayed by the community in which they are surviving.

The past only becomes history on condition that it will be remembered. This, presumably, is what Ricoeur means when he calls joyful memory "in retrospect the lodestar of the whole phenomenology of memory".[48] Attempting to give the victims of former oppression a past to look forward to is a highly ambivalent enterprise. It is bound to fail if there is no future to look forward to, for instance in the sense of a prospect of a more decent life for one's children. This is why any process of transitional justice will fail if there is no political upshot in the form of reparations to be paid by the former oppressors; in other

47 Agamben (1999).
48 Ibid., 643.

words if it just boils down to public confessions, quasi-catharsis and warm feelings.[49] This is also why a process of transitional justice cannot be restricted to mere reparations and socio-economic redistributions.

5.2. AGAINST

One of the least discussed problems of transitional justice processes is that people tend to believe that the label is right. Having left the *terminus a quo* (injustice) one imagines having the *terminus ad quem* (justice) already in sight, and having a just order almost achieved but for a few steps that would bring it to perfection. It is only in the back of one's mind that one would know that, in a profound sense, justice is transitional by definition. Justice is always in transit to better constellations than the established ones, with no blueprint for what is best. In spite of this implicit awareness, from the first moment it is proclaimed, "never again" already contains the seeds of the re-iteration of oppression in the very act of rebutting it. How else does one go about transitional justice but by suppressing all residual and embryonic manifestations of oppression? How should one label those grey zones where such suppression intertwines with new oppression? After all, most oppressive regimes (even Nazism) could flourish only through a credible enough appeal to justice. This does not mean that "never again" is a false or cynical vow. Rather, that in an important sense, its pledge has to be reflexive and has to be accompanied by self-constraint. It not only has to be "joyful memory", as Ricoeur explained, it also has to be "dangerous memory" in the sense of J.B. Metz. In the words of Steven T. Ostovich:

> Dangerous memories keep alive *Leidensgeschichte* or the history of a suffering that disrupts any controlling myth of progress. Modern reason is supposed to be about

---

[49] Cf. what Heidi Grunebaum-Ralph said in her contribution to the public discussion "Transforming Society Through Reconciliation: Myth or Reality" (Cape Town, 12 March 1998), where she said she wanted "to link memory to questions of poverty, lack of resources, anger and bitterness, to social justice and reparations. I want to think about how, when speaking about reconciliation, there may remain or there may be the danger that we forget who is wronged, who has been victimised, where culpability lies and how the types of amnesia that are written into the very Act which mandates the compromise out of which the TRC grew – and I am thinking, for example, of amnesty as well as of the definitions of human rights violations which side-step the issue of apartheid as a crime against humanity – are present in the way we talk about reconciliation." And, further: "After the bitter pill that the amnesty provisions have presented to so many the debate around reconciliation needs to be linked to reparations and reparation policy; to questions of how to address the powerful and empowering gesture of material reparation. If reconciliation is used as fixing, closing, ending the past, the concept could promote a forgetting, a disavowal of the past and the dangerous obliteration of the victimised."

> freedom, but there is a performative contradiction entailed by the relation of freedom to domination. Dangerous memories offer an alternative: "the memory of the 'history of suffering of the world' becomes a medium for the realization of reason and freedom that critically opposes an unreflective as well as banal idea of the undialectical 'progress of reason.'" ... "Brushing history against the grain" therefore requires an "anamnestic solidarity" with the dead, a solidarity with the victims of injustice whose memory precludes closure of the story of the past so long as the struggle for justice continues (and there appears to be no end to this struggle short of the eschaton).[50]

Metz argues that it would be an error to take the abstract idea of "human dignity" as a rational or moral touchstone for an account of what it means "to be human", either individually or collectively, i.e., as a polity. If it means anything, then "remembrancing suffering" (*memoria passionis*)[51] is the only human universal that is truly historical.

> When I assert that the *memoria passionis* is the only universal category of humanity that is open to us, I am not thinking of a memory that only serves to affirm us or to secure our identities. Rather, it is the opposite: it calls into question our tightly sealed-up identities. It is a "dangerous" memory; it makes one rather "weak"; it creates an open flank.[52]

This open flank, it should be said, is the core of restorative justice.[53]

References

Agamben, G. (1999) *Remnants of Auschwitz: the witness and the archive.* New York: Zone Books.

Arendt, H. (1981 [1978]) *The Life of the Mind.* New York/London: Harcourt Brace Jovanovich.

Arnesen, A. (2002) "The Myth of Anamnesis" in *Theology* **105**, no. 828: 436–443.

Bratman, M.E. (1999) *Faces of Intention. Selected Essays on Intention and Agency.* Cambridge: Cambridge University Press.

—— (2007) *Structures of Agency. Essays.* Oxford: Oxford University Press.

Chaparro Amaya, A., B. van Roermund, et al. (eds.) (2015) *¿Quiénes somos "Nosotros"? O cómo (no) hablar en primera persona del plural.* Bogotá: Editorial Universidad del Rosario and others.

50 Ostovich (2005) 49, with references to Metz (1977) 171 (translated as Metz (1980)). See also his elaborated contribution to Confino and Fritzsche (2002).

51 "Remembrancing" (in German "*Eingedenken*") is the neologism Metz proposes to capture "ana" in anamnesis.

52 Metz (1999) 33–34.

53 See Reyes Mate (2003) 115ff in a similar vein regarding Metz. For a more extensive argument see Reyes Mate (2008). Thanks are owed to Catalina Uprimny for referring me to his work.

Christodoulidis, E. (2001) "Law's Immemorial" in E. Christodoulidis and S. Veitch (ed), *Lethe's Law. Justice, Law and Ethics in Reconciliation*. Oxford/Portland O.R.: Hart Publishing, 207–228.

Christodoulidis, E. and S. Veitch (eds.) (2001) *Lethe's Law. Justice, Law and Ethics in Reconciliation*. Oxford/Portland O.R.: Hart Publishing.

Confino, A. and P. Fritzsche (eds.) (2002) *The Work of Memory. New Direction in the Study of German Society and Culture*. Urbana I.L.: University of Illimois Press.

Descombes, V. (2004) *Le complément de sujet. Enquête sur le fait d'agir de soi-même*. Paris: Gallimard.

Gilbert, M. (1996) *Living Together. Rationality, Sociality and Obligation*. Lanham M.D., etc.: Rowman & Littlefield.

—— (2000) *Sociality and Responsibility. New Essays in Plural Subject Theory*. Lanham M.D., etc.: Rowman & Littlefield.

—— (2006) *A Theory of Political Obligation: Membership, Commitment, and the Bonds of Society*. Oxford: Oxford University Press.

Ginn, R.J. (1989) *The Present and the Past. A Study of Anamnesis*. Allison Park P.A.: Pickwick Publications.

Herman, J.L. (2005) "Justice From the Victim's Perspective" in *Violence Against Women* **11**, no. 5: 571–602.

Kolimon, M., Wetangterah, L. et al. (ed), (2015) *Forbidden Memories. Women's Experiences of 1965 in Eastern Indonesia*. Clayton, Victoria: Monash University Publishing.

Leibowitz, Y. (1992) *Am, Erets, Medina*. Jerusalem: Shorashim Institute / Keter.

Liebenberg, I. (1997) "Die Waarheids- en Verzoeningskommissie (WVK) in Suid-Afrika en die implikasies daarvan vir 'n Suid-Afrikaanse Historikerstreit en eietijdse geskiedskrywing" in *Journal for Contemporary History – Joernaal vir Eietijdse Geskiedenis* **22**, no: 98–114.

—— (1998) "Debating our past: the road to a human rights culture. The role of the Truth and Reconciliation Commission (TRC) and the need for a South African *Historikerstreit*" in *Focus Forum* **5**, no. 5: 24–30.

List, C. and Pettit, P. (2011) *Group Agency. The Possiblity, Design, and Status of Corporate Agents*. Oxford: Oxford University Press.

Lyotard, J.-F. (2004) "Anamnesis: On the Visible" in *Theory, Culture & Society* **21**, no. 1: 107–119.

Marx, K. (1844 [1971]) "Zur Kritik der Nationalökonomie – ökonomisch-philosophische Manuskripte" in H.-J. Lieber and P. Furth (eds.), *Karl Marx Frühe Schriften, Bd I*. Darmstadt: Wissenschaftliche Buchgesellschaft, 506–665.

Merleau-Ponty, M. (1964) *Le Visible et l'Invisible*. Paris: Gallimard.

Metz, J.B. (1977) *Glauben in Geschichte und Gesellschaft*. Mainz: Matthias Grünewald.

—— (1980) *Faith in History and Society: Toward a Practical Fundamental Theology*. New York: Seabury.

—— (1999) *Hope Against Hope: Johann Baptist Metz and Elie Wisel Speak Out on the Holocaust*. New York/Mahwah, N.J.: Paulist Press.

Montesquieu (1979 [1748]) *De l'esprit des lois* (2 vols.). Paris: Garnier-Flammarion.

Ostovich, S.T. (2005) "Dangerous Memories and Reason in History" in *KronoScope* **5**, no. 1: 41–57.

Polanyi, K. (1977) *The Livelihood of Man*, H.W. Pearson (ed.), New York etc.: Academic Press.

Radbruch, G. (1973 [1932]) *Rechtsphilosophie*. Stuttgart: Koehler Verlag.

Reyes Mate, M. (2003) "En torno a une justicia anamnética" in J.M. Mardones and M. Reyes Mate (eds.), *La ética ante las víctimas*. Rubí (Barcelona): Anthropos Editorial, 100–125.

—— (2008). *Justicia de las víctimas: terrorismo, memoria, reconciliación*. Rubí (Barcelona), Anthropos Editorial.

Ricoeur, P. (1983–1985) *Temps et récit, tomes I-III*. Paris: Du Seuil.

—— (2000) *La mémoire, l'histoire, l'oubli*. Paris: Du Seuil.

Van Roermund, B. (1997) *Law, Narrative and Reality. An Essay in Intercepting Politics*. Dordrecht/Boston/London: Kluwer Academic Publishers.

—— (2001) "Rubbing Off and Rubbing On: The Grammar of Reconciliation" in E. Christodoulidis and S. Veitch (eds.), *Lethe's Law. Justice, Law and Ethics in Reconciliation*. Oxford/Portland O.R.: Hart Publishing, 175–190.

Waldenfels, B. (1994) *Antwortregister*. Frankfurt am Main: Suhrkamp.

Wittenberg, D. (2004) "'Blanco amnestie is amnesie'. Dr. Alex Boraine over opmars van waarheidscommissies" in *NRC Handelsblad*, 20 March 2004.

CHAPTER 6

REFLECTIONS ON THE WORK OF THE TRUTH AND RECONCILIATION COMMISSION IN SOUTH AFRICA

Memory, Counter-Memory and Restorative Justice

Anél Marais

Amnesia appoints another Commission, the Lethe Commission, Limbo Commission, Nirvana Commission, Justice van deFerred Commission.

Jeremy Cronin[1]

1. INTRODUCTION

The South African Truth and Reconciliation Commission (TRC) formed part of what is now regarded as an emergent trend of official state attempts at coming to terms with the aftermath of repressive regimes.[2] This kind of

1 From his poem "Even the Dead", as cited by Harlow (2000) 183.
2 There is a record of at least 15 Truth Commissions between 1974 and 1994. *Human Rights Quarterly* Vol 16 No. 4 (November 1994) pp. 597–655.

process, by necessity, involves a myriad of political, ethical and often also very personal complexities. In the same way as previous commissions of this kind,[3] the TRC had to find a balance between so-called "truth finding", retribution, reparations and the rather elusive concept of reconciliation. The mandate contained in the title of the Promotion of National Unity and Reconciliation Act (the 1995 Act)[4] already established what were to be regarded as the priority concerns, namely "truth" and "reconciliation". In the context of transitional justice this was regarded by many as a "middle road", somewhere between impunity/amnesia at the one extreme and retribution/prosecution on the other. However, in the painstaking process of structuring the TRC proceedings it became clear that the trump ingredient, the *panacea*, was the concept of "truth".

It is important to remember, first, that this rather fragile process took place under heavy influences of divergent political concerns, and, second, that due to the volatility of the political situation and the real danger of an outbreak of uncontrollable violence, the stakes were regarded as extremely high. Although the TRC process is now regarded as part of the legal and social history of South Africa, it is important to not relegate the insights gained at the time of the hearings to a fixed historical archive, but to rather regard it as an ongoing and open process mediating between past and future. Evidently the past, even a very dramatic past, as experienced by many South Africans, gets overtaken by new political agendas and alliances and new social problems. There is, however, an enduring legacy of a nation struggling, still struggling, in the aftermath of a painful past. The argument will be that keeping the past open, *not* to seal the archive as "done and dusted", even in the face of new and difficult circumstances, is called for. This chapter will therefore revisit and re-open the contested concepts of the "past" and of "truth", and also of the future, within the wider perspective of restorative justice.

Section 2 presents a condensed version of the historical and political context of Apartheid and its demise. The protracted history of colonisation and racial discrimination permeates every aspect of South Africa's political background. It is only against the backdrop of this long and iniquitous history that the significance and legacy of the TRC can be comprehended. Section 3 concentrates on the concept of *truth* as the perceived cornerstone of the TRC proceedings. This is discussed, first, against the background of the "right to truth", articulated as an emerging right under international law.[5] Secondly, a

---

3 Examples include the Commission of Inquiry into "Disappearances" of People in Uganda Since 25 January 1971; the National Commission of Inquiry into Disappearances in Bolivia in October 1982 and the National Commission for Truth and Reconciliation in Chile in March 1990.

4 The Promotion of National Unity and Reconciliation Act 34 of 1995.

5 Following an expert workshop on the right to the truth, organised by OHCHR in October 2015, the following was stated: "The study concludes that the right to the truth about gross

more nuanced expression of different types of "truth" is examined. The question here is whether one can ever refer to a single "truth" rather than multiple "truths". It also considers the differentiation between micro/personal truth and political/collective truth, and the purposes of such a distinction. Section 4 takes the form of a short exposition of three different but related "meditations" on the philosophical impulse to come to terms with the past and, by definition, also with the future. Nietzsche's short essay "On the Uses and Disadvantages of History for Life" calls for the critical use of history. This implies, on the one hand, a just treatment of the past, but, on the other, also a dismissal of one's traditional reverence of the past. It may demand that one sees oneself and one's own history in a way other than how one might have preferred. This is followed by Foucault's reading of Nietzsche in his essay "Nietzsche, Genealogy, History", as well as, more generally, Foucault's concept of counter-memory. A case study of the TRC's Women's Hearings illustrates Foucault's insight as to the importance of radical openness and also of the processes of radical openness of remembering and forgetting. The fifth section focuses on Derrida's short work, *Archive Fever*, and on the power associated with interpreting and constituting the past.

2. FROM POLITICAL INIQUITY TO TRUTH AND RECONCILIATION

The history of racial discrimination and segregation in South Africa began very soon after the first colonisation of the Cape by Dutch settlers in the mid-seventeenth century. The area now known as Table Bay, where the modern city of Cape Town is located, in the mid-seventeenth century was inhabited by the Khoikhoi, who were pastoral farmers moving around the area in search of fresh grazing for their cattle. The territorial expansion of the Dutch settlers and their gradual invasion of KhoiKhoi territory led to continuous and often violent confrontations.[6] In the 1670s the Dutch East India Company agreed to upgrade the Cape trading post to a permanent settlement. The colony grew relatively fast, and in 1795, at the time of the first British invasion, it comprised roughly 32,000 inhabitants, half of which were slaves.

In 1806 the Cape was permanently occupied by the British. In the same year the British authorities in the Cape initiated a pass law, also known as the

human rights violations and serious violations of human rights law is an inalienable and autonomous right, linked to the duty and obligation of the State to protect and guarantee human rights, to conduct effective investigations and to guarantee effective remedy and reparations."

6 This led to the first Khoi-Dutch war in 1659–60.

"Hottentot Proclamation", which was aimed at controlling the free movement of farm workers. Each "Hottentot" (KhoiKhoi) worker had to register a fixed address and was allowed to leave only when a pass had been obtained from the master. During the nineteenth century many discriminatory legislative acts followed, including the Kaffir Pass Act of 1857, which "prohibited Xhosa from entering the Colony except to work".[7]

Throughout the nineteenth and early twentieth centuries Africans continued to live under conditions of legal and *de facto* segregation and discrimination. They were not allowed to own land[8] and had only very restricted voting rights. Their freedom of movement was generally constrained and employment conditions were often extremely harsh, especially in the case of migrant mine workers from the early twentieth century onwards.

However, when the National Party gained control of Parliament in 1948, a systematic and large-scale programme of racial segregation was implemented underpinned by an ideology of racial superiority. The theory was that South Africa was comprised of four distinct "racial groups", namely White, Coloured, Indian and African. Furthermore, the best interests of these groups required that they "develop separately". All whites were regarded as members of a single nation, while Africans formed part of several (around 10) distinct nations or "potential nations", each of which was provided with a so-called "homeland". This also had the implication that the "White nation" was in the majority. On a practical level, the segregation of the different nations – now known as *Apartheid* – brought about the traumatic process of the forced relocation of around 3.5 million people between 1960 and 1983. This was accompanied by a litany of legislation enforcing and policing racial segregation. The most infamous acts included: the Mixed Marriages Act of 1949 prohibiting interracial marriages; the Group Areas Act regulating where members of each race could live; the Reservation of Separate Amenities Act ordering segregated public amenities; and the Immorality Act criminalising sex between people of different race groups.

Already in the early stages of implementing the Apartheid regime criticism emerged from the international community. In 1962 the United Nations General Assembly passed a non-binding resolution calling for sanctions against the South African government.[9] This was strongly opposed by western countries, with the UK and the United States most unwilling to support the growing anti-Apartheid campaign. In 1973 the UN General Assembly declared Apartheid

7 Crais (1992) 212.

8 The Natives Land Act, 1913, subsequently renamed Bantu Land Act, 1913 and Black Land Act, 1913; Act No. 27 of 1913.

9 In November 1962, the United Nations General Assembly passed Resolution 1761, a non-binding resolution establishing the United Nations Special Committee against Apartheid and called for imposition of economic and other sanctions on South Africa.

to be a "crime against humanity", and in 1977 the Security Council imposed trade sanctions and an arms embargo on South Africa. Individual countries, such as the United Kingdom and the United States, persisted in their view that Apartheid did not pose a threat to international peace and security and therefore the imposition of sanctions would be "illegal", with a secondary argument that sanctions would harm the poor black population more than they would the wealthy white population. The Apartheid regime chose to regard this as tacit support by major western powers and proceeded with its policies with impunity.

Twenty years later, with the National Party (by then called the New National Party) still in power, the political situation underwent a rapid and drastic turnaround. On 11 February 1990 Nelson Mandela walked out of the gates of the Victor Verster Prison in Paarl as a free man after 27 years of imprisonment and hard labour. He punched the air in a victory salute. By then there had been a considerable relaxation of Apartheid laws, including lifting of the longstanding ban on the African National Congress (ANC), by the then President F.W. de Klerk. It soon became clear that Mandela was not intent on seeking revenge for the past and that his main concern was a peaceful transition to full democracy. This remarkable attitude led to Nelson Mandela's iconic status as a peacemaker. The Nobel Peace Prize of 1993 was awarded jointly to Nelson Mandela and Frederik Willem de Klerk.

Despite the cautious optimism prevailing in the international community and also in South Africa, the negotiations concerning the transitory arrangements were complex and often fractious. In December 1993, at the so-called "Kempton Park negotiations", a crucial decision was made that determined the direction and outcome of the entire peace process. Negotiating parties agreed to insert a clause in the postscript of the Interim Constitution of 1993 providing for the granting of amnesty to perpetrators who met certain criteria. Amnesty would be granted "in respect of acts, omissions and offences associated with political objectives and committed in the course of the conflicts of the past".[10] The subsequent Act provided for amnesty from criminal and civil prosecution for so-called "politically-motivated acts".[11] There were two conditions: first that the acts were proportionate to the political objective in question, and, secondly, that a full disclosure was made by the perpetrators. Hence the principle of "truth for amnesty" was established.

Like other truth commissions, or similar processes of transitional justice, the TRC mandate represented a heavy political compromise. The first impetus for setting up a commission came from an internal inquiry conducted by the

10 This is based on the final clause of the Interim Constitution. See www.justice.gov.za/trc/legal/justice.htm.

11 As defined in section 20(2) and (3) of the 1995 Act.

ANC in 1993 into allegations of torture and killings in its own military camps. At the same time, gruesome details started to emerge concerning so-called "third force" killings by the South African security forces, which were allegedly aimed at provoking violence between the ANC and the *Inkatha* Freedom Party. The first non-racial elections, planned for April 1994, came under threat from white right-wingers as well as from Pan-Africanists, who committed public violence with impunity, while security forces were regarded as remaining mostly passive.

From 1996 to 2001 the TRC conducted public hearings throughout the country. These, however, was not restricted to amnesty hearings. In an attempt to gain access to as much information as possible, a second category of hearings was held entitled the Human Rights Violations Hearings. Although the term "hearings" was used for both types of procedures, they had little in common as far as their nature and aims were concerned. Amnesty hearings were legal proceedings aimed at establishing whether individual perpetrators of human rights violations complied with the legal requirements for receiving indemnity for offences committed. The aims of human rights violation hearings were equally important to the overall project of "reconciliation", but much more difficult to explain in a legal context. Suffice to say for the moment that these hearings, where victims of human rights abuses had the opportunity to "relate their own accounts of the violations of which they [were] the victims"[12] played an important part in the therapeutic process of coming to terms with past violations. It was also hoped that this would contribute to the provision of reparation, in its widest possible sense.

Although the overall process of the TRC was based on the two elements of truth and reconciliation (and some complex links between the two), it became clear that there was a third important element which was unaccounted for, namely reparations. The total amnesty granted to perpetrators who met the criteria for it had the effect of depriving victims of human rights violations of their legal rights to seek redress from the courts. This was rectified by the inclusion of Chapter 5 (Reparation and Rehabilitation of Victims) in the 1995 Act. Thus, a third element was added to the TRC's mandate. Section 3(1)(c) of the Act required the TRC to formulate a policy of monetary reparations, as well as to recognise the "human and civil dignity of such victims by granting them an opportunity to relate their own accounts of the violations of which they are victims". In the context of other transitional justice models, it was clear that South Africa had chosen a middle ground: neither criminal prosecutions, nor blanket amnesty, but an exchange of "amnesty for truth".

The above events leading up to the establishment of the TRC are well known. It is, however, the remarkable events during the public hearings which

[12] Section 3(1)(c) of the 1995 Act.

left the strongest impression on the national consciousness. The mandate and aims of the TRC had much in common with other transitional justice models around the world. However, it was its radically public procedure that made it unique. The hearings were aired on radio and television, often broadcast live, and the TRC's transcripts of most of the testimony could be accessed on the internet. Testimonies from victims and perpetrators were often very personal and harrowing in their detail. Outbreaks of emotion, including from the commissioners and famously from the chairperson, happened regularly.[13] Despite the wealth of academic publications and analysis of the legal work that the TRC undertook, it was always the visual impact and the raw emotion of the public hearings which defined the TRC in the country's imagination.

Before the structural elements of the TRC hearings are analysed, it may be useful to put the magnitude of the TRC's task in perspective: 7,112 amnesty applications were heard and decided (of which 849 were successful); more than 20,000 people made submissions concerning human rights violations (of whom about 2,000 testified in public); 20 so-called "special hearings" took place, including the women's hearings, armed forces' hearing, business hearing and children's hearing. The final TRC Report spanned roughly 2,700 pages over seven volumes.

3. TRUTH AND TRUTHS

For the TRC "finding the truth" was regarded as the key, or one can maybe say the cornerstone, of their mandate. The idea that exposing the truth is a prerequisite for regaining equilibrium in a divided society is not new. This is especially the case in the aftermath of an oppressive regime that committed gross human rights abuses. For instance, in the wake of the Argentine dictatorship from 1976–1983 and the widespread "disappearances" of political opponents, finding the truth became a central outcry: Where are my loved ones? Are they alive? Where are their bodies? Here, in the realm of private and intimate life, the value of finding the truth seems to reside in the value of human compassion, perhaps even as part of humanitarian law, in our modern parlance. The Working Group on Enforced Disappearances expressed the opinion that long-term uncertainty related to the suppression of information on the fate of loved ones can constitute an act of torture. Revealing the truth about the fate of family members and friends, however painful the details, may facilitate the process of individual grieving and hence, so the argument goes, may also contribute to some oblique and symbolic form of reparation.

[13] See, for example, http://adst.org/2015/11/south-africas-truth-and-reconciliation-commission/.

Archbishop Desmond Tutu, Chair of the TRC, echoed this sentiment and explained thus: "However painful the experience, the wounds of the past must not be allowed to fester. They must be opened. They must be cleansed. And balm must be poured on them so they can heal."[14]

In analysing this position, the first difficulty is the semantic slipperiness of its concept of truth. Unfortunately, the ideal of truth being consistent and readily verifiable very often remains just that, an ideal. Signification is very seldom reliable and, even more problematically, it is also very seldom innocent. There is, however, a view that it may be possible and useful to separate individual truth, so-called elementary/micro-truth, from political/collective truth. De Frouville argues that on a micro level there is an absolute and intangible right for families to "know the truth of the tragedies that have affected their life, which have radically changed them".[15] "Forgetting" cannot be forced on anyone. It is a sovereign and individual choice that is beyond judgment. The subject here is the suffering human, who can make a choice between remembering and forgetting. This choice is personal and depoliticised and cannot be judged. However, there is also the victim, the person bearing rights, the person who has the right to have rights. The suffering human is thus re-positioned in the social and political realm. The claims of the re-politicised victim, the *public* victim, can be calculated and weighed, and may very well be in competition with claims by other social and political groups.

Although the scope of individual/micro-truth has no limits, the magnitude of the question of public truth may be contained to a certain degree by using the restraints provided by law, and maybe also the restraints provided by politics. The TRC, in quite an innovative way, employed both these techniques.

At the time of the TRC hearings the so-called "right to truth" was not yet articulated as an emerging right under international law. Despite this, the process exhibited many features which were later incorporated as part of the *Joinet Principles* (or "Principles against impunity"). These principles incorporated three values, namely the right to know, the right to justice and the right to reparation. Drawing on the South African example, the Principles incorporated the "right to truth" as inherently linked to the right to reparations. It also made provision for a rather oblique duty on the state to "give effect to the right to know". This is generally interpreted as the duty of the state to set up and preserve national archives, to facilitate criminal prosecutions and to establish a non-judicial process to supplement the judicial processes. Further developments followed and December 2006 saw the adoption of the first treaty

---

14 Tutu (2000).

15 UN Working Group on Enforced or Involuntary Disappearances, *General Comment on the Right to the Truth in Relation to Enforced Disappearances*. Available at: http://www2.ohchr.org/english/issues/disappear/docs/GC-right_to_the_truth.pdf.

in this regard, the International Convention for the Protection of All Persons from Enforced Disappearance. The Convention made explicit mention of the "right to know the truth" and the duty that rests on each State Party to take appropriate measures to investigate disappearances and, when necessary to locate and return human remains. These are legally-binding measures that are clearly aimed at dealing with post-conflict and, by definition, politically-laden situations. Despite the veneer of official procedures and legal sanctions, their focus still seems to be on less calculable aspects: the healing power of truth, the possibility of *symbolic* reparations and an acknowledgment of the dignity of victims and survivors.

When focusing on public/political truth, the approaches to and consequences of the process shift. The main aim of establishing "political truth" is to preserve or restore the moral value of the state. Acknowledging and exposing the moral corruption of the state and the fact that the state turned against its own citizens, often through criminal means, should be established as an incontestable political truth. In other words, it needs to be clear that all parties were not equally to blame. Despite possible excesses, and possibly even human rights violations on both sides, there is nevertheless a moral hierarchy. In the South African context one can say that the Apartheid state was to blame without the possibility of exonerating itself by referring to the criminal behaviour of the ANC resistance movement. This does not mean that the gross human rights violations committed by ANC resistance fighters are morally justifiable. It simply means that those violations cannot be used to "even the political scales".

Listening to and recording testimonies of both victims of gross human rights abuses and the perpetrators of such abuses formed the greater part of the TRC's remit. Following from the analysis above, it is clear that the Commission had to sit on two chairs, or rather, they had to constantly shift from one chair to the other. In their legal capacity in the context of hearing perpetrators' applications for amnesty, the TRC made use of normal juridical procedures. This included adhering to the required standard of proof, requiring corroboration of relevant facts, cross-examination of witnesses, and so on. The outcome of this forensic procedure would be either the granting or denying of amnesty to the applicant, and the consequences would be dramatic either way. However, during the Human Rights Violations Hearings the meaning of the word "truth" shifted and became much more opaque and diffuse. Testimony by victims was not subjected to cross-examination or to rigorous scrutiny and was regarded as more akin to personal narrative. Victims and witnesses could unburden themselves from their experiences and memories that had been hitherto untold. The simple human action of narrating events that you have witnessed, in public and without fear or shame, became part of the process of reparation.

The TRC acknowledged that this was a very uneasy conceptual pairing and in its report it tried to make a distinction, quite remarkably, between four notions of truth: "factual or forensic truth"; "personal and narrative truth", "social truth" and "healing and restorative truth" The Commission, however, also admitted that "official truth", established on a case-by-case basis and forensically verified during the amnesty hearings, was privileged: "The familiar legal or scientific notion of bringing to light factual, corroborated evidence, of obtaining accurate information through reliable (impartial, objective) procedures, featured prominently in the Commission's findings process".

The Commission, however, also had a mandate "[to] report on the broader patterns underlying gross human rights violations and to explore the causes of such violations". This meant that, parallel to its judicial methodology, the TRC also engaged in a so-called "social scientist's approach". Before individual testimonies could contribute to the Commission's findings, the Commission's investigators in its research department had to frame them in a socio-historical context. The Commission insisted that it did not set out to write the history of the country. The end result, or cumulative effect, as many agree, was exactly that, however. This postulated "history" seems to be fully and rather simplistically equated with a catalogue of gross human rights violations. The complexity of experiences and the intermingling of "the truth" and many individual and contested "truths" remain unacknowledged. As Jeremy Cronin, celebrated poet of the resistance, rightfully asked: "Was [the past] peopled only by victims and perpetrators ...? Was there no active heroism?" He then answers his own question "The past was not just peopled by victims and perpetrators. There was a struggle, a just struggle. There were strugglers."

In relation to the value of "personal and narrative truth", Desmond Tutu, chair of the TRC, said: "This Commission is said to listen to everyone ... [E]veryone should be given a chance to say his or her truth as he or she sees it". This opened the TRC procedure to radically democratic consequences. The TRC directive not only allowed, but also *required* reciprocal telling and listening, and these mandated activities were aimed at "[restoring] the human and civil dignity of the victims by granting them an opportunity to relate their own accounts of the violations of which they are the victims".

The ambiguous roles of testimony provided by individual witnesses are difficult to understand and to reconcile. On the one hand, individual witnesses assisted in uncovering existing facts about past abuses – the "truth" as they saw it and experienced it. On the other hand, they were also co-workers in the creation of an agreed "narrative truth", a concept that was never quite explained. It was not enough for discrete events to be recalled; these events also had to be processed and incorporated into a coherent and wider context. It was felt that there had to be an effort to collate individual "truths" into a single and comprehensible truth to be archived and to be accessible to future generations.

The problem clearly centres on the question of verification, or rather on the impossibility for narrative testimony to be verified. The question is whether the Commission sometimes was listening in order to verify and sometimes was listening simply in order to listen. The second option, listening for the sake of listening, would imply that the most important aspect was not *what* is being told, but the fact that *telling occurs*. The language used in the TRC Report to describe the TRC's aim is subtle: "The Commission sought to capture the widest possible record of people's perceptions, stories, myths and experiences". No allusion is made to the truth in its forensic sense. Instead, the Commission turns to the African continent: "In the (South) African context, where value continues to be attached to oral tradition, the process of storytelling was particularly important." The first observation one can make is that the act of "telling", in a specific cultural context, is regarded in itself as being a valuable therapeutic activity. This arguably cannot be claimed as exclusively "African" and hence not necessarily ascribable to African culture alone. The beneficial significance of narrating one's story in public was also, for instance, acknowledged as an unintended function of the war crimes tribunal for the former Yugoslavia.[16] The difference is perhaps that "listening and telling" were *legally* prescribed activities for the TRC. By narrating one's story to an official and attentive audience, one can restore dignity on a personal level. From such a perspective, one can perhaps assume that the basic human action of communicating the fact of personal loss and grief, and sometimes also one's anger and bitterness, can *somehow* "repair" the injuries of the past, and therefore it can be regarded in a very wide sense as part of reparations.

4. UNTIMELY MEDITATIONS, COUNTER-TRUTH(S) AND THE ARCHIVE

From a political and legal perspective, the impression can be created that post-conflict resolution and the addressing of past excesses of oppressive regimes are modern phenomena. Although what we now call truth commissions or post-conflict tribunals are indeed recent phenomena, the philosophical impulse to come to terms with the past is far from new. In order to put "our history" in the wider theoretical context of "the history of history", this section will provide a short exposition of three accounts on dealing with the past and, by definition, dealing with the future.

The first inquiry is into Nietzsche's early, and rather idiosyncratic, analysis of historical consciousness in his essay "On the Uses and Disadvantages of History for Life".[17] The second sub-section will turn to Foucault and his reading of Nietzsche in his essay "Nietzsche, Genealogy, History", as well as, more generally, Foucault's concept of counter-memory. The third sub-section focuses

16 White (2008).
17 Nietzsche (1983 [1874]).

on Derrida's short work *Archive Fever*, and more specifically, on the power associated with interpreting and constituting the past.

4.1. NIETZSCHE'S "UNTIMELY MEDITATIONS"

In the second essay of *Untimely Meditations*, Nietzsche deals directly with what he calls "the uses and disadvantages of history for life". The "untimeliness" of this work lies in the fact that Nietzsche, in an epoch of historicism, seems to have gone against the grain by being sceptical of the value of history and of the value of the past in general. He makes it clear that "thinking historically" has its uses, but, because *life* is the primary concern, "thinking unhistorically" may sometimes be required. It is interesting that Nietzsche throughout uses the word *Historie*, rather than the word *Geschichte*. Although the difference between the two terms is somewhat contested, in general *Geschichte* refers to the "living experience" of events, including things such as stories and oral accounts of what has really happened, or may have happened, even if the event cannot be objectively verified. *Historie*, by contrast, refers to facts that have been objectively validated and falls within the formal academic discipline of History. This distinction shows some interesting semblance to the TRC's procedures, whereby the Amnesty Hearings were led by *Historie*, and required objectively verified facts, but the Human Rights Violations Hearings rested on *Geschichte* and comprised mostly subjective accounts of what victims had experienced.[18]

Nietzsche's concern seems to be not with the past *as such*, but rather with the past as a potential influence on the present and the future. This focus on the present and the inhabitants of the present is what represents the "untimely" return to humanism. Nietzsche refers to the cultivation of history as something potentially "injurious" and states that "we are all suffering from a consuming *fever of history*" (emphasis added).[19] The ability to forget – or differently stated, the ability to exist *unhistorically* – is crucial to happiness as well as to the possibility of present and future action. Rather dramatically Nietzsche explains:

> He who cannot sink down on the threshold of the moment and forget all the past, who cannot stand balanced like a goddess of victory without growing dizzy and afraid, will never know what happiness is – worse, he will never do anything to make others happy.[20]

---

18 McGrath suggests that this distinction will be better explained by using objective-historical for *Historie* and existential-historical for *Geschichte*. McGrath (1997) 149.

19 Nietzsche (1983 [1874]) 60.

20 Ibid. 62.

This historical sense, which he describes as a "degree of sleeplessness", he regards as potentially harmful, even fatal, not only to an individual, but also to the collective. The ideal individual, the one with the "most powerful and tremendous nature", would not be overwhelmed by history, but would be able to draw a protective boundary around themselves and "forget" that which they could not subdue.

Nietzsche insists on a sharp dividing line, a firm boundary, between the past and the future, thus separating "the bright and discernible from the unilluminable and dark".[21] The mandate of the TRC can possibly be regarded as facilitating such a radical break with the past. The cathartic processes and experiences during the hearings illuminated the contrast between the dark past and the brighter future to come. The future, however, first demands the disclosure of past truths. The dividing line can only be drawn once we are certain of where the past ends and the future begins. It is impossible to step over a line that one cannot see.

Nietzsche acknowledges that this radical cut-off point, the dividing line between the past and the future, can only be imagined by considering the historical *and* the unhistorical in equal measures. Living unhistorically, by definition, narrows the horizon to that of, in Nietzsche's colourful metaphor, "a dweller in the Alps" – someone who mistakenly believes that all his experiences are unique. The temptation to regard one's own experiences as singular, especially in the case of life-changing personal or political events, is considerable. After the first democratic elections in South Africa, South Africans very often regarded their own situation and the dramatic political changes around them as not only remarkable, but also unique. It is only by introducing one's own experiences into the historical that it becomes possible, in Nietzsche's idiom, to "employ the past for the purposes of life" and to "introduce into history that which has been done and is gone".[22] It is, however, very important for the historical and the unhistorical to remain balanced. In *Untimely Meditations* Nietzsche calls for the critical use of history. This implies, on one hand, a just treatment of the past, but, on the other hand, also a dismissal of one's traditional reverence of the past. It may demand that we see ourselves and our history in a way other than we might have preferred.

4.2. FOUCAULT: HISTORY AND COUNTER-HISTORY

In his essay *Nietzsche, Genealogy, History*,[23] Foucault engages with and expands on the arguments Nietzsche put forward in *Untimely Meditations*.

[21] Ibid. 63.
[22] Ibid. 64.
[23] Included in Foucault (1980) 139–164.

Foucault builds on aspects of Nietzsche's theory but also provides a new, and maybe again "untimely" and uncomfortable perspective on history, knowledge and discursive practices.

At the outset Foucault rejects the classic perception of history as following a linear trajectory. According to him, this is a wholly erroneous attitude, which he labels as "an English tendency". The first problem is the rather obvious fact that words do not keep their meaning, and the second, that "ideas do not retain their logic". Perceiving the past as having a discernible and stable origin and an objective essence is challenged by a myriad of singular events. Such events, which one will normally not classify as "history", for Foucault, include aspects such as "sentiments, love, conscience, instincts".[24] History comprises that which cannot be "fitted" into a coherent and straight path. It includes what happened, but also what did not happen, or what may have happened.

Foucault, in approximate agreement with Nietzsche, distinguishes between traditional or metaphysical history, on the one side, and effective or *wirkliche* history on the other. The latter coincides with what he calls genealogy. Foucault strongly opposes the way that traditional history endeavours to capture the essence of things, events and identities. Such history assumes that there is some original site of truth and knowledge that is accessible and which can be recovered, something that is fundamental to human nature. Genealogy, in contrast, provides no sense of stability. Rather than offering foundations and a stable structure, it is discontinuous and shows the heterogeneity of everything we regard as constant and secure. Foucault explains, as one commentator observes, that the genealogist does not "set out to study the beginning – [but rather] its numberless beginnings".[25] He explains thus:

> [W]e should not be deceived into thinking that this heritage [referring to the past] is an acquisition, a possession that grows and solidifies; rather, it is an unstable assemblage of faults, fissures and heterogeneous layers that threaten the fragile inheritor from within or from underneath.[26]

With history providing no foothold and no handrails, the question turns to the future. If Nietzsche is correct in calling for a sharp divide between the past and the future, but neither of these can be clearly delineated, how to proceed is not obvious. However, taking a wider perspective on Foucault's views on epistemology, discursive practices and especially what he refers to as "subjugated knowledges"[27] may provide new possibilities.

---

24 Ibid. 139–140.
25 McWhorter (1999) 41.
26 Foucault (2003) 146.
27 Foucault (2003) 7–9.

The first important point is that, for Foucault, the practices of remembering and forgetting are never neutral. Rather, such practices are always embedded in the context of power relations. These are epistemic negotiations, which determine what we (can) remember and what we (should) forget. Such negotiations are seldom harmonious and there will always be some memories/truths which become dominant and get absorbed into prevailing hegemonic structures, and others which get subjugated and consequently marginalised and even forgotten. According to Medina, the task of genealogy is to resurrect such subjugated knowledges and, in the process, ensure that coercive epistemic closures are re-opened. We know from experience that there are always people whose memories do not fit the dominant narrative and who "remember against the grain". Such non-dominant versions of history lead to the production of so-called counter-histories, which normally are experiences and memories that are not integrated or accepted in official versions.

The key concept in understanding Foucault's position is that discursive practices have consequences for epistemic knowledge *as well as* for power. What we can *do* depends on what we *know* and on what we can *say*. Power and knowledge therefore cannot be separated. Medina points out that marginalised groups are not without knowledge and power. In other words, they are not ignorant or powerless, but their powers and knowledges have been demeaned and obstructed".[28] Foucault explains that the battle is "not one between knowledge and ignorance, but an immense and multiple battle between *knowledges in the plural*" (emphasis added). He explains that there is a critical struggle against establishing a monopoly on knowledge-producing practices. Such a monopoly of the episteme can be avoided by "an insurrection of subjugated knowledges". Counter-history produces disunity and counters hegemonic closure.

In the context of the TRC hearings and the aspiration of drawing a firm line demarcating the past and the future, counter-histories produced variable consequences. One example of this, amongst others, is the so-called "women's hearings" conducted by the TRC between 1996 and 1997. During the process of drafting the 1995 Act, very little, if any, awareness was shown of the gendered aspects of past human rights violations. A number of reasons have been provided for this "blind-spot" in the TRC structure. It was clear from the beginning that the overriding concern during the negotiations was addressing past and present *political* violence. In subsequent legislation, the mandate of the TRC was to investigate "gross human rights violations". These were defined as "the violation of human rights through the killing, abduction, torture or severe ill-treatment of any person" or the "attempt, conspiracy, incitement, instigation,

---

28 Medina (2011) 13.

command or procurement to commit such acts".[29] The definition did not include any references to rape or other forms of sexual violence, although this was later obliquely included under "severe ill-treatment" after lobbying by women's groups.[30] Gendered human rights abuses, however, remained on the periphery. Kusafuka provides an example of this. During the Amnesty Committee hearing for Jabu Jacob Nyethe, certain details of rape were reported. The Chairperson reminded those present that there was no application for amnesty against rape and that the hearing should "limit collecting testimonial evidence on rape".[31] The counter-truth was simply swept off the table.

The emphasis on politically-motivated, race-, class- and gender-led violence became subsidiary. Also, the narrow focus on so-called "political" offences, especially in the context of amnesty hearings, led to a disregard of structural abuses, including gendered abuses against women. One of the reasons why sexual violence was particularly difficult to deal with was that the demarcation between political and personal motives was not always clear.[32] In framing violence as either "political" or "personal", political violence was always prioritised. Civil society groups noticed that although the TRC conducted extensive outreach campaigns in local communities, there was a marked lack of women coming forward to present their own experiences of violence and abuse. Where they did testify before the Commission, it was normally on behalf of someone else – mostly a male family member, a brother, or husband or son, who had been killed or went missing during the struggle.

In 1996 the TRC recognised that there were certain gaps in its fact-finding procedures and decided to conduct a range of thematic hearings, including special women's hearings.[33] The aim was to gather information on women's first-hand experiences of human rights violations. The hearings were conducted before a women-only panel and mostly *in camera*. According to Goldblatt and Meintjies "these hearings clearly indicated that women were afraid and ashamed to speak about their experiences but when provided with an opportunity to do so in a safe environment, were more willing to come forward."[34] In general, women felt ashamed of their experiences of torture, especially if this included, as it mostly did, a direct or oblique sexual threat or sexual

---

29 Promotion of National Unity and Reconciliation Act no 34 of 1995.

30 Goldblatt and Meintjes (1997).

31 Kusafuka (2009) 58. Special Women's Hearings, Johannesburg, 28–29 July 1997. TRC women's hearings were not published due to the sensitive nature of the issues. Hence I cannot refer to pages.

32 There was evidence of instances where rape was sanctioned by the security forces. See Goldblatt and Meintjes (1997).

33 These took place in Cape Town (August 1996), Durban (October 1996) and Johannesburg (July 1997).

34 Goldblatt and Meintjes (1997) 9.

violence. During the women's hearing in 1997 in Johannesburg, the following testimony was heard:

> The way women experience detention is totally different from the way men do. I burst into tears when a security policeman said to me, I really enjoy interrogating women. I can get things out of them and do things with them that I cannot do to a man.[35]

Returning to Foucault, it can be confirmed that we cannot regard the history of some as the history of all. The women's hearings are examples of counter-history not only filling the gaps in official history, but also revealing the disunity and oppositions within the political body. Foucault explains that the counter-history

> ... also breaks the continuity of glory. It reveals that the light – the famous dazzling effect of power – is not something that petrifies, solidifies, and immobilizes the entire social body, and thus keeps it in order; it is in fact a divisive light that illuminates one side of the social body, but leaves the other side in shadow or casts it into darkness.

4.3. DERRIDA AND THE ARCHIVE

In August 1998, during his brief visit to South Africa, Derrida participated in a seminar at the University of the Witwatersrand in Johannesburg. The topic of the seminar was Derrida's short work *Archive Fever, A Freudian Impression*, first published in 1995. The choice of theme and the timing were impeccable: it was two months prior to the TRC's submission of the first five volumes of its report, a document which would stand as the official archive of the "conflicts of the past", as it was called in the Interim Constitution.

During the seminar, Derrida spoke in very cautious terms to the work of the TRC. In referring to the forthcoming report he remarked that "we could say that it is a problem of archive".[36] Without doing justice to the complexity of the arguments put forward in Derrida's essay, three aspects of archive/archive fever and how they relate to the TRC and its work will be examined. The first theme concerns the TRC as the official custodians of the past, and by implication the relationship between power and memory. The second is the archive's relation to both the future and the past and the political responsibility of maintaining an open archive. The third consideration is the key role of

35 The sexual abuse of women was not exclusively at the hands of the security police and prison wardens, but also included abuses in ANC training camps. See: http://www.justice.gov.za/trc/media%5C1996%5C9606/s960618b.htm.

36 Derrida (1996) 48.

"forgetting" and how, according to Derrida, this may be "the unconfessed desire of the Truth and Reconciliation Commission".

In *Archive Fever*, Derrida refers to the custodians of the official archive as the *archons*. The *archons* were the supreme magistrates of the Greek polis, "those who commanded", and their residence, the *arkheion*, was the official site of power. Thus, there was an intersection of *nomos* and *topos*, of law and place. The *archons*' political authority was first determined by the fact that they were the keepers or guardians of all official documents. According to Derrida, however, they not only commanded the right to physically secure and guard the archive, but also "the hermeneutic right and competence" to interpret the archive and to "represent the law".

In his 1998 seminar in Johannesburg, Derrida observed that "the TRC could be considered a place of archive". A feature of the archive is that it is *located* somewhere; it has a specific external site. There is no concept like an internal/private archive. Because of its structural exteriority, it has to exist somewhere, it is inescapably *public*. Derrida says of the then forthcoming TRC Report:

> It's going to be a public archive. And the very publicity, the inscription in public space, of these testimonies and these *interpretations* of the testimonies will have no doubt a powerful effect on the history and the future of South Africa (emphasis added).[37]

It is clear that the archive is not a mass of objective facts, gathered and disseminated in a neutral manner. Its "truth" is "interpreted truth". Those who have the power to interpret, modern-day *archons*, have their own motivations and their own pre-shaped schemes of interpretation. As an example of this, Derrida points to the interpretation of "reconciliation" as being conditioned by "confession, repentance, forgiveness, and so on and so forth".[38] In an oblique reference to the chairperson of the TRC, he notes that such an interpretation introduces values or assumptions which may be linked to the interpretation of a particular religious tradition.

The second aspect of the archive, and closely related to the first, is its relationship to both the past and the future. In the 1998 seminar Derrida explains that "the archive doesn't simply record the past. It also, of course, constitutes the past, and in view of a future which retrospectively, or retroactively, gives it its so-called final truth".[39] Not only is the archive something which is shaped by a certain selective power, as discussed above, it is also shaped by the future and its openness to the future. Despite the evident relationship between

---

37 Derrida (1996) 48.
38 Ibid. 54.
39 Ibid. 42–43.

the archive, memory and the past, Derrida insists on its futurity and the fact that "the archive [is] an irreducible experience of the future".[40]

The archive's "openness to the future" can be understood on more than one level. First, there is the fact that the archive will inevitably remain incomplete. There will always be new materials coming to light, new facts "emerging", hitherto suppressed information "discovered" and so on. In Foucauldian terms, one can say that counter-truths will always emerge. Because of this inescapable imperfection, the archive can never be closed and it can never be declared to be a complete or accomplished "project". This future-orientated structure of the archive comes with an ethical and political responsibility – the responsibility to allow for re-interpretation and the responsibility to resist any attempts at official closure of the past. The possibility of counter-history is thus not only one of many alternatives, but also a moral imperative.

On another level, the future-to-come of the archive also refers to a more radical impossibility of knowledge *as such*. As a messianic order the *avenir*, the "to-come", does not fall within the domain of theoretical knowledge or of *epistēmē*. It keeps the possibility of knowledge, and thus also the ordering/archiving of knowledge, conditional on "a coming or an event which one *allows* or *incites* to come ... in an experience which is heterogeneous to all taking note ... to all stabilizable theorems as such."[41]

The third aspect of the archive can be classified under what Derrida refers to as "archive fever" or maybe rather "archive madness" (*le mal d'archive*). This complex and internally divided concept points, on the one hand, to Freud's death drive, an instinct of utter destruction, not only of the thing, but also of the memory of the thing and even of the name of the thing. On the other hand, it indicates a "burning with passion" *for* the archive, to have an overpowering and nostalgic desire to return to the origins of the most archaic place. It indicates an obsession to find and possess the moment of beginning, the beginning of beginning, the *arkhě*, unmediated by the archive.

Both types of "fever" are reliant on the fact that the archive is not "living" or "true" memory. It is, in fact, quite the opposite. The archive, like a notebook or a diary, allows one to forget. Derrida gives a practical example: When I handwrite something on a piece of paper, I put it in my pocket or in the safe, it's just in order to forget it, to know that I can find it again while in the meantime having forgotten it. Through archiving, live/internal memory is consigned to some external place for "safekeeping". This creates the possibility that one can always, in the future, return to the archive and retrieve or reproduce that which has been forgotten. The exteriority of the archive, however, also marks its vulnerability. There is always the possibility that the archive can be completely destroyed,

---

40 Ibid. 68.

41 Ibid. 68.

burned to the ground, leaving no traces of the history that we have forgotten. At a psychic level the drive to preserve (archive) is threatened or comes into conflict with the death drive, the drive to destroy.

Evident in Freud's writing is, however, also the reverse type of "archive fever". This is the intense desire for finding and possessing the *original* "archive". The desire here is not for the archive as prosthesis of live memory (the notebook), but rather a desire for the *thing itself*, the live experience, the living memory. In the procedures of the TRC, and especially in the recordings and transcripts of the live hearings, this kind of fever is often evident. The search is for *unmediated* and *self-evident* "truth"; to find the place where the "stones speak for themselves". We know, however, that finding this kind of truth is not possible. Truth is made, it is mediated, and it can be changed. A burning desire for something more than that, something pure and eternal, can be as destructive as the desire for annihilation.

Harlow explains that truth commissions form part of "strategies (complex, conflicted, compromised as they might be) for rewriting the historical legacies left to the late twentieth century."[42] Such a view produces more questions than answers, many of which confront the South African political community now more than ever.

Crucial to their work, whether in Latin America, the former Yugoslavia, or South Africa, are the determinations of just how to retrieve those legacies, where to place them, and who will have access to these archives, the new additions to the modern library, the expanded stacks. What will be the new geographies, and what the revised chronologies? Who are the participants and what are the roles assigned to them?[43]

5. CONCLUSION

When Nelson Mandela walked out of the gates of the Victor Verster Prison in the Paarl and raised his fist in a freedom salute the world changed. It was in Badiou's vocabulary, an *event*[44] in true style, an event with irrevocable consequences. For the majority of South Africans, freedom was no longer a political slogan, but a realistic possibility. However, despite the compelling narrative pull of this remarkable tale of redemption and freedom, history did not come to an end. In the "new" South Africa questions surrounding the reform of the moral order, communal solidarity, civil responsibilities and

42 Harlow (2000).
43 Said (2000) 183–184.
44 Badiou (2005).

public accountability are heavily contested. One can perhaps, with Nietzsche, call for the *critical* use of history, which may even imply mild amnesia. Foucault could perhaps remind us of the uncomfortable fact that the past is never neutral and that history is not always shared history. Counter-memory pushes against a monopoly of the episteme; it illuminates the fissures and counters a hegemonic "closure" of knowledges. This process, one can argue, is fundamental both to the present and to the future.

References

Adorno, Th. (2003) *Negative Dialectics*. transl. E.B. Ashton, London: Routledge.

Badiou, A. (2005) *Being and Event*. transl. O. Feltham, London: Continuum.

Bové, P.A. (ed.) (2000), *Edward Said and the Work of the Critic: Speaking Truth to Power*. Durham N.C./London: Duke University Press.

Crais, C.C. (1992), *White Supremacy and Black Resistance in Pre-Industrial South Africa: The Making of the Colonial Order in the Eastern Cape 1770–1865*. Cambridge: Cambridge University Press.

De Frouville, O. (2006) "The Human Right to the Truth in International Law: On Some 'Untimely Meditations'". *Sorbonne-Assas Law Review*, Panthéon-Assas, Université Paris II.

Derrida, J. (1996) *Archive Fever: A Freudian Impression*. Baltimore M.D.: Johns Hopkins University Press.

Foucault, M. (1980) [1977] *Language, Counter Memory, Practice. Selected Essays and Interviews*. D.F. Bouchard (ed.), transl. D.F. Bouchard and S. Simon. Ithaca N.Y.: Cornell University Press.

—— (2003) *Society Must Be Defended, Lectures at the College de France 1975–1976*. New York: Picador.

Goldblat, B. and Meintjies, S. (1997) "Dealing with the Aftermath: Sexual Violence and the Truth and Reconciliation Commission" in *Agenda: Empowering Women for Gender Equity*, **13**, no. 36: 7–18.

Harlow, B. (2000) "Sappers in the Stacks: Colonial Archives, Land Mines and Truth Commissions" in P.A. Bové (ed.), *Edward Said and The Work of the Critic: Speaking Truth to Power*. Durham N.C./London: Duke University Press.

Kantsteiner, W. (2002) "Finding Meaning in Memory: A Methodological Critique of Collective Memory Studies" in *History and Theory*, **41**: 179–197.

Krog, A. (2001) "Locked into Loss and Silence: Testimonies of Gender and Violence at the South African Truth Commission" in C. Moser and F. Clark (eds), *Victims, Perpetrators or Actors? Gender, Armed Conflict and Political Violence*. London: Zed Books.

Kusafuka, A. (2009) "Truth commissions and gender: A South African case study" in *African Journal on Conflict Resolution*, **9**: 45.

McGrath, A.E. (1997) *The Genesis of Doctrine: a Study in the Foundations of Doctrinal Criticism*. Grand Rapids M.I.: Eerdmans; Vancouver: Regent College Publishing.

McWhorter, L. (1999) *Bodies and Pleasures. Foucault and the Politics of Sexual Normalization*. Bloomington/Indianapolis I.N.: Indiana University Press.

Medina, J. (2011) "Towards a Foucaultian Epistemology of Resistance: Counter Memory, Epistemic Friction and Guerilla Pluralism" in *Foucaultian Studies*, no. 12: 9–35.
Motsemme, N. (2004) "The Mute Always Speak: On Women's Silences at the Truth and Reconciliation Commission" in *Current Sociology*, 52, 909–932.
Nietzsche, F. (1983) [1874] *Untimely Meditations*, transl. R.J. Hollingdale. Cambridge: Cambridge University Press.
Tutu, D. (2000) *No Future without Forgiveness: A Personal Review of South Africa's Truth and Reconciliation Committee*. New York etc.: Image.
—— (2002) "Foreword" to R. Helmick and R., Petersen, *Forgiveness and Reconciliation*. Philadelphia P.A.: Templeton Foundation Press.
White, G. (2008) "Witnessing Proceedings: The Hague War Crimes Tribunal, Narrative Indeterminacy and the Public Audience" in *War and Other Bad Shit*, **52**: 75–86.

CHAPTER 7

"BEGGING TO BE BLACK"

Liminality and Critique in Post-Apartheid South Africa

Stewart Motha*

This is a republication of an article I wrote a decade ago and published in the journal *Theory, Culture, and Society.* Since that time there have been numerous political and juridical developments in South Africa that are pertinent to the themes explored in this chapter. Among these are the growing dissatisfaction with the constitutional settlement negotiated by the African National Congress (ANC) in 1994, and the palpable lack of progress in land and wealth redistribution. The gist of the criticism is that resorting to constitutionalism at the moment of the shift from white to black rule juridicalised and thus stilled the radical momentum of popular social movements, thereby leading to a compromise that suited white and black elites. There is now a resurgent black nationalism, and a call for "settlers" and "natives" to have a new reckoning to address the history of colonial violence and dispossession in South Africa.

Reflecting now on what I wrote many years ago, my concern remains with the problem that belonging is too readily and simplistically determined and mediated through concepts like "settler" and "native". I called for an engagement with postcolonial epistemologies precisely to counter the argument that who

* Professor of Law, Birkbeck, University of London.

is "proper" to a place can be determined by a binary opposition of settler/ native. My concern has always been, and remains, the danger of political and juridical arguments that turn on an essential identity linked to the notion of "blood and soil". Strategies informed by such notions will ineluctably lead to yet more camps and gulags. Any argument that seeks to undergird sovereignty (including a decolonised one) through such essential identities needs rigorous interrogation. It remains the case, then, that I believe that Antjie Krog and Mogobe Ramose, the primary thinkers with whom I engage in this chapter, provide useful intellectual resources to address the problem of belonging in South Africa. Their encounter is one that I have staged in the chapter by making their respective concerns and arguments speak to each other.

The wider global proliferation of transitional justice has also come under sustained and meaningful challenge. Mechanisms such as truth and reconciliation commissions have become the favoured methods of political reconstitution when societies confront or are involved in transitioning from colonial violence, dispossession, and racist discriminatory orders. Such institutions face the challenge of whether they represent the "true" path to decolonisation. The choice is often presented starkly as one between revolutionary justice (comprehensive redistribution of land and property for instance) or "justice-as-reconciliation" (Meister 2011, 24–31). For Meister, the latter is a result of "Human Rights Discourse" delegitimising revolutionary politics by turning erstwhile revolutionaries into participants in a new "moral consensus" about how to address the "evil" of the "past". Transitional societies such as South Africa are then regarded as constituted by a new cast of political actors: individual perpetrators (who can be dealt with as pathological villains or "bad apples"), "collective beneficiaries" (who retain their unjustly acquired gains), and reconciled victims (who are regarded as "undamaged" if they heed the call to forgive). In a revolutionary trajectory, on the other hand, a beneficiary is a perpetrator, so the re-introduction of the distinction between beneficiary and perpetrator enables so-called transitional societies to retain inequalities. Closing a chapter of violence is, on Meister's account, too readily launched by disavowing a revolutionary horizon. "Human Rights Discourse" is the political and juridical trope that Meister usefully identifies to herald a time after the Cold War when a new revolutionary dawn seems to have come to an end.

The epistemology and ontology of being and becoming remains a key challenge for political and juridical transformation today. There is no more pressing symptom of this than the re-racialisation of nationalist claims in the name of progressive politics in South Africa and elsewhere. On this and many other things, the world must learn from South Africa. Addressing the plurality of being must involve plural ways of knowing. Krog and Ramose are exemplary companions for such an endeavour.

1. INTRODUCTION: FROM ANTI-COLONIAL LONGING TO POSTCOLONIAL BECOMING

Each generation must discover its mission, fulfil it or betray it, in relative opacity.

(Frantz Fanon, *The Wretched of the Earth* (2004) [1961]: 145)

Fanon wrote these lines as a wave of anti-colonial revolution and transformation swept aside the erstwhile imperial orders in Asia, Africa, the Caribbean and the Middle East. The opacity he speaks of conveys a quieter and more contemplative message than that of the fervent Fanon whose call to revolutionary violence was embraced by those engaged in anti-colonial struggle.[1] In the face of a totalising, brutal, violent, racist colonial order, Fanon's aim was to authorise every anti-colonial revolt including the claim to nation (Fanon, 2004 [1961]: 146). Engaging with the psychic and affective lives of coloniser and colonised, he gave particular attention to how a fragile and anxious colonised consciousness could assert and arrive at national liberation. Throwing out the old order through national liberation usually resulted in a transfer of sovereignty. But postcolonial sovereignty often replaced imperial sovereignty with a suppression of minorities, ethno-national chauvinism, new racisms and the rise of "private indirect rule" (Mbembe, 2001). The objective of this chapter is not to hammer yet another nail into the coffin of colonial sovereignty; nor is it to claim that postcolonial imperatives have not yet been met because the anti-colonial revolution failed or is yet to happen. Instead, it is to signal the need to move beyond "anti-colonial longing" towards postcolonial becoming as the condition for grappling with the challenges of divided polities still emerging from colonial violence, and social and economic inequalities that remain the stubborn legacies of colonialism (Scott, 2004: 7).[2]

The move from anti-colonial longing to postcolonial becoming is one that is located among liminal beings and the spaces they occupy. The focus here will be on the "new" South Africa that emerged following the juridical and political transition from Apartheid in 1994 (Madlingozi, 2007).[3] What mode of becoming, this chapter asks, might secure a postcolonial future? The liminal figure on which most attention is focused here is South African poet and writer Antjie Krog, and her book *Begging to Be Black* (2009). This might immediately rile some readers. Why focus on a white Afrikaner woman who has written a book about becoming black, in a country where the vast majority of the black population are living in conditions of violence and inequality that

1 See Homi K. Bhabha's "Foreword" to *The Wretched of the Earth* (2004: xli) for an evocative discussion of this opacity.

2 This move away from 'anti-colonial longing' is influenced by Scott (2004: 7).

3 See Madlingozi (2007) for a critique of the terms of transition, and a problematization of the 'new' in post-Apartheid discourse.

hardly provide much opportunity for becoming otherwise? Such a question does not do much justice to the multiple forms of black becoming. What Krog is attempting is an epistemic move towards another ontology of being. She is seeking to de-centre herself and a coloniser's way of seeing, knowing and being. She does not seek to deny or hypostatise difference. Her approach has risks and contradictions. The objective here is to discuss some of these.

"Becoming otherwise" is not only a challenge for South Africans attempting to deal with 350 years of colonialism, and 50 years of Apartheid.[4] South Africa is not a place for Europeans and North Americans to sharpen their good consciences. Apartheid, despite its singularity, was a metonymic violence through which to decipher so many different kinds of violence going on in the world (Derrida, 1994: xv). The inequality between white and black people in South Africa reflects a global crisis of wealth disparity and the failures of radical political transformation.

South Africans share the problem of political horizons with people from other parts of the world. When Chris Hani, leader of the South African Communist Party and chief of staff of *Umkhonto we Sizwe*, the armed wing of the ANC, was assassinated in Boksburg on 10 April 1993, and quite possibly well before that, a paradigm of communism and socialist nationalism was being lost not only to South Africa, but also to the world.[5] Democracy, human rights, the rule of law, capitalism and de-regulation of markets constitute a global institutional consensus implemented in South Africa and many other countries. They form a structural limit on deeper political and socio-economic transformation. While anti-capitalist rebellion and revolt is urgently needed, so many alternatives hinge on forms of nationalist sovereignty that carry their own disasters. At least one modest task, therefore, is to chart some of the modes of becoming for living here and now, in this world and not in a Utopian future.

To return to Fanon, then, what is the postcolonial injunction or mission for "becoming otherwise" in South Africa today? How will it be discovered, fulfilled or betrayed? Taking my cue from Fanon, I want to suggest that the South African poet and writer Antjie Krog might be finding a way to dwell in the opacity of the present in ways that open, however tentatively, some pathways of postcolonial becoming. The epistemology and ontology of postcolonial becoming is the crux of this chapter's concern. It thus compares Krog's approach with that of the leading South African philosopher of ubuntu, Mogobe Ramose (Ramose (2002); (2006); (2007)). Both Krog and Ramose give us the epistemological and ontological resources for grappling with the relationship between past, present and future. But there are important differences between

4 For an excellent history of colonial expropriation in South Africa, see Terreblanche (2003).

5 See Jacques Derrida's discussion of Chris Hani's assassination in his lecture "Whither Marxism?", later published as Derrida, *Spectres of Marx* (1994) – a book dedicated to Chris Hani.

the two thinkers. The key difference is between anti-colonial longing (Ramose's project) and postcolonial becoming (Krog's project). Although this author favours Krog's approach, it is with the hope that the onto-epistemology for its fulfilment might be found in Ramose's philosophical writings. Whether Krog succeeds or fails may quite aptly, as Fanon suggests, remain opaque.

The more general concern of the chapter is what questions and approaches will animate postcolonial becoming? The tension here is between a past that resists correction (the problem of justice) and a future that demands adjustment (the problem of invention). To put it another way, will the future be driven by an adjustment of the past (recovering sovereignty for instance), or by the creation of new missions directed at new problems and questions? What is needed is a turning towards a future but always with the spectres that disrupt the linear unfolding of time. The narratives of past, present and future are the spaces where movement is possible. But what mission, what horizon, drives the narratives and work of becoming?

I am not a South African. I was born in Sri Lanka in 1970. I became a Tamil on 25 July 1983, when my family and I were attacked in our home in the violence unleashed on Tamils in Colombo and throughout the country. A discussion of that forced becoming is for another time and place. But it is an experience that radicalised me against any essential conception of being. The enforcement of identification that struck my otherwise multiply-constituted and -situated body in July 1983 conditioned my close interest in non-sovereign forms of becoming. South Africa has been an exemplary setting for thinking through the problem of becoming in the face of colonial violence and sharply divided communities. Although I now live and work in the UK, I have found myself regularly returning to South Africa after my first visit in 2003.

Unlike Sri Lanka, with its now triumphant Sinhalese majority, or Australia, with its belated apologies for genocidal acts and tightly circumscribed native title rights, South Africa is driven to confront a stark reality. The descendants of the waves of colonial settlers remain a minority. And despite their relative affluence, preserved in the political compromise that ended Apartheid in 1994, there is a strong sense that more radical transformation is urgently needed. This chapter explores some of the more imaginative and inventive approaches to becoming postcolonial that are emerging in South Africa.

2. BECOMING MINOR

Antjie Krog is a celebrated South African poet who was born in Kroonstad and grew up on a farm in the Free State. While her poetry has been translated into many languages, she gained significant international prominence among critical theorists following her work with a team that covered the Truth and

Reconciliation Commission (TRC) hearings for SABC Radio in 1995. She later brought her formidable literary skills to bear on transmitting the power of the testimonies at the TRC to a wider international audience through her book *The Country of My Skull* (1998). She conveyed something of people's trauma in that book, but importantly also the limits of addressing this through testimonies before commissions, strained apologies or seemingly cathartic spectacles of forgiveness. This was followed by *A Change of Tongue* (2003), which combined fact and fiction to explore how South Africans were living with the legacies of Apartheid: its traumas, but also the beauty and anxiety in what has slowly emerged over time – the Afrikaans language, food, dramatic landscapes with layers of agriculture, and mixed and divided communities. The challenge of becoming different after Apartheid is captured in the title *A Change of Tongue*. Language is one contested and complex site of becoming. The Constitution guarantees 11 languages, but English is in the ascendant. In some cases the rise of English only serves to sustain white enclaves, crowding out members of the "coloured" community who speak Afrikaans as their first language. The rise of English over Afrikaans, partly a result of globalisation, is also due to the fact that few South Africans have bothered to learn Sepedi, Sesotho, Setswana, siSwati, Tshivenda, Xitsonga, IsiNdebele, IsiXhosa or IsiZulu, across the boundaries of their respective communities. Beyond language, what Krog has been concerned with is the question of what it means to become different across racialised lines of community when continued co-existence demands transformation. Addressing that question is at the heart of Krog's latest book, *Begging to Be Black* (2009).

It is of course significant that the title to Krog's book about "becoming black" carries the somewhat shocking title of "Begging to Be Black". Again, one can imagine the reactions: a white person can never know what it means to be black; how can this privileged white woman pretend to cast herself in such a "needy" light by using "begging" in her title; is she appropriating an experience of oppression that white people can never know about; or is it a willed submission from a place of plenty, or "identity suicide"? The title should be read more generously as invoking a passivity and necessity that moves away from a strong sense of subjectivity or judgement. "Begging" opens a relation of gifting. But as is suggested below, it is not an identity that is being sought. Rather it is an attempt to share an onto-epistemology of becoming. *Begging to Be Black* explores the possibility of white people becoming otherwise in post-Apartheid South Africa. The project of "becoming black" eschews any essentialist meaning of being "black/white", colonial/postcolonial. Those who hold to a notion of race as a substance with presence in the world will tend to misunderstand this book. This is not to deny that racial logics produce real and actual consequences in the lived reality of those with racialised bodies. Nor is there a suggestion that a movement towards black can be (or ought to be) replicated with a move away from black. We should by now be well past the time when race is treated as having such a substantial essence. This is not an easy thing for liberals who have built their careers in Identity Inc.

Begging to Be Black is a work of literary non-fiction. Krog weaves several narrative strands together: the murder of a gang leader shot by ANC cadres in 1992 and her own involvement in the case after the killers hid incriminating evidence and the weapon in her home; an account of the Boer and English land grabs of the nineteenth century in what is now Lesotho, told through the encounter between the Besotho King Moshoeshoe and French missionaries; Krog's visit to the *Wissenschaftskolleg* (Institute for Advanced Study) in Berlin; more intimate reflections contained in letters to her mother while in Berlin; and Krog's visit to Lesotho. Each of these strands is placed in conversation with the other. Krog is experimenting with the genre of literary non-fiction, where past and present, inner thoughts and outer events are folded into each other. While each strand of the book might be treated individually as the recounting of actual events, their being placed beside each other constitutes a mytho-poetic narrative. The reader is drawn into that powerful imaginary space where characters and events across time and space speak to each other. *Begging to Be Black* is a mytho-poetic narrative because a world is imagined where King Moshoeshoe, missionaries from the nineteenth century, Antjie Krog and her friends and colleagues, ANC cadres, the Deleuzian philosopher Paul Patton, Krog's husband "J.", Nelson Mandela, Archbishop Desmond Tutu and the ANC Youth League are placed in the same narrative space where they can intermingle. And this is done to respond to a crisis of the present – the difficulties South Africans face in grappling with the legacies of colonialism and Apartheid, and the fact that there is a process of un-homing and re-homing that Krog feels white South Africans in particular need to think about more deeply. Although facts are recounted, the form of the text produces a powerful *as if*. The wisdom of this illusion, this *as if*, is that it composes a conversation across time and space (Part One of the book is "The Long Conversation: First Perceptions and Un-hearings"), and then creates the conditions for drawing out insights and examining errors and failures of perception (Part Two: "Understandings, Assumed Understandings, and Non-understandings"). In the final part ("The Long Conversation: Whose Context?"), she returns to key moral and political dilemmas raised in the narrative to find that her own line of thinking needs to be altered in order to face up to a philosophical and existential un-homing. Each character, each position and perspective, is put into question in its intermingling with others. This approach to history takes seriously the fact that it is narrative that constitutes the relation between past, present, and future (Scott, 2004: 7).

Begging to Be Black begins with the killing of Wheetie, leader of the Three Million Gang, by ANC cadres in the Town of Kroonstad on 25 February 1992. Two possible reasons for killing Wheetie emerge. Wheetie had set up an Inkatha branch in a township with the support of the police and was spreading violence in Kroonstad. He was thus eliminated by his political enemies. However, one of the members of the ANC youth group involved in the killing, the Young Lions, had also been caught in bed with Wheetie's wife and Wheetie had threatened revenge. So was his killing personal or political? When Krog is drawn into assisting the killers to escape, and later finds that the pistol and balaclava used in the killing were hidden in her garden, and a T-shirt worn by one of the accused is left in her possession, she faces a number of moral and political dilemmas. Here the context of the killing becomes relevant. In what way, and to what extent, should it have a bearing on whether she will report the matter to the police, or give evidence for the state in the prosecution of the killers?

By the time of Wheetie's killing Nelson Mandela had been released from prison and the ANC had been unbanned. F.W. de Klerk was negotiating with the ANC and Mandela. However, the Apartheid state and the security police were fomenting and orchestrating violence in the townships by exploiting rivalries, setting Inkatha members against the ANC. As Krog puts it within her narrative, "The TRC also heard that more South Africans were killed between 1990 and 1994 than in the twenty years of Total Onslaught before." "Is this possible?", Krog wonders, and phones one of the TRC lawyers to find out. "It's true", she says. "Remember that the majority of amnesty applicants are black and many many of them formed part of these roped-in groups, especially through Inkatha" (Krog, 2009: 257).

Krog's initial dilemma about what to do when she finds out that she is going to be implicated in assisting Wheetie's killers to escape is set within a paradigm of the struggle against Apartheid. If the killing is part of the struggle then is what Krog does in taking the incriminating evidence to the police justified? Is the killing about sex, revenge or politics? What difference should each of these possibilities make to the dilemmas of a white woman at a time when South Africa was in the throes of a violent transition to democratic rule? Krog was not given much of a choice when she was unwittingly drawn into driving the killers to Maokeng. She is a white woman, a member of the ANC, working in solidarity with the black and coloured communities to bring down the Apartheid state. In that context what she has to offer the struggle are her middle-class advantages – a car, a fax machine, her profile as a celebrated poet. For Krog "[i]t's a moral decision, but the thing is, to what extent can you make a moral decision within an immoral context?" (2009: 13).

In one sense the killing of Wheetie involved the murder of a murderer. She believes murder is wrong – respect for life should be a basic principle. Is she frightened?, the police ask her, as they search her home soon after the killing. She refutes this vehemently: "If I look frightened to you, it is because I'm upset that you and the politicians have made sure that an honourable position is no longer possible for an ordinary person in this country" (Krog, 2009: 39). Krog grapples with the conundrum of respect for life in a society that has never formed "a coherent enough whole" to decide on which principles it agrees (2009: 46). But can this be the basis for deciding whether a death, a killing, is legitimate? Would the killing be any more legitimate if there was a communal consensus about it? This is the well-worn decision on the political – the decision between friend and foe that Carl Schmitt (1996) wrote about. Is loyalty to the cause, supporting the struggle, enough reason to support a killing or killers? Does this simply shift the moral responsibilities of the individual? Put differently, Krog is fighting for a moral space in conditions where most of the population, including her, don't live within a common, stable moral environment. She seems to conclude that an "honourable position" is not possible where death-dealing and violence is justified in the name of the "struggle". Will such instrumental reasoning only prepare the ground for a sacrificial union – a Republic of friends and enemies?

Krog was ultimately drawn into the case as a state's witness in the prosecution of the killers. She took the red T-shirt that implicated the killers to the police. This was by no means the end of the violence in Kroonstad. The accused were convicted and received prison sentences but later received amnesty through the TRC. She faced a terrible choice – to risk becoming an accessory to murder by trying to cover up a murder that went against all the principles of valuing life that she believed the ANC was fighting for, or to work with the police who were fomenting and facilitating the violence between Inkatha and the ANC. But the question remains – is the murder of a murderer any less a murder because the killers get an amnesty? Krog made her decision as a middle-class white woman who believed murder was wrong – though the decision is not specific to her class, race or gender. Whether murderers remain "murderers" after being granted amnesty is a question that continues to haunt South Africa.[6] It is from this setting, with these dilemmas, that she turns to consider how to understand her choices as the majority of South Africans might do.

Krog poses difficult questions. Is morality or ethics relative to one's conditions of existence? Is there a distinction between black and white morality in South Africa, given the very different conditions in which people live? How can white people even think this when Krog knows that during Apartheid other white mothers like her were making torture bags on their sewing machines for use by the police (2009: 69)? She yearns to be in another ethos or life, "unpolluted by human" (2009: 69). To be human, then, is precisely to confront

[6] On 30 September 2010, the Constitutional Court of South Africa heard the appeal in *The Citizen (1978) (Pty) Ltd and Others v McBride* (CCT 23/10) concerning whether a newspaper's reference to a person as a "murderer" after he was granted amnesty by the TRC constituted defamation. Does the recognition of the "political" nature of a killing mean that it ceases to be a "murder"? Can newspapers or relatives of the victim refer to the perpetrator as a murderer?

these moral and ethical dilemmas in the face of what humans unleash on other humans in the name of humanity. Having told herself that she would not draw lines (not make ethical judgements), that white people should be prepared to live 300 years under other people's terms, she draws a line:

> I can't exist in a space where certain things don't count, old-fashioned things like respect for life, respect for each other as human beings, honesty and something that perhaps I'll call beauty … something uncontaminated by people – like trees, grass, birds. (Krog 2009: 69)

There is a yearning here for "truth" in conditions where colonialism and Apartheid have destroyed the conditions for an ethical consensus. There is also a powerful ethic of putting the "world" as conceived by "humans" into question. There is a distrust of human values, human ethics and human truths – a search for something uncontaminated by people. It is a going beyond human that conditions the onto-epistemic transformation it seems she would like all South Africans to undergo, especially white South Africans. It is a going beyond human that sets the scene for the "becoming minor" that she develops later in the book. In this moment of marking the need to go beyond human, one feels she is putting herself in a liminal space from which to think postcolonial alternatives.

The liminal space between a colonial order and a postcolonial future can only be grasped through the beings that occupy it. It cannot be opened by legislation, or inaugurated in a spectacular declaration, even though law and its origins might be born of this liminality. Liminality is a lived condition which presents itself in the everyday existence of ordinary and extraordinary people. Krog occupies this space herself when she confronts tough choices, dwelling in the in-between space of dishonourable safety (reporting to the police) and dangerous possibility (going beyond the humanism that has previously authorised critical judgement). But more importantly, she draws out this liminality through two other central figures who populate her book – King Moshoeshoe of the Besotho, and Petrus, a character in J.M. Coetzee's novel *Disgrace* (1999). Moshoeshoe's story is drawn from the past to circulate in the present, while Petrus is here now (albeit in literature), but his story and the conditions for its telling are yet to come (to be discussed below).

Moshoeshoe was a Bosotho King who united numerous tribes to withstand the onslaught of Boer and English settlement, as well as the killing sprees of Shaka, Manthatise and Mzilikazi. He enters the records of Western history in June 1833 when Eugène Casalis, a young missionary of the Paris Evangelical Missionary Society, arrives in his kingdom. The diplomatic strategies and techniques of government that Moshoeshoe developed to unite his people, and to grapple with Boer and English land grabs, disclose flexibility and openness. Moshoeshoe's struggle was to understand and inhabit the terrain of shifting sovereignties – to remain true to his own ancestral spirits and customs while preparing himself and his people for the colonial onslaught. Moshoeshoe occupied and negotiated a liminal space.

By juxtaposing the stories of Moshoeshoe's encounter with the missionaries and colonisers with her own encounter with post-Apartheid transition, Krog confronts the dilemma of finding a new sense of being in a place that never was home. This is a relatively unique approach where the descendant of the erstwhile coloniser un-homes herself in the new dispensation rather than retreating to the safety and security of the European metropolis, or disavowing the morality, ethics and abilities of the new rulers. Canadian, US and Australian settler-descendants can experience and learn much from this enterprise of being un-homed, of becoming a minority. As Krog puts it:

> I want to be part of the country I was born in. I need to know whether it is possible for somebody like me to become like the majority, to become "blacker?" and live as a full and at-ease component of the South African psyche. (Krog 2009: 93)

The conditions for this need not be a choice between African or Western philosophy. Krog sees it rather as a mingling or entanglement of roots (2009: 95). However, philosophies are not so easily deployed or readily set aside. It is in the register of stories recovered, recounted and imagined that the challenge of making a shift is enunciated. It is a strategy of writing and living that will disturb those who live and work in the shade and shadow of weighty traditions such as historiography, philosophy and law. Such readers will want to dismiss Krog as nostalgic and moralising, but hopefully with the niggling suspicion that their regular authorities are hardly up to the task of the challenges posed in a postcolonial setting.

Krog moves between the story of Moshoeshoe, whose conversion to Christianity was the much-sought-after prize of successive missionaries in the nineteenth century, and her own personal dilemma of being un-homed in South Africa. Though she does not explicitly make the connection, Moshoeshoe and his people, and Krog and her people, confront the dilemma of living with an "Other" in power. Though Moshoeshoe never converted to Christianity, he encouraged his people to do so, and took advantage of the education about Western values and practices that the missionaries brought with them. Krog folds the story of Moshoeshoe with that of her own ambivalent support for ANC cadres in troubled and violent times. How is one to understand and figure the postcolonial present when one wants to appreciate both Wagner and Moshoeshoe, the freedoms of the Berlin academy and the mountains of Lesotho? Becoming minority, in a Deleuzian sense, is marked in both Moshoeshoe's and Krog's individual fates. Christianity, colonialism, liberalism and ubuntu – each secures the limits of what one might become. But they also constitute the ground from which Krog is becoming otherwise. This chapter turns, then, to the problem of becoming-minority, becoming black, as the possibility of the emergence of a critical being, capable of challenging both African and Western philosophical and political paradigms.

Being-becoming is an epistemic and ontological problem at the heart of decolonisation and transformative politics. Krog has responded to the urgent need to transform ways of being beyond the juridical and institutional transformations by elaborating what it would mean for an Afrikaner woman such as herself to "become black" in multiple senses. Although she makes much of "interconnectedness" in *Begging to Be Black*, there are very few explicit references to ubuntu. And despite her disavowal of European philosophy, and being conscious of having a white, male philosopher as her primary philosophical interlocutor in the book, she relies very heavily on a Deleuzian theory of becoming. It is thus apt to provide some suggestions on ways of directly engaging ubuntu philosophy, and the implications of this for anti-colonial struggle and postcolonial thinking.

3. BECOMING SOVEREIGN

In Conscripts *of Modernity: The Tragedy of Colonial Enlightenment* (2004), David Scott focuses on the narrative form in histories of anti-colonial struggle – especially C.L.R. James's treatment of the Haitian Revolution of 1791–1804 in his magisterial work, *The Black Jacobins* (2001 [1938]). Scott makes many incisive observations – a key one being that narratives of the past are often told with the discontent of the present in mind (Scott, 2004: 22). James's account of Toussaint L'Ouverture's heroic and ultimately tragic struggle against French imperialism and slavery was told with mid-twentieth-century decolonisation, and anti-imperial nationalism, as the near horizon. *The Black Jacobins* was thus a work of anti-colonial longing. Scott's point of departure is that we should move away from anti-colonial longing and examine the relationship between past, present and future as historical conjunctures constituted by different "problem spaces" (Scott, 2004: 4). The conceptual-ideological problem space of the anti-colonial struggle is one that is concerned with sovereignty and national liberation. Ramose's philosophy of ubuntu is tentatively read here as caught between this anti-colonial longing for sovereignty (as his conceptual-ideological problem space), and a postcolonial potential that his own account of the philosophy of ubuntu conveys. It is this liminal space between anti-colonial longing for the recovery of sovereignty, and a postcolonial longing for becoming otherwise that his critique opens. Critique is this opening of a liminal space – a "conceptual-ideological problem space" that both Krog and Ramose occupy but in very different ways.

Mogobe Ramose begins his essay "In Memoriam: Sovereignty in the 'New' South Africa" (2007) with a prayer. For Ramose, speaking of sovereignty in

South Africa is a requiem mass – a gesture that marks a death. He asserts the need to resurrect a sovereignty that has been buried, displaced and misrecognised. Ramose refuses to allow the "lost sovereignty" of all peoples conquered in the "unjust wars of colonialism" to remain a memory. Recovery and restoration are claimed as the twin exigencies of justice and as the "necessary means to the construction of peace in South Africa" (2007: 311). The process of decolonisation, in Ramose's (2007: 319) view, is not yet concluded, and certainly was not achieved through the elimination of Apartheid and the guarantee of civil rights since April 1994. While those who pushed a compromise in the early 1990s argued that they were averting a civil war, Ramose's claim is that since colonisation South Africa has been "practically in a state of war" (2007: 320). In his view it was gullible and misleading to think that Apartheid was the fundamental problem. This is why freedom was reduced to the guarantee of fundamental rights (2007: 320). The morality and political legitimacy of the colonial "right of conquest" was left untouched by the post-1994 dispensation. Ramose thus challenges the reasoning that asserted, from the Freedom Charter onwards, that "South Africa belonged to all who lived in it". We might then conclude that for Ramose decolonisation involves "becoming sovereign" or a longing for true national liberation.

A post-conquest South Africa, Ramose argues, must recognise that indigenous communities have been deprived of their sovereignty through an illegitimate war and usurpation. Abiding by community in African culture – the "interconnectedness" that Krog refers to – requires that the three dimensions of the living, the living dead and the yet to be born are taken to be the critical ethical concern. Thus the survival of customary kingship, and the memory of the heroes and heroines who fought against colonialism, require that parity – horizontality – be restored between the "indigenous conquered peoples" and the successors in title to the questionable "right of conquest". For Ramose, the "reaffirmation" of such "horizontal reasoning" is a necessary condition for a genuinely autochthonous constitution (2007: 326). Here the challenge to Krog's approach to becoming black is a stark one. It says: "if you want to establish genuine parity between yourself as coloniser and the indigenous population, then return sovereignty to the colonised". The institutional expression of this would be parliamentary sovereignty rather than the constitutional supremacy that South Africa adopted in 1994.

For Ramose, the denial of parity and "authentic liberation" took at least two forms: the subordinate status accorded to Indigenous, Bantu or customary law in the Constitution of the Republic of South Africa 1996, and the racial ideology that converted parliamentary supremacy to constitutional supremacy in the transition to a post-Apartheid legal order. For Ramose:

> Ubuntu ... represents the epistemological paradigm that informs the cultural practices, including the law, of the Bantu-speaking peoples. Excluding it from the

> constitution is tantamount to denying the Bantu-speaking peoples a place in the constitutional dispensation of the country. The current Constitution is, therefore, not the mirror of the legal ideas and institutions of the indigenous conquered peoples of South Africa. It follows then that a truly South African Constitution is yet to be born. On this reasoning, Act 108 of 1996 [the Constitution] has, perhaps inadvertently, set the stage for the struggle for a new constitutional order in South Africa. (Ramose 2006: 366)

Examining the move to constitutional supremacy ushered in by the new Constitution of 1996, Ramose asks why the turn to "colour-blind" majority rule engendered fear of a black constituency. The reason behind the conversion from parliamentary to constitutional supremacy, despite the principle of anti-racism in the Constitution, is "racialist thinking": "The fact that the conqueror considered the black majority as a race, coming into the constitutional process, was itself racialist thinking" (Ramose 2006: 367). There was a fear that the putative "black race" would have unanimity on all matters and thus threaten all "other" interests if they were granted legislative or parliamentary supremacy. Rather than signalling the return of sovereignty to the colonised population, the terms of the transition from Apartheid to post-Apartheid are viewed by Ramose as further inscriptions of a colonial racial logic. Parliamentary sovereignty – and the consequent threat of majoritarianism – was dealt with by the introduction of constitutional supremacy. Equality and civil rights would be guaranteed by the Constitution – as would the ill-gotten gains of several centuries of colonial violence and usurpation. For some this compromise opened a sacrificial logic that marks the new constitutional dispensation.

The case that epitomises the post-Apartheid order of sacrifice is *Azapo and Others v President of South Africa* in which the families of victims of the Apartheid state's violence, including the family of Steve Biko, challenged the constitutionality of the Truth and Reconciliation Commission's capacity to grant amnesty for political crimes.[7] Sacrifice was at the heart of the Constitutional Court's denial of the families' challenge, and a key feature of democratic transition. Why should the state avoid responsibility from delictual claims for the actions of its agents as the applicants in *Azapo* claimed? According to the Court the state can either compensate the families of those killed, and the victims of torture and other violations of human rights, or state funds can be directed towards the social and economic well-being of the living and of future generations. According to the Court in *Azapo*, the negotiators who brought into being the Constitution could have chosen to saddle the state with liability for claims made by insurance companies which had compensated institutions for delictual acts performed by the servants of the state, and to that extent again divert funds otherwise desperately needed to provide food

7 *Azapo and Others v. President of South Africa* (1996) CCT 17/96.

for the hungry, roofs for the homeless and black-boards and desks for those struggling to obtain admission to desperately overcrowded schools. The architects of the Constitution were entitled to permit the claims of such school children and the poor and the homeless to be preferred. (*Azapo*, para. 44)

The new democratic order, according to the Epilogue to the interim Constitution, would represent "reconciliation between the people of South Africa and the reconstruction of society". It is worth paying attention to this account of reconciliation. This is not a reconciliation between previously conflicted polities – coloniser and colonised – or between the beneficiaries of Apartheid and the disenfranchised of that system. It is not reconciliation of a fractured society coming together to form a unified whole. It is not a restoration of a lost sovereignty. It is precisely a sacrificial reconciliation – a case of becoming reconciled to what will be forgone when amnesty is granted for political crimes; when property rights are guaranteed despite the unjust conditions of accumulation; when redistribution will be balanced with social and economic stability. And so reconciliation must be understood through its verb – to become reconciled to a particular liberal constitutional project. It is not a reconciliation of the laws of the conqueror and conquered, or of their respective and multiple philosophical traditions. Indeed, the status of ubuntu philosophy is such that it might even be said, as Ramose has argued, that the "struggle for reason" in Africa remains. If reconciliation is to be the restoration of sociality, then we must still ask: what is being restored? What is this sociality?

Krog's intervention in *Begging to Be Black* must be read in this contested setting, where embracing "interconnectedness", ubuntu or being-becoming black is articulated in terms of recovering sovereignty as a mode of establishing political and epistemic parity. There is an anti-colonial longing in Ramose's thinking that is tied to concrete demands about democracy, customary law and parliamentary sovereignty. Here the distinction that Scott draws between anti-colonial longing and postcolonial becoming is a useful one. Becoming postcolonial cannot, in this author's view, hinge on the recovery of a "lost sovereignty". Nor can it be achieved by replacing imperial sovereignty with indigenous sovereignty. This chapter is interested in the fragmentation of the sovereign "I" or unity. The sovereign being (imperial, national, corporate or indigenous) whose command, sanction and legitimacy assert a global presence needs urgent undoing wherever it is found. Both Ramose's and Krog's thinking contain the resources for postcolonial becoming. The following section elaborates this.

4. LIMINALITY AND INTERCONNECTEDNESS

What does it mean to "become black" in a territory where an "original sovereignty", as Ramose claims, is still in contention? In Krog's work "becoming black" is a mode of contending with being colonial, being white, being Afrikaner. It adopts the Deleuzian orientation of "lines of flight", where a discrete subjective agent is undone by a being whose becoming is minoritarian. This process of becoming is signified by "becoming minor" – and by extension here, "becoming black".

The discussion of Deleuzian lines of flight takes place between Krog and the Australian philosopher Paul Patton, while both are visiting the Institute for Advanced Studies in Berlin. Patton is a translator of some of Gilles Deleuze's major works, and has also written an essay on Coetzee's *Disgrace* where he discusses the arc of transformation of characters like David Lurie in Deleuzian terms as becoming-animal or becoming-woman (Patton, 2006). Krog sees writing as a process of "becoming towards" what she is trying to understand, and Patton explains that this is akin to what Deleuze means by a "line of flight" (Krog, 2009: 92). In a line of flight:

> [o]ne moves from an established known identity by transforming oneself. But transformation always moves in a particular direction and writing is often the best way to trace these directions. Expressed in different words: the aim of good writing is to carry life to the state of non-personal power. (2009: 92)

Liminality, exposure at the margins, being in-between – all these terms explain the kind of understanding that Krog is trying to reach by exploring the possibility of "becoming black". She is clear that she is seeking neither an essential identity nor a difference. What she seeks is a framework of understanding – acknowledging what she perceives as a shift from Western and European frameworks after the end of Apartheid. One example she offers to characterise this shift is the fact that Robert Mugabe is "read" differently by the South African government and Zimbabweans themselves when compared with Western reactions (2009: 93).

Krog might be too hasty in even claiming that such a shift of frameworks of understanding has taken place. That, of course, is Ramose's point. The Constitution and many of South Africa's institutions continue to be informed by liberal values and ideologies. And Robert Mugabe is not far from framing his own actions with direct reference to the West and its leaders as the erstwhile masters with whom he is engaged in a "heroic" dialectical struggle; a struggle for which his "people" are paying the highest price. But the example of reactions to Mugabe might be obsolete for other reasons. The process of becoming worldwide, of globalisation or what Jean-Luc Nancy has called "mondialization", undermines the possibility of a discrete or delimited "sense" of the world (Nancy, 1997; 2007). When systems of economic valuing and exchange are worldwide, what scope is there for ethical and political values to maintain a discrete, localised quality? Krog is attempting to open an understanding of what resists these processes of globalisation.

Is it the case that Krog is seeking a sort of communal completeness to be shared with all South Africans that is distinct from Euro-American conceptions? Or is it another instance of the coloniser being convinced that the colonised are utterly different, and thus subtly keeping ingrained racism alive?

Krog wants to move towards "blackness" as black South Africans understand it (2009: 94). She is seeking to understand and live within an African paradigm, and is not necessarily interested in "African philosophy versus Western philosophy". She is not seeking an "entanglement" or "mingling" but a "synapse" – inquiring into how "one root can become or link to another" (2009: 95).

Deleuzian philosophy forms the context of Krog and Patton's discussions of these questions – and so it is worth quoting the gist of Deleuze's idea of becoming as it is reproduced by Krog:

> Plants and animals, inside and outside, and even organic and inorganic, cannot really be told apart. All these things are themselves, *yet* on another level they are transforming towards one another. Things continue to become the other, while continuing to be what they are. (2009: 99)

Transformation, becoming, multiplicity – each expresses a process of "becoming-other", becoming-minor in terms of "becoming-child, becoming-animal, becoming-woman, becoming-black" (2009: 99). Krog wants to take up the opportunity to do what South African writer Njabulo Ndebele had called for – to move away from the "international sanctity of the white body and share the vulnerability of the black body" (2009: 100).

The question is whether the "sanctity of whiteness" or its philosophical extensions can be undone at the level of the "understanding"? And can the vulnerability of the "black body" ever be understood? Such an understanding, if it were possible, would be very distinct from living that vulnerability. In their discussions, Patton explains to Krog that what she seeks might be achieved through the capacities of an affective being. Krog might become an "inter-individual assembly or assemblage" that has the capacity to affect and be affected by the "other side of the pact" (2009: 101) Listening to stories is the device that Krog suggests for moving towards such a pact:

> Stories have different characters and threads and plots; they leave space for variety. Stories are boundary crossings, making it possible to move, justifying different kinds of behaviour and also behaviour that is not necessarily justified – no single line holds things together, because the spaces contain contradictions in which one variety is as valid as the other. (Krog 2009: 101)

In listening to stories in order to become, Krog opens a liminal space. Liminality is the space of a movement, contact with an outside, un-homing and re-homing at the same time. The liminal space is hazardous, the site of risk, exposure – but also opening the possibility of sharing, being-with, refusing the safety of clear positions and certain outcomes. Stories, the mytho-poetic, seem to enable this liminality. But in what language will these stories be heard and told?

Krog reminds us of those powerful words from Coetzee's *Disgrace* where David Lurie remarks that Petrus's story cannot be told in English. Perhaps the deepest opacity of the South African condition is revealed in the story that is not yet told – Petrus's story. One is left with the sense, in reading Krog's book, that the key to postcolonial becoming is for the space to be created for Petrus's story to be told. Krog's book is dedicated to Petrus, it seems to be oriented towards him – but it is still about Krog's becoming rather than his. This is, then, the most opaque of liminal moments, a vanishing point at which Krog's text deconstructs itself. Krog does not have the language to tell Petrus's story. He must tell it, and in his language. And then the difficulty will be that the community that must share in this telling will be circumscribed by the politics of language in South Africa. How will stories told by black people enable access to becoming-minor – generate the affective feelings across assemblages – if English dominates and becomes the medium for truth in South Africa? Despite these distortions, what Krog is starting to hear is the communal ethics that guides the actions of black South Africans. So there is not only a postcolonial voice, but also a postcolonial listening in Krog's book. This section will return below to the notion of "interconnectedness" that Krog deploys as the black paradigm or framework of understanding that white South Africans need to move towards. First it will consider the telling of stories in another register.

Towards the end of her conversation with Patton in Berlin, Krog is asked whether she is writing a novel. She insists that she is not. Why so, Patton asks, when she could explore the inner psyche of characters – imagine being black, for instance? Krog responds that she does not want to give up on the "strangeness" that can be preserved in non-fiction. It is a strangeness that is not invented: "the strangeness is real, and the fact that I cannot ever really enter the psyche of somebody else, somebody black. The terror and loneliness of that inability is what I don't want to give up on" (2009: 267). She goes on to state that at this stage, for her, "imagination is overrated" (2009: 268). Krog then says that:

> to imagine black at this stage is to insult black. That is why I stay with non-fiction, listening, engaging, observing, translating, until one can begin to sense a thinning of skin, negotiate possible small openings at places where imaginings can begin to begin. (2009: 268)

In exploring the interconnectedness that underpins the actions of black people in Southern Africa, Krog dismisses the suggestion that this is also present in many Western philosophies. There is an exceptionalism in her treatment of Bantu philosophy – and she has no truck with Patton's suggestion that

Spinoza, Feuerbach, Levinas, Freud, and indeed Jewish and many other cultures, are characterised by this interconnectedness (2009: 155–56). But there is also merit in eschewing the sense that Europe has always already thought it (interconnectedness, and everything else), and can encompass everything within its philosophical frameworks. Instead Krog sees the interconnectedness at the heart of black leaders like Mandela or Tutu as one inherited from the First Peoples of Southern Africa, the San and Khoi (2009: 184).

Krog's objective is to draw on the onto-epistemes of Bantu, and Western philosophies, as well as oral and literary traditions. Rejecting the option of "white flight" – the "take the money and run" attitude that some white South Africans have adopted – she has used the genre of literary non-fiction to pose and respond to the question of what it would mean for white South Africans to undergo epistemic and ontological decolonisation as a condition of being-becoming otherwise. In a philosophical register, her inquiry is into ways of constituting a decolonising "sense of being". The verb "decolonising" rather than "decolonised" is significant here. It accords with the verbal character of ubuntu which operates as a gerund, a noun that functions as a verb (see discussion of Mogobe Ramose's philosophy of ubuntu below). "Decolonising" also signals the ongoing, and possibly endless, task of undoing colonial legacies.

It is at this juncture that it is useful to read Ramose's account of ubuntu against his anti-colonial longing for a recovered sovereignty. It is clear from Ramose's account of ubuntu that "wholeness" of society should not be read as stasis or fixity.[8] If anything, what is clear about the concept of be-ing in ubuntu is that "Ubu-" is "marked by uncertainty" because it is "by definition motion involving the possibility of infinite unfoldment and concrete manifestation into a multiplicity of forms and organisms" (Ramose, 2002: 50). This resonates quite strongly with Deleuzian accounts of being as an "inter-individual assemblage". "Ubu-" expresses the notion of "be-ing in general", the widest generality of be-ing (Ramose, 2002: 41). "Umu-" shares a similar ontology, but is more specific. "Umu-", joined with "-ntu" – umuntu – marks the emergence of homo loquens and in "common parlance means the human being: the marker of politics, religion and law" (2002: 41). The inquiry into being, experience, knowledge and truth is conducted by umuntu – but this is "an ongoing process", an "activity rather than an act" (2002: 41). Hence "ubu-" is regarded as "be-ing becoming" (2002: 41). It implies a notion of be-ing as incessant motion (2002: 41).

8 See Drucilla Cornell, "The Significance of the Living Customary Law for an Understanding of Law: Does Custom Allow for a Woman to be Hosi?" (2009) 2 *Constitutional Court Review* 395–408. Here Cornell discusses the case of *Shilubana v. Nwamitwa* (CCT 03/07) [2008] ZACC 9; 2008 (9) BCLR 914 (CC); 2009 2 SA 66 (CC) concerning the manner in which custom and customary law develops over time, and the distinction between that and changes in the common law.

Umu-ntu / ubu-ntu in incessant motion can then be expressed with the emphasis on the "verbal" rather than the verb "-ntu". Ubuntu is then a "verbal noun" – that is to say, in grammatical terms, it is a "gerund" ("a form of verb functioning as a noun" – in English ending in -ing and used with a verb – OED) (2002: 41–42, 82). This is a disruption of the regular Western opposition between being and becoming. "Be-ing becoming" places the emphasis on motion, and is thus against the fragmentation of being (2002: 42–43). The association of "being" with order and "becoming" with chaos is broken by the "flow" (the Greek verb, *rheo*) of "be-ing becoming". The general view is that the "apparent structure of language determines the sequence of thought" (2002: 43). As language breaks the silence of be-ing, "be-ing becoming" must be understood in and through the "rheomode" language (2002: 45). This has implications for how the legal subject is conceptualised, and can be explained at that more concrete level.

The logic of ubu-ntu follows that of a rheomode language. A rheomode language places emphasis on the gerund, and opposes the "subject-verb-object" linguistic structure (2002: 46). Of course this linguistic structure which privileges the name/noun as the acting moving subject has been undone by many philosophers, including by Jacques Derrida in his work on the "trace" which marks and exceeds the appearance of all signification, as well as in his deconstruction of the metaphysics of "presence". These insights are incorporated by Ramose (2002: 101). The "subject-verb-object" structure asserts an ontology where subject/object are distinct entities and the verb acts as mediator. It is in this way that what Ramose terms the "fragmentation of be-ing" takes place. It is through this ontological structure that Western legal thought attributes rights and duties to the "nounized legal subject" (2002: 82).

The whole-ness that the philosophy of ubuntu is supposed to inspire is thus not the absolute of community-as-law or communitarianism. Rather wholeness through ubuntu is the recognition that be-ing is not fragmented as the subject/noun "be!" as it is in (some) Western ontologies (2002: 46–47). African law:

> is law without a centre since the legal subject here is an active but transient participant in the be-ing, that is, the musical flow of law. … Ubuntu law is not only the ontology of the do-ing subject. It is contemporaneously the epistemology of the discern-ing subject continuously harmonising the music of the universe. In this sense, ubuntu philosophy of law is a dynamology. Law here is thus dynamic because it is in the first place rheomodic. (Ramose, 2002: 92)

The subject is then not obliged to live "within the law" as with the Western legal subject, but to "live the law" (2002: 93). The object of law inspired by ubuntu is to maintain equilibrium (2002: 93–94).

Ubuntu thus provides a mode of becoming otherwise that will not guarantee individual freedoms at all times, as some Western liberal philosophers demand.

According to Krog, ubuntu promotes a mode of interconnectedness which is at the heart of the great deeds of men like Mandela and Tutu. But it also goes wrong when the interconnectedness is conflated with race – when identifying with being black and against the "West" leads to defining community without interrogating what this community is or should be. Krog suggests that this explains the mistaken support for Mugabe – a sense of black community and interconnectedness that has gone wrong. She contrasts this with Mandela and Tutu, who always use interconnectedness to redefine their religious and political communities (Krog, 2009: 236–237).

5. CONCLUSION: RESTORING BEING-BECOMING

The history and politics that conditions living beside and with Petrus is at the heart of *Begging to Be Black*. Indeed the book is dedicated to Petrus – the character in J.M. Coetzee's *Disgrace*. Here the fictive inaugurates an ethical moment and political event. *Begging to Be Black* is not a work of fiction. Krog insists that she will not write fiction. Instead, literary imagination, the creation of worlds, listening to stories, is folded into history, philosophy, transformative politics and the juridical order. Krog thus inaugurates a critical event through her book. It is an inauguration (an event) because it is at once the creation of a world in text – but also the recovery of nineteenth-century colonial history, and an engagement with the pressing social and political problems of the present. *Begging to Be Black* is a critical event in that it responds to a crisis of identity, belonging, violence, home and colonial epistemicide. True to the double demand of critique, it identifies the crisis or limit and suggests a restorative way forward. Being-critical, being-with, restoring a sense of the world – Krog shows how these are not only post-Heideggerian attitudes to philosophy and politics. They are also the urgent demands of decolonisation – and Krog finds the resources in Western and Bantu philosophy for addressing them. Through this work of literary history a newness enters the world. It is a newness always already conditioned by a colonial history. Becoming black might be the *as if* that opens and sustains a new political dispensation in post-Apartheid South Africa.

The space of postcolonial becoming opened by Krog is a liminal space. Liminality is the space of a traversal – a point of contact between past and future. Liminality works more subtly and does not carry the temporal weight of "post" (in postcolonial or post-Apartheid). Liminality invokes a fragility. It refers to beings, bodies or events that are the site of exposure to a new accommodation that eschews a sovereign mode of being. Liminality is opaque. Liminality is quite centrally tied to the task of critique. Postcolonial becoming through liminal beings is one of the important sites where the work of critique takes place. The "vanishing point" is another way of expressing the liminal, the threshold momentarily occupied by a new subjectivity in the face of a crisis of law and society. The liminal subject of critique opens a new accommodation, refusing the state and its rights, and thus dissociating sovereignty from a new ethics and politics.

References

Bhabha, H.K. (2004) "Foreword" in Frantz Fanon, *The Wretched of the Earth*. New York: Grove Press.

Coetzee, J.M. (1999) *Disgrace*. London: Secker and Warburg.

Derrida, J. (1994) *Spectres of Marx*. New York: Routledge.

Fanon, F. (2004 [1961]) *The Wretched of the Earth*. New York: Grove Press.

James, C.L.R. (2001 [1938]) *The Black Jacobins*: Toussaint L'Ouverture and the San Domingo Revolution. New York: Penguin.

Krog, A. (1998) *Country of My Skull: Guilt, Sorrow, and the Limits of Forgiveness in the New South Africa*. Cape Town: Random House.

—— (2003) *A Change of Tongue*. Cape Town: Random House.

—— (2009) *Begging to Be Black*. Cape Town: Random House.

Madlingozi, T. (2007) "Post-Apartheid Social Movements and the Quest for the Elusive 'New' South Africa" in *Journal of Law and Society* **34**, no 1: 77–98.

Meister, R. (2011) *After Evil: A Politics of Human Rights*. New York: Columbia University Press.

Motha, S. "'Begging to Be Black': Liminality and Critique in Post-Apartheid South Africa" in *Theory, Culture & Society*, **27**, no. 7: 285–306.

Mbembe, A. (2001) *On the Postcolony*. Berkeley: University of California Press.

Nancy, J.-L. (1997) *The Sense of the World*. Minneapolis M.N.: University of Minnesota Press.

—— (2007) *The Creation of the World or Globalization*. Albany N.Y.: SUNY Press.

Patton, P. (2006) "Becoming-animal and Pure Life in Coetzee's *Disgrace*" in *A Review of International English Literature (ARIEL)* **35**: 101–119.

Ramose, M. (2002) *African Philosophy through Ubuntu*. Harare: Mond Books.

—— (2006) "The King as Memory and Symbol of African Customary Law" in M.O. Hinz and H. Pateman (eds), *The Shades of New Leaves: Governance in Traditional Authority, a Southern African Perspective*. Berlin: LIT Verlag.

—— (2007) "In Memoriam: Sovereignty and the 'New' South Africa" in *Griffith Law Review* **16**, no. 2: 310–329.

Schmitt, C. (1996) *The Concept of the Political*. Chicago I.L.: University of Chicago Press.

Scott, D. (2004) *Conscripts of Modernity: The Tragedy of Colonial Enlightenment*. Durham N.C.: Duke University Press.

Terreblanche, S. (2003) *History of Inequality in South Africa 1652–2002*. Natal: University of Kwazulu Natal Press.

PART III

RESTORING LAND

CHAPTER 8

LIMITATIONS TO THE PRINCIPLE OF *RESTITUTIO IN INTEGRUM* AND FULL REPARATIONS IN TRANSITIONAL JUSTICE CONTEXTS

What Reparation does not Repair

Beira Aguilar Rubiano*

> "They, their ancestors, had killed and captured, conquered and defended their lands in full-fledged combat, but they had never dared to imagine individual property: already an enormous crime was committed by stealing the substance of the earth, and in order to appease it, precise ceremonies were to be performed, to which they had tried to adhere, trying to maintain a balance in the natural order of life, until they failed to do so and as punishment, to see some day appear among the pastures, some men whose skin gave off the smell of death, who sowed death and for death they procreated since their law inevitably spread discord."
>
> Marvel Moreno, *En Diciembre llegaban las Brisas* (2014), 243–244[1]

---

* I am deeply grateful to Professor Bert van Roermund and my colleagues and friends Wilson Herrera and Iván Mahecha for their help in reading drafts of this chapter, asking probing questions, and providing useful commentaries, all of which contributed to its final production. In particular Iván Mahecha provided me with information on the debate over whether absolute rights are subjective, like personal and real rights are. Thanks also to Andy Klatt who helped in the English translation of this text.

1 M. Moreno, *In December the Breezes Arrived* (Bogotá: Alfaguara (2014) [1987] at 243–244): "*Ellos, sus ancestros, habían matado y pillado, conquistado y defendido sus tierras en combates sin cuartel, pero nunca habían osado imaginar la propiedad individual: ya de por sí crimen enorme se cometía al robarle a la tierra su sustancia y a fin de apaciguarla debían realizarse ceremonias precisas a las cuales ellos habían intentado conformarse a tientas buscando mantener un equilibrio en el orden natural de la vida hasta equivocarse y como castigo, ver aparecer un día entre los pastizales a unos hombres cuya piel despedía el olor de la muerte, que sembraban la muerte y para la muerte procreaban puesto que su ley secretaba inevitablemente la discordia.*"

1. INTRODUCTION

Victims who survive a period of widespread, systematic, and atrocious violence run the risk of transitional justice (TJ)[2] being but a brief interruption in the injustices they suffer, and that the justice it promises will be too vague to truly fulfil the promise of a transformation from one condition to another. Such promises of change may be from violence to peace, from dictatorship to democracy, or from a society with grave and systematic violations of human rights to one in which human rights are recognized and respected. The very meaning of *justice* in the context of transitional processes supported and given legitimacy by the international community is still very much a matter for debate, despite continuing to be the *sine qua non* of transition. The temporality and duration of transitional justice can mean anything if the process is focused merely on re-establishing order, "pacification", and achieving what has been called *negative peace* that is limited to the ending hostilities and the prevention of an early return to violence (Mani 2002, 12). Its meaning is something entirely different, however, when the goal is a *positive peace* that emphasizes the consolidation of peace through political and structural reforms that prevent violence in the long-term, including the cessation of hostilities as one of its prerequisites (Mani 2005; Galtung 1998, 15–18).[3]

2 A standard definition of transitional justice, provided by the International Center for Transitional Justice (ICTJ), is as follows: "Transitional justice is a response to systematic or widespread violations of human rights. It seeks recognition for victims and promotion of possibilities for peace, reconciliation and democracy. Transitional justice is not a special form of justice but justice adapted to societies transforming themselves after a period of pervasive human rights abuse. In some cases, these transformations happen suddenly; in others, they may take place over many decades." (ICTJ 2015).

3 Note that the temporality of the TJ process is a function of the objectives that are established for it, which are directly related to the (variable) conception of justice. This is a matter

Furthermore, the goals and purposes of the TJ process also reflect other things beyond a mere demand for recognized and enforceable justice. For example, the short-term goal of a cessation of hostilities or pacification may be incompatible with, or present an obstacle to, structural reforms that *positive peace* or an inclusive democracy may require. It may be that the search for *negative peace* and a suspension of violence requires granting concessions to those who perpetrated that violence or benefited from the human rights violations that occurred during it, if they are in positions of power during the process and are not inclined to lose or to risk their privileges, sacrifice their interests, or answer for all that they have done.[4] In this context of concessions, hostilities may be provisionally suspended and deferred rather than brought to an end, and the legacy of violence may threaten to impose itself on the transitional process and the establishment of order in its wake, thereby continuing the violence or engendering its eventual renewal and intensification.

Whatever justice has been demanded, who has demanded it, and how it has been conceived have all taken on different nuances in the course of the development of TJ, as it responds to varying local contextual considerations, forms of social mobilization, and international precedents. The different conceptions of justice that have arisen in TJ processes have included fundamentally punitive or retributive approaches that focused on the punishment of perpetrators – principally entailing trials, convictions and sentences – as well as other conceptions oriented towards victims and the injustices they have suffered.[5] Under these latter conceptions, punishment and sentences continue to be important, but are primarily so in relation to victims' demands, for example demands for truth regarding the fate of disappeared relatives and the specific

that is still disputed, despite some consensus on certain minimum norms or tools now established for the implementation of TJ in different contexts arising from its own history of consolidation as a legal field. For more on the notion of the "field" and its development in TJ, see De Greiff 2011. The distinction between negative and positive peace has also been worked on by Johan Galtung, who argues that is not enough to stop direct violence (which would constitute negative peace), but that TJ processes must also attack structural causes, both social and cultural.

4 This was the case in Argentina. After its transition from dictatorship to democracy and in a context of extreme political polarization, President Raúl Alfonsín promulgated the *Ley de Punto Final* (Full Stop Law), which ended all criminal investigations and actions regarding crimes committed in the context of violent political action up until 10 October 1983. Part of the justification for this law was the need to avoid another military coup, given that many of those responsible for disappearances and human rights violations during the dictatorship had remained in positions of power, from where they continued to exert pressure and threaten a military uprising.

5 It may be said that victims are also taken into account under the first conception, given that perpetrators are judged, sentenced, and punished based on what they have done. Nevertheless, actions taken in the transitional process under this conception focus on what perpetrators have done and on legal determinations of their responsibility and their punishment, rather than on the condition of victims resulting of the crimes committed.

circumstances in which they lost their lives, or demands that perpetrators recognize the damage that they caused, as is the case in the most recent approaches to restorative and reparative justice.

The restorative and reparative perspectives in the field of TJ have emerged as attempts to address the limited capacity of punitive justice to respond to different kinds of demands by victims that are not limited to demands for trials and sanctions against perpetrators. In recent years, a focus on the demands of victims and the debts owed to them has made reparations one of the constituent elements of transitional justice, along with punishment, truth-seeking, guarantees of non-repetition, and institutional transformation.

Despite our awareness of these constituent elements (truth, punishment, reparation and guarantees of not repetition), the overall conception of justice itself in the context of TJ is still not fully clear. However, this question will only be answered once the dispute over the scope and limitations of TJ is resolved. Despite the dominant role of reparations in current TJ processes, it is nevertheless still continuously challenging to conceptualize and apply reparative measures in the variety of circumstances that they face, including the variety of kinds of injustice that were perpetrated in societies undertaking TJ processes.[6]

This chapter presents some of the limitations and challenges that one faces when conceptualizing reparation as one of the normative elements of TJ in the case of countries that have long histories of distributive injustice, misrecognition and participatory injustices, such as poverty, inequality, exclusion, oppression, discrimination, unequal participation and so on.[7] Such injustices can be considered structural, having pre-existed and been sustained during the period of violence that a TJ process is hoping to end, and being likely to persist even after the transition period comes to an end. I am particularly interested in seeing how a reparation process that is governed and configured

---

6 As will be demonstrated in the following section, the emergence of the TJ paradigm took place in a particular context and under particular conditions that have changed and do not characterize many of the current experiences where TJ is applied. These changes have introduced, and continue to introduce, challenges and problems with respect to the conceptualization of TJ and its normative elements. This text focuses on the particular case of dispossession of land and forced displacement followed by victim reparation through TJ in societies characterized by structural injustices that differ greatly from those where the TJ paradigm originated.

7 As noted by Knut Andreas Lid, transitions from one political regime to another are different from transitions from an armed conflict to peace. The former are more easily identifiable, while in the latter it may be difficult to determine when the transition has in fact taken place, and whether it has been complete; sometimes some but not all of the groups involved in the conflict also participate in the transition. The Colombian case falls into this category. I concur with Lid in that despite these differences among transition processes, all such processes have had one thing in common, which is the goal of creating something new through the correction of actions that took place in the past (Lid 2012).

by the standards of international law under the principle of *restitutio in integrum* and the notion of full reparation operates in relation to a specific kind of damage to be repaired. Damage that includes the dispossession and forced displacement of rural people close to the land or peasants (*campesinos*)[8] is particularly interesting, since it is in this type of phenomenon that structural injustice of a social, cultural, economic and political nature can be better evidenced. In transitional contexts, these structural injustices introduce tensions and problems that cannot be fully resolved with approaches based on the principle of *restitutio in integrum* and full reparation. This is even more the case when the legal order is not only an objective to be reached but is also part of the oppression and systematic violence of the past. As stated by De Gamboa Tapias and van Roermund, in the eyes of those who have suffered violence at the hands of the legal order, the law and its administrators will be suspect. This is where TJ faces its main challenge. It is here where reasons emerge to associate it with a notion of restorative justice as well as a requirement to go beyond criminal penalties for perpetrators and aim to restore life in society itself, in which Reparation for victims is as fundamental an aspect as is the Truth, Accountability and Reconciliation (TARR-Model). Restoring land would then imply what these authors have noted in the Introduction to this book, namely a call to memory in terms of reclaiming the past to reform the future, and in this way call for a heuristic model of restorative justice.

In order to understand the context in which reparation is consolidated as one of the normative elements of TJ, taking on the specific characteristics that international standards dictate, Section 2 briefly describes the development of the field of transitional justice, in which the reparation of victims is now considered to be a fundamental aspect of moving beyond conflict and implementing and/or strengthening the democratic rule of law in countries where TJ is applied. Secondly, Section 3 describes how the focus on reparation based on the principle of *restitutio in integrum* and full reparation is tied to implementing and strengthening the rule of law and to restoring victims' rights. It is also tied to a particular way of understanding property rights, especially when applied to land and to dealing with the damage and injuries suffered

8 The notion of reparation as applied to the restitution of property lost by victims of the conflict, and in particular the loss or forced abandonment of land, presents certain tensions and problems that an understanding of TJ based on the restitution of rights necessarily implies for societies characterized by structural injustice closely tied to human rights violations. While I am thinking of the Colombian case and its Law of Victims and Land Restitution (Law 1448 of 2011), I will limit myself here to a conceptual analysis regarding land restitution as a means to make reparation to victims of dispossession and forced displacement. I have discussed the Colombian case itself elsewhere, in my doctoral thesis ("Vidas Dañadas y Sentidos de la Tierra. La Reparación a Victimas Campesinas Desde el Enfoque de las Capacidades" (Aguilar 2020)), so any allusions to that case in this text are merely for purposes of reference.

by those who lost land due to systematic violence imposed in a context of conflict. Thirdly, Section 4 indicates the principal difficulties that this focus encounters, in particular four matters: (i) the introduction of the rule of law as a goal of TJ and a fundamental part of how victim reparation is conceived; (ii) the notions of damage, responsibility, and reparation for victims that this approach introduces; (iii) notions of legal personhood and victim as they are defined for TJ; and (iv) how land is conceived of as a particular kind of property for appropriation.

2. THE DEVELOPMENT OF THE FIELD OF TRANSITIONAL JUSTICE AND THE MODEL OF REPARATION

In recent decades, transitional justice has been increasingly seen as the paradigmatic process to use to help societies that have experienced armed conflict or periods of systematic and widespread abuse and violations of human rights to achieve a cessation of hostilities and confront the challenges of the post-conflict period.[9] While the term refers more generally to a conception of justice that is associated with periods of political change (Elster 2006; Teitel 2003), the paradigm as currently understood has more specific connotations.[10]

Following the genealogy proposed by Teitel, in its first phase the objective of traditional justice was to establish responsibility and achieve accountability in the context of applying international humanitarian law to non-state individuals and groups who had committed human rights violations, and to provide legitimacy for the punishment of those responsible (Teitel 2003). In the case of Nuremberg and other post-war trials, human rights abuses were criminalized by the winning party, the Allies, who invoked universal standards and the international rule of law to assure individual accountability for atrocities that were committed (Carrillo 2006).

Subsequently, with the collapse of the Soviet Union and the proliferation of political and democratic modernization processes – including the end of the Latin American dictatorships and the post-1989 transitions in Eastern Europe, Africa and Central America – transitional justice processes began to be characterized by the particularities of different national contexts, which introduced changes to the post-war model. The dissimilarity of these contexts

9 The fact that the transitional justice process is paradigmatic does not mean that there is only one way to conceive of and apply it. The notion of transitional justice and experiences of its application have been varied and have a history of tension, changes, and modifications. For a record of these variations, see the now classic text by Ruti Teitel (Teitel 2000).

10 These connotations can be traced to the period following the Second World War and the Nuremberg trials.

illustrated the need for local models of extraordinary and imperfect justice in order to respond to novel tensions that were emerging. One example of these responses was the promulgation of amnesty laws which, by virtue of their very nature, implied sacrificing punitive justice in the interest of achieving peace, sometimes characterized as reconciliation.

According to Pablo de Greiff, despite these differences the emergence of the TJ paradigm responded to particular problems that required specific responses. One such problem was the abusive exercise of state power in countries where state power was institutionalized and efficient, and therefore able to commit massive and systematic abuses and violations. In these cases, the concern facing the TJ process was a breakdown of justice institutions in need of repair. The goal of TJ in such cases was to address these breakdowns of justice by establishing accountability (De Greiff 2011, 18, 26).

The field of TJ, over time, has broadened beyond post-authoritarian contexts. It is now applied to post-conflict scenarios in general, and even, as de Greiff notes, to active and ongoing conflicts, which are very different scenarios from the circumstances that led to the emergence and development of TJ and the way that it was originally applied (De Greiff 2011, 26). Over the past 20 years, TJ has largely been applied in the context of weak or failed states whose institutionality is weak or non-existent, whose resources are scarce, and where violent conflict is rooted in structural injustices of a distributive nature or in problems of recognition. In these cases, TJ mechanisms – including truth commissions, criminal proceedings and trials, individual and collective reparations, and institutional reforms – have been flexibly applied while still governed by international legal standards. As such, despite their differences, they retain their original characteristics in terms of their conceptualization of TJ, the definition of their goals, and what it is believed that they may be able to accomplish.[11]

The major goals of these different transitional justice measures are as follows: (i) the recognition of victims in terms of the violations and abuses

[11] This introduces a series of challenges that are worth considering. Despite the unique characteristics of different individual contexts and the serious difficulties that confront societies in transition, international standards play a fundamental role in limiting the concessions that can be made to address apparently conflicting goals of transitional justice. One example of these limits is the inadmissibility of amnesty for crimes against humanity in order to achieve peace. For the genealogy of the term itself, see "Transitional Justice Genealogy" by Ruti Teitel (Teitel 2003). In addition, international legal standards inform and govern TJ measures and TJ processes must conform to them. See: Carrillo, 2006; De Greiff, 2006a; and Rincón, 2010. Furthermore, it should be noted that the UN considers that in cases of human rights violations, states have an obligation to proceed with the prosecution of crimes and reparation to victims: "[I]n the face of widespread human rights violations, States have the obligation to act not only against perpetrators, but also on behalf of victims – including through the provision of reparations" (UN Security Council 2004).

that they suffered, the obligation to repair them, and their status as subjects with rights (De Greiff 2011, 29); (ii) constructing peace, both in its negative sense, such as the absence of direct violence and the cessation of hostilities, as well as in its positive sense, such as the elimination of structural violence (Mani 2002);[12] (iii) the establishment or reestablishment of democratic legality, including the restoration of the rule of law[13] and the institutionalization and strengthening of inclusive democracies that guarantee the non-repetition of violent conflict and widespread violations of human rights.[14]

To accomplish these broad and general goals, societies facing transition must take the difficult step of determining who should be held responsible for the crimes committed during the period of conflict, recognize and redress the damages suffered by victims, and construct or reconstruct social confidence among citizens as well as between citizens and institutions.

Although all the means and mechanisms of transitional justice (truth, justice, reparation, guarantees of non-repetition, and institutional reforms), are typically conceived of as complementary measures to respond to past systematic abuses, reparation is a specific mechanism that focuses on recognizing harms suffered by victims and ways to redress them. Much like the field of TJ, this measure can be understood by its genesis,[15] and here the principle of

---

12 Although these two aspects of peace are related, achieving them requires different tasks. Negative peace requires preventing the repetition and reappearance of violence by reaching or maintaining a cease-fire agreement in the short-term, while the construction of positive peace includes providing assistance to the national recovery and hastening the elimination of the war's underlying causes (Mani 2002, 12).

13 This can be understood in a narrow and minimalist way or in a broader and more substantive fashion. Conceptually, the rule of law can be understood as a means of protecting us from the arbitrary and abusive use of power by a state, which requires human behavior to be subject to publicly promulgated and universally applied laws that introduce certainty and predictability in juridical relations and in all that takes place within the constraints of legality (Mani 2002, 26). The minimalist perspective (where justice is strictly formal) prescribes a government that is subject to and operates within the law and that guarantees citizens protection from the state; the maximalist perspective (where justice is substantive) demands the inclusion of structural, procedural, and substantive elements that incorporate values such as human rights or a commitment to democracy in addition to the institutionality and predictability entailed in the minimalist version (De Greiff 2011, 30 et seq; Mani 2002, 26, 27).

14 Focused on rectifying past abuses, this corrective justice has adopted different approaches based on specific social and cultural needs and circumstances, which have included truth commissions, trials and other court proceedings, compensation, symbolic measures, commemorations, and memorials (Mani 2002). More recently, and due to the difficulties of achieving lasting peace in the context of grave structural injustices not always directly or immediately tied to the conflict, transitional justice has begun to be conceived of in a distributive sense, responding to deeper structural causes of conflict that is understood in terms of social, economic, political, and cultural injustices (Mani 2002).

15 In her book *Verdad, justicia y reparación: la justicia de la justicia transicional*, Tatiana Rincón demonstrates that the concept of reparation has a long history in general international law,

restitutio in integrum is of central importance[16] as it directs restitution processes to re-establish the victims' situations as they were before harms were incurred, thereby restoring their lives to the conditions that they enjoyed before the conflict in question took place. Understood this way, reparation operates within the framework of a compensatory conception of justice that supposes first, that it is possible to compensate for damage suffered, and second, that such compensation can and should be proportionate to damage incurred. This specific criterion to restore a previous situation can be better understood as restitution, and is complemented by other measures and instruments to achieve just, adequate and proportional reparation for violations and damage suffered. Thus, we can speak of comprehensive or full reparation that considers both the material and symbolic dimensions of reparation and includes different measures such as restitution, compensation, satisfaction, indemnification, etc.[17] Given the atrocious forms of harm that are involved in cases of TJ, however, and their

referring to the obligations of states in relation to moral and material damages suffered by individuals or collectivities. She also demonstrates that in the context of human rights and International Humanitarian Law, this concept is embodied in measures whose goal is to efface the effects of human rights violations that have been committed. (Rincón 2010, 75–118).

16 "While there is solid consensus about the criterion of reparatory justice for the relatively isolated case, namely *restitutio in integrum* – the effort to reestablish the situation that existed prior to the wrongful act (or omission), or to compensate the victim in proportion to the harm suffered – there is no consensus yet around a criterion of justice for the massive cases [but] the ideal behind reparations is 'full restitution' (*restitutio in integrum*), that is, the restoration of the *status quo ante*." (De Greiff 2006b, Introduction, 14–19). "Now, in an isolated case of a human rights violation, this ideal of complete reparation (*restitutio in integrum*) understood in terms of the restoration of the *status quo ante* or of compensation in proportion to the harm suffered, is unimpeachable. Its justification should be obvious: from the perspective of victims and survivors; it attempts to neutralize the consequences of the violation they have suffered. From another perspective, the ideal hopes to prevent perpetrators from enjoying any benefit they may have derived from their criminal actions, or to obligate the state to take responsibility for having allowed, by act or omission, certain violations to occur. But there are circumstances in which this ideal is unrealizable, either due to insurmountable constraints such as the impossibility of bringing someone back to life, or due to constraints that although not absolute, are still severe, such as real scarcity of resources of the sort that makes it unfeasible to satisfy, simultaneously, the claims of all victims and of other sectors of society that in fairness, also require the attention of the state." (De Greiff 2006a 455, 456).

17 "*Restitution* seeks to *restore* the victim, to the extent possible, to his or her situation as it was before the violation of rights (by restoring freedom, rights, social position, family life, citizenship, possessions, returning him or her to the previous place of residence or the recovery of employment, among other measures). *Indemnification* seeks to *compensate* for material damages suffered as a consequence of the violation of rights, or moral, physical, or mental damage suffered in the same context … *Rehabilitation* seeks to provide medical, psychiatric, psychological, or legal services that will allow for the victim *to be rehabilitated in the most complete sense possible* … *Satisfaction* seeks to *recover* the name, history, and dignity of the victim … And *guarantees of non-repetition* seek to assure that the victim *will not again suffer* a violation of his or her rights." (Rincón 2010, 83, 84; Van Boven 2010; van Boven 1997).

widespread and systematic nature, the strict application of this restitutive principle is impossible. In some cases, the nature of the damage is so extensive that it is impossible or undesirable to re-establish the previous condition or to provide compensation proportionate to the damage suffered, making it problematic to find the just, adequate and proportional reparation that full reparation demands.[18]

While reparation in TJ processes is governed by international standards that are based on the principle of *restitutio in integrum*, it is necessary to consider the particular nature of the damage, victims and circumstances that are involved in any given case, and doing so requires a certain flexibility with respect to those standards (Rincón 2010, 116–118).[19] In the face of widespread, systematic and grave violations, reparations have also been structured around a standard of "fair and adequate" reparation, which according to Rincón, offers a broader understanding of justice that focuses not on the principle of proportionality or the re-establishment of the *status quo ante*, but on the re-establishment of social confidence and above all on recognizing the dignity of victims (Rincón 2010, 114–116). The restitution of their rights is understood as the means that will accomplish this end.[20]

---

18 We refer here to cases of homicide, sexual violation, torture, etc., where damage inflicted, or property lost cannot be undone or returned. In the case of homicides, disappearances, or extrajudicial executions, for example, the life of the victim has been taken and cannot be restored. In such cases, it would be extraordinarily difficult to establish criteria for compensation. We also face situations where, in addition to violations of human rights, we see cases of structural injustice (both distributive and with respect to recognition) where returning victims to their prior situations would mean leaving them in a state of devastating vulnerability and/or poverty. In addition, reparation based on the principle of *restitutio in integrum* refers to individual cases, while in cases where social groups have been victimized, the proportionality that figures into this principle, together with the scarcity of resources, make the concept unviable as a basis for TJ.

19 This approach has been incorporated into human rights treaties at the international level, producing a corpus of the elements that should be included in reparation. The model is based on international standards and seeks to avoid claims by victims for any other purposes that could imply sacrificing any that should be included, thereby guaranteeing that necessary elements be addressed in the transitional process. Due to its one-size-fits-all nature, however, this model does not address the specificities and contexts of different societies, which may be inherently heterogeneous (De Greiff 2006a; Carrillo 2006). Given that the application of international standards is intended to promote legal reform and re-establish the universally applicable rule of law, the policies and mechanisms needed to implement these goals are conceived and incorporated in a top-down fashion, leading to inadequate participation by direct victims.

20 There are different proposals that offer alternatives to the dominant approach of TJ on how to understand reparation for transitional contexts. One of them is transformative reparations, which seeks to be sensitive to transitional contexts that present deep inequalities and distributive structural injustices. Uprimny and Guzman's proposal identifies serious problems with the paradigmatic approach of integral reparation in the transitional contexts that are discussed here, insofar as it introduces difficult conflicts between corrective and

In the next section, I will analyze the assumptions that are implicit in a focus on reparation involving the restitution of victims' rights, as understood by a given legal system.

3. THE FOCUS ON REPARATION WITH AN EMPHASIS ON THE RESTITUTION OF RIGHTS

As mentioned above, reparation is one element of a broader approach that, from an institutional point of view, sees one of the goals of transition to be the (re)establishment of the rule of law.[21] In order to consolidate long-term peace and guarantee the non-repetition of violence, legitimate structures must be (re)established for the peaceful resolution of disputes and the administration of justice. At the same time, however, difficult social problems and circumstances in these societies can make (re)establishing the rule of law difficult. The normative basis for promoting the rule of law as established in international human rights norms and standards is the principle of *restitutio in integrum*, the goal of which is to efface the effects of damage and return victims to the conditions and circumstances that prevailed before it was suffered. In transitional contexts, however, this approach encounters difficulties relating to the nature of the damage as well as the scale and magnitude of the violations that took place that make its strict application both impossible and undesirable.

In the case of crimes such as murders, massacres, forced disappearances, torture and sexual violation, among others, it is often not possible to re-establish

---

distributive justice, particularly with respect to two of the duties that states have: on the one hand, the duty to make every effort to rectify unjust harms perpetrated against a victim and, on the other hand, the duty to make every effort to achieve an equitable distribution of goods and burdens between all members of society (Uprimny and Guzmán 2010, 236). In opposition to the proposal for structurally transformative reparations, especially the more ambitious ones supported by Anne Saris and Katherine Lofts, Margaret Urban Walker has pointed out the danger of neglecting corrective justice and replacing it with a notion of transformative reparation, arguing that the latter can dilute the importance of recognizing a duty of reparation to the victims as individuals, in order to achieve the advances of distributive justice. For Walker, the current practice of reparations has already gone beyond focusing on returning victims to their previous situations, and instead is the outcome of various tests and struggles in legal, social and political environments at local, national and international levels. In order to respond to the structural injustices suffered by oppressed groups, such as women, for example, Walker proposes using an aspirational principle of non-discrimination for reparations (Walker 2016).

21 Understood as a principle of governance in which both people and public and private institutions, including the state itself, are responsible and equally subject to publicly promulgated laws that in practice are consistent with international human rights norms and standards.

the pre-damage life conditions of surviving, nor is it often possible to extirpate the effects of those crimes from their lives. After a period of widespread, systematic and atrocious violations, the lives of survivors will never be the same. Nevertheless, the negative effects of atrocities can be minimized. Given the nature and dimensions of the damage, its effects cannot be eliminated from the lives of survivors. The restitution of the *status quo ante* is conceived of in the broader framework of full reparation, based on a belief that the most effective way to repair damage done to victims lies in the institutional (re)establishment and guaranteeing of their rights as well as opportunities for them to meaningfully enjoy the rights that they lost, or were never able to enjoy, and measures to prevent any further violations. Thus, a goal of reparative measures is to recognize rights that were violated and to contribute to re-establishing the rule of law (Teitel 2000), the most robust understanding of which includes the reconstruction of civic confidence and democracy.

As we have seen so far, the system of rights constitutes the normative core of the rule of law (Shelly 2007, 67; UN Security Council 2004). From a juridical point of view, when we speak of *derechos*[22] we should distinguish between two points of view: the objective (law) and the subjective (rights). The word "law" refers to juridical norms, a specific set of social norms that discipline the behavior of community members and dictate sanctions for their violation. Community members are considered permanently subordinate to such norms since they derive from an authority considered to be legitimate. Citizens are bound to comply with these norms and do so voluntarily. Juridical norms are usually produced by state or government institutions, and are established through various means that produce laws, regulations, ordinances, etc., which are disseminated through the publication of documents containing codes, regulations and other juridical texts. This kind of *derecho*, in its objective sense, includes all the juridical norms in a particular community and entails the establishment, promulgation, recognition and communication of those norms and sanctions for their violation.

In their subjective sense, in contrast, *derechos* are the rights, powers, or privileges to which people are entitled under the law. Although rights are individual, the existence of these rights, powers, or privileges reflects relations that are determined by fields of power and the freedom to act in relation to other people.

The powers that form the basis for rights[23] can be understood as powers to act and freedoms to do, be, or possess *x* that those endowed with them may unilaterally exercise. First, in relation to freedom, rights may define licit acts

---

22 [Translator note: In different contexts, the word *derecho* that is used throughout this text in the original Spanish can mean either *law* (jurisprudence) or *a right.*]

23 This explanation follows W.N. Hohfeld's analysis of rights as described in Hohfeld 2004.

that subjects may undertake as well as prohibited acts that the law determines to be sanctionable. Second, rights can also be considered juridical powers that authorize certain kinds of acts that people have the capacity to carry out. In this sense, the law establishes a juridical relation between two or more people participating in the juridical act and specifies the scope of the power to act to which the subject is entitled. Third, while legal codes delimit the scope of powers, they also establish corresponding duties or obligations, and in this sense can be seen as making real and effective demands on the behaviors of others, behaviors that, as duties, are imposed by juridical norms that stipulate powers to enforce the juridical relationship (Hohfeld 2004).

Since rights allow people to act in relation to other people, they can be conceived of as: (i) *the freedom* of subjects to do or refrain from doing *x*, if *x* is not prohibited or sanctioned under the law; (ii) legal *powers* to carry out act *x*, if the person has the capacity to carry it out, which produce juridical relations that subject parties to a defined field of action with corresponding duties and obligations; and (iii) the *capacity* to demand specific behaviors from others under certain circumstances, supported not only by the power to impose certain consequences for non-compliance, but also the power to determine those consequences and to exercise discretional authority to use juridical mechanisms and procedures for this purpose.

Both "law" and "rights", then (both meanings of *derecho*) are configured through juridical norms that give rise to a specific field of power that is translated into a set of freedoms, powers, capacities, and also responsibilities with which subjects are invested, though they may or may not make use of them. By law, the subjects who enjoy these rights, powers and capacities fall into the juridical category of persons. This is a category that brings together a group of attributes and qualities (e.g. name, legal capacity, marital status) and attributes rights, duties and obligations to those subjects, such as the right to freely act in the sense that they can choose to do or be *x*; that they have legal sovereignty over themselves; that they are responsible for complying with their duties and obligations insofar as they are able; that they have the capacity to be accountable for their acts in relation to themselves and others; and that they assume the consequences of not fulfilling those duties.

The category of person not only covers those circumstances in which subjects comply with all the attributes with which they are endowed, but also has implications for the scope of the law in those situations in which there is a temporary or permanent deprivation of those attributes and qualities.[24]

---

24 The focus on rights also allows for the protection of those who are unable to exercise the rights as described, either temporarily or permanently, and in different ways, such as: minor children, people with mental illnesses, and those affected by other circumstances defined by the law as disenabling or disentitling people from exercising their rights, although they continue to legally possess them.

The idea of dominion is essential to the nature of subjective rights when understood as the powers or rights of subjects with sovereign will, firstly because people have sovereign power over themselves, and secondly because in exercising their sovereignty people have the power to determine the actions they may take to satisfy their own interests. In relation to the former sense, the law establishes the juridical relations that people have with themselves. All people possess and have ownership of themselves, of their bodies, of their names and of their ideas. These attributes form part of persons and their self-identification. As a result, sovereignty over one's own person is inalienable, for which reason slavery and human trafficking are impermissible. The recognition of all persons' personal sovereignty over themselves constitutes a form of inalienable property that disallows any transfer or usurpation of the rights of persons over themselves.[25] In relation to the latter sense, the legal sovereignty of persons over themselves is extended to those actions that are required to satisfy self-interests, many of which suppose access to objects that are external to the person and the use of those objects. In this context, the subjective rights model establishes a difference between that which is intrinsic to the person and therefore not transferable, and that which may be appropriated by the person but is external to him or her.[26] The posited sovereignty of subjects over their own persons likewise grants them sovereignty over those objects that may be appropriated by them, categorized as property. By virtue of their being empowered to exercise dominion over appropriated objects, property owners – a legal category that describes subjects who exercise dominion over and thus property rights to those objects – have the *freedom* to use and dispose of these goods as they wish, as long as such use is not prohibited by the law. Furthermore, they can benefit from the juridical *power* and *capacity* to participate in established juridical relations with those objects, including transfer, sale, gifting, exchange, etc. Finally, through mechanisms and procedures established by law, they can have an *ability* to effectively exercise such power and demand that others comply with their obligations in conformity with the law.

These relations to things or assets make up what are called real rights, principal among which is the right to property. In the juridical context,

---

25 These rights are known juridically as *absolute rights*, i.e. rights that one has over oneself and that cannot be separated from the person. These include the right to life, personal liberty, etc. They are distinguished from other rights called *real rights* or *ius in re* (those rights that people have over property), and personal *rights* (which people can establish among themselves, for example to regulate the payment of debts or the provision of services). What makes a right subjective is that it can be exercised with respect to an object of that right. This is not the case with respect to the absolute rights of a person. Nonetheless, this discussion is not central to the focus in this text.

26 Consider the distinction between subject and object in jurisprudence. People can be subjects of a juridical relationship and things can be objects of such a relationship. In the context of these relations, people cannot be objects and things cannot be subjects.

this right was initially considered absolute and exclusive, but the broadest rights that an individual may enjoy over things are nevertheless subject to juridical norms that limit these rights and impose certain responsibilities and restrictions over the way they may be used. Such regulations may focus on either (i) the *subjects* enjoying these rights to possess, or (ii) the *objects* that are susceptible to being possessed. In the former case, those regulations that focus on the *subjects* who possess things take the form of limitations and/or responsibilities that are applied to the powers of free and sovereign property owners who exercise dominion over the things. In the traditional conception of the right to own property, this absolute sovereignty is understood in the sense that property owners are fully empowered to make use of (or not make use of) their property in any way that pleases them, including destroying it, or, in the case of land, leaving it uncultivated or unproductive. From this traditional perspective, the property rights regime is limited to the regulation and resolution of conflicts that may arise among property owners and the prescription of duties and obligations that are based on the utility of properties and the freedom of property owners.[27] In the latter case, when regulations are focused on the *objects* and the characteristics that make them goods susceptible to being possessed, there are also specific juridical constructions that regulate the relations of subjects regarding those goods. This is the case when the right to property takes on a functional meaning that emphasizes the specificity and diversity of goods and their social meaning through which their social function is determined.[28] In this case, a property owner is no longer an omnipotent sovereign with full and absolute domain over the thing possessed. Rather, obligations based on social benefits and usefulness that may be derived from an asset become a factor in defining the relations between owner and possession.

Placing objects and their specific characteristics at the center of legal regulations also allows for a certain categorization of assets whose principal characteristic is that they are external to the person but necessary to that person's life and the pursuit of his or her interests. It is because of this necessity that their loss, damage, or dispossession is also legally regulated and categorized within a notion of harm. At the same time, the law categorizes the victim as an individual or collective person who has suffered damage, injury, or loss to their own person, their capacities, rights, or property,[29] and

27 Under current conceptions of property rights, these rights are subject to limits and are not absolute.

28 This is not merely a question of juridical relations between people and things, but also of relations between people regarding a thing, and relations among people, things, and a third party, i.e. society. The law establishes a category of damage that is applied in cases where a thing is taken away illegitimately.

29 According to the United Nations General Assembly, the definition of a victim is as follows: "Victims of Crime. 'Victims' means persons who, individually or collectively, have suffered

also establishes the means by which the harm or damage suffered by victims may be repaired.

In transitional contexts, the rights of survivors have been violated or suppressed in some way. Their lives, their physical integrity and/or their freedoms have been threatened and seriously infringed upon, affecting their capacity and power to work and make choices and their ability to effectively demand their rights and that others fulfill their legal duties. In transitional justice, such violations of rights are assumed to be reversible through the model of reparation that is based on the re-establishment of the rights of surviving victims. It is for this reason that urgent protection is lent to victims so that they may regain their ability to act in the juridical context,[30] i.e. to use, exercise and fully enjoy their rights, and thereby overcoming their condition as victims.

Among the rights to be repaired in transitional contexts is the right to land, and more specifically rural land. In societies that are characterized by structural injustices and past or ongoing violent conflict, it may be said that the right to property has been violated not only due to the conflict, but also due to pre-existing historical conditions that may come to bear during the transition. Land restitution has been thought of as a transitional mechanism that can repair violations of land and property rights, but when land restitution is undertaken exclusively on the basis of rights as described in previous paragraphs, problems emerge when reference is made not only to the period of violent conflict to which TJ is theoretically circumscribed, but also to long traditions of structural injustice regarding recognition and land distribution.[31] These problems are addressed in the next section.

---

harm, including physical or mental injury, emotional suffering, economic loss or substantial impairment of their fundamental rights, through acts or omissions that are in violation of criminal laws operative within Member States, including those laws proscribing criminal abuse of power. A person may be considered a victim, under this Declaration, regardless of whether the perpetrator is identified, apprehended, prosecuted or convicted and regardless of the familial relationship between the perpetrator and the victim. The term 'victim' also includes, where appropriate, the immediate family or dependents of the direct victim and persons who have suffered harm in intervening to assist victims in distress or to prevent victimization. The provisions contained herein shall be applicable to all, without distinction of any kind, such as race, colour, sex, age, language, religion, nationality, political or other opinion, cultural beliefs or practices, property, birth or family status, ethnic or social origin, and disability." (Declaration of Basic Principles of Justice for Victims of Crime and Abuse of Power, proclaimed on 29 November 1985 through Resolution 40/34 of the United Nations General Assembly).

30 Also their ability to act in relation to other aspects of their lives, for example citizenship rights (political life), the right to life, to health, etc.

31 As indicated, this text does not refer directly to any specific case. Nevertheless, the Colombian case is an illustration of this point. The South African case also provides elements of analysis on this topic (Christodoulidis and Veitch, 2008).

4. PROBLEMS REGARDING LAND RESTITUTION AND REPARATION

One of the principal assumptions that is made when looking at reparation from the paradigmatic perspective of rights is that victims find themselves in conditions of particular vulnerability that impede, impair, or deprive them of their capacity to genuinely exercise, use and enjoy their rights. On the institutional level, it has been said that societies engaging transitional justice processes should focus on re-establishing the rule of law, the normative bases of which are international human rights standards that stipulate reparation and the restitution of lost property after an armed conflict or a period of violence.

Despite the importance of this objective, societies embarking on transitional justice processes face the task of transforming the existing political, social and economic order that co-existed with and often gave rise to the past violence that the processes are trying to deal with. In contexts where rights were systematically violated but the juridical order, whether precariously functioning or not, was unable to resist the violence, a reparation process that is focused on the restitution of rights will face practical limitations and problems both on the conceptual level and in application. Below four problems are outlined relating to reparation and the restitution of land property rights in societies with structural injustices regarding recognition and distribution of property.

4.1. THE GOAL OF RE-ESTABLISHING THE RULE OF LAW

In the paradigmatic conception of transitional justice, re-establishing the rule of law is not only one of the objectives of the transition, it is also a prerequisite for democratizing society, re-establishing social confidence and maintaining a social order in which the rights of all members of the political community can be guaranteed and justice can be provided to those whose rights have been violated. It is a widely held belief among international organizations that in order to meet these objectives, re-establishing the rule of law is essential since it seeks to reduce the arbitrary and discretional actions of officials in positions of power that may have contributed to past human rights violations.

In addition to holding officials accountable, the rule of law is public, stable, general and clear. As such, it favors the creation of an atmosphere of juridical certainty, predictability and security, which is indispensable for confident social relations – both the vertical kind, i.e. between citizens and government, and the horizontal, i.e. among citizens. Since juridical norms are known beforehand and applied to all persons equally, it is much easier to coordinate practices and transactions among citizens and to maintain control and vigilance over those who conduct government business.

Yet, despite the supposed benefits that the rule of law brings to TJ, its relation to the democratization of society and overcoming the effects of systematic and atrocious violence is not obvious. Some criticize the efficacy of these objectives, whether considering vaguer or more substantial versions of the concept of the rule of law, i.e. defining the rule of law either in formal terms focused on institutions and procedures that allow for holding citizens and officials to compliance with the law, or also in terms of substantive criteria regarding justice and democracy that underlie the concept.

The principle criticism of the more formal, procedural version of the rule of law is that the existence of public, general and stable laws does not guarantee that they will be just or that they will not represent the interests of particular groups in societies and represent dramatic differences in types and degrees of oppression, inequity and exclusion. These are conditions that may be present in societies that have experienced periods of grave violations of human rights. In addition, the fact that norms are publicly known beforehand does not necessarily guarantee that people will follow them; nor does it mean that all people will use them or follow them in the same fashion.[32]

In a society characterized by extremes of structural inequality and injustice, even when equality before the law meets the requirement of being public, general and stable, it may nevertheless still deepen social disadvantages that were experienced by some groups during the period of the conflict or even earlier. An approach that privileges legality over other social aspects loses sight of a broader reality that cannot be captured by focusing on the law, because it is general and loses sight of the specific. In the same sense, reducing discretional government action by instituting the rule of law can be problematic in societies in transition that are also quite unequal. The law is general and may not always be applied appropriately in cases that merit a more specific and sometimes exceptional evaluation by judges wishing to promote necessary social change.

For these reasons, the defenders of more substantive conceptions of the rule of law insist on including measures to protect rights in order to further human development, justice and democracy. These measures include international human rights standards that include, among other things, provisions relating to reparation and the restitution of property that victims may have lost due to an armed conflict or a period of social violence. These more substantive versions of the rule of law, however, face practical problems related to the necessary transformation of the political, social, economic and juridical *status quo* that are associated with, and may promote logics of, social distrust, violence, oppression and other injustices that resist change. In addition,

---

32 Referring here to the problem of the different capacities that people require to follow and use established norms.

the substantive approach must confront the vagueness of notions such as democracy and justice, which are closely tied to political projects that require a putative "we" that may not yet exist or that has been constructed in a non-inclusive sense.[33] In both practical and conceptual terms, introducing substantive versions of the rule of law entails the questions of what kind of democracy is required and under what criteria will justice frame the juridical norms that are promulgated and sanctioned by an authority in order to regulate the juridical relations in a society in which individual and collective interests, needs and prerogatives diverge and may be incompatible? The reconstruction of social confidence that is indispensable for building a sense of community cannot be established if the existence of a "we" that would sustain the process is in crisis and if there is a lack of confidence in the authority that promulgates juridical norms, their contents and their sanctions, and that defines the field of power within which subjective rights become operative.

It is not unusual to see that during a period of transitional justice the legal and institutional order that prevailed during periods of past violence continues to operate, precarious though it may be. Transition processes experience tension when searching for certain guarantees of stability with juridical certainty, predictability and security, while at the same time necessarily transforming the rules and structures that govern society and define the limits of responsibility and of rights. The goal of a new and inclusive society is called into question when it is found to be difficult to define which juridical frameworks should be maintained and which should give way to new, different or extraordinary structures and norms.

The transformative logic of TJ, together with the regularity and stability of the rule of law, as well as the content of the legal norms that shape it, remain suspended as long as they are not discussed and defined by the political community to which they apply; that is the meaning of the "we", the rules that will govern it and the powers that will authorize it. If issues related to the punishment of perpetrators or the restitution of civil and political rights are included in the discussion about the scope of the transitional process and any transformation of (or exceptions made to) social norms, but the rules that regulate economic life and private property are not considered, then the scope of transformation is limited as these latter aspects are implicitly not subjected to political debate.

In fact, there appears to be a tendency to depoliticize economic issues and relegate them to non-negotiable aspects of transition as efforts instead

33 Referring here particularly to current transition experiences, which differ from those that gave rise to the field of TJ. These are characterized by situations in which state institutions, where they existed, were "completely absent from large parts of the national territory, [countries or societies] in which large elements of relations among citizens, and especially between citizens and State institutions, were yet to be regulated." (De Greiff 2011, 18).

concentrate on advancing the democratization of the political sphere. Emilios Christodoulidis and Scott Veich, for example, state that this distinction between non-negotiable economic questions and democratically debated political issues in South Africa was established not only *by* the law, but indeed *as* the law itself (Christodoulidis and Veitch 2008). In this context, property rights, land rights, and rights to sovereignty were guaranteed and enshrined as the rules of the game according to which future policies could be measured, but by the same logic were exempt from political disputes or disagreements (Christodoulidis and Veitch 2008). In the Colombian case, pre-existing juridical criteria applicable to the restitution of land to victims of the conflict determine who can legally claim property rights over land, but they are also the same criteria that have produced and frequently intensified dynamics that have led to the dispossession and forced displacement of *campesinos* without title to the land. If the existing economic model and private property system are not addressed under a given TJ process, they will be excluded from consideration under the democratic process, thereby protecting the *status quo*. If land restitution is carried out based on pre-existing rights that are said to have been lost or disregarded, they then become established as operative and as non-negotiable at the time of the transition and understood as the transformation of a society in crisis.

As mentioned, the juridical certainty, predictability and security that are provided by established regulations are fundamental to the rule of law; namely those regulations that are not questioned or disputed in the initial stages of the transition because they are considered the basic and necessary rules that will allow a successful transition to democracy. However, when these essential elements operate in a context that allows for debates over political but not economic outcomes, they cease to be neutral. They are more closely correlated with market-based economic systems that require the certainty and predictability of contracts and transactions, allowing economic actors to predict the costs and benefits of future economic activity. They protect property and property owners, and importantly give legal standing to existing property relations, thereby precluding questions about the bases and justifications for that right to property in the first place.[34]

In this sense, the establishment of the rule of law faces problems when it demarcates what is and is not negotiable in the transition, a distinction that is imposed not by an inclusive "we", but rather by an authority representing a partial "we" with private interests that are juridically protected and that form part of the legal system itself that frames the transition and upon which it depends.

---

34 When a thing is accepted as indisputable simply because it is an accepted frame of reference or an established premise, it is far from being neutral. It serves an end, and that end is to maintain what has existed before the discussion.

4.2. DEPENDENCE OF REPARATION ON TYPE OF DAMAGE SUFFERED

Reforms to pre-existing laws or the establishment of new legislation to deal with the injustices and past atrocities are fundamental parts of any transitional process in societies where confidence in institutions is impaired. Indeed, they are central to providing redress for damage that victims have suffered from the systematic violation of their rights.

The reparation approach based on the principle of *restitutio in integrum* and the later and broader notion of full reparation both focus on restoring the rights of victims. Reparation has a strong moral justification, both discursively and in the concrete experiences of transitional justice, that is tied to the urgent duty to redress widespread and atrocious damage that has been inflicted systematically and that the existing political and juridical order has been unable to prevent or curtail, leaving citizens defenseless. Victims and damage suffered in an isolated and occasional fashion in "normal" social situations, are distinguished from victims of acts that were widely and systematically committed, considered atrocious, and linked to the conflict or the period of violence that a TJ process attempts to overcome.[35]

In the latter case, when the damage that is suffered is considered to be profound, the principle of *restitutio in integrum* that seeks to return the victim to his or her state before having suffered the damage cannot be fully applied. Nevertheless, full reparation that seeks to minimize the effects of damage and contribute to the victim's ability to overcome his or her situation[36] through

---

35 The kind of damage for which reparation under transitional justice is applied is different from damage caused in an isolated and individual manner where such appalling cases are not the norm. While there are individual instances of sexual violence, violence leading to death, and other horrifying acts, systematic and widespread violence is in its own category and justifies legal procedures and responses that differ from those offered in isolated cases. The exceptional nature of both the damage and reparations for such acts is configured by an approach that seeks to restore rights during a period of transition. Under these exceptional circumstances, there is a sense of urgency for reparation that is not present in responses to more common kinds of damage that result from the violation of rights or their inadequate protection. In exceptional circumstances, the loss of freedom, capacities, powers, and of the ability to use established mechanisms to address these losses does not result from acts by any agent or group of agents who can be held directly responsible. Rather, it reflects the unfortunate socioeconomic position into which some people are born and live, as well as the unfortunate natural distribution of talent. In the case of damage directly caused by agents or groups of agents, the responsible parties, damage, and victims can be clearly identified. Reparation in transitional justice, however, responds to injustices that are suffered by those who find themselves in the least advantageous social positions due to society's endemic or structural failures. Here our discussion contrasts the scope of action within the transitional justice process with the scope of action to further the goal of distributive justice.

36 Usually expressed in the sense that people cease to be victims and return to being – or become for the first time – citizens exercising their rights.

reparation should not be based exclusively on a *restitution* of previous rights – which focuses on returning the victim to his or her condition before the violation – but rather on the *re-establishment* of his or her rights by rehabilitating their capacity to take legal action, which has been diminished by his or her specific situation of vulnerability. As mentioned above, this capacity refers to juridical freedoms and powers and the ability to use juridical mechanisms and procedures to do or not do *x*, as established by law.

Such damage, however, goes beyond the violation of these subjective rights. The dominion that a person exercises over him- or herself is essential, as is the dominion over external objects that allows one to realize one's own interests and make one's life possible. Injury either to a person's subjective rights or to a person's dominion over him- or herself is considered an element of the damage that should be repaired; therefore reparation calls for the re-establishment of a person's dominion over self.

There is a distinction at the very heart of the law between that which affects a person's dominion over him- or herself and that which affects a person's dominion over external objects that enables the realization of his or her goals and interests. This distinction has consequences with respect to how damage is conceptually assessed. Damage to a person and to a person's dominion over him- or herself comes much closer to the notion of "irreparable", which thereby requires that reparation based on the principle of *restitutio in integrum* be interpreted in such an elastic fashion that it emphasizes people's rights more than their conditions. Think of injuries to people's physical integrity or to their bodies and psyches resulting from torture, sexual abuse, injury, and the like, where physical and psychological effects leave their marks on the personal histories and identities of surviving victims. Damage to external objects over which people exercise dominion, on the other hand, may take the form of legally sanctioned loss, destruction, or depreciation by actors during a conflict or during a period of widespread and systematic violence.

Those objects are important because they are useful means through which people accomplish their life goals, including goals related to their dominion over themselves. It is that particular usefulness that is susceptible to damage. In such cases, it is an object and not a subject that has been affected by the damage, however, the object is nevertheless important to the subject because of its utility or the capacity it gives to the subject to accomplish the life goals that define his or her identity. However, there are objects such as land in rural areas, which for many people and communities are not separable from their identities, and thus, seem to have a special meaning. Rural land is a good that is inhabited, and in that sense is like urban areas, but unlike urban areas, for some people in rural areas the space they inhabit can be an extension of themselves and their identities.

Identifying types of damage and what is to be repaired is done on the basis of categories established under the law. In dealing with injuries to a person, to his or her body, their physical integrity, memories, or ideas, such damage directly impacts on personal identities, self-conceptions, and personal plans and projects. In such cases, a policy or norm promoting reparation will have to focus on the parts of the person that have been negatively affected and on the idea that irreparable harm has been done. A different concept of legal damage arises when we think of damage such as the dispossession or theft of objects that are useful for life. It is understood that objects are mere objects, bereft of any meaning other than their usefulness in maintaining a body that may be mine, yours, or someone else's. Things may be useful for individual or social purposes, but at the end of the day, important only inasmuch as they are means used by people to accomplish their goals.

This is not the case with respect to the dispossession or forced abandonment of land. The idea that land is an object external to the subject whose relationship with the subject is primarily one of utility is too narrow a conception of what land property means to the people who build and inhabit their homes on it, along with their life plans, their expectations, their dreams and their identity. This idea also leads to an equally limited conception of what the loss of land entails. The loss or forced abandonment of land affects not only the property, an object that is external and differentiated from the person. It also attacks and injures the person as such: his or her conception of self, life plans, and ways of understanding that have mediated his or her relations with others and with the social and natural environment.[37]

4.3. WITH RESPECT TO THE LEGAL CATEGORIES OF PERSON AND VICTIM

As mentioned in the first section of this chapter, transitional justice in recent decades has been putting much more emphasis on victims and the reparation

37 This argument is also operative in relation to what constitutes the home space in urban areas, where such an inhabited space can also be conceived by people as an extension of themselves and of their identity, or at least an intimate space that they expect will be respected by others. Nevertheless, there are differences between what these spaces can mean in cities and in rural areas, where spaces are not only inhabited but are also where people learn what it means to be and to carry out life tasks. It is a space that is both home and territory; the place where an important kind of knowledge is created that allows for sustenance and nurtures the creation of life plans. The Brazilian film *Aquarius* (2016), directed by Kleber Mendoça, provides a beautiful representation of the multiple meanings and tensions surrounding inhabited spaces in urban areas with an exclusively economic view of housing. The film is about a retired film critic named Clara, who is the last resident in an old building called Aquarius. The rest of the apartments in the building have been acquired by a group of real estate investors with plans for redevelopment, but even after receiving a very lucrative offer and despite multiple pressures to which she is subjected, Clara refuses to sell her apartment because it contains the memories of her life and family who also lived there.

of damage they have suffered. As we have seen, this emphasis has been inspired by an international standard based on the principle of *restitutio in integrum* which has been adapted to be part of the full reparation, related to the restitution of rights. This approach recognizes different forms of damage, responsibility, and reparation[38] tied to the notions of person and victim.

Certain characteristics are attributed to the juridical person, including free agency, autonomy, free will, and the ability to make choices and act to assume responsibilities and duties. The victim, on the other hand, is generally thought of as a patient, one who has suffered damage, about whom it can be said that all the attributes enumerated above are diminished, compromised, or non-existent.

Within transitional and reparative processes, specific kinds of damage are identified in distinction to those considered to be typical of "normal" or "ordinary" times. Also distinguished here is a special category of victims who will be the beneficiaries of reparation during the transition as opposed to those who suffer other kinds of damage or harm. These categories of damage seem to be differentiated by virtue of a specific type of damage suffered that correlates with a particular conception of justice and injustice associated with the process.

We find that the definition of victim which is associated with transitional justice processes refers to damage stemming from widespread and systematic violations of human rights in what are considered abnormal contexts, when efforts are made to overcome these violations, which are related to "actions or omissions that violate existing law in member States, including legal prohibitions of abuse of power."[39]

---

[38] These forms of damage, responsibility, and reparation are described in subsection 4.2 above.

[39] In the Colombian case, for example, people are assigned to the category of victims based on temporal criteria, the characteristics of the perpetrators or those who caused the damage, and the nature and extent of their involvement and participation in the conflict (Martínez 2013; "Ley de Víctimas y Restitución de Tierras" 2015; Amnistía Internacional 2012). Victims are those who have suffered damage perpetrated by armed actors in the context of the Colombian armed conflict under these criteria. The recognition of victims with rights to some kind of reparation depends on when they suffered the damage, and recognizes only damage suffered after 1985, although the Colombian conflict and widespread and systematic violations of human rights began long before that year. With respect to land restitution, only those who have suffered dispossession of their lands or forced displacement since 1991 and before 2021 have a right to access the reparation mechanism. Only victims of forced displacement who hold land titles or those who can protect their property rights by virtue of having occupied their land for the length of time legally required to formalize possession are legally entitled to have their land returned to them. This excludes tens of thousands of *campesinos* and other victims of forced displacement from recovering their land because, as mentioned, the Law of Victims and Land Restitution does not apply to victims displaced from their land as a result of abuses and human rights violations committed before January 1991 (Amnistía Internacional 2012). The following criteria are stipulated in the Law on Victims and Land Restitution: "Article 72. Actions for Restitution of the Dispossessed …

These criteria that define and demarcate a universe of qualifying victims exclude other victims of the conflict from policies for reparation if they don't meet legally defined requirements. Whatever criteria are used to set apart different kinds of victims, having a specific category of victims with the right to this or that type of reparation runs the risk not only of homogenizing a group of victims based on suffering damage recognized as unjust and therefore deserving of reparation, but also entails the exclusion of a much broader community of victims who will be barred from the transitional justice regime. The categorization of victims with rights to reparation during the transition also supposes a differentiation between different kinds of injustice based on what the law determines to be their sources or causative factors rather than how those injustices compromise the capacities of victims or how they diminish the attributes of the person as agent, as discussed above.

These are the ways to set apart the subjects whose injuries should be redressed under transitional processes, and thus to categorize certain kinds of injustices as central. When it is established under the law that the right to reparation is accorded to those who have suffered a certain kind of damage due to an armed conflict or during an exceptionally violent, atrocious, or oppressive period, a context and a scope are also defined with respect to what is understood as justice and injustice in TJ, implicitly delimiting the TJ process.[40]

In the case of unassigned properties, granting property rights over the unassigned property will continue in favor of the person who has been making economic use of the property if the conditions for allotting the land were met during the dispossession or abandonment … Article 75. Holders of Rights to Restitution. Those people who were property owners or who were in possession of land properties, or conducted economic activities on unassigned properties and seek to obtain property rights over those properties by judicial action, who have been dispossessed of that land or who have been forced to abandon it as a direct or indirect result of acts constituting violations as described in article 3 of this Law, between 1 January 1991 and the expiration of the Law, may seek juridical and material restitution of the lands they have been dispossessed of or from which they have forcibly displaced in the terms established in this chapter." ("Law of Victims and Land Restitution"). In addition, a regulatory decree governing the implementation of the Law of Victims and Land Restitution speaks of a 10-year period during which the Law will be applied (Decree no. 4800 of 2011): "Victims of forced displacement and other abuses against human rights committed before 1985 may only benefit from symbolic reparation, not land restitution or economic compensation. Victims of abuses against human rights committed between 1985 and 1991 will have a right to economic compensation but not to land restitution. Only those victims whose lands were improperly appropriated or illegally occupied through human rights abuses after 1991 and before the expiration of the law will have access to land restitution. Given that the effective life of the Law is 10 years beginning at the time of its approval, this will apply until 10 June 2021."

40 Of course, the gravity of atrocious violations of human rights is such that their victims deserve urgent reparation and special attention in transitions that are intended to lead society to times of peace and democratic institutions. What is really terrible about these violations, however, are their consequences for the lives of those who suffer them, i.e. the defenselessness, vulnerability, and humiliation to which they have been subjected, and the fact that there are many people outside the universe of legally defined victims. These people, although they also

This may produce inconsistencies with respect to the objectives laid out for transitional justice. The distinction between victims with the right to reparation[41] and those without such a right but who are nevertheless in situations of extreme vulnerability assumes that the reparation of the harm done to the former is essential to achieving peace and democratization, and they therefore require urgent and prioritized attention during the transition, while action to redress the injustices suffered by the latter is secondary and should be postponed or disregarded, depending on the availability of the resources of society.

This distinction is even more problematic when it comes to land restitution. Definitions of the injustice that should be repaired and the relevant period in the past should be added to the definition of the damage and of the victim. It is important to note how legislation and policy set apart certain periods in the past as relevant to the process while other periods are excluded.[42]

4.4. THE CATEGORIZATION OF LAND AS AN EXTERNAL OBJECT/POSSESSION

As has been mentioned, the law categorizing forms of damage distinguishes between those that relate to a person's dominion over him- or herself and others that relate to objects or entities external to the person, i.e. property over which a person can and must exercise dominion to guarantee his or her own life. In the former case, even if rights associated with the sovereignty of the individual over him or herself were not recognized or guaranteed before the period of violence to which the reparation refers, in TJ it is assumed that such rights will nevertheless be established through reparation. If the pre-existing juridical and political systems did not recognize or guarantee those rights, there is no question that TJ reparation is not limited to simply restoring the *status quo ante*, but also extends to recognizing essential rights for the first time.

The latter situation operates differently in some situations, however; especially with respect to the private ownership of land. Reparation in such cases

suffered and continue to suffer the terrible consequences of defenselessness and vulnerability, are not eligible for reparations, and there is no clear way for them to be brought into an inclusive democracy as stipulated in the field of TJ.

41 A limited group in the Colombian context, which, as stated above, excludes a larger group of the conflict's victims.

42 In the case of land distribution in Colombia, for example, one could go back to the Spanish conquest and the colonial period, or, under other interpretations, to the 19th or early 20th centuries. With respect to the categorization of victims and related problems, I have benefited from the writings of François du Bois about a group of victims who were eligible for reparation in another TJ process, and the larger group of victims who were not included in that process (du Bois 2008, 117).

does not involve recognizing people's rights independently of whether or not they were previously recognized. Property restitution is limited to those cases in which the ownership of the property in question was previously established or the requisite means of establishing the property relationship were available. The restitution of property rights takes place when it has been established that the people in question previously possessed those property rights.[43]

This distinction is critical to restitution because it excludes from public discussion the legal principles that justify and protect ownership of private property external to the subject. In the case of land property, these foundational principles do not consider the diversity of relations by which people establish their claims to land. When the law considers relations between subjects and objects, it may focus on the owners of property or the external objects that constitute it. In either case, it determines the way that property relations and property itself are understood. From the liberal point of view of rights in Western jurisprudence, the sovereign dominion that a person (subject) exercises over his or her possessions (objects) establishes a relationship of absolute dominion in which the property owner has the power to decide on the use, enjoyment, and disposition of the thing, and the power and freedom to do or not do so.

With land property, however, the concept of the social function of the object[44] has been introduced, which may subject a landowner to a set of duties and responsibilities that limit the powers conferred by the property title. In other words, the concept of the social function of land as property not only grants powers to the landowner but also subjects him or her to legal responsibilities by taking into consideration the value or utility that the land has to society. In societies in transition where disputes over land property were at the center of the recent conflict and where they were one of the causal factors behind human rights violations, the social function of land[45] and the

---

43 In the Colombian case, for example, those who can assert the right to land restitution are those who can prove that they previously enjoyed such a right, or who meet certain conditions for eligibility and belong to the category of victims with this right. Such proof can take the form of them having a registered or unregistered land title or by providing witnesses and evidence of the payment for public services, indicating that they had possession of the property, or by demonstrating that they have inhabited and worked a specific piece of land for a period of no less than five years. Many of these conditions that are found in the Law of Victims and Land Restitution also appear in previous legislation, and in some cases are intended to facilitate the granting of unassigned property to landless *campesinos* and to curb the accumulation and concentration of land. Nevertheless, the concentration of land in the hands of a few continued to increase, along with the forced displacement of *campesinos* to prevent them from claiming land ownership.

44 This social function has been defined in relation to the public utility ascribed to land property.

45 In the Colombian case, this social function of land has been conceived of predominantly from an economic point of view, privileging an understanding of land as a means of production. This productivist point of view is but one of the many meanings ascribed to land, especially

manner in which land can be reclaimed in reparation should be at the center of whatever TJ process they undertake. Indeed, the juridical separation of the person (subject) and the property (object) obscures the different kinds of relations that private property may be understood to legitimize, and when the powers and rights of a landowner over land are regulated, even when they take account of their possible social significance, the question of what is being repaired and why we are repairing it is not taken into consideration.[46]

5. CONCLUSIONS

The previous reflections presented some of the problems inherent to the paradigmatic model of reparation based on the principle of *restitutio in integrum*,[47] in relation to four aspects of the process as described below:

(i) The emphasis on re-establishing the rule of law to reach peace and the restoration of rights tends to privilege a legal and procedural dimension to

---

for *campesinos*, for whom land is part of their identity and their understanding of a full and rich life.

46 In the Colombian case, those who have the right to land restitution are people who can prove that they previously had the rights to a property, be it because they held title to it or because they can demonstrate that they possessed, occupied, or productively used the land. Unless the transfer or acquisition of land titles was unjust, i.e. illegal, the legality of the land property is not challenged or questioned. However, in relation to the problem that I am raising here, two concerns arise: (i) What happens to those *campesinos* who are unable to prove either titles or possession, occupation, or productive use for five years, but whose way of life and sustenance have been fundamentally linked to rural land throughout their entire lives, albeit not to any particular piece of land? This situation is very widespread in the context of the long period during which forced and violent displacement has taken place in Colombia. (ii) Since damage is thought of as the dispossession of property external to and different from the subject, the reparation of this damage is thought of as the restitution of that property. However, its meaning, use and enjoyment may depend on other things, including some things related to what has been identified as the dominion of the subject over him or herself, including his or her life plans, expectations, and freedom. In relation to such matters, it should be pointed out that many *campesinos* have continually had to move from place to place due to the conflict, and have never been incorporated into the juridical category of those with property rights, i.e. those owning, in possession of, or occupying land – the stipulated criteria for the restitution of property rights – leaving these *campesinos* at a disadvantage. Others may be categorized as victims of land dispossession and thus demand restitution, and they may even possess property titles, but this does not mean that they will escape from their precarious living conditions – because their legal freedoms, powers, capacities, and ability to make use of mechanisms to demand respect for the rights that are recovered along with their property rights are mere words. In addition, the restitution of land property may not contribute to the reparation of damage to some victims, i.e those for whom their land property has lost the meaning that it once had and no longer plays a role in their life plans or their conceptions of a good life.

47 This model is centered on the re-establishment and institutional guarantee of victims' rights and their genuine enjoyment based on the establishment of the rule of law, the end of

transition that presupposes a political community, a "we", as well as defined rules of the game in a context where these are, by definition, in crisis. Establishing a universally-applicable procedural perspective obscures the particularities of each case and does not take account of the difficulties of translating changed juridical normativity into changes in the lives of citizens and their social, economic, and cultural relations.

(ii) Reparation seeks to redress exceptional damage of a particular nature affecting a specific type of victim, and differentiates them from forms of damage and victims that the juridical order deems to have arisen from contexts of social normality. The restitution of such rights, understood as the freedom, power, capacity and authority to act in a juridical context, relates to damage to a person and also to external means and objects separate and distinguishable from that person but nonetheless necessary for the accomplishment of his or her personal goals. Based on this understanding of reparation, when the damage has been suffered to those means or to property, such as land in the case of forced dispossession and displacement, the restitution of rights is conceived of as a way of repairing the lost dominion over those objects, which are external to and distinguishable from the subject. This restitution takes place under criteria established that relate to that dominion but that do not examine presuppositions that link the primary dominion of a person over him or herself with that person's secondary dominion over external objects. This link between primary and secondary restitution should be examined, since in some cases, simply restoring victims to the conditions under which they lived before the conflict may be questionable, given that in some cases such conditions may have been miserable.

(iii) The specific kind of victim who is recognized as a subject for reparation in a transition period is one who has suffered a particular kind of damage whose gravity is considered different than other kinds of damage that may occur in normal contexts. In an ongoing transitional justice process, we confront widespread and systematic violations of human rights that call out for urgent reparation. In cases of forced dispossession and displacement, attention is paid to the conditions under which damage took place, such as an armed conflict for example, but excludes other conditions such as structural poverty or inequality that may be endemic to the society. Thus, the recognition of certain kinds of victims and determination that damage suffered by them will be repaired during the transition is based on a relatively limited range of perceived injustices to be

hostilities, and the elimination of structural violence, implying guarantees of non-repetition of the violent conflict and the violation of their rights.

corrected. This excludes other forms of injustice that may also be related to the violent past and that may have produced similarly prejudicial impacts on the lives of people who do not fit the accepted category of victim. In the case of victims of forced dispossession and displacement, a specific kind of injury to their property rights is recognized and deemed worthy of redress, but no concern is given to the victimization of others who never owned property. Under this approach to reparation, the restitution of property rights is intended to correct past injuries, however, it also restores property ownership without concern for the way that the present and future lives of people are affected when they are dispossessed of the means necessary to achieve their goals.

(iv) When applied to the restitution of rights to victims of land dispossession and forced displacement, this approach to reparation tends to consider land as a good over which dominion is established through property rights, and the restitution of dominion is supported by the juridical recognition of a previously held right that was violated. However, under conditions of structural injustice, poverty, and inequality a central contributing factor to the prior conflict may have been the unequal distribution of land to begin with. Thus to presume that land is nothing more than property external to the subject and that dominion over it should be established and protected by pre-existing juridical orders avoids any consideration of how those property rights are justified, or how property is socially and culturally constructed.

Public discussion is in theory fundamental to the construction and strengthening of an inclusive democracy. However, the problems discussed above indicate that the conception of justice that underlies reparation, with its original principle of *restitutio in integrum* as adapted to the restitution of rights, *a priori* excludes from that public discussion certain aspects of the damage that victims have suffered and the criteria for reparation. This entails a certain assumption about what is and is not disputable and negotiable in transitional justice processes that is far from neutral and depoliticizes all that it excludes. In the case of a program focused on land restitution, the question of who has the right to land and on what basis such rights can be established is excluded from that public discussion, leaving existing juridical determinations in the balance.[48]

[48] This is not something that only happens in relation to reparation, but rather points in general to the model of transitional justice. In this regard, Emilios Christodoulidis and Scott Veitch, this time in relation to the issue of reconciliation, responsibility and memory in South Africa in 1994, affirm that reference to the economic struggle was eliminated from the political register of transition, which allowed the survival of a system of deeply racialized economic exploitation that made the construction of a common future impossible: "What conditions are assumed as negotiable and what not, and how are the boundaries drawn between what is

References

Aguilar, B. (2020) "Vidas Dañadas y Sentidos de la Tierra La Reparación a Victimas Campesinas Desde el Enfoque de las Capacidades" PhD Thesis, University of Tilburg.

Amnistía Internacional (2012). "Colombia: La Ley de Víctimas y de Restitución de Tierras. Análisis de Amnistía Internacional."

Carrillo, A. (2006). "Justice in Context: The Relevance of Inter-American Human Rights Law and Practice to Repairing the Past" in P. de Greiff (ed.), *The Handbook of Reparations*. Oxford: Oxford University Press.

Christodoulidis, E. and S. Veitch (2008). "Reconciliation as Surrender: Configurations of Responsibility and Memory" in Fr. Du Bois and A. Du Bois-Pedain (eds.), *Justice and Reconciliation in Post-Apartheid South Africa*. Cambridge: Cambridge University Press, 9–36.

De Greiff, P. (2006a) "Justice and Reparations" in P. de Greiff (ed.), *The Handbook of Reparations*, New York: Oxford University Press, 451–477.

—— (ed) (2006b) *The Handbook of Reparations*. New York: Oxford University Press.

—— (2011) "Algunas Reflexiones Acerca Del Desarrollo de La Justicia Transicional" in *Anuario de Derechos Humanos*, 7: 17–36.

Du Bois, Fr. (2008). "Reparations and the Forms of Justice" in Fr. Du Bois and A. du Bois-Pedain (eds.), *Justice and Reconciliation in Post-Apartheid South Africa*. Cambridge: Cambridge University Press, 116–143.

Elster, J. and Zidenwerg, E. (2006) *Rendición de Cuentas: La Justicia Transicional En Perspectiva Histórica*. Buenos Aires: Katz Editores.

Galtung, J. (1998) *Tras La Violencia, 3R: Reconstrucción, Reconciliación y Resolución. Afrontando Los Efectos Visibles e Invisibles de La Guerra y La Violencia*. Bilbao: Gernika Gogoratuz.

Hohfeld, W.N. (2004) *Conceptos Jurídicos Fundamentales*. 1st edn. México: Distribuciones Fontamara.

taken as politically contestable, and what is deemed beyond the reach of politics? These are of course deeply political questions. But when the boundary between politics and economics is drawn in a particular way, they quickly become de-politicized. ... To put it in terms of 'constituencies', we might observe that whilst the political constituency is democratized, the economic constituency is not. Responsibility for the latter is hived off to the market, in such way that suffering consequent on economic immiserisation does not register as a matter of political choice." "This leads to a key observation concerning the way in which this distinction was established not only by, but as the law. That is, the demarcation between what contestable within a transitional politics of reconciliation is, and what is beyond such contestation, was put in place with respect to the central issues of property, land and sovereignty through legal means in the 1993 'transitional' Constitution." "The constitutionalization of rights, even rights deemed allegedly progressive, sealed them off from political, or to be precise, democratic contestation by entrenching them as only judicially reviewable. In this way property rights, land rights and the rights of sovereignty became 'guaranteed' as the rules of the game according to which any further politics had to be played, rules which themselves were taken as immune from immediate political contestation. And hence the categorization of resources, benefits or harms in legal terms, narrowed the range of permissible forms of dissensus by setting limitations on who or what is responsible for what." (Christodoulidis and Veitch 2008, 19–20).

International Center for Transitional Justice (2015) "What is Transitional Justice?" ICTJ Factsheets. https://www.ictj.org/sites/default/files/ICTJ-Global-Transitional-Justice-2009-English.pdf.

"Ley de Víctimas y Restitución de Tierras." (2015). http://www.unidadvictimas.gov.co/normatividad/LEY+DE+VICTIMAS.pdf. http://www.centrodememoriahistorica.gov.co/micrositios/caminosParaLaMemoria/descargables/ley1448.pdf.

Lid, K.A. (2012) "La Restitución de La Tierra en la Justicia Transicional: Retos y Experiencias. El Caso de Colombia" in M. Bergsmo, C. Rodríguez, P. Kalmanovitz, and M.P. Saffon (eds), *Justicia Distributiva en Sociedades en Transición*. Oslo: Torkel Opsahl Academic ePublisher & Peace Research Institute Oslo (PRIO), 193–231.

Mani, R. (2002) *Beyond Retribution. Seeking Justice in the Shadows of War*. Cambridge: Polity Press.

—— (2005) "Reparation as a Component of Transitional Justice" in K. De Feyter, S. Parmentier, M. Bossuyt and P. Lemmens (eds), *Out of the Ashes. Reparations for Victims of Gross and Systematic Human Rights Violations*. Antwerpen: Intersentia, 53–82.

Martínez Cortes, P. (2013) "Ley de Víctimas y Restitución de Tierras en Colombia en Contexto. Un Análisis de Las Contradicciones Entre el Modelo Agrario y La Reparación a Las Víctimas" Amsterdam: Transnational Institute. https://www.tni.org/files/download/martinez-victims-law-web.pdf.

Moreno, M. (2014) *En Diciembre Llegaban Las Brisas*. Bogotá: Alfaguara.

Rincón, T. (2010) *Verdad, Justicia y Reparación. La Justicia de La Justicia Transicional*. Bogotá: Universidad del Rosario.

Shelly, R. (2007) "The Discourse Concept of the Rule of Law and Democracy" in *Southern Cross University Law Review* 11: 59–80.

Teitel, R. (2000) *Transitional Justice*. New York: Oxford University Press.

—— (2003) "Transitional Justice Genealogy" *Harvard Human Rights Journal* **16**: 69–94.

UN Security Council (2004) "The Rule of Law and Transitional Justice in Conflict and Post-Conflict Societies Report of the Secretary-General Summary." http://www.un.org/es/comun/docs/index.asp?symbol=S/2004/616&referer=http://www.un.org/es/sc/documents/sgreports/2004.shtml&Lang=E.

Uprimny, R. and D. Guzmán (2010) "En Búsqueda de Un Concepto Transformador y Participativo Para Las Reparaciones En Contextos Transicionales" in *Revista Colombiana de Derecho Internacional* 17: 231–286.

Van Boven, Th. (1997) "Revised Set of Basic Principles and Guidelines on the Right to Reparation for Victims of [Gross] Violations of Human Rights and International Humanitarian Law".

—— (2010) "The United Nations Basic Principles and Guidelines on the Right to a Remedy and Reparation for Victims of Gross Violations of International Human Rights Law and Serious Violations of International Humanitarian Law." *United Nations Audiovisual Library of International Law*, 1–7.

Walker, M.U. (2016) "Transformative Reparations? A Critical Look at a Current Trend in Thinking about Gender-Just Reparations" in *International Journal of Transitional Justice* 10 (December 2015): 108–125.

CHAPTER 9

PROBLEMS AND INCONSISTENCIES IN THE PROTECTION OF WOMEN IN THE COLOMBIAN LAND RESTITUTION PROCESS

Lina M. Céspedes Báez

1. INTRODUCTION

This contribution to a book about restoration in the aftermath of political violence is a snapshot of a particular moment in the quest for truth, justice, and reparation for victims in the context of the Colombian armed conflict. It aims to explore the promises and shortcomings of restorative justice from a feminist legal standpoint through the examination of the introduction of the gender perspective in the land restitution scheme that the Colombian state put in place in 2011. In this sense, it explores the intersection between law, as a means to achieve accountability, land tenure, as the embodiment of the most salient form of property, and women, as a category minted to redress discrimination and violence against a particular group. It is based on research that the author undertook for a doctoral degree in law and speaks to a longstanding interest in the interplay between gender, armed conflict, and property. It relies on a reading and examination of more than one hundred land restitution cases that were brought in the two years (2012–2014) that followed the establishment of the land restitution process in the country. This material can be considered pivotal, since it sheds light on the difficult encounter between private and public law in transitional justice that occurs in the process of offering redress to victims related to the armed conflict.

The strategy of this chapter is to illustrate this challenging interaction between these two areas of law and their different rationales and logics, and in so doing bring to the fore the legal mandate that introduced a gender dimension in the adjudication of Colombian land restitution claims. It asks whether that dimension has been operative in the concrete resolution of the cases that land restitution judges and tribunals have had to decide. Answering this question is essential for determining whether the lines of legal action that have been implemented by a society entrenched in conflict to achieve certain distributive justice goals and to acknowledge the particular predicament of certain groups like women are germane, pertinent, and effective.

Beginning in the late 1990s, the three most influential Colombian women's rights NGOs, Casa de la Mujer, Corporación Sisma Mujer, and Corporación Humanas, have been producing knowledge about women in the context of the Colombian armed conflict. Their documentation and study of the fate of women in this setting have been key to *genderizing* understandings of the conflict, training state officials and the general public on women's rights, and to positioning themselves as strategic actors/experts in national and international arenas. Their narratives about women in conflict have been rooted in the emergence and consolidation of sexual violence as the paradigmatic gender-based crime in international public law that have been spurred by radical feminists worldwide.[1] Their discourse has been the basis for drawing a hegemonic legal subjectivity for women in the Colombian conflict ingrained in bodily and psychosocial damage.

While this legal subjectivity has played an essential role in construing women in conflict as a differentiated group in need of affirmative action from legislation and public policy, it has also fostered a partial approach to their predicament in this context and legal regulation that is not contributing effectively to the complete eradication of violence and discrimination against them. One of the most salient examples is the introduction and operationalization of the differential approach for women in Law 1448's hybrid land restitution process.[2] This instance is of the utmost interest because it demonstrates how a

---

1 Halley (2009); Miller (2004); Engle (2005); Céspedes-Báez (2017).

2 Ley 1448 de 2011, *por la cual se dictan medidas de atención, asistencia y reparación integral a las víctimas del conflicto armado interno y se dictan otras disposiciones*, Diario Oficial Año CXLVII No. 48.096, Bogotá, D.C., viernes, 10 de junio de 2011.

category structured around a public law issue, such as sexual violence in armed conflict, is not easily adaptable to a transitional justice scheme that depends on private law categories to a great extent. It shows how a particular narrative about women in conflict that is entrenched in international and national *public law* was turned into a normative category to redress damages that are not related to the body and mind, and that are mostly readable through *private law* categories.

This study also contributes to the identification and better understanding of the problematic encounter between private and public law and their amalgamation in a transitional justice hybrid judicial process. Armed conflict is not only seen in terms of the heinous crimes committed during it but also in terms of the daily undermining of the bases for property, contracts, and liability. Adequate redress for the consequences of armed conflict will have to consider the different levels at which individuals' lives were impacted. That will entail designing transitional justice schemes that aim to right private and public law wrongs and that thoroughly comprehend the "*immanent rationality*"[3] of each of these fields of law, to prevent incoherence, erratic adjudication, and even stagnation.

Based on an examination of 14 land restitution cases that were singled out by this author from the database built while doing dissertation research, the contention in this chapter is that there was evidence to suggest that the mainstream understanding of the experience of women in the Colombian armed conflict between the late 1990s and 2000s was incapable of effectively *genderizing* the land restitution process in the period under examination. Analysis of these cases indicates that the legal subjectivity of women that emerged during these years was not functional in the litigation of real-property-related claims. Its public law breadth did not offer clear guidance to adjudicate on Law 1448's land restitution cases in which women were either claimants and/or "opponents" (i.e. defendants) of real property rights. Its rhetoric of victimhood based on the knowledge acquired through the documentation of sexual violence was unfit to identify and describe in precise legal terms the issue of women's access to, control of and recovery of property in the context of the Colombian conflict.

This chapter proceeds as follows: Section 2 offers a brief overview of the emergence of a legal category in Colombia, namely "*women in conflict*", that is based on the international public law narrative of sexual violence against women in the context of armed conflict. Section 3 explores the land restitution process as an instance in which private and public law meet and the resulting difficulties in defining the relationship between both rationales. Section 4 examines how the introduction of the public law category of *women in conflict*,

---

[3] Weinrib (2012), 4–5, 19, 206–214.

drawn from radical feminist readings of the predicament of women in conflict settings, interplayed with private law categories in the adjudication of specific cases. The final section outlines some conclusions and issues for further research.

2. WOMEN IN CONFLICT: A NORMATIVE CATEGORY

The Colombian armed conflict escalated in the 1990s. Drug trafficking and administrative decentralization in the country, among other factors, contributed to the strengthening of guerrillas and paramilitary groups.[4] Attacks on civilian populations increasingly became a means by which both groups could attain territorial and strategic control.[5] Massacres[6] were a favored tactic to achieve that end, especially for paramilitary groups.[7]

Amidst increasing violence and forced displacement, the Colombian women's movement faced the challenge of tuning its agenda and translating women's experiences in conflict into the language of rights and gender. With recent experience in the constitution-making process of the late 1980s, the women's movement had tailored a peacetime agenda that was based on the premise of equal civil and political rights for men and women.[8] The intensification of

---

4 Pécaut (2004), 73–102; Martínez and Ávila (2010).

5 Strategic and territorial control seek the domination of a territory without paying heed to popular adherence of the population settled in that location. The former refers to controlling territories' political, military, and economic advantages. The latter pertains to the domination of territories and their populations through coercion or fear in order to involve them in the achievement of the oppressor's aims or at least to prevent their interference with them (Pécaut (2002) 27–34; Martínez and Ávila (2010) 122–123).

6 The National Center of Historic Memory defines massacre as "the intentional killing of four or more defenseless persons in the same temporal and locational circumstances, and during which violence is displayed publicly" (author's translation from Spanish). Centro Nacional de Memoria Histórica. "Bases de datos ¡Basta ya!", http://www.centrodememoriahistorica.gov.co/micrositios/informeGeneral/basesDatos.html. It is worthwhile to note that "massacre" is not a legal concept and that its definition varies nationally and internationally, especially when it is necessary to define the number of necessary killings (in Céspedes et. al. (2014) my co-authors and I discussed the conceptual downsides of using the concept of massacre as a category of analysis in the investigation of sexual violence in Colombia). The equivocal concept of massacre has affected specifically the accurate gathering of data in Colombia.

7 According to the Center of Historic Memory's database, between 1997 and 2005, paramilitaries committed 782 massacres, unidentified armed groups 176, guerrillas 172, and the public forces 44 approximately, making a total of 1174 reported massacres for this period. These figures stand in contrast to 695 massacres reported between 1980 and 1996, and illustrate the transformation the armed conflict experienced after different paramilitary groups confederated and implemented their counterinsurgent strategy, and guerrillas tried to reach different regions and sources of power and income. Bases De Datos ¡Basta Ya!", http://www.centrodememoriahistorica.gov.co/micrositios/informeGeneral/basesDatos.html.

8 Quintero (2005).

the conflict required them to modify their platform to maintain the political space they had carved out with great effort.[9] The Colombian public and state spheres were about to make the armed conflict their main topic of interlocution, a source of specialized knowledge, and an avenue to international arenas and funding.

During the 2000s, the most visible women's rights NGOs outlined and honed legal arguments to make a case for the disproportionate and differential impact that the armed conflict was imposing on women. To do so, they developed what is here called the *code of disproportion*:[10] a particular narrative of what happens to women in this context based on a radical feminist reading of the causes of violence and discrimination against women. Radical feminism understands that women's disadvantaged position vis-à-vis men emerges from patriarchy, a power that creates the two sexes (gender),[11] organizes the unequal relation between them through the imposition of mandatory heterosexuality, and maintains this imbalanced distribution of entitlements through sexual violence or the threat of it.[12] This feminist trend became hegemonic in international public law after the international ad-hoc tribunals for the former Yugoslavia and Rwanda, and the Rome Statute of the International Criminal Court adopted it to make women visible in conflict settings.[13]

This *code of disproportion* was the device that was needed to make women stand out in an internal conflict that impacted both men and women, irrespective of their sex. Massacres, forced displacement, enforced disappearances, and homicides were not easily read through a gender-based lens. The *code*, sketched throughout the 2000s in several reports, enabled this reading by establishing the following:[14] (i) women have been subjected to historical discrimination, in

---

9 Wills (2007), 219–238.

10 Céspedes-Báez (2017), 305.

11 The term *gender* in this chapter refers to Catharine MacKinnon's understanding of it, where gender is not understood as difference but rather as the creation of hierarchies through the production of two sexes and mandatory heterosexuality. Therefore, gender means sexual domination; sexuality is about power of men over women; and sexual violence, particularly rape, and/or the threat of sexual violence, is the main device to maintain this order. MacKinnon (1982) 517, 529. MacKinnon (1991), chapters 6 and 7. MacKinnon (1987), 5–10; 40–45. This author does not personally share this notion of gender, but it is nevertheless used here in reflection of the great influence it had in the 1990s and early 2000s in the advocacy and legal work that ultimately positioned sexual violence against women in conflict in international public law as an urgent and serious issue. Halley, Kotiswaran, Shamir and Thomas (2006). Halley (2009). It is acknowledged that there are different notions of gender at play in the Colombian armed conflict, such as the one that includes violence against lesbian, gay, bisexual, transsexual and intersex people, and that the very definition of gender in Colombia is a site for contestation and debate.

12 MacKinnon (1982), 517, 529; (1987), 5–10; (1991), Chapters 6 and 7.

13 Halley (2009).

14 Corporación Sisma Mujer along with Confluencia Nacional de Redes Mujeres in 2001 drafted a document that would lay down the foundations of the *code of disproportion*: "Documento

the sense that they have always been on the losers' side vis-à-vis men in the game of society; (ii) this has led to a lack of recognition of their rights and entitlements, as well as their exclusion, and violence; (iii) males are not only the winners of this social game; they are also the agents of violence against women in the form of government representatives and officials, armed group members, civilians, and relatives; (iv) discrimination is deployed through violence against women, and violence against women is discrimination, the most evident illustration of this symbiosis being sexual violence, which affects women differentially and disproportionately; and (v) this precarious situation is the same in peace and wartime, but exacerbated during the latter.

In 2008, through Order 092 of 2008 (Auto 092/98), the Constitutional Court turned the *code* into the basis for a legal identity and category to allocate rights in the context of conflict. The Court issued this order as part of the follow-up process for Decision T-025 of 2004, in which the Colombian state was held accountable for its lack of compliance with internally displaced people's (IDPs) fundamental rights. The extent of the state's resistance to fulfilling its obligations led the Court itself to monitor in detail the government's steps to implement the T-025 orders. Hearings in which the government was confronted by IDPs, international organizations, activists, and NGOs became the Court's favored strategy for closely inspecting the implementation of its decision.

Order 092 was in part the outcome of pressure that influential Colombian women's rights NGOs put on the Court through advocacy and report production. Influential women's rights NGOs like Sisma Mujer filed information with the Court to contribute to T-025's follow-up process,[15] and prepared and attended when the Constitutional Court extended an invitation to hold a hearing on the subject along with other organizations such as Casa de la Mujer. This hearing was a unique opportunity for them to deliver in person the information and theses – particularly the *code of disproportion* – which they had honed over the previous seven years, to the Court, the government, and the general public.

Marco Conceptual", http://webs.uvigo.es/pmayobre/textos/cecilia/documento_marco_conceptual.pdf. In the years that followed, this and other influential NGOs, such as Casa de la Mujer and Corporación Humanas, and the coalitions in which they participated, such as the Mesa de Mujer y Conflicto and Mesa de Seguimiento al Auto 092 – Anexo Reservado, would polish and give traction to this rationale. To get a sense of the evolution of the *code of disproportion* see Mesa de Trabajo Mujer y Conflicto Armado (2003); Mesa de Trabajo Mujer y Conflicto Armado (2005); (2009); (2010); Corporación Sisma Mujer (2007); (2009); Corporación Humanas – Centro Regional de Derechos Humanos y Justicia de Género (2009); Mesa de Seguimiento al Auto 092 de 2008 – Anexo Reservado (2009); (2010).

15 Céspedes-Báez (2014).

Order 092 revolved around sexual violence. Even though the decision touched on other topics, such as forced disappearance, land seizure and loss, and political participation, the Constitutional Court legally operationalized the *code* by emphasizing sexual violence. To do so, it (i) openly underscored the seriousness and generalization of that conduct, falling short of stating that sexual violence in conflict amounts to a crime against humanity; (ii) outlined its own categorization of strategic uses and objectives for sexual violence in the Colombian conflict; (iii) devoted a significant part of its decision to proving this assertion; and (iv) collected all the cases of sexual violence that had been reported to the Court in a Confidential Annex (*Anexo Reservado*) and ordered the Attorney General's Office to investigate them.

Drawing on the *code*, the Constitutional Court crafted the "*women in conflict*" category that contained within it a particular narrative about sexual violence, derived from radical feminism. It crafted a legal identity to which to allocate rights, thereby creating a legal "script" to which real women in conflict had to conform to express their claims to the Colombian state. The pervasive nature of this reading and its contribution to halting any broader analysis of the situation of women in the context of the Colombian conflict is evident when one examines the discussion of the Bill that was going to become Law 1448 of 2011. Even though this piece of legislation aimed at offering redress for a wide array of harms related to armed conflict, its gender approach remained firmly anchored to sexual violence as the paradigmatic gender-based crime, and introduced a one-sided category into the land restitution process that did not fully grasp the complexity of women's lives. Through this category it is almost impossible to see women as entrepreneurs or productive peasants since its logic and, therefore, its deployment, is so heavily focused on their victimization.

3. THE COLOMBIAN LAND RESTITUTION PROCESS, A CASE OF HYBRIDIZATION

On 10 June 2011, the Colombian Congress passed Law 1448, "by which measures for attention, assistance, and integral reparation of victims of the internal armed conflict are enacted."[16] This piece of legislation, commonly known as the "Victims and Land Restitution Law" (*Ley de Victimas y Restitución de Tierras*), was a turning point in the way in which the Colombian state approached the internal armed conflict. Leaving behind legal schemes centered on illegal armed groups' demobilization, the government, Congress, civil society and

16 Above, n. 2 (author's translation from Spanish).

international organizations worked towards drafting and sanctioning a body of law aimed at redress for victims of armed-conflict-related harms.[17] Law 1448 is grounded on more than a decade of knowledge that different stakeholders had built up on the impact of armed conflict on the civilian population. The discussion, approval, and content of this law summarized common understandings of the time about the victims and harms generated by Colombian internal armed conflict.

Forced displacement and loss of land had been at the forefront of analyses of the conflict since at least the late 1990s and early 2000s.[18] It took a decade to translate those insights into a specific legal mechanism that aimed to correct land seizure and forced abandonment.[19] The final product was the establishment of a land restitution process through Law 1448, a hybrid scheme that combines private and public law concepts, rationales and objectives. Its very existence illustrates the difficult encounter between human rights and private law,[20] and it exemplifies the complexity of the issues that are at play whenever private law is employed to redress gross human rights violations and provide closure to armed conflict. The inclusion of the *women in conflict* category is just one of the various expressions of that imbrication.

The Victims and Land Restitution Law and various congressional debates related to it provide scarce guidance on how to integrate the institutions of private and public law into one transitional justice scheme.[21] Law 1448's procedure establishes causes of action unlike any previous other and its specific assemblage from among pre-existing private and public categories, rules and principles is far from clear. At the time of writing, there is an ongoing discussion in Colombia on the matter, since its definition will guide future interpretation and implementation of Law 1448. Some scholars have drawn parallels between the land restitution process and *tutela*, the constitutional action to enforce fundamental rights, such as due process, privacy, and equality.[22] The Constitutional Court, the Supreme Court, and land restitution judges and tribunals have struggled

---

17 Céspedes-Báez (2012).

18 Consultoría para los Derechos Humanos y el Desplazamiento – CODHES (1999); Women's Commission for Refugee Women and Children (1999); Meertens (2000); Corporación Sisma Mujer (2006); Meertens (2006).

19 Government reluctance, paired with a lack of political momentum, impeded any serious effort to design and implement such a mechanism. The government of President Álvaro Uribe Vélez (2002–2010) instead privileged the demobilization of paramilitary structures when confronting the internal armed conflict.

20 Paraphrasing Horatia Muir Watt, human rights language has become the "most disruptive common vocabulary that can be mobilized today." Muir Watt (2014).

21 Congreso de la República de Colombia, *Gaceta Del Congreso no. 107, 170, 213, 692, 1004* of 2010; Congreso de la República de Colombia, *Gaceta Del Congreso no. 63, 88, 116, 247, 253, 338, 339, 340, 469, 483, 1139* of 2011.

22 Quinche et al. (2015).

to define how deep the difference is between land restitution and private law causes of action and where they converge.[23]

Private and public law are two distinct areas of law. Each of them has its own "*immanent rationality*" that uses particular "concepts", "institutional settings", and "modes of reasoning".[24] The uniqueness of these features arises from the specificity of the legal subjects and situations that each of them regulates. Private law is concerned with placing private parties on equal footing and dealing with their transactions and the harms that they suffer at each other's hands. In this sense, concepts such as tortfeasor, third-party bona fide purchaser, and possessor are intelligible only within this domain. Causes of action and litigation based on the rights and obligations attached to those private law legal subjects are the institutional settings that guarantee equality between the parties and rectify imbalances. Corrective justice is the backbone of this structure and informs its mode of reasoning.[25]

Public law, in this case embodied in human rights law, is understood differently, as the ordering of the polity's common good and the site of substantive equality. It is concerned with disparities of individuals' experiences in political, economic and social landscapes, and it draws its fundamental insights from what it understands to be the primary location of inequality: the relation between the state and its citizenry. To grasp the full meaning of this imbalance and to provide avenues to remedy it, human rights law thus relies on a logic of distributive justice.[26]

Hybrid judicial processes are those that combine one or more of the elements of the immanent rationalities of private and public law. Such encounters could involve either the instrumentalization of one field to the benefit of the other, or an interaction in which both remain independent but resort to the other to improve outcomes.[27] From the outset, therefore, the land restitution process facilitated an encounter between private and public. Law 1448 established a cause of action for owners and possessors of plots, occupants of

---

23 Corte Suprema de Justicia, Sala de Casación Civil, Radicación no. 11001020300020140285100, enero 14 de 2015. *T-679* (Corte Constitucional de Colombia 2015); *T-244*, (Corte Constitucional de Colombia 2016); *C-330* (Corte Constitucional de Colombia 2016); Juzgado Primero Civil del Circuito Especializado en Restitución de Tierras de Guadalajara de Buga, *Junio 27 De 2013, Rad. 20120004100* (2013); Tribunal Superior del Distrito Judicial de Bogotá, Sala Civil Especializada en Restitución de Tierras, *Agosto 26 De 2013, Rad. 2012-00088* (2013); Ministerio de Agricultura y Desarrollo Rural (2012); Presidencia de la República de Colombia (2015).

24 Weinrib (2012), 5, 16, 206–214.

25 Weinrib (2012), 5, 18–19, 114, 207–231; Barnard-Naudé (2013); du Bois (2013).

26 Ibid. Barnard-Naudé (2013) and du Bois (2013).

27 Drawing on du Bois' insights, one can say the former refers to what is called "*horizontal application*" and the former to "*indirect horizontal application*". "*Vertical application*" endorses the total independence of these fields of law. Ibid.

wastelands (*baldíos*), and their spouses or domestic partners who were living with them at the time of the displacement,[28] to legally and materially recover their seized or forcibly abandoned land through an expedited administrative and judicial procedure with lenient rules of evidence that favored them.[29] The rules of this process draw on and followed private law and transitional justice standards, since it pertains to property, contracts, and liability in the context of conflict. The process pursues private and public law goals, respectively: the clarification and formalization of land tenure through a contentious judicial proceeding between two parties, and the reparation of armed conflict wrongs through the deployment of public law insights in the particular adjudication process.

Even though Law 1448 and its regulatory decrees do not make any substantial mention of the Civil or Commerce Codes or establish them as sources of complementary regulation, it is contended here that private law is nevertheless the main foundation of the land restitution process. This is because this area of law provides the content and breadth of key concepts that the process uses, such as property, ownership, and possession, and it lays out the basic interplay between rights, obligations, damage, and redress among private parties.[30] The presence of public law, however, is also intensely felt through the attenuation of private law rules via the inclusion of certain public law principles, such as the differential perspective, and legal assumptions (described below).

The differential perspective established in Article 13 of Law 1448 mandates that the heightened risks that certain groups – such as women, children, and people with disabilities, among others – experience in conflict must be taken into account when applying this body of law. The meaning of *women* in that provision does not refer to any lay definition of ordinary language but to a very specific notion that women's rights NGOs and the Constitutional Court had crafted in previous years to genderize the conflict in a specific way. "*Women*", in this sense, encompasses a legal subject whose particularity resides not only

---

28 Although that is the letter of the law, it is nevertheless possible to find at least one case in which that rule was not followed and where the tribunal instead decided to restitute land rights to the woman who was the female domestic partner of the beneficiary of the judicial decision at the time of the forced displacement as well as to his current domestic partner: Juzgado Primero Civil del Circuito Especializado en Restitución de Tierras de Villavicencio, *Abril 22 De 2013, Rad. 50001-31-21-001-2012-00111-00* (2013). This case will be analyzed in detail later in this chapter.

29 According to Law 1448, a "land seizure" takes place when somebody takes advantage of the context of violence and acquires real rights over a plot of land through contracts, administrative acts, judicial decisions, the perpetration of crimes, or by simply taking it over. "Forced abandonment" happens when the claimant leaves her or his land due to violence related to the conflict. Forced abandonment is always present in land seizure, but not all events of forced abandonment inevitably result in land seizure.

30 Weinrib (2012), 9–10.

in its sex but in its interrelation to men through discrimination and violence. In this sense, it is a relational concept that necessitates *men* as its counterpart, and a very precise radical feminist narrative to explain why the latter discriminates and exerts violence against the former.[31]

Two main assumptions sustain the land restitution proceedings: (i) that claimants are defenseless and act in good faith; and (ii) that opponents act correlatively in bad faith and have a greater capacity to fare successfully in the judicial process vis-à-vis claimants. These assumptions stem from the notion that this process was primarily intended to address crystal clear cases in which claimants were IDPs who had a real right (right *in rem*), or a legitimate expectation to acquire it, over the land they asked in restitution, and that opponents were either armed conflict criminals who had seized it, or were bystanders who had taken advantage of the conflict to acquire rights over abandoned plots.[32] Land restitution claimants enjoyed a lenient burden of proof along with correlated legal and conclusive presumptions,[33] while "second occupants" or opponents were subjected to a more stringent burden of proof.[34]

In summary, Law 1448 denies the possession of land by opponents,[35] obliges its restitution, and recognizes compensation only to those opponents who can prove that they meet a stringent "good faith with no fault" (*buena fe exenta de culpa*) standard of care. This demand requires proof not only that the opponent consciously acted correctly but also that he or she took the necessary steps to avoid any error or fault, and that any other skillful person in the same position could have made the same mistake.[36] This body of law is an outcome of the hybrid nature of the land restitution process that pursues both corrective and distributive justice goals.

31 Congreso de la República de Colombia, *Gaceta Del Congreso no. 865*, 2010.

32 Congreso de la República de Colombia, *Gaceta Del Congreso no. 865* of 2010 pp. 17–18; Congreso de la República de Colombia, *Gaceta Del Congreso no. 116* of 2011 pp. 35–36.

33 There are two types of presumptions in the Colombian legal system: Legal presumptions or *presunciones legales* (*praesumptio iuris tantum*), which are rebuttable, and conclusive presumptions or *presunciones de derecho* (*iure et de iure*) which are not.

34 In 2016, the Constitutional Court issued its decision C-330 on the issue of second occupants (*segundos ocupantes*) in the land restitution process. The issue at hand was the stringent standard of proof that second occupants have to meet if they want to protect their rights to land vis-à-vis claimants, especially when they are part of vulnerable groups, such as in the case of other armed-conflict-related victims who were forced to flee to other parts of the country and find new land to establish their homes. The Constitutional Court ordered land restitution judges and tribunals to take into account this vulnerability and the absence of any relation to the claimant's land loss on a case-by-case basis to make the standard of proof more flexible in such situations. It is important to note that the Constitutional Court underscored throughout its decision the hybrid nature of the land restitution process and noted that this feature poses serious challenges to its interpretation and implementation. *C-330* (Corte Constitucional de Colombia, 2016).

35 Below, n. 47.

36 Gómez Jiménez (2009); Torrado (2011).

The interplay between the introduction of the *women* category through the differential perspective and these two assumptions reinforced a static and overarching idea of women in conflict as victims of a patriarchal system rooted in sexual domination. In this sense, it paved the way for including an extraneous consideration in an adjudication process that was dominated by private law language and rationality.

4. THE GAP BETWEEN SEXUAL VIOLENCE AND THE LAND RESTITUTION PROCESS

Legal categories are pivotal in legal reasoning and litigation. They are devices that encapsulate legal knowledge, and provide guidance to resolve actual and potentially contentious issues. *Women in conflict* was structured using radical feminist understandings entrenched in international public law revolving primarily around sexual violence. It did not encompass any meaningful insight into women and the private law, or women and their access to, and control and recovery of rural real estate.

The fact that the most influential Colombian women's rights NGOs prioritized the documentation of sexual violence did not contribute to an in-depth analysis of the hurdles that women have faced in acquiring real property and the role that the conflict has played in that situation. Apart from pointing out how their relation to land was mediated through men and the implications that this state of affairs had in armed conflict, they did not develop a robust diagnosis of this issue as they had in the case of sexual violence.[37] Before the discussion on the Bill that would lead to Law 1448 started, the farthest that influential women's rights NGOs had gone in this analysis was to establish that there was a relationship between sexual violence and forced displacement, and therefore a correlation between sexual violence and land seizure and forced abandonment.[38] This imbrication paved the way for the identification of land-related harms suffered by women as direct or indirect consequences of sexual violence, and then and thereby explaining them in terms of how and why sexual violence takes place in conflict.

---

37 Corporación Sisma Mujer, (2008); (2009); (2011); Falcón (2008); Corporación Humanas – Centro Regional de Derechos Humanos y Justicia de Género (2009); Mesa de Trabajo Mujer y Conflicto Armad (2008); Mesa de Trabajo Mujer y Conflicto Armado (2003); Mesa de Seguimiento al Auto 092 de 2008 – Anexo Reservado (2009); Mesa de Trabajo Mujer y Conflicto Armado (2010); Mesa de Seguimiento al Auto 092 de 2008 – Anexo Reservado (2010).

38 Corporación Sisma Mujer, (2009); Mesa de Trabajo Mujer y Conflicto Armado (2009).

This focalization of knowledge about women in conflict enabled women's rights NGOs and activists to propose particular substantive and procedural provisions around sexual violence, such as rules of evidence, to facilitate the prosecution of sexual crimes. However, at the same time it impeded them from doing so for land restitution.[39] While they advocated for the introduction of specific articles to provide, among other things, access to abortion for women victims of sexual violence and HIV and STD tests, in the matter of land restitution their main call to Congress was for the recognition of women's right to land restitution as individuals and not as spouses and domestic partners. They did so without properly exploring the reasons why women have had such difficulty acquiring, controlling, and recovering real estate rights within a legal regime that has recognized the legal capacity of both sexes to enter into contracts and administer their property since Law 28 of 1932.[40]

Deeper research on the question of women and land would have shown, however, how the interpretation of evidence had been a key factor in the curtailment of women's access to property rights, just as happens in sexual violence prosecutions. An examination of how women had been faring in private law proceedings would have revealed the importance of testimony in the acquisition of property through possession and acquisitive prescription, and how certain forms of evidence were prone to gender biases. Since informality in rural land tenure is common, possession and occupation of wastelands have been the main available modes of acquisition of real estate rights for the peasant population.[41] Such knowledge would have proved strategically important for furthering peasant women's property rights.

---

39 It is also possible that aggregated legal knowledge increased the ability of women's rights NGOs to draft precise and operative proposals for the prosecution and redress of sexual violence. International public law and related prosecutions offered them a valuable source of causes of action and strategies in this subject. The Rome Statute of the ICC and its Rules of Procedure and Evidence were key in this matter. In the case of women and land, international public law does not have anything that is closely related to it apart from general calls to ensure women's access to land as a resource.

40 Corporación Sisma Mujer et al., "Declaratoria Conjunta De Las Organizaciones Sociales Sobre Aspectos Fundamentales Con Relación a Los Derechos De Las Mujeres Para Ser Tenidos En Cuenta En: El Trámite Legislativo Del Proyecto De Ley no. 107/10 Cámara – 213/10 Senado 'Por La Cual Se Dictan Medidas De Atención, Reparación Integral y Restitución De Tierras a Las Víctimas De Violaciones a Los Derechos Humanos e Infracciones Al Derecho Internacional Humanitario y Se Dictan Otras Disposiciones'"; Corporación Sisma Mujer et al., "Propuesta Conjunta De Las Organizaciones Sociales Sobre Aspectos Fundamentales Con Relación a Los Derechos De Las Mujeres Para Ser Tenidos En Cuenta En: El Trámite Legislativo Del Proyecto De Ley no. 107/10 Cámara – 213/10 Senado 'Por La Cual Se Dictan Medidas De Atención, Reparación Integral y Restitución De Tierras a Las Víctimas De Violaciones a Los Derechos Humanos e Infracciones Al Derecho Internacional Humanitario y Se Dictan Otras Disposiciones'".

41 According to the Ministry of Agriculture's Unit for Rural Agriculture Planning (*Unidad de Planificacion Rural Agropecuaria*), as of 2012 informality in land tenure affected 40% to 50% of rural lands; cf. Unidad de Planificación Rural Agropecuaria (2014).

An analysis of Supreme Court case law demonstrates that in order to succeed in acquiring property through possession and occupation the plaintiff has to produce robust testimony to prove not only that he or she dwells on and works the land (*corpus*), but also that he or she engages in those activities as an owner and not as a mere tenant (*animus domini or animus rem sibi habendi*).[42] In these cases, such testimony comes from third persons who narrate what they perceive. Gender bias might influence those perceptions. Men's activities could be more prone to be read as an expression of ownership, while women's could remain invisible or be read just as household chores, as expressions of mere tenancy or as ancillary to men's initiatives.[43]

Gender bias in private law proceedings is also evident in cases involving a declaration of de facto marital property between unmarried couples who started cohabiting before the Colombian state recognized domestic partnerships and civil unions in 1990. Since the legal system did not recognize the existence of those sentimental unions, the only avenue to resolve common property issues between the partners in case of death or separation was to resort to the regulation of de facto corporations (*sociedades de hecho*). This recourse, applied in Colombia for the first time in 1935, intended to offer women an effective way of claiming their share in property to which they had made contributions in order to acquire and/or increase their shared holdings that were usually held under men's names.[44]

However, to do so, women had to prove that they behaved like corporate partners, and not as significant others. In order to determine that there was a de facto corporation between them, women had to offer evidence showing that (i) there was a common enterprise between her partner and herself; (ii) they pursued profit; (iii) they considered themselves equals in this enterprise; (iv) the de facto corporation was not established to create or sustain the cohabitation, since that was against the law; and (v) the activities developed therein were different from the ones that usually spring out of life in common.[45] Women had a hard time proving all those premises, chiefly because they had to rely on the perceptions that other people, i.e. third parties and the judge, had of their activities. For that reason, they had to downplay their domestic

42 Corte Suprema de Justicia, Sala de Casación Civil, mayo 6 de 1953.

43 See for instance, Corte Suprema de Justicia, Sala de Casación Civil, agosto 28 de 1942; Corte Suprema de Justicia, Sala de Casación Civil, Expediente no. 4990, marzo 16 de 1998; Corte Suprema de Justicia, Sala de Casación Civil, Expediente no. 11001 3103 029 1997 23485 01, mayo 31 de 2006.

44 Although this doctrine was initially crafted with women in mind, men have also benefited from it. Corte Suprema de Justicia, Sala de Casación Civil, julio 8 de 1976; Corte Suprema de Justicia, Sala de Casación Civil, Expediente no. 54001-3103-001-2006-00164-01, diciembre 5 de 2011.

45 Corte Suprema de Justicia, Sala de Casación Civil, noviembre 30 de 1935.

role and highlight their role as entrepreneurs, an approach that was not always feasible.[46]

Had women's rights NGOs and activists paid closer attention to the interplay between case law related to the acquisition of real estate rights through adverse possession and the declaration of de facto marital property, they would have seen how the judiciary tends to presume that men's activities are productive, generate wealth, and amount to *animus domini*, while women's are intimate, domestic, and driven towards providing care, and not to producing or increasing wealth. This knowledge would have given them the expertise to advocate with a more complex understanding of the differential perspective in land restitution proceedings. Even though they presented a proposal to establish a presumption of bona fide possession, occupancy, and tenancy for women claimants, they did not address specific matters of evidence in the land restitution proceedings, nor did they otherwise explore how these proceedings would work in practice. For instance, no initiatives were proposed to include gender-sensitive readings of crucial property terms like "economic exploitation", or evidence guidelines to consider activities that were typically done by or ascribed to women as expressions of *animus domini*.

Furthermore, had they made the link between the pervasiveness of possession among the rural population and its dismissal without further consideration in Law 1448 when applied to seized or abandoned lots, they would have realized that the land restitution process was likely going to have a negative impact on some women. If possession is the most common mode of acquisition and legal relationship that rural women have with land, then the way that Law 1448 ruled it out in these cases, without taking into account the bona or mala fides of the individual who takes over the land, was likely going to generate undesirable consequences for women in conflict.[47]

---

46 Corte Suprema de Justicia, Sala de Casación Civil, octubre 1 de 1953; Corte Suprema de Justicia, Sala de Casación Civil, marzo 30 de 1954; Corte Suprema de Justicia, Sala de Casación Civil, noviembre 25 de 1966; Corte Suprema de Justicia, Sala de Casación Civil, noviembre 30 de 1967; Corte Suprema de Justicia, Sala de Casación Civil, septiembre 20 de 1972; Corte Suprema de Justicia, Sala de Casación Civil, septiembre 23 de 1988, Corte Suprema de Justicia, Sala de Casación Civil, expediente no. 3639, mayo 6 de 1993

47 Above, n. 28. Article 77 of Law 1448 introduced certain presumptions to strengthen the ability of victims to succeed in land restitution proceedings. One of them rules out possession as a mode of acquiring property if it took place during the period to which the regulation applies, namely 1 January 1991 until Law 1448 came into force. As a transitional justice measure, Congress established a ten-year period of validity. Article 77 as a whole is a clear, radical, and problematic departure from private law reasoning in the name of providing justice to armed conflict victims and to expedite the redress of dispossession. This provision rules out the possibility of possession without qualifying the good or bad faith of the possessor. Generally, in Colombian private law, when Party A fails to deliver ownership to Party B in a property sales contract, either because he was not the owner of the plot or because there was a problem with contract formalities, and if Party B takes possession of the plot he becomes its possessor

Litigation in sexual violence and land restitution cases follows different rationales. The genderization of each of them therefore must employ different strategies and rationales. Although definitions of rape and sexual violence have evolved recently to include same-sex conduct, these crimes traditionally have been associated with heterosexuality and gender difference. Therefore, "*women*" has not normally been an extraneous category in this area. On the contrary, since the late 1800s and early 1900s, the western world has seen the gradual but steady erasure of *women* as a relevant category in property, contracts, and inheritance, among other private law matters. Feminism as a movement has been key in achieving that goal, which was seen as a way of guaranteeing a woman's right to ownership and a capacity to use private law institutions to participate in commerce. For this reason, one must be cautious about redeploying *women* in any of these spheres and pay heed to its interplay with pre-existing categories. Had *women* had a private law breadth of its own that reflected an understanding of the predicaments of real women in accessing, controlling, and recovering real property, then its inclusion in the land restitution process would not have been so problematic. However, what this category brought to the table instead was knowledge accrued around sexual violence that offered no clear guidance to adjudicate land restitution issues. At the time that this research was done, the evident outcome of its introduction to land restitution processes was a deficient genderization of the land restitution procedure, erratic case law, and a reinforcement of the idea that women are mainly victims.

5. THE IMPACT OF AN IMPRECISE DIAGNOSIS: A FLATTENED NOTION OF WOMEN IN CONFLICT

The introduction of the *women* category in the land restitution process meant the addition of a new and alien criterion to resolve questions of property in this context alongside longstanding private law concepts, such as third party, possessor, and usurper, among others. However, contrary to what happens with these traditional legal categories, whose substance and eventual protection or sanction stems directly from their specific relation with property and/or other legal subjects who have an interest in it, the content of *women* as a category is delineated only according to sex and a presumed history of violence and discrimination. For this reason, while the traditional private law categories provide clear guidance for the adjudication of conflicts in this area (since the way that they draw rights and obligations takes into account their

---

and he could become the owner once the statute of limitations has passed. The same also happens if Party B consecutively sells his non-existent right to Party C, in which case Party C becomes the possessor, or if Party B finds a plot and starts living and working it as if he was its owner (*corpus* and *animus*).

situations vis-à-vis property and other interested parties), the legal category of *women* cannot do so given its lack of a situation-specific approach.

An examination of 14 land restitution cases selected from a universe of 135 judicial decisions provides some preliminary insights on the effect that the introduction of the *women* category and the differential perspective had in this transitional justice scheme during the period under analysis (2012-2014).[48] These judicial decisions were selected taking into account the presence of (i) a defendant (opposition); (ii) at least one woman as claimant or opponent; and (iii) a legal issue that involved at the outset the interplay between the new category of *women* and traditional private law categories.[49] This exploratory analysis suggested that regarding the analyzed period:

a) there is a growing consensus among the land restitution judiciary that the topic of disproportionate gender inequality in the context of conflict is an issue that should be resolved when adjudicating these claims;

48 The Specialized Administrative Unit for the Management of the Restitution of Dispossessed Land, which oversees implementation of Law 1448, has a website with information about the land restitution process. It was difficult to establish criteria to search for relevant cases, as initially relatively few cases had been published and decisions were uploaded without any accompanying abstracts or keywords. I therefore began by exploring the website and read what was available to try to understand how land restitution judges and tribunals were applying the law and the differential perspective. I decided to read around 100 cases to try to sort out decisions that were relevant for this analysis. In so doing, I concluded that only cases where there was a defendant (opponent) and at least one female party would help me understand how the gender-sensitive perspective was working in land restitution proceedings. At my request, some of my colleagues assisted me with finding further information regarding such cases. In particular, I thank Juan Francisco Soto and other colleagues who preferred to remain anonymous for their invaluable collaboration in this search. At the time of editing this piece, the Colombian foundation Forjando Futuros has made available a land restitution case law search engine that incorporates certain criteria such as year, plot type, differential approach, among others, to facilitate the identification of relevant decisions. Forjando Futuros, *Buscador*, http://sifff.eaconsultores.com.co/Buscador/Index.

49 I reached these selection criteria after organizing in a spreadsheet the information that I had distilled from 135 cases: information pertaining to parties, facts, claimants' alleged relationships to the land, causes of abandonment and/seizure, the rule of law, and my commentaries. Only cases in which one of the parties was a woman and where there was opposition could illuminate how the *women* category was interacting with other traditional private law concepts. That does not mean that the remnant cases were not pertinent to the topic of women and land. On the contrary, some of those cases indeed strengthen the conclusion of how gender equality in land tenure has become a mandatory issue that calls for the invocation and/application of the differential perspective: see Juzgado Primero Civil del Circuito Especializado en Restitución de Tierras de Santa Marta, *Julio 19 De 2013, Rad. 470013122001-2012-0066-00* (2013); Juzgado Primero Civil del Circuito Especializado en Restitución de Tierras de Villavicencio, *Abril 22 De 2013, Rad. 50001-31-21-001-2012-00111-00* (2013); Juzgado Primero Civil del Circuito Especializado en Restitución de Tierras de Villavicencio, *Abril 22 De 2013, Rad. 50001-31-21-001-2012-0093-00* (2013). However, if there was no opposition to a claim in a certain case, that then meant that the interplay between *women* as a category and traditional private law concepts was not going to be a matter of adjudication.

b) there is an incorporation of a new legal subject that competes with longstanding private law subjects for protection in the context of the process; and
c) the new subject of protection does not provide a clear rule that both fulfils the distributional outcomes for which it aims as well as resolves the specific cases that land restitution judges have to adjudicate. This contrasts with the longstanding private law subjects, whose conception and protection are closely tied to the legal relations under discussion in ways that provide clear standards that judges can use to resolve the specific cases in which they are invoked.

Twelve of these cases explicitly mentioned gender inequality as a prevailing issue and the differential perspective principle as the tool to address that situation. However, the extent to which they developed the subject and used the principle as a standard to reach a decision varied among them. Some made brief references to gender as something to take into account in the context of the land restitution process, especially in the introductory part of the reasoning where the tribunal laid out the pertinent rules. Others also developed and applied these general standards to the particular case at hand.

For instance, on 22 October 2014, the Tribunal of Cúcuta's Chamber of Land Restitution invoked the differential perspective in the opening of its reasoning but it did not use it to resolve the particular case it had at hand. Instead, it resorted to Law 1448's general provisions on land restitution and traditional private law categories to find that the contract that the claimant's deceased husband had concluded back in 2007 was voidable due to lack of consent given the situation of violence in which it was negotiated.[50] In contrast, decisions such as the one the Tribunal of Cali's Chamber of Land Restitution issued on 7 February 2014 illustrate a sophisticated and operative deployment of the differential perspective and the *women* category. On that occasion, the Tribunal went beyond merely invoking them and turned them into key concepts that, alongside other evidence, supported its conclusion that both female parties, claimant and opponent, were victims.[51]

Having women and gender inequality as an issue to be addressed through the land restitution procedure is a direct outcome of the differential perspective principle. This move to establish a legal presumption of the vulnerability of women and the necessity of offering them special treatment in these proceedings raises a number of questions regarding the meaning and extent of that protection, and the utility of introducing this kind of distributive goal – without further guidance – to a transitional justice model that is mainly designed to achieve land restitution. What these cases demonstrate is the difficulty of coherently

50 Tribunal Superior de Cúcuta – Sala Civil Especializada en Restitución de Tierras, *Octubre 22 De 2014, Rad. 540012221002-2013-00147-00* (2014).

51 Tribunal Superior de Cali – Sala Civil Especializada en Restitución de Tierras, *Febrero 7 De 2014, Rad. 761113121001-2012-00030-00* (2014).

integrating the *women* category into the land restitution process, since doing so either does not effectively contribute to the resolution of the conflict and turns it into a mere token, or, when it is used effectively as the criterion to adjudicate a case, creates incoherence and competing issues between traditional private law categories.

The 25 February 2014 decision of the Tribunal of Cúcuta's Chamber of Land Restitution is an example of the first.[52] In 1999, Carmen Cecilia Chiquillo and her husband bought the right to occupy a lot identified here as "A". In 2001, members of a paramilitary group started to harass her and her family and accused her sons of being guerrilla collaborators. She therefore abandoned the lot with her family. Her husband later moved to Venezuela without her. In 2007, the opponents in the case offered to buy lot A from her, to which she agreed, allegedly because she was in a difficult economic situation and needed to support her ill husband.[53] To decide the case, the land restitution tribunal highlighted the context of violence and the low price that the opponents paid to acquire their right to occupy lot A. Even though it made reference to women's vulnerability and the fact that the claimant's husband had left for Venezuela, the differential perspective had little to no operative application in reaching the final outcome. Consent and bad faith were the key concepts that the tribunal used to resolve this case. Similar cases in which tribunals made no explicit reference to the differential perspective were solved in a similar vein.[54]

Acknowledging gender as an important issue to have in mind when resolving land restitution cases but not using the differential perspective to adjudicate them illustrates the difficulties of translating that principle into rules to resolve private law issues without disrupting private law's logic. When land restitution tribunals have tried to break that barrier, the results have only reiterated this predicament. In the following subsections this preliminary finding is supported by analyzing five cases.

5.1. WOMAN vs. WOMAN: WHO IS THE VICTIM?

On 27 August 2013, the Tribunal of Cartagena's Chamber of Land Restitution adjudicated a case involving two women: Elina de la Cruz, the claimant; and

52 Tribunal Superior de Cúcuta – Sala Civil Especializada en Restitución de Tierras, *Febrero 25 De 2014, Rad. 540012221002-2013-00086-00* (2014).

53 The decision does not specify for how long her husband stayed in Venezuela or when he came back to cohabitate with the claimant.

54 Tribunal Superior de Cúcuta – Sala Civil Especializada en Restitución de Tierras, *Agosto 12 De 2014, Rad. 540012221002-2013-00004-00* (2014); Tribunal Superior de Cúcuta – Sala Civil Especializada en Restitución de Tierras, *Octubre 31 De 2014, Rad. 540012221002-2013-00122-00* (2014).

Sandra Holguín, the opponent.[55] In 1991, Cruz, along with other peasants, took possession of a certain plot of land. They informally divided it among the families and each of them started to dwell on and work the allocated land. They also initiated negotiations with the Colombian government and the owner of the land to acquire ownership through state subsidies. Elina de la Cruz was selected as one who would receive that subsidy. However, by the time this happened, she had already sold her rights to the lot to the father of Sandra Holguín, who then passed them to her. De la Cruz therefore declined the subsidy. In 1999, Sandra Holguín obtained the state subsidy and acquired ownership over the plot. However, the very same year she had to abandon it due to the armed conflict. She returned afterwards.

These facts beg the questions: who is the "protected women" subject and what kind of protection does she deserve? According to the available evidence and its analysis throughout the decision, there is little doubt that de la Cruz concluded the contract to sell her rights over the plot in a difficult context in which she felt her life and that of her family was at risk. Therefore, if private law had been seen as the controlling body of law to decide the case, and the Tribunal had found evidence of de la Cruz's vitiated consent, then it should have (i) declared the contract void; (ii) ordered the restitution of de la Cruz' and Holguin's rights to the *status quo ante*; and (iii) determine Señora Holguin's good or bad faith in concluding the contract, to decide whether Sandra had a right to compensation for her improvements to the lot and for its produce. However, if there was not proof of de la Cruz's vitiated consent, the other avenue for the Tribunal to take under private law would have been to determine the liability of those who contracted with her in a context in which she was forced to flee.

An application of Law 1448 with no consideration of the differential perspective for women would restore the plot to the claimant once she proved her condition as a victim of the internal armed conflict, her legal relationship to the plot, and that the loss of her land was related to violence from the armed conflict. Holguin would have only enjoyed a right to compensation after proving she had exercised the pertinent standard of care when she acquired the rights over the plot under contention, thereby requiring the tribunal to evaluate Holguin's behavior to conclude whether it fulfilled the standard of care.

In the end, the Tribunal did not reach any of these conclusions. Instead, it considered both women – claimant and opponent – to be specially protected subjects under Article 13's differential perspective. In this fashion, it stated

55 Tribunal Superior del Distrito de Cartagena – Sala Civil Especializada en Restitución de Tierras, *Agosto 27 De 2013, Rad. 200013121001-2012-00143-00* (2013); Tribunal Superior del Distrito de Cartagena – Sala Civil Especializada en Restitución de Tierras, *Mayo 9 De 2013, Rad. 200013121001-2012-00141-00* (2013).

that the opponent could retain ownership of the plot since declaring otherwise could entail her re-victimization, but also ordered the Colombian government to award the claimant a similar plot. The decision did not even cursorily explore why, in its judgment, this outcome did not re-victimize the claimant, de la Cruz.

What this case shows is that the harmonization of the transitional justice scheme of land restitution and the introduction of women as a distributional category depends on an erroneous assumption: that women, given their history of discrimination and vulnerability, would always be claimants but not opponents. One of the biggest flaws of this assumption is that it disregards the fact that in a protracted armed conflict like that in Colombia, internally displaced populations flee from their land and sometimes enter into possession of plots that other IDPs have earlier left. It overlooks the possibility that they are victims of land seizure or abandonment, but also potential agents of land seizure, even if they act in good faith.

The presence of a woman as an opponent in this decision therefore disarticulated the underlying rationales of both private law and Law 1448 and forced the Tribunal to cast a solution outside the boundaries of both of these bodies of law by disregarding the logic of traditional private law categories. One of the essential questions here is whether the Tribunal could have ignored the inconsistencies of the opponent's declarations regarding her status as a single mother – which made her part of a particularly vulnerable population – if it had not applied the *women* category to her. Perhaps dispensing once and for all of this category for both parties could have allowed a deeper analysis of the case overall, especially of the opponent's good or bad faith. Such an examination would have strengthened the rationale of an otherwise confusing and unconvincing decision.

5.2. THE DISPENSABILITY OF THE DIFFERENTIAL PERSPECTIVE

On 22 September 2014, the Tribunal of Bogota's Chamber of Land Restitution adjudicated the case of Ana Olga Ruíz v. Cecilia Díaz.[56] Since 1988 the claimant had been the occupant of the plot of land in question. In 1998, she had to flee due to violence in the area. In 2000, she allegedly authorized Cecilia Díaz to occupy the plot temporarily until some future date when she would ask for it back. The opponent contended instead that the claimant had donated the land to her and that Ruíz had told her that she wanted to leave the region and had

[56] Tribunal Superior de Bogotá – Sala Civil Especializada en Restitución de Tierras, *Septiembre 22 De 2014, Rad. 50001 31 21 02 2013 00086 01* (2014).

another plot somewhere else. Both the claimant's and opponent's evidence were inconclusive. However, using the principle of good faith of victims and the differential perspective, the Tribunal concluded that the claimant had a right to restitution and the opponent to compensation.

On 11 February 2014, the Tribunal of Cartagena reached an identical conclusion in a similar case by just resorting to private law and Law 1448's land restitution provision.[57] No significant mention of the differential perspective was made to support judgments where the claimant won the restitution and the opponent was awarded compensation. Lack of consent due to the context of violence and voidability of the contract were the only bases upon which those conclusions rested, which illustrates the futility of the differential perspective and the specific terms that it introduced in the Victims and Land Restitution Law.

5.3. WHEN PROTECTING WOMEN MIGHT PLAY AGAINST WOMEN

On 4 July 2013, the Tribunal of Bogota's Chamber of Land Restitution decided the case of Mr. Aniceto Jaspes.[58] In 1994, Jaspes acquired the right to occupy a plot in Puerto Gaitán, Meta, to which he moved with his partner, Sonia Milena Daza, and their family. In 1998 guerrillas accused Jaspes of collaborating with paramilitary groups and kidnapped him for two days. After he was released, Jaspes left town with his partner and family. While they were away, other people seized the lot. Later on, he filed a land restitution claim to recover it.

Jaspes succeeded in having his lost land restituted to him. He did not have any problem proving his relationship to the plot and his status as victim. What is interesting about this case, though, is the judgment's order to restore the piece of land to the claimant, his domestic partner at the time of the seizure, Sonia Milena Daza, and his current domestic partner, Luz Mercy Macías. It is not possible to find any reasoning in the decision, apart from abstract references to the differential perspective, to support an outcome that clearly goes against the clear mandate of Article 118 of Law's 1448, which only recognizes joint title to a claimant's spouse or partner who had suffered forced displacement in relation to the same plot the claimant has sought in restitution. The primary aim of that provision is to protect women and private law standards forcing land restitution judges to recognize spouses' and domestic partners' contributions

57 Tribunal Superior de Cartagena – Sala Civil Especializada en Restitución de Tierras, *Febrero 11 De 2014, Rad. 20-001-31-21-001-2012-00222-00* (2014).

58 Tribunal Superior de Bogotá – Sala Civil Especializada en Restitución de Tierras, *Julio 4 De 2013, Rad. 50001 31 21 001 2012 00117* (2013).

to the acquisition of real property. In this particular case, though, only Sonia Milena Daza had the right to joint title since it was she who had occupied and worked the plot that Aniceto Jaspes was seeking in restitution. According to the decision, however, Luz Mercy Macías was also to be a beneficiary, even though there is no evidence that she dwelled and worked on that lot, or made any contribution to its acquisition, and thus there was no proof that she had accrued any right to it. It is possible that the rhetoric of women's vulnerability had influenced this outcome, and that this is another example of how unpredictable outcomes could result from the introduction of *women* as a distributional category in the land restitution proceedings. Perhaps the intention to protect *women* in this case ended up in encroaching on one woman's rights in order to benefit another whom the Tribunal perceived as being a vulnerable subject.

On 22 January 2014, the Tribunal of Cúcuta's Chamber of Land Restitution decided the case of Ilia María Barbesi v. Martha Isabel Leguizamo.[59] This case exemplifies not only the dangers of advocating for the protection of women without taking into consideration the context, but also the risks of not paying heed to private law to solve real estate-related questions. In 1979, the government awarded the La Esperanza lot to Barbesi's husband, Nepomuceno Ariza, who later died in 2007. In 1993, the two left the lot after their foster son was killed and paramilitary members threatened to do the same to Ariza. Before they fled, Ariza sold the plot to María Trinidad Rincón and during the same year the government revoked Ariza's award and issued one for Rincón. In 1999, María Trinidad Rincón sold La Esperanza to her sister who in turn sold it in 2001 to Ascensión Peña, the opponent's mother. In 2010, the opponent, Martha Isabel Leguizamo, inherited the lot from her mother.

A harmonious application of Law 1448's land restitution provisions in combination with private law rules would have voided the 1993 sale, ordered restitution to the claimants, and established the opponent's good faith with no fault as third-party acquirer, to recognize her right to compensation. The logic of this last conclusion is especially true when one takes into account the passage of time between the 1993 contract, the 2001 purchase, and the 2010 inheritance. The existence of different purchasers between the moment at which the claimants sold their property and when the opponent acquired it made it difficult for Leguizamo and her parents to determine in what circumstances Ariza had sold his lot to María Trinidad Rincón. Even if Leguizamo's mother had failed to closely analyze the deeds to La Esperanza's in the public record, only an expert on the highly specialized regulation of wastelands would have noticed that the revocation of Ariza's award was suspicious.

[59] Tribunal Superior de Cúcuta – Sala Civil Especializada en Restitución de Tierras, *Enero 22 De 2014, Rad. 2013-00051* (2014).

However, the Tribunal did not follow this rationale. Instead, it decided to deploy the rhetoric of *women in conflict* to void the 1993 contract, order the restitution to Ilia María Barbesi, and establish that Leguizamo was a mala fide third party and thus not eligible for compensation. Although the Tribunal did not say it explicitly, the differential impact might not have been applicable to her because she did not allege that she was a victim of the conflict as well or, that she was a "woman" who fit into Law's 1448 category of *women*.

6. CONCLUSION: RETURNING TO PRIVATE LAW?

This examination of this group of land restitution judicial decisions demonstrates several things. First and foremost, there appears to be a wide gap between understanding sexual violence against women in conflict as a phenomenon and grasping the full extent of other harms that they experience in this context, especially in relation to access to economic resources, such as land. Although women's rights NGOs were aware of the problems that women in conflict faced in acquiring, controlling, and recovering property in the context of armed conflict, they did not have the required expertise to propose operative and concrete measures to tackle them. For that reason, they had to deal with the imminent discussion, approval, and implementation of a land restitution scheme based on their knowledge on sexual violence.

The same happened also with other relevant actors, such as members of Congress, state officials, academics, and human rights defenders who participated in some way or other in the discussions that led to the promulgation of Law 1448. They either replicated the rationale which these women's rights NGOs had been able to craft to genderize the conflict or did not contribute at all to this specific discussion. Even though the competent work of women's rights NGOs was able to put women at the forefront of the analysis of the internal armed conflict and receive acknowledgement that sexual violence committed against them was a serious crime, this research suggests that this approach has had its shortcomings in this particular instance, and that there is an urgent to need examine thoroughly other situations in which women bear other heavy burdens in this context.

Second, the legal notion of *women in conflict* that was introduced in the land and restitution proceedings through a differential perspective, incorporated a distributional device into this process. Although its main goal was to improve women's chances of succeeding in this transitional justice scheme, nobody, whether women's rights NGOs and activists or any other interested actor, explicitly pointed out or appeared to understand that the *women* category might be incoherent and a source of legal instability. The concept was pre-configured on certain assumptions that did not have any relation to the regulation of property, specifically the *code of disproportion*, and discrimination and violence against women stemming from male actors and structures. In this sense, *women* established a standard for the allocation of property that relied basically on those assumptions and did not pay heed to the very substance of private law.

Third, the introduction of the *women* category has had unexpected distributional impacts.[60] Every law reform or variation in legal standards redistributes rights and power within the legal system. That is, every variant, no matter how superficial, creates new winners and losers in the game of law, or at least increases the chances of some groups succeeding while decreasing those of others. In this particular case, the deployment of the differential perspective to protect a certain idea of women seems to have disadvantaged other women who do not quite fit in the description of women in the context of conflict, or women who have to litigate their case before other women. Land restitution proceedings as litigation were designed to have only one winner, and the downsides of using *women* as a category in those proceedings become evident when two opposing parties in a case were competing for the same protection of the differential perspective.

What this chapter demonstrates is the importance of taking into account the specialty of each area of the law when designing transitional justice schemes. The expertise that women's rights NGOs and activists had developed in the 2000s to address the situation of women in armed conflict revolved around just one kind of harm, sexual violence, which was not easily translatable to a land restitution model. Although genderization means acknowledging the disadvantages that certain individuals face due to their gender and introducing remedies to neutralize or compensate for them, this does not happen by simply including the word *women* in a legal provision. Categories have a history and a context that turn them into meaningful devices that anticipate legal outcomes and resolve specific problems. If that history and context do not correspond to the legal field, or are incomplete, then the presence of any such category will likely lead to tokenism or mere incoherence.

References

Martínez, A. and Ávila, F. (2010), "Injerencia Política De Los Grupos Armados Ilegales" in C. López Hernández (ed.), *Y Refundaron La Patria ... De Cómo Mafiosos y Políticos Reconfiguraron El Estado Colombiano.* Bogotá: Random House Mondadori, 79-213.

Barnard-Naudé, J. (2013) "The Politics of Private Law: Sexual Minority Freedom in South Africa and Scotland" in E. Reid and D. Visser (eds.), *Private Law and Human Rights. Bringing Rights Home in Scotland and South Africa.* Edinburgh: Edinburgh University Press, 37–80.

---

60 Halley et al. (2006); Halley and Rittich (2010).

Casa de la Mujer (2011) *The First Survey on Prevalence on Sexual Violence Against Women in the Context of the Colombian Armed Conflict 2001–2009* Bogotá: G2 Editores.
Centro Nacional de Memoria Histórica (2014) "Bases De Datos ¡Basta Ya!", http://www.centrodememoriahistorica.gov.co/micrositios/informeGeneral/basesDatos.html.
Céspedes-Báez, L.M. (2017) "En los Confines de lo Posible: inclusión del enfoque de género en el Acuerdo de la Habana" in L.M. Céspedes-Báez and E. Prieto-Ríos (eds), *Utopía u Oportunidad Fallida. Análisis Crítico del Acuerdo de Paz*. Bogotá: Universidad del Rosario, 295-326.
—— (2014) "Far Beyond what is Measured: Governance Feminism and Indicators in Colombia" *International Law. Revista Colombiana De Derecho Internacional* **2**: 311–374.
—— (2012): "Colombia's Victims Law and the Liability of Corporations for Human Rights Violations" *Revista De Estudios Socio-Jurídicos* **14**, no. 1: 177–213.
Céspedes-Báez, L.M. et.al. (2014) "Metodologías para el Estudio de la Violencia Sexual en el Contexto del Conflicto Armado Colombiano" *Colombia Internacional* **80**: 19–56.
Congreso de la República de Colombia. *Gaceta Del Congreso no. 1004* of 2010.
—— *Gaceta Del Congreso no. 107* of 2010.
—— *Gaceta Del Congreso no. 1139* of 2011.
—— *Gaceta Del Congreso no. 116* of 2011.
—— *Gaceta Del Congreso no. 170* of 2010.
—— *Gaceta Del Congreso no. 213* of 2010.
—— *Gaceta Del Congreso no. 247* of 2011.
—— *Gaceta Del Congreso no. 253* of 2011.
—— *Gaceta Del Congreso no. 338* of 2011.
—— *Gaceta Del Congreso no. 339* of 2011.
—— *Gaceta Del Congreso no. 340* of 2011.
—— *Gaceta Del Congreso no. 469* of 2011.
—— *Gaceta Del Congreso no. 483* of 2011.
—— *Gaceta Del Congreso no. 63* of 2011.
—— *Gaceta Del Congreso no. 692* of 2010.
—— *Gaceta Del Congreso no. 865* of 2010.
—— *Gaceta Del Congreso no. 88* of 2011.
Consultoría para los Derechos Humanos y el Desplazamiento - CODHES (1999) *Un País Que Huye. Desplazamiento y Violencia En Una Nación Fragmentada*.
Corporación Humanas - Centro Regional de Derechos Humanos y Justicia de Género (2009a) *Guía Para Llevar Casos De Violencia Sexual. Propuestas De Argumentación Para Enjuiciar Crímenes De Violencia Sexual Cometidos En El Marco Del Conflicto Armado Colombiano*. Bogotá, Colombia: Ediciones Ántropos.
—— (2009b) *Situación En Colombia De La Violencia Sexual Contra Las Mujeres*. Bogotá: Ediciones Ántropos.
Corporación Sisma Mujer. "Comunicación Dirigida Al Secretario Ejecutivo De La Comisión Interamericana De Derechos Humanos. Información Corporación Sisma Mujer. Seguimiento Sobre El Cumplimiento De Las Recomendaciones Informe Las Mujeres Frente a La Violencia y Discriminación Derivadas Del Conflicto Armado En Colombia. Septiembre 18 De 2009." Bogotá.

—— "La Impunidad De La Violencia Sexual Perpetrada En El Conflicto Armado En Colombia. Ponencia Presentada En El Seminario Internacional: 'Del Dicho Al Hecho: Políticas Públicas En Violencia Sexual Contra Las Mujeres En Contexto De Conflicto Armado Interno: Promesas y Realidades. -PCS Consejería En Proyectos.'"
—— *Las Invisibles. Mujeres, Desplazamiento y Política Pública. 2002–2005*. Bogotá: Papelería Atlas E.U., 2006.
—— *Mujeres En Conflicto: Violencia Sexual y Paramilitarismo*. Bogotá: Litoxpress S en C.S., 2009.
—— *Violencia Sexual, Conflicto Armado y Justicia En Colombia*. Bogotá,: Torreblanca, 2007.
Corporación Sisma Mujer, Mesa de Incidencia Política de las Mujeres Rurales, Comité de América Latina y el Caribe para la Defensa de los Derechos de la Mujer, Colectivo de Abogados José Alvear Restrepo, Corporación Humanas - Centro Regional de Derechos Humanos y Justicia de Género, Grupo de Trabajo Sobre Protección, Centro de Estudios de Derecho, Justicia y Sociedad Dejusticia, Colectivo Mujeres al Derecho, et al. "Declaratoria Conjunta De Las Organizaciones Sociales Sobre Aspectos Fundamentales Con Relación a Los Derechos De Las Mujeres Para Ser Tenidos En Cuenta En: El Trámite Legislativo Del Proyecto De Ley no. 107/10 Cámara - 213/10 Senado 'Por La Cual Se Dictan Medidas De Atención, Reparación Integral y Restitución De Tierras a Las Víctimas De Violaciones a Los Derechos Humanos e Infracciones Al Derecho Internacional Humanitario y Se Dictan Otras Disposiciones.'"
—— "Propuesta Conjunta De Las Organizaciones Sociales Sobre Aspectos Fundamentales Con Relación a Los Derechos De Las Mujeres Para Ser Tenidos En Cuenta En: El Trámite Legislativo Del Proyecto De Ley no. 107/10 Cámara - 213/10 Senado 'Por La Cual Se Dictan Medidas De Atención, Reparación Integral y Restitución De Tierras a Las Víctimas De Violaciones a Los Derechos Humanos e Infracciones Al Derecho Internacional Humanitario y Se Dictan Otras Disposiciones.'"
Corte Constitucional, sentencia T-679 de 2015, M.P. Luis Ernesto Vargas Silva.
—— Sentencia T-244 de 2016, M.P. Gloria Stella Ortiz Delgado.
—— Sentencia C-330 de 2016, M.P. María Victoria Calle Correa.
Corte Suprema de Justicia. Sala de Casación Civil, mayo 23 de 1932, M.P. Tancredo Nannetti.
—— Sala de Casación Civil, noviembre 30 de 1935, M.P. Alberto Zuleta Ángel.
—— Sala de Casación Civil, agosto 28 de 1942, M.P. Fulgencia Lequerica Vélez.
—— Sala de Casación Civil, mayo 6 de 1953, M.P. Gerardo Arias Mejía.
—— Sala de Casación Civil, octubre 1 de 1953, M.P. Rodríguez Peña.
—— Sala de Casación Civil, marzo 30 de 1954, M.P. Alfonso Márquez Páez.
—— Sala de Casación Civil, noviembre 25 de 1966, M.P. Aníbal Cardoso Gaitán.
—— Sala de Casación Civil, noviembre 30 de 1967, M.P. Flavio Cabrera Dussan.
—— Sala de Casación Civil, septiembre 20 de 1972, M.P. Ernesto Cediel Ángel.
—— Sala de Casación Civil, julio 8 de 1976, M.P. Humberto Murcia Ballén.
—— Sala de Casación Civil, mayo 6 de 1993, expediente No. 3639, M.P. Carlos Esteban Jaramillo Schloss.
—— Sala de Casación Civil, marzo 16 de 1998, expediente No. 4990, M.P. Nicolás Bechara Simancas.
—— Sala de Casación Civil, septiembre 23 de 1988, M.P. Rafael Romero Sierra.

—— Sala de Casación Civil, febrero 14 de 2006, expediente No. 05001-3103-012-1999-1000-01, M.P. Carlos Ignacio Jaramillo.
—— Sala de Casación Civil, mayo 31 de 2006, expediente No. 11001 3103 029 1997 23485 01, M.P. Pedro Octavio Munar Cadena.
—— Sala de Casación Civil, diciembre 5 de 2011, expediente No. 54001-3103-001-2006-00164-01, M.P. William Námen Vargas.
—— Sala de Casación Civil, enero 14 de 2015, expediente No. 11001020300020140285100, M.P. Luis Armando Tolosa Villabona.
Du Bois, Fr. (2013). "Private Law in the Age of Rights" in E. Reid and D. Visser (eds.), *Private Law and Human Rights. Bringing Rights Home in Scotland and South Africa.* Edinburgh: Edinburgh University Press, 12–36.
Engle, K. (2005) "Feminism and its (Dis)Contents: Criminalizing Wartime Rape in Bosnia and Herzegovina" *American Journal of International Law* **99**: 778–816.
Gómez Jiménez, J.C. (2009) "El Pacto Reserva De Dominio" in A. Venegas Franco, J.P. Cárdenas Mejía and F. Mantilla Espinosa, *Estudios De Derecho Privado. Tomo I. Liber Amicorum En Homenaje a César Gómez Estrada.* Bogotá: Universidad del Rosario, 336–368.
Halley, J. (2009) "Rape at Rome: Feminist Interventions in the Criminalization of Sex-Related Violence in Positive International Criminal Law" *Michigan Journal of International Law* **30**, no. 1: 1–123.
Halley, J., Kotiswaran, Pr., Shamir, H. and Thomas, Ch. (2006) "From the International to the Local in Feminist Legal Responses to Rape, Prostitution/Sex Work, and Sex Trafficking: Four Studies in Contemporary Governance Feminism" *Harvard Journal of Law and Gender* **29**, no. 2, 335–423.
Halley, J. and Rittich, K. (2010) "Critical Directions in Comparative Family Law: Genealogies and Contemporary Studies of Family Law Exceptionalism" *The American Journal of Comparative Law* **58**: 753–775.
Juzgado Primero Civil del Circuito Especializado en Restitución de Tierras de Guadalajara de Buga. *Junio 27 De 2013, Rad. 20120004100* 2013.
Juzgado Primero Civil del Circuito Especializado en Restitución de Tierras de Santa Marta. *Julio 19 De 2013, Rad. 470013122001-2012-0066-00* 2013.
Juzgado Primero Civil del Circuito Especializado en Restitución de Tierras de Villavicencio. *Abril 2 De 2013, Rad. 50001-31-21-001-2012-0093-00* 2013a.
—— *Abril 22 De 2013, Rad. 50001-31-21-001-2012-00111-00* 2013b.
Mackinnon, C. (1982) "Marxism, Method, and the State: An Agenda for a Theory" *Signs* 7, no. 3: 515–544.
—— (1987) *Feminism Unmodified: Discourses on Life and Law.* Cambridge M.A.: Harvard University Press.
—— (1991)*Toward a Feminist Theory of the State.* Cambridge M.A.: Harvard University Press.
Mantilla Falcón, J. (2008) "Violencia Sexual Como Crimen De Lesa Humanidad a La Luz De Los Avances Del Derecho Internacional" in Corporación Sisma Mujer (ed.), *Más allá De Las Cifras.* Bogotá: Omar Gutiérrez Acevedo, 11–34.
Marín Ortega, I. (2008) "Violencia Sexual, Paramilitarismo e Impunidad. Análisis y Propuestas Desde Una Mirada De Género" in Corporación Sisma Mujer (ed.), *Más allá De Las Cifras.* Bogotá: Omar Gutiérrez Acevedo, 35–82.

Meertens, D. (2000) *Ensayos Sobre Tierra, Violencia y Género. Himbres y Mujeres En La Historia Rural De Colombia. 1930–1990*. Bogotá, Colombia: Universidad Nacional de Colombia.

—— (2006) *Tierra, Derechos y Género. Leyes, Políticas y Prácticas En Contextos De Guerra y Paz* (Informe Final De La Consultoría Sobre Derechos De Las Mujeres a La Tierra. UNIFEM - Programa Paz y Seguridad - Colombia). Bogotá.

Mesa de Seguimiento al Auto 092 de 2008 - Anexo Reservado (2009) *Primer Informe De Seguimiento Al Cumplimiento De La Orden Del Auto 092 Referida Al Anexo Reservado De 183 Reportes De Violencia Sexual*. Bogotá, Colombia.

—— (2010)*Tercer Informe De Seguimiento Al Auto 092 De 2008*. Bogotá, Colombia.

Mesa de Trabajo Mujer y Conflicto Armado (2003) *III Informe Sobre Violencia Sociopolítica Contra Mujeres, Jóvenes y Niñas En Colombia*. Bogotá: Ediciones Ántropos,.

—— (2005) *V Informe Sobre Violencia Sociopolítica Contra Mujeres, Jóvenes y Niñas En Colombia*. Bogotá: Ediciones Ántropos.

—— (2008) *VIII Informe Sobre Violencia Sociopolítica Contra Mujeres, Jóvenes y Niñas En Colombia*. Bogotá, Colombia: Ediciones Ántropos.

—— (2009) *IX Informe Sobre Violencia Sociopolítica Contra Mujeres, Jóvenes y Niñas En Colombia*. Bogotá: Ediciones Ántropos.

—— (2010) *X Informe Sobre Violencia Sociopolítica Contra Mujeres, Jóvenes y Niñas En Colombia*. Bogotá: Ediciones Ántropos.

Miller, A.M. (2004) "Sexuality, Violence Against Women, and Human Rights: Women make Demands and Ladies Get Protection" *Health and Human Rights* 7, no. 2 (Sexuality, Human Rights, and Health), 16–47.

Ministerio de Agricultura y Desarrollo Rural (2012). *ABC Para Jueces En Materia De Restitución De Tierras*.

Muir Watt, H. (2014) "The Contested Legitimacy of Investment Arbitration and the Human Rights Ordeal: The Missing Link" in W. Mattli and Th. Dietz (eds), *International Arbitration and Global Governance. Contending Theories and Evidence*. Oxford: Oxford University Press, 214–240.

Observatorio de los Derechos Humanos de las Mujeres en Colombia (2013) *Documento Marco Conceptual.*, http://webs.uvigo.es/pmayobre/textos/cecilia/documento_marco_conceptual.pdf.

Pécaut, D. (2004) "Guerra, Proceso De Paz y Polarización Política" in G. Sánchez and E. Lair (eds), *Violencias y Estrategias Colectivas En La Región Andina*. Bogotá: Editorial Norma, 73–102.

Presidencia de la República de Colombia (2015) *La Restitución De Tierras En Colombia: Del Sueño a La Realidad.*

Quinche, M.F. et al. (2015) *El Amparo De Tierras. La Acción, El Proceso y El Juez De Restitución*. Bogotá: Universidad del Rosario.

Quintero, B. (2006) "Las Mujeres Colombianas y La Asamblea Nacional Constituyente De 1991 - Participación e Impactos" in S. Montano and V. Aranda (eds.), *Reformas constitucionales y equidad de género: informe final seminario internacional*. Santiago de Chile: Naciones Unidas/CEPAL, 269–285.

Sánchez, O.A. (2014) *Interview 2 December 2014*.

Torrado, H.A. (2011) *Código Civil Comentado*. Bogotá: Librería Ediciones del Profesional Ltda.

Tribunal Superior de Bogotá - Sala Civil Especializada en Restitución de Tierras. *Diciembre 18 De 2013, Rad. 50001 31 21 001 2012 00082/90/06/24/33 01* 2013a.

—— *Julio 4 De 2013, Rad. 50001 31 21 001 2012 00117* 2013b.

—— *Mayo 14 De 2013, Rad. 50001 31 21 01 2012 00083 01* 2013c.

—— *Octubre 24 De 2013, Rad. 50001 31 21 001 2012 00092 01* 2013d.

—— *Septiembre 22 De 2014, Rad. 50001 31 21 02 2013 00086 01* 2014.

—— *Septiembre 23 De 2013, Rad. 50001 31 21 001 2012 000110 01* 2013.

Tribunal Superior de Cali - Sala Civil Especializada en Restitución de Tierras. *Febrero 7 De 2014, Rad. 761113121001-2012-00030-00* 2014.

Tribunal Superior de Cartagena - Sala Civil Especializada en Restitución de Tierras. *Febrero 11 De 2014, Rad. 20-001-31-21-001-2012-00222-00* 2014.

Tribunal Superior de Cúcuta - Sala Civil Especializada en Restitución de Tierras. *Agosto 12 De 2014, Rad. 540012221002-2013-00004-00* 2014a.

—— *Enero 22 De 2014, Rad. 2013-00051* 2014b.

—— *Febrero 25 De 2014, Rad. 540012221002-2013-00086-00* 2014c.

—— *Octubre 22 De 2014, Rad. 540012221002-2013-00147-00* 2014d.

—— *Octubre 31 De 2014, Rad. 540012221002-2013-00122-00* 2014e.

Tribunal Superior del Distrito de Cartagena - Sala Civil Especializada en Restitución de Tierras. *Agosto 27 De 2013, Rad. 200013121001-2012-00143-00* 2013a.

—— *Mayo 9 De 2013, Rad. 200013121001-2012-00141-00* 2013b.

Tribunal Superior del Distrito Judicial de Bogotá, Sala Civil Especializada en Restitución de Tierras. *Agosto 26 De 2013, Rad. 2012-00088*, 2013.

Unidad de Planificación Rural Agropecuaria (2014). *Bases Conceptuales. Procesos De Regularización De La Propiedad Rural y Acceso De Tierras.*

Weinrib, E.J. (2012) *The Idea of Private Law.* Cambridge M.A.: Harvard University Press.

Wills, M.E. (2007) *Inclusión sin Representación. La Irrupción de las Mujeres en Colombia (1970–2000).* Colombia: Editorial Norma.

Women's Commission for Refugee Women and Children (1999). *La Farsa De La Preocupación: El Abandono De La Población Desplazada Por La Violencia En Colombia.* New York.

CHAPTER 10

LETTING GO AND CREATING NEW OPPORTUNITIES IN PALESTINIAN WOMEN'S WORDS

"'They' Entered and Took 'us'"

Fatma KASSEM

1. INTRODUCTION

Life stories are powerful. They are politically, socially, and culturally constructed. Stories reveal what we want to tell ourselves and the world but they also censor and silence what we do not want to tell. This author interviewed 37 women living in Lyd and Ramleh, using the life story method to collect data. Despite living on the margins, and being excluded and silenced as women, as Palestinians and as Israeli citizens, they were nevertheless able to keep and maintain a distance from an elitist, intellectual and masculine meta-national narrative, while fostering an open space that allowed them and others to learn about modern national ideology, where they could clarify who and what they endorsed, who and what they censored, and for which purposes. When referring to the *Nakba* – the expulsion and dispossession of Palestinians that they witnessed in 1948 – these women used phrases like "they came and took us", or "when

Israel came and took us". This chapter asks what this phrasing means and what options it carries and offers? What are the limitations and the opportunities they suggest in relation to the Palestinian-Zionist conflict?

It is argued here that in these words of these Palestinian women, in particular those referring to 1948, although replete with memories of displacement, dispossession, and both personal and collective pain and sorrow, nevertheless the seeds of new opportunities are found. With their peculiar choices of phrases and terms, they signal their resistance to the narrative constructs of Zionist ideology and reveal its oppressive practices and policies. Simultaneously, however, they also challenge a parallel intellectual-masculine Palestinian national narrative. Despite the limitation of the patriarchal forms of expression, in resisting both narratives these women create opportunities and alternatives to abusive familial relationships that pervade each of the conflicted groups and their interrelations. Their mixture of political and personal, private and public discourses carries with it the potential to resolve the bitter conflict between the two nationalist ideologies, liberating both parties from their oppressive masculine dominant presumptions about freedom. Their words also indicate an innovative and subversive potential for a radical re-organization of Palestinian and Israeli social life, including gender relations.

2. A META-NATIONAL NARRATIVE

Palestinians and Israelis commonly construe their meta-national narratives based on historical rights that give precedence to their claim over the others'. Moreover, both, in different ways, have continuously recruited the transcendent power of "God" to justify the "legitimacy" of these historical rights and their exclusive claims to the Land of Palestine. Let me illustrate the point before looking at both narratives in greater detail. The following brief anecdote from 1 February 2014 at the "peace" negotiation conference in Munich, between Palestinians and Israelis, reflects the master national ideology that each party endorses, and how it prevents them from reaching peace. Saeb Erekat, the chief Palestinian negotiator, sitting on a panel with a senior Israeli politician, Tzipi Livni, replied to Livni's repeated demand for Palestinians to recognize Israel as a Jewish state in the following way:

> When you say "accept Israel as a Jewish state", it means you are asking me to change my narrative. I am the son of Jericho, the proud son of the Natufians and the Canaanites; I have been there 5500 years before Yehoshua Bin-Nun came and burned my home town Jericho.

The Zionist national narrative is based on the transcendental idea of a "God-given land" for his "chosen people", the Jews, in Palestine. This idea is derived from a specific reading of the Hebrew Bible. Although, according to the Old Testament, the Land was given to Abraham and his offspring,[1] and not exclusively for the Jews, God's offer in the Old Testament was distorted to comply with the discourse of the Zionist ideology. Specifically, it transforms the founding myth of a particular people, Jacob's descendants exclusively, into a universal law that binds every other people. This transformation is made possible by the suggestion that an historical fact can acquire normative force by virtue of divine command. According to the biblical story, Moses said to Joshua: "Choose men for us and go out, fight against Amalek" (Exodus 17: 9). When mythical narratives like the Zionist one collapse "history under the cloak of God", they make war sacred and provide an inviolable basis upon which assault and continuous aggression toward the Palestinians can be legitimized, with no distinction made between living and inhabiting the land and destroying, controlling, exploiting and dominating others on it. This historicist fallacy makes use of God and presents Him as a narrow-minded landlord, discriminatory and unjust in the service of Zionist historiography. An historiographical narrative would in fact assert that Joshua occupied the land, committed genocide on its people and destroyed its cities, all by the command of his God. The fallacy, then, carries the myth of Joshua's founding mission over into an inalienable right in the contemporary conflict, supported by history and granted by God as the eternal law-giver.

This fallacy is omnipresent in Israel. For instance, the Rachel Sculpture at Ramat Rachel, a prominent monument in Jerusalem, demonstrates how the Zionist narrative intertwines, deliberately and inextricably, religion and state ideology to legitimize the exclusive Jewishness of Israel while at the same time justifying the subjugation of its women. The monument bears a quote from Jeremiah 31: 17: "Sons returned, to their own border" [*Veshavu Banim, Le'gvulam*, i.e. "their homeland"]. Known as Rachel's consolation for her grief over those who died on the battlefield, this phrase depicts sons rather than daughters as Israel's warriors. Sons will not just return, but will return as guardians of the land, of its borders, and of its women. A comment by Margalit Shilo bears out the ideological slant of the quote. She argues ((Shilo 2006) 217) that:

> Rachel was not just one of the Four Matriarchs. Jeremiah's famous words of consolation lifted her out of the historical context and placed her above and beyond time. She became the eternal mother of the nation, whose tears had moved God to bring her sons back to their homeland.

These words of Shilo lend a religious dimension to the image of Rachel as the eternal mother of the Jewish nation, transcending both history and social life.

---

1 See Genesis 12:7.

The words of Jeremiah are omnipresent in Israel and featured at many sites and in many books, poems and songs in language that refers to imprisoned soldiers. They not only remind the Jews in Israel of the bond between God and his "chosen people", but also reassure Zionist fellow-travelers of their absolute right to occupy the land. On another, though related note, to which I will later come back, the same phrase also perpetuates the idea that mothers and women are in need of masculine protection. Among an already privileged people, Zionist ideological discourse specifically addresses the "sons" as more privileged than the daughters. In this way, the failure to separate God and religion from the state not only dictates virtually every relationship between the Jews in Israel and the Palestinians, but it also determines, as I will show, the status of women within Israeli society as subjugated to men by God, by Zionist ideology and by the military.

Even though the Zionist movement from its inception has been a secular movement by any standard, this religious Jewish discourse of historic rights to the "promised holy land" was introduced at the first Zionist congress in Basel 1897. Consequently, it has always been a part of Israeli politicians' demands that Palestinian peace negotiators recognize Israel as an exclusively Jewish sovereign state. According to Azmi Bishara, such a demand is the

> Israeli drive to wrest from the Arabs a recognition that extends beyond the acceptance of the state. It wants them to recognize its Zionist creed ... its ethical and historic legitimacy ... In addition to negating the Palestinian right to return ... On top of gaining legitimacy for the tangible existence of the state, it would win legitimacy for Zionist culture, ideology and political discourse. (Bishara 2011)

Furthermore, such a demand for recognition also requires Palestinians to deny any historical rights accrued to them by their mere existence and for having inhabited the land for centuries through to the present and into in the future. The Palestinian recognition of Israel as a Jewish state, rather than as a state were Jews live, or a state for all of its citizens, therefore entails Palestinians giving up their collective rights to self-determination in all respects: politically, economically, socially, and culturally; that they refrain from claiming rights in the future; and that they put their destiny into the hands of the leaders of the Jewish state that is subjecting them.

Palestinians, in turn, construe their own national narrative as a claim of historical precedence as descendants of the Cạnaanites, which also grants the Palestinians an exclusive right to the land, not just to own it but also, and more importantly, to exercise sovereignty over it. Thus, their narrative also has a strong historical precedence argument playing in the background. Furthermore, Palestinians have a duty to guard *al-haram al-qudsī ash-sharīf*, i.e. the Al Aqsa Mosque, on behalf of the Muslim faith due to its religious importance for Muslims. In this view, all Palestine is *waqf* that they must control and protect in the name of God. In Islamic law, the concept of "*waqf*" normally refers to property owned for charitable purposes. In the Palestinian national discourse, though, Palestine itself is considered to be a holy Muslim *waqf*. In this way, Palestinians like Zionists, also fail to separate God from their national ideology. They, too, call on statehood to realize and practice freedom in society. They, too, endow their struggle for liberation with a form of sacredness that blends God/religion and historical precedence as a nationalist aspiration for emancipation. This blending is evident in Erekat's speech quoted earlier. His words speak to the oppression of and aggression towards Palestinians by Israelis, but also allude to a counter-narrative to the biblical justification that Zionist state ideology usually puts forward to legitimize the occupation of Palestine, namely the story of Joshua first exploring and then occupying the land of Canaan. History and religion are forced into a single continuum when Erekat says: "Yehoshua Bin-Nun came and burned my home town Jericho."

In sum, although nationalism evolves as secular thought and as a movement demanding that God/religion be separated from the state, both Zionist and Palestinian meta-narratives fail to do so. Instead, they lump God/religion, history, and national ideology together in order to justify their positions in the current conflict. Both turn war into a sacred notion with only one acceptable political outcome: total victory of one side over the other. In this way, they serve to reproduce the power of those who can control and dominate the "other", ignoring reality and denying any responsibility for past and present injustices, thereby fueling the conflict over and over again. Such mindsets certainly will not lead to a just solution of the Palestinian–Israeli conflict. When partisans from both sides bring God/religion into the conflict, they overtly and covertly claim the right to destroy each other in the name of God.

Therefore, in order to live in sustainable peace in the land of Palestine/Israel, Palestinians and Israelis have to change their narratives. This means a commitment to the day-to-day actuality of political, social, and familial life in the area. It requires placing the highest value on life for all, instead of on conflict and war. If both parties would commit themselves to just, egalitarian relationships, i.e., respecting decent living and peace as fundamental values, then war and the inextricable cycle of violence would dissipate and conflicts would be resolved. However, the emotional element of such a change should not be underestimated. Palestinians and Jewish Zionists base their national narratives on their being victims of oppression and injustice. Jews in Europe created Zionism in response to anti-Semitism that culminated in the Holocaust, whereas Palestinians feel that they are victims of Jewish Zionism that was supported by imperial and international power hierarchies. Both groups need a new paradigm to shift their collective consciousness from victimhood to agency and responsibility. In order to establish their freedom they must liberate themselves from the goal of the exclusive domination of the land of Palestine/Israel and move instead towards cooperation, consolation, and forgiveness.

This chapter will now turn to the ways in which this message is voiced, both substantively and emotionally, by Palestinian women from the contested cities of Lyd and Ramleh, where this author listened to their stories.

3. CONTESTED CITIES

The scale of this chapter allows for only a small sampling of the data gathered. It is therefore necessary to provide some context to place that data in the right light, in particular with regards to the received view of the cities selected and of the place of women in them.

In writing the history of Palestine, most scholarly work considers Palestinians to be a peasant society. Such a label ignores the fact that 30 to 35 per cent of the Palestinian population were city-dwellers involved in the general historical process of urbanization throughout the Middle East. Such a construction of Palestinians as peasants often serves to distance Palestinians from "civilized" western communities by instead presenting them as primitive. This is manifest in Zangwill's prominent phrase about "a Land *without a People* for a People without a Land" (emphasis added), not to mention others where he says that in Palestine "there is at best an Arab encampment" ((Masalha 2003) 13). A similar perception and attitude of superiority was expressed by Weizmann when he stated: "The British told us that there are hundreds of thousands of negroes [*kushim* in Hebrew] and [apparently] there is no value." (ibid). By these and similar statements Zionist leaders have identified themselves as belonging, as Edward Said put it, to the "Occident/Western superiority" as opposed to the "Oriental inferiority" ((Said 2003) passim) of Palestinians. Thus, they have depicted Palestinians as "'conniving', 'dishonest', 'lazy', 'treacherous', 'liars', 'murderers', and 'Nazis'" ((Masalha 2003) 12). In brief, akin to any other colonial movement, Zionism legitimizes the theft of the land and the property of Palestinians by degrading, indeed demonizing and dehumanizing them.

However, in point of fact, many cities within the 1948 borders were densely populated when those borders were first drawn. This certainly applies to the cities of Lyd and Ramleh, both located in the central part of Palestine/Israel on the coastal plain, close to what is today the metropolis of Tel Aviv. Around 1948, other cities like Safad, Tabarias, Besan, Beer el Sabih, Asqalan, Isdud and al-Majdal were depopulated and cleansed of their Palestinian residents. Morris writes that, "[t]he fall of Tiberias, Safad, Samahk, Jaffa, Haifa, and Acre [Akka] engendered in their wake many waves of emigrants" ((Morris 2003) 198). In contested cities, like Yaffa, Haifa, Akka, Lyd, and Ramleh, only a handful of pre-1948 Palestinians inhabitants remained behind. Families were not allowed to continue living in their own homes, as they were dispossessed and displaced from their properties. This occurred with the use of force: "About noon on 13 July … Lydda inhabitants were forced to walk eastwards … many of Ramle's inhabitants were ferried in trucks or buses" ((Masalha 2003) 30). According to the website *Palestine Remembered*,[2] in July 1948 the vast majority of the inhabitants of both cities were expelled. In Lyd, out of 19,000 inhabitants in 1947, only 1,052 were still there in 1950. In Ramleh, out of a population of 17,000, only 400 remained in 1950. In the official state lexicon both cities became "mixed cities", a term reflecting their ongoing Judaization ((Yacobi 2002; Yacobi 2004); (Bashir 2004)). Today, of the 74,604 inhabitants of Lyd, 22,600 are Palestinians. In Ramleh, of 75,668 inhabitants, 17,600 are Palestinians.[3] Most of these Palestinians live in segregated districts and suffer from exclusion, marginalization, home demolitions, which manifest in poverty, deteriorating educational and health systems, crime, high rates of unemployment, and many forms of violence and drugs.

4. WORDS AS EXPRESSION OF POWER RELATIONS

Palestinian women from the cities of Lyd and Ramleh represent the most marginalized of people in the broader Palestinian community and in Israel. Their marginalization is complex and multiple: as Palestinians, as women, as elderly people. Most lack any formal education or any independent sources of income. They are regularly subjected to many forms of oppression and deprivation of rights under an age-old societal patriarchy that intersects with the Zionist colonization of the country and their cities. Women have received no recognition of their losses, and certainly not for their pre-1948 dispossessed properties. They have been excluded from the formation of the collective Palestinian national narrative and deprived of any real political legitimacy in the public domains of their cities today.

The protracted violent conflict between Palestinians and the Jewish Israeli-Zionist state in which they are citizens also situates these women in an intersectional position that compounds their multiple marginality, oppression, and invisibility. Living in contested Palestinian-Jewish cities exposes them to tension and confrontation on a daily basis. In spite of their predicaments, these women's words were nevertheless powerful enough to rupture the Zionist narrative underlying the colonial invasion of their cities in 1948, as well as the

2 https://www.palestineremembered.com/al-Ramla/al-Lydd/index.html#Statistics, 2017.

3 Central Bureau of Statistics, 2017. https://www.cbs.gov.il/he/settlements/Pages/default.aspx?subject=%D7%90%D7%95%D7%9B%D7%9C%D7%95%D7%A1%D7%99%D7%99%D7%94.

Palestinian national narrative that countered it. This can be explained with an excerpt from one of the life stories gathered.

> When I asked Salma to tell the story of her life, she smiled and said, "The story of my life? Who would that interest?"
>
> "Me", I said.
>
> "What do you want to hear about, exactly?", she asked.
>
> "What do you want to tell me about?" I replied.
>
> She looked at me and asked, "Do you want me to tell you about the time when we migrated?".
>
> "Whatever you want", I answered.

It is important to note that most of the women told their stories while surrounded by family members from different generations, all attentively listening with me.

Salma narrates:

> I want to tell you that I am from Lyd; from here originally and by origin we are from here. We are from Lyd. Then I got married and we migrated. We migrated to Amman; at first to Ramallah, then from Ramallah to Amman. At first, I had four kids here [in Lyd], two girls and two boys. One girl and both boys died here before we were out, before we migrated. Then we migrated and I was pregnant with a girl too … We were here at the hospital, washing for the injured ones in the hospital when the Jews entered … My husband was there and I was sitting there, me and the Christian woman from the town, here it is in Lyd … we were showering the injured casualties and changing them and washing their clothes.
>
> A Lydian man, came and said, "Come on, come on, go out!" The Jews came in [dakhalo] and expelled us right away. They got us out right away. I did not have time to say anything to him [her husband]. I did not see him. They [the casualties] were on the second floor and we were under that, washing … At the beginning of Israel there was a war … the Jews entered, the Jews took us ["*dakhal el yahud wakhaduna*"]. They started to hit the cars with cannons. He [her husband] got injured and his cousin died … I was with him in the hospital [and] he told me go with them, with the people that the Jews had expelled. They did not let anyone stay here in town. They just allowed the elderly to stay here, like me [today]. The ones that cannot walk, they [the Jews] allowed them to stay and they [the Jews] expelled all of the other people. We went out. The people were not recognizing each other because they were so many and they were pushing each other … People couldn't even recognize their own brother or son … What can I tell you? Like the snake or something. Many, many people from all over the country were expelled. The Jews expelled the whole country. Yalla yalla to Abdallah to Abdallah, yalla! We did not have anything – no clothes and not even bread for the kids; my daughter in my hands, and without any piece of bread. We did not have anything.

Salma continues:

> We went out like that. If anyone had something, they [the Jews] were taking it from him. Jewellery, money, they were taking it, they were piling valuable things on bed sheets at the road junction here outside of the city and if anyone had anything, they were taking it and putting it on the white bed sheet. They [women soldiers] were searching the women and the men were searching the men and putting all they have, whatever they had, they were putting it and not taking anything with them. The Jews … [unfinished sentence and silence] did not leave anything with us. They did not leave half a [piece of] bread for a child. They did not allow water for a child. They were expelling the people to the mountains, barefoot and tired. We were so miserable, you can say. God, what can I tell you? What we saw in our days … We were fasting the first day. It was the third day of Ramadan. People died on their way. My husband's cousin died and his aunt and my cousin died on her way. The poor ones, they did not find anyone to say a prayer for them. It was so hot, so hot. The other people did not look at them. They died, they died. Yes, the old ones were dying. Bodies were left by the road. There is no one that took care of them. There is no drop of water. No water. We were fasting … I know someone who left his mother. She was old, and he left her on the road and she died … On the third day he came back, as infiltration, brought [the body of] his mother, carried her back and buried her. ((Kassem 2011))

The women interviewed often narrated their stories in the present tense, leaving no doubt that their memories of 1948 had been constitutive of their pasts and continued to profoundly influence their present lives. The unresolved trauma of the 1948 forced expulsion and dispossession is vividly present in Palestinian daily life. Memories like Salma's transfer it, consciously and unconsciously, to the next generation of Palestinians.

Palestinians, in particular, researchers, politicians, intellectuals, authors and poets, use the concept of *Nakba* [catastrophe] to describe the 1948 expulsions. *Nakba* has become one of the most widely known and fundamentally constitutive concepts of the modern collective Palestinian national awareness, for both men and women. For example, Palestinian author Salman Natur (1985: 49) writes, "I belong to the generation born one year after the *Nakba*." By doing so, Natur marks the *Nakba* as a constitutive marker of time that is carved in stone, distinguishing those born before it from those born during it and those born after it.

In stark contrast, the word *Nakba* was conspicuously absent in the narratives of the women interviewed. Only three of the 37 interviewees mentioned the word, and all three were political activists in the Communist Party. Instead, the women commonly used phrases like "when the Jews came into the country" ["*laman dakhal elyahud liblad*"] or "when Israel took us" ["*laman ijat Israel wakhdatna*"]. The men interviewed also rarely used the term "*Nakba*", although their language nevertheless diverged from that of the women in their preference for descriptive phrases like "when the Israelis occupied" or "the days of the Jewish conquest".

Although the hegemony of the Zionist discourse, which seeks to erase the use of the term *Nakba* from daily language and political consciousness, may offer a partial explanation for the word's absence in the narratives of the interviewees, it is possible to identify other more productive possibilities by focusing on and analyzing further the meaning of the phrases that these women *do* use instead.

5. MICRO–MACRO FORMS OF PATRIARCHAL VIOLENCE

Joan Wallach Scott argues that "we construct history through the language we use, just as we do the society in which we live" ((Hutton 1993) 121)). This is apparent in the language patterns of the women interviewed. If attention is paid to their language to describe the occupation of their cities in 1948, it is noticeable that they say: "when the Jews entered", "when Israel came in", "when the Jews took us" and "when Israel entered and took us", or "they entered and took us".

In literary Arabic, the word "enter" ["*dakhala*"] is commonly used in public political discourses to denote the military occupation of land and territory. In colloquial Arabic, however, the terms "entered" ["*dakhala*"] and "came in", when accompanied with the term "took us", are commonly used to describe the penetration of a woman's body by a man, especially on their wedding night. In accordance with Palestinian cultural and social norms of the generation of the interviewees, it was customary to say: "The bridegroom entered ['*dakhala*'] the bride" and "the bridegroom took the bride ['*akhad'ha*']." The word choice these women make to describe 1948 in this way reflects the norms and values of Palestinian social and cultural life at that time. In patriarchal traditional societies, like Palestinian society was in 1948, sexual intercourse was carried out without adequate preparation of the bride and with the knowledge of the bride's family, giving the husband their tacit approval by "keeping a low profile". Thus, secrecy and a conspiracy of silence legitimized the sexual act carried out between women and men.

One should note in this regard that, whether in politics, literature or art, Palestine is often portrayed not only as a homeland ["*Watan*"] but also as a beloved female body. The national Palestinian poet Mahmoud Darwish, for instance, describes his homeland in terms of such a beloved geo-female body:

> My homeland is not a traveling bag.
> Nor am I a passing traveler.

It is I who am the lover
And the land is my beloved

Mahmoud Darwish ((Darwish 1996) 347).

This image of Palestine as a beloved female body is a prevalent part and parcel of the modern national narrative of the *Watan* homeland, portrayed as an erotic but subjugated woman: an object of love "to possess". In the words of Najmabadi, *al Watan* "was imagined as the outlines of a female body: A body to love and be devoted to, to possess and protect, to kill and die for." ((Najmabadi 1997) 445) In the wake of 1948, Qustantin Zurayk referred to the loss of the land of Palestine as having been raped by Zionist forces ["*Falastin el Mug'tasabah*"], as he unfolded short and long-term strategic plans for the liberation of Palestine.

In this author's reading, the symbolic language of the "entry" of the Zionist Brigades into the Palestinian cities and villages in 1948 consistently links the occupation of Palestine to the penetration by a man of the most private and intimate part of a woman's body. It equates it to the occupation of the most private parts of Palestinian lives: their homes; their shattered family lives, their communities and their land. As the women interviewees were inadequately prepared for the sexual act at the time of their marriages, so too were Palestinians exposed to and unready for the violent and forcible penetration of Zionist Brigades into their land, cities and villages. "No one believed this [i.e., the uprootedness] would happen to us", as the women repeatedly said in so many words. In the same way that a new bride faces a conspiracy of silence that legitimizes the sexual act on her wedding night, so too did Jewish Zionist Brigades occupy Palestinian territory under a secret cloak of legitimacy given to them by the broader "family" of Arab states, most of whom were not yet sovereign, as well as by the world's Empires: Britain, the United States and the international community, formerly represented by the League of Nations, all of whom knew what was going to happen.[4] This interpretation is reinforced by the interviewees' use of the verb "took us", indicating that "something" has been taken away against their will, in this case Palestine.

The images that the interviewed women used to describe the occupation of their home cities in 1948 provide a distressing mirror of the macro-level politics pursued by the imperialistic powers concerning Palestine and the Palestinians. This is reflected in the Balfour Declaration of the British Empire of 2 November 1917, which approved the Basel Program that had been declared earlier at the first Zionist congress in 1897: "Zionism seeks to establish a home for the

4 Some kept silent despite their knowledge, offering passive agreement; others actively supported Zionist violence. Moreover, this pattern of support for the State of Israel continues today.

Jewish people in Palästina[5]/Palestine secured under public law."[6] In contrast to the hypostatization of "Jewish people" as "the Jewish people", the idiom of the Balfour Declaration divided Palestinians into different religious groupings and communities. In this way, the Declaration recognized that Palestine was not an empty land, while at the same time refusing to define it in terms of a collective political entity. These quasi-subtle changes manifest the support that imperial powers lent to the Zionist effort to reinforce and disseminate among themselves and the international community the idea that no national collective of Palestinians existed.

It is striking to observe the strong parallels between, on the one hand, the sexualized image of a woman who has been handed over by her family to her new husband, who subsequently "takes" or "enters" her, and, on the other hand, of Palestine as given away by the "Patriarchal Family" of the imperial powers and the international community to a people who did not dwell on it, to take coercively and without any consideration for the needs and desires of the Palestinian people who dwelled there. The Council of the League of Nations in spirit approved the Balfour declaration on 24 July, 1922, declaring itself "responsible for placing the country under such political, administrate and economic conditions as will secure the establishment of the Jewish national home."[7] The "mandate" was supposed to come into operation in September 1923; however, in reality the British "mandate" in Palestine effectively began in 1920 with the UK's implementation of the San Remo agreement before the League of Nations had approved it. In Article 4 of the agreement the League of Nations argued for

> an appropriate Jewish agency [that] shall be recognized as a public body for the purpose of advising and cooperating with the Administration of Palestine in such economic, social and other matters as may affect the establishment of the Jewish national home.

Thus, when it comes to memories, one could argue that the *Nakba* of the Palestinian people began at this moment, when the British Empire adopted the Zionist Basel Program. The international community saw to it that imperial or other control over Palestine did not end. Like parents conceding their newly-

5 Palestina is a biblical term; its use in the Zionist narrative has religious, historical and political implications.

6 "Der Zionismus erstrebt für das jüdische Volk die Schaffung einer (öffentlich-)rechtlich gesicherten Heimstätte in Palästina." Note the use in 1897 of "Palestina" as the name of a geographical region under imperial rule rather than a full-blown polity, as well as the last minute insertion (by a curved bracket) of the word "öffentlich" ["public"] before "rechtlich" ["by law"] – all of which was ignored or rather put aside by Balfour in 1917.

7 http://avalon.law.yale.edu/20th_century/palmanda.asp.

wed daughters to the patriarchy, the international community remained silent, knowing what was going to happen to the Palestinians and to Palestine, as they still do.

6. HEALING WOUNDS BY WOMEN'S AGENCY

Despite her initial lack of knowledge about the impending sexual act and the pain and injury of the first penetration, the bride overcomes the experience and establishes a respected subject position from which she grows a new family life. This, too, is reflected in the verbatim recordings of the broader experience of the interviewees. All of those interviewed who were married, for example, stated that "we raised the children and married them off" ["*Rabina liwlad, wjwaznahum*"]. They also used other phrases, like that their children "established a home" ["*Banina beit*"] or "everyone opened a home" ["*Wkol wahad fatah beit*"]. These phrases have special meaning, as they are used in conjunction with phrases like "we were the only family who stayed here and now there are many of us" and "I am the only one who remained in the country [the city] and my children built their homes around me". Such language indicates that these women perceive themselves as capable of action, choice, and control in their lives, despite the on-going trauma visited upon them by Israel through the 1948 invasion of the land, and the destruction of their family and community lives. They describe how, as they did with their weddings, they managed to overcome ruin, destruction, loss, and insecurity, even after their families and communities had been ripped apart and dispersed. In the wake of these experiences, they rehabilitated their lives, rebuilt their homes, raised families, and re-established their communities in Lyd and Ramleh.

Nonetheless, their use of sexual metaphors relating to procreation as a woman's affair reflects the gender power imbalance in Palestinian society, and reveals not only their reproduction, but also how difficult it is to challenge these structural relations. At the same time, however, the way these women use the phrase "(we) raised the children" in juxtaposition with "(they) entered and took us" demonstrates their capacity to both subvert gender relations within Palestinian society and transform the broader political situation that defines their lives.

7. FAMILIAL NATIONAL FORMATION

As Najmabadi points out,

> Modern nations have often been explicitly imagined through familial metaphors. In particular, the construction of the national community as a brotherhood (*a fraternity)*

has pointed both to the centrality of male bonds in the production of nationalist sentiment, and to the exclusion of women from the social contract ((Najmabadi 1997) 442).

Nationalism as a social and gender construction qualifies mothers as the producers or birth-givers of the nation, but only in an entirely passive sense. In such a role, women save the nation in every respect thinkable as keepers of the social reproduction of tradition and national culture (Yuval-Davis 1997). However, they lack genuine political agency: the power that constitutes society. Spivak makes a similar claim, namely that the national project has been imagined by men and has been designed as a masculine construct. Patriarchal hierarchies have become the foundation of the nation as much as the foundation of both gender and sexuality (Spivak 1992; Spivak 2007). Both Palestinian and Zionist constructions of national identity follow these patterns.

Palestinian national narratives, such as those that represent the land of Palestine as a beloved geo-female body, also portray it as a country that was raped by Israeli invaders in 1948. As can be seen in Joseph Massad's argument (Massad 1995), for instance, the protagonists of Palestinian nationalism conceive of national agency in masculine terms. Thus, while signifying the conquest of Palestine as a rape, they also disregard women's independent resilience, and subordinate them in advance to young male Palestinian nationalist liberators. Furthermore, what happened to Palestine and the Palestinians in 1948 was not an isolated event, but rather the beginning of a forceful abusive relationship that has continued until now with many subsequent acts of violence and dispossession. Through various mechanisms of oppression, aggression and humiliation, the Israeli state continues to persecute the Palestinian people, both women and men, but in Palestinian nationalist discourses, the response to this violation appears as a masculine impulse to protect and liberate Palestine that disregards women's own strength.

Yet, the fact is that women are contributing their share to the maintenance of the family that is taken for granted; in addition, the historical record shows that Palestinian women actively participated in the liberation struggle against British imperial rule and Zionist colonialism. Islah Jad reminds us that "In August 1929, out of 120 Arabs killed by the British as they put down nationalist protests, 9 were women." ((Jad 2007) 251) Women demonstrated and formed committees, unions, and national movements, but they chose not to draw special attention to their emancipation from social, political and economic oppression while doing so. Women initially justified their choice as strategic: "They believe that during the national liberation struggle they should focus on resistance and not open secondary fronts." ((Jad 2007) 265). However, women's attitudes shifted during the *Intifada*, as women began to play an increasingly crucial political role that "has led to the emergence of a new ideal of women as saviors rather than weak creatures needing protection." ((Jad 2007) 266).

Jad wonders: "Will this trend be reflected in a new social agenda for the women's organization?" The answer she proposes is that it depends on women's awareness (ibid).

These patterns of gender inequality are similarly reflected in Zionist nationalist narratives that also speak of a nationalist identity defined in terms of male ownership of the land, where Jews are the fore*fathers* of the land of Israel or Jacob. This ignores any equal consideration of Jewish women as the fore*mothers* of the land in the same way. Furthermore, while we know that the 12 sons of Jacob formed the Jewish community, we only know about one of Jacob's daughters, Dina, and the only thing we know about her is that she was the object of revenge for two of her brothers. In this way, she was an (allegedly) passive object that masculine forces possessed and protected without her consent and even against their father Jacob's will. Eretz Yisrael itself is construed as a beloved geo-female body that must be rescued and liberated from its Palestinian "occupiers", and therefore is in constant need of masculine warriors. Jewish-Israeli women have been construed to serve this purpose as "national reproducers" of the "new Jew" in Israel (Yuval-Davis 1989), which is shaped and affected by a sexual division of labor. Even the obligation for Jewish-Israeli women to serve in the army has not erased differences between men and women in this regard (Yuval-Davis 2004). The Zionist national project, therefore, failed to liberate, and also continued to oppress, many segments of the Jewish society, such as the Mizrahi "Oriental" Jews. Ella Shohat (Shohat 1988) has argued that the Zionist claim of being a liberation movement for all Jews is a false one, since in Israel European Jews dominate not only Palestinians but also Oriental Jews. Shohat shows, in great detail, how Ashkenazi Zionist Jewish politicians, social scientists, educators, writers and mass-media orientalize Sepharadi/Mizrahi Jews by depicting them as having a "primitive mentality", lacking the most elementary knowledge, as savages and barbarians who came from backward countries that belong to a low culture and therefore need to be elevated to a suitable level of civilization. As a result, they are widely discriminated against and they are not equally integrated into Jewish-Israeli society or the state that was specifically established for all Jews.

Related to this masculine and racial bias, another problematic aspect that dominates the Jewish-Israeli mindset and culture today is the militarization of "civil society". Sociologist Baruch Kimberling (Kimmerling 1993) speaks of a society in military uniform, and describes how this process has developed since the inception of the Jewish state. He shows how militarism has not only socio-political, but also strong cultural and cognitive dimensions in Jewish-Israeli society due to the prevailing perception that the conflict is absolute and therefore inevitable. This has created a military doctrine that places the army center-stage and militarizes thinking across society. In the context of the persistent conflict with the Palestinians, Jewish warriors become the paradigm of what is most needed to guard the nation. As long as this persists,

Jewish communities will maintain a preference for the masculine over the feminine. In brief, the militarized mindset that pervades society as a whole is utterly unable to guarantee equity and equality to its women or to any other "disadvantaged" group or form of citizenship within Israel's borders.

In both the Palestinian and the Zionist national narratives, women are depicted as subordinated to a construction of the land of Palestine/Israel as feminized and therefore in need of liberators, defenders and protector warriors. As such, these are narratives that constitute nationalism on the basis of very strong "male bonding" on both sides, whether understood as imagined communities (Anderson 1991) or as men sharing the same culture (Gellner 1983). Such is the paradigm of patriarchal nations, and hence nation states. Both of these masculine and intellectualized national narratives fail to recognize the other's collective right to live in Palestine/Israel, although they do so from different positions in the overall configuration of power relations between them. However, whether they like it or not, the fate of both peoples is linked to the same territory and thus both the Palestinian question and the Jewish question are similar questions of liberation and emancipation from victimhood and all forms of oppression and domination within the group and between them.

As Anne McClintock observes, "all nations depend on powerful constructions of gender" ((McClintock 1993) 61), and thus in line with geo-feminine concepts of territory that these two nationalist discourses share, female identity is consistently constructed by each in terms of an on-going need for possession and protection by men. This construction of female identity is subject to male domination whether or not the geo-body/territory is liberated. As such, the potential liberation of the land offers no corresponding option for the liberation of women within the context of either of these masculine nationalist narratives. For women, then, these are doubly dangerous discourses. Not only do they maintain gender inequalities, but they keep in perpetual conflict the societies to which women belong.

In addition to their obvious gender biases and structured inequalities, whatever value these national narratives may have is further limited by their inaccurate portrayals of the experiences of 1948 and beyond. For instance, the word *Nakba* mostly applies to a situation drawn from Arab history. Typically, it represents total defeat, where overcoming catastrophe is practically impossible. However, it is evident that despite past defeats and prevailing weaknesses, Palestinians are nonetheless capable of on-going struggle against and resistance to what happened to them in 1948. They also cannot ignore the current political reality of the existence of the Jewish-Israelis in Palestine/Israel. The voices of the interviewed women call on others to face the challenge through female and male emancipation rather than masculine/patriarchal power domination and oppression, and in so doing speak more closely to the post-1948 reality than either of the nationalist narratives.

In stark contrast to the patriarchal narratives of national identity that simply turn the tables of oppression, the choice of words used by the ordinary women interviewed for this research offers an inherently different perspective, but one that is no less political. To say: "Israel entered and took us" metaphorically mixes the private with the political. It rejects the proposition that the private realm is just left-over or peripheral to the public realm as established by the powers that be. Instead, it returns the private to the public realm in the form of the politics of persons out of which polities are born. It also criticizes the power relations between Israel and Palestine for the ways that the latter (i.e., those who were "entered") is the feminized other, unprepared for Zionist penetration, while the state of Israel becomes the masculinized aggressor.[8] However, from another perspective, this phrase also links Jewish-Israelis and Palestinians in an abusive familial relationship and is critical of the masculine ideal of political fraternity which separates each side of the conflict into its world and ignores women's rights. In particular, the "entry of the Israelis" metaphorically resembles Palestinian women's experiences of violence, whereby men engage in violence because they are seen as physically able to do so while such behavior is supported by patriarchal social norms and values. The on-going violent aggression of the state of Israel against Palestinians since 1948 is rooted in a similar logic: they do it because they are able to do so, because of their superior military capacity, because this behavior is implicitly and/or explicitly supported by the democracies of the First world, backed by most of the international community of nation states, and because the negation of Palestinian rights has become the political norm. This pattern is reinforced further by the silence of most Arab countries in the face of continued Israeli aggression. Taken together, this begs the question of how will it be possible for Palestinians to stop this violence if they continue to practice it in their own homes?

It is true that Israel, supported by a "modern imperial power ... tries to separate the bride from her dowry, to force a relationship on the bride, and to illegally appropriate her dowry out of wedlock" ((Grinberg 2009) 106). Indeed, this coercive and abusive "wedlock" happened because people on both sides linked their destinies to the same land. True, the "bride" [Palestinians] was not asked about the entrance of the "groom" [Zionist-Israelis] to her "body" [the Palestinian homeland]. However, the lesson to be taken from the interviewees is this: It does not matter if it is within a cohesive marriage or a divorce; both sides know today that they must share the "bride's dowry", namely the land of Palestine/Israel. No less importantly, both sides now have a chance to deconstruct the abusive patriarchal power relationships in their families and their respective nations, and to create an alternative that is based on equal access to resources, shared sovereignty, and the mutual right to develop resources in order to constitute a new social and political contract.

8 Granted, this perspective is also endorsed in Palestinian nationalist narratives.

8. CONCLUSION

In other words, this mixture of the political and the private carries a need to radically de-patriarchalize the mindset of the Palestinians and re-organize Palestinian society based on mutual respect and liberation. As for Jewish-Israelis, a de-militarization of their mindset is required for achieving a decent social life, particularly with regard to Palestinians and gender relations, without violence and domination. Palestinians and Zionist nationalists must understand that the repetitive call for priority and privilege – as it appeared in the claims of chief negotiator Saeb Erekat and others, or in the demand of Tzipi Livni that Palestinians recognize the exclusivity of the Jewish state – will not resolve the conflict. They must also leave God/religion out of the pursuit of a political settlement and instead refer it to the private/personal sphere in the traditional, non-political sense. Unlike the masculine meta-narratives of Palestinian and Israeli nationalist identities, the women's phrases mentioned above contain within them an opportunity to constitute a new form of political family relations within each party and in between the two, based on a partnership.

This appeal to non-violence is directed to both sides. Palestinians' preferred form of struggle should be non-violent and concern the interests of "people" in general, rather than "the people". The state of Israel and the Zionist movement, in turn, should recognize, acknowledge and take responsibility for their aggressive actions and practices toward the Palestinians. They should choose to de-Zionize the oppressive apparatuses of the state, opting instead to include and serve all inhabitants of Palestine/Israel, and look for a mutual solution to the refugee problem together with the Palestinians. Fulfilling these preconditions has the potential to create a new negotiation atmosphere that is built on trust and that can establish new relationships that are not based on patriarchal values or nationalist identities founded on aggressor-victim dualities of master–slave or ruler–ruled. Rather, this would be a mature relationship grounded in mutual recognition that recognizes the suffering of the other and takes responsibility for the collective life they desire and seeks to establish. A new social and political contract must be formed based on equal rights and the equitable distribution of sovereignty, land and other resources for the common good of all people, including women and men, Palestinians and Jews alike.

Websites

Central Bureau of Statistics, (2017) Israel.
https://www.cbs.gov.il/he/settlements/Pages/default.aspx?subject=%D7%90%D7%95%D7%9B%D7%9C%D7%95%D7%A1%D7%99%D7%99%D7%94

Exodus 17: 9: Old Testament.
http://bible.oremus.org/?passage=Exodus+17.

Genesis 12: 7: Old Testament
http://bible.oremus.org/?passage=Genesis+12

Jeremiah 31: 17: Old Testament.
http://bible.oremus.org/?passage=Jeremiah+31

Palestine mandate: The Council of the League of Nations.
http://avalon.law.yale.edu/20th_century/palmanda.asp

Palestine Remembered.
https://www.palestineremembered.com/al-Ramla/al-Lydd/index.html#Statistics

References

Anderson, B.R.O.G. (1991) *Imagined communities: reflections on the origin and spread of nationalism*. London: Verso.

Bashir, N. (2004) *Judaizing the Place: Misgav Regional Council in the Galilee (Arabic)*. Haifa: Mada el Carmel.

Bishara, A. (2011) "On a Jewish and Democratic State". https://www.dohainstitute.org/en/ResearchAndStudies/Pages/On_a_Jewish_and_Democratic_State.aspx.

Darwish, M. (1996) "Diary of a Palestinian Wound (Arabic)" in S. el Khadra'a el-Jausi (ed.), *Maousoua'ah ala'db alfalastini alma'asr*. Beirut: Dar el Awada.

Gellner, E. (1983) *Nations and nationalism*. Oxford: Blackwell Press.

Grinberg, L. (2009) "Speechlessness: In Search of Language to Resist the Israeli 'Thing Without a Name'" in *International Journal of Politics, Culture, and Society* **22**, no. 1: 105–116.

Hutton, P.H. (1993) *History as an art of memory*. Hanover, N.H.: University Press of New England.

Jad, I. (2007) "From Salons to the Popular Committees: Palestinian Women, 1919–89" in I. Pappé (ed.), *The Israel/Palestine question: a reader*. London: Routledge, 217–233.

Kassem, F. (2011) *Palestinian Women. Narrative Histories and Gendered Memories*. London/New York: Zed Books.

Kimmerling, B. (1993) "Militarism in the Israeli Society (Hebrew)" in *Theory and Criticism* **4**: 123–139.

Masalha, N. (2003) *The politics of denial: Israel and the Palestinian refugee problem*. London: Pluto Press.

Massad, J. (1995) "Conceiving the Masculine: Gender and Palestinian Nationalism" in *Middle East journal* **49**, no. 3: 467–484.

McClintock, A. (1993) "Family Feuds: Gender, Nationalism and the Family" in *Feminist Review*, no. 44: 61–80.

Morris, B. (2003) "The Causes and Character of the Arab Exodus from Palestine: the Israeli defense forces intelligence service analysis of June 1948" in I. Pappé (ed), *The Israel/Palestine Question. A Reader*. London/New York: Routledge, 193–210.

Najmabadi, A. (1997) "The Erotic Vatan [Homeland] as Beloved and Mother: To Love, to Possess, and To Protect" in *Comparative Studies in Society and History* **39**, no. 3: 442–467.

Said, E.W. (2003) *Orientalism*. London: Penguin.

Shilo, M. (2006) "Self-sacrifice, National-Historical identity and Selfdenial: the experience of Jewish immigrant women in Jerusalem, 1840–1914" in *Women's History Review* **11**, no. 2: 201–230.

Shohat, E. (1988) "Sephardim in Israel: Zionism from the Standpoint of Its Jewish Victims" in *Social Text*, no. 19–20: 1–35.

Spivak, G.C. (1992) "Woman in Difference: Mahasweta Devi's 'Douloti the Bountiful'" in A. Parker, M. Russo and others (eds.), *Nationalisms and Sexualities*. New York: Routledge, 96–117.

—— (2007) "Nationalism and the Imagination" in C. Vijayasree, M. Mukherjee and others (eds.), *Nation in Imagination: Essays on Nationalism, Sub-nationalism and Narration*. New Delhi: Orient Longman, 1–20.

Yacobi, H. (2002) "The Architecture of Ethnic Logic: Exploring the Meaning of the Built Environment in the 'Mixed' City of Lod, Israel" in *Geografiska Annaler. Series B, Human Geography* **84**, nos. 3–4: 171–187.

—— (2004) "In-Between Surveillance and Spatial Protest: the Production of Space of the 'Mixed City' of Lod?" in *Surveillance & Society* **2**, no. 1.

Yuval-Davis, N. (1997) *Gender & nation*. London: Sage Publications.

—— (2004) "Gender, the Nationalist Imagination, War, and Peace" in W. Giles and J. Hyndman (eds.), *Sites of Violence. Gender and Conflict Zones*. University of California Press, 170–190.

PART IV

RESTORING LAW

CHAPTER 11

LEGAL ARGUMENTATION IN TRANSITIONAL JUSTICE ADJUDICATION

A Land of New Arguments, a Land of New Law*

Juan Francisco SOTO HOYOS

* This chapter is an adjusted version of my Master's thesis submitted for the Advanced LLM in Public International Law at the Law School of Leiden University in July of 2016. Professor Dr. Carel Smith supervised it.

ANECDOTE

The elder peasant listens carefully to my explanation. I am talking about the Victims and Land Restitution Law. This law, I am saying, has created, among other things, a new legal action and process designed to guarantee the land restitution right of internally displaced persons (IDPs) who are victims of land seizures and forced abandonment in the context of the Colombian armed conflict. I am trying to expose the characteristics, benefits, and innovations of this transitional justice mechanism. These features, alongside their comparison with ordinary legal actions and processes, seem not to persuade the elder peasant and he is skeptical of my reasoning. I try to convince him by describing how this new law will benefit him by incorporating international human rights standards regarding the rights of victims of gross human rights violations and international humanitarian law breaches. I remark, using the rhetoric of transitional justice, how his right to truth, justice, and reparation with guarantees of non-recurrence can be satisfied by this new process. Nevertheless, he is not persuaded at all, and after taking a breath, he raises his hand and interrupts me by saying: "Here in Colombia one law replaces another law, and then another new law replaces that law; our reality is made out of laws and laws, but in the end there is no law at all."[1]

1 This anecdote arose during a meeting with a peasant community in the north of Colombia in November 2014. The meeting was part of the author's work as a lawyer in the Colombian Commission of Jurists where he represented victims of land seizures and forced abandonment within the context of the Colombian armed conflict. The author also used this anecdote in a

1. INTRODUCTION

The rustic wisdom of the peasant points to one of the main dilemmas of transitional justice adjudication. His words contain two claims. On the one hand, he implies that the process by which a new law is created to replace another law is indicative of a context of "no law", a context in which the Rule of Law can be undermined by the instability of the legal framework and by uncertainty regarding the applicable law, or what to do when old and new laws collide. On the other hand, his skepticism refers to the incapability of law exercised by the judiciary to actually produce desirable consequences in his reality. He has been disappointed by the law several times: it failed him when his rights were violated and his land seized; and it failed him when his claims were dismissed and his rights remained unprotected. With this new law, he says, there is nothing to indicate that this time it will be any different. He is skeptical whether the law's promises can be achieved and of the true effectiveness of this transitional justice mechanism. In short, therefore, his words are claiming two things: an adjudicative process whose consequences can transform his reality while truly establishing the Rule of Law. He seeks a transformation and the establishment of a kind of restorative justice in which reparation implies a restoration of the peasants' land and which, out of necessity, is able to deal with the tensions between the needs of today and the integrity of the legal order.

The dual claim of this peasant, while consistent with the UN's approach to transitional justice, is not free of tensions and paradoxes.[2] As some transitional justice scholars have highlighted, the nature of transitional justice sometimes implies a dynamic and flexible understanding of the Rule of Law.[3] Consequently, in transitional justice adjudication, judges might need to go beyond formalistic approaches to the Rule of Law in order to fulfill its goals.[4] Rather, they may need to apply a "purposive interpretational approach" that better enables

presentation to the Institute for Global Law and Policy – IGLP – Conference that took place at Harvard Law School in June 2015.

2 See: UN General Assembly (2004) UN Doc. S/2004/616.

3 As it will be developed below, this is the central thesis of Teitel (2000).

4 The formalistic approach of the Rule of Law, according to Tamanaha, incorporates three elements: (i) Rule-by-law (meaning law as an instrument of government action); (ii) Formal legality (which implies generality, prospectivity, clarity and certainty); and (iii) Democracy (which propounds that consent determines the content of the law). Tamanaha explains that the substantive approach, on the other hand, involves three different elements: (i) Individual rights; (ii) Right to justice; and (iii) Social welfare (which involves substantive equality, welfare, and the preservation of the community). These elements run from thinner to thicker accounts to the Rule of Law, although the latter usually involve the former. The tensions between transitional justice mechanisms and the Rule of Law usually arise from the formalistic elements; however, this does not mean that tensions with some of the elements of the substantive approach cannot also arise, specifically because the three last elements can pursue contrary goals. See: Tamanaha (2004) 91.

them to fulfil the aims of transition.[5] In doing so, however, the judge may impinge upon certain values of the Rule of Law, which can undermine its (re)-establishment in the long term.[6] This presents a dilemma or paradox of how a transitional judge can apply, through his legal reasoning, the "new law" while simultaneously going beyond its merely formal implementation? Furthermore, how can the judge ensure that for this peasant there is actually a law for him this time? How can he persuade the peasant that this time things are going to be different?

Answering these questions is not easy. It is true that in some cases a judge will not have to face this tension and will be able to fulfill the peasant's requirements by adjudicating in a conventional way without undermining the dual purpose of transitional justice. However, the adjudicative context of transitional justice often involves complex legal, political and social-economic realities that would pose several challenges to a transitional judge's legal reasoning. From a legal perspective, such challenges would include: the indeterminacy of the legal language that is typical of the drafting language of these mechanisms; the co-existence of different and colliding norms; the difficulty of being able to find applicable law to fill legal gaps; a high degree of discretion in the interpretation of principles, values and purposes of the "new" laws; and/or the legacy of legal reasoning from the former legal order that makes new understandings necessary to begin with. Furthermore, a transitional judge will need to face the complex contextual reality upon which his decision will have an impact. A fragile political environment requires balancing the powers and interests of different actors within an unstable social situation in which social actors have short- and long-term expectations regarding the results of the transitional justice mechanism. This situation is accompanied by an economic reality in which victims require reparation for harms suffered while society at large expects structural changes to restore normalcy and to guarantee a sustainable future.

This complex and difficult context in which adjudication must occur justifies the peasant's skepticism. It seems unlikely that there is an "ideal" model of transitional justice adjudication that can guarantee the (re)-establishment of the Rule of Law and achievement of its restorative aims of transition. However, by acknowledging the rawness of this reality, the transitional judge is called upon to decide the case and to persuade the peasant that his decision is an appropriate one. For that reason, it is necessary to pave the way for a suitable model of adjudication in which the judge can achieve this goal: one that can offer the judge adequate tools to justify his decision and satisfy the "dual-purpose" of transition, while also satisfying the double claim of the peasant, namely for

5 See: Yusuf (2007) 1.

6 McAuliffe highlights this paradox. See: McAuliffe (2010).

an adjudication that is capable of transforming and restoring his reality while simultaneously establishing the Rule of Law.

This chapter will propose such a model in order to open a debate regarding the interaction of transitional justice and legal argumentation. To contribute to this debate, this chapter offers (i) an inquiry about the context and complexities of adjudication in transitions; (ii) a proposal regarding what would be a suitable theoretical foundation for a model of transitional justice adjudication; and (iii) a test of the model through the analysis of transitional justice adjudication by land restitution judges and tribunals in Colombia. Its ambition is that these inputs might motivate transitional justice actors and legal theorists to pursue the debate that it is necessary to have in order to ensure that there actually is a law for this peasant.

2. TRANSITIONAL JUSTICE ADJUDICATION: A THEORETICAL INQUIRY

Imagine a scene. A transitional judge is sitting at his desk studying a case. The decision is complex and the judge has to analyse several factors in order to adjudicate it. He wonders about the context in which he has to decide and the implications that it has for his legal reasoning. The judge thinks about the difficulties he needs to overcome. On the one hand, he can turn to the law governing the type of case before him and engage with new legislation that "attempts to come to terms with a legacy of large-scale past abuses, in order to ensure accountability, serve justice and achieve reconciliation".[7] On the other hand, this legislation also seeks to (re)-establish the Rule of Law understood as "a principle of governance in which all persons … are accountable to laws that are publicly promulgated, equally enforced and independently adjudicated, and which are consistent with international human rights norms and standards".[8] Furthermore, it promotes a Rule of Law that requires measures to ensure adherence to the principles of legality, certainty, due process and for the avoidance of arbitrariness.[9] The judge will require tools to deal with specific complexities that arise from this tension. For instance, new legislation may incorporate human rights provisions that are often ambiguous, vague or indeterminate, largely because they are statements of values or principles.

7 UN General Assembly, Secretary-General, above n. 2 at para. 8.

8 Ibid. para. 6.

9 This definition of the Rule of Law incorporates the three elements of the formalistic approach as defined by Tamanaha. However, one can also assert that from the UN's perspective some of the elements of the substantive approach are also implied, especially considering that the definition declares that these elements should be consistent with international human rights norms and standards. See: Tamanaha above n. 4.

Such ambiguity might impinge upon the strict adherence to these same rights in a consistent and coherent way.[10] Furthermore, such provisions may clash with domestic laws, and the principle of legality or legal security may be undermined if a judge is required to pay heed to both within the applicable international legal framework.[11] He is aware that his decision will impact on a complex and unstable transitional political context in which there are myriad competing interests that at times may be directly conflicting, but that are nonetheless equally worthy of recognition. Thus, it becomes necessary for the judge to understand the structural socio-economic causes underlying the violent past, and therefore it is likely that he will need a new approach to his adjudicatory process in order to fulfill both these aims. Although a judge may find such contextual complexities overwhelming, he or she nevertheless has to decide. But how?

2.1. THE CONTEXT OF TRANSITIONAL JUSTICE ADJUDICATION

Providing an answer to this question is not an easy task, particularly because the context of transitional justice adjudication may vary. However, a common dilemma may arise regarding achieving transitional aims and the role of the Rule of Law. As Rincon has asserted, it is true that transitional justice, depending on context or focus, pursues various different goals.[12] Generally speaking, however, transitional justice mechanisms are designed to deal with past gross human rights and/or humanitarian law violations, and therefore the goal of transitional justice mechanisms generally involves some new ideal as well as overcoming and restoring the consequences of that past to build a different future.[13] In this transition from the past to the future, the process of adjudication must somehow operate amid constant legal tension.

Teitel has identified three phases on the historical progression of transitional justice in which this tension is present. In the first phase, namely the "Post-War phase", accountability through the application of international law raises tensions around legitimacy vis-à-vis values arising from the domestic notions of the Rule of Law such as the principle of legality.[14] In the second, "Post-Cold War" phase, the aim of transitional justice was to overcome authoritarian or oppressive regimes, which created tensions between punishment and amnesty, retroactivity and tampering with existent law, and the contradiction between

---

10 Tobin (2010) at 1.

11 Ní Aoaláin, Campbell and Bell (2004) at 308.

12 Rincón (2012), at 112–113.

13 Ibid.

14 Teitel (2003) at 73.

prevailing human rights standards and contrary policies, among others.[15] The third and current "Steady-State" phase, was one of a "normalization" of transitional justice mechanisms in diverse contexts (internal armed conflicts, political flux, etc.), but also where tensions with the Rule of Law arose in liberal democracies as a result of adjudicatory fragmentation, the high degree of politicization in the uses of justice, and debates about the continuity or discontinuity of transitional justice mechanisms.[16]

2.1.1. Legal Complexities of Transitional Justice Adjudication

Christine Bell has argued that this common tension between transitional justice and the Rule of Law mainly implies that transitional justice mechanisms do not fit easily within existing legal regimes. Specifically, in the context of transition, different legal regimes often interact, the most obvious being domestic law, transitional legislation, and international law. Their interactions can be labelled "regime conflict and legal pluralism", which helps in understanding how the adjudicative process will often face complex legal dilemmas regarding the legality or illegality of certain measures, normative hierarchies, or questions of priority.[17] Such complexities can produce a "legal chaos" in which it is difficult to find the applicable norm or to determine legality.[18] In practical terms, during the process of adjudication in transitional contexts, judges frequently face "hard cases" or "problem cases". According to Moreno, in every legal context, "hard cases" arise because of the ambiguity, vagueness and indeterminacy of legal norms, normative conflicts and legal gaps, and from diverse ideological interpretations about the purposes of the law.[19]

The number of "hard cases" is likely to increase in transitional adjudication due to (i) the indeterminacy of human rights provisions, leaving them open to different and/or contrary interpretations;[20] (ii) normative conflicts among different applicable branches of law and the challenge of filling legal lacunae either with domestic law or international law;[21] and (iii) ideological difficulty in finding solutions to "hard cases", given the multiple aims that transition can pursue.[22] Therefore, as Bell says, this reality requires

---

15 Ibid. 75–77.

16 Ibid. 89–93.

17 Bell (2008) at 19–20.

18 Zajac Sannerholm (2012) at 109.

19 Moreno also analyses the existence of "hard cases", that arise out of the difficulty of establishing the facts of the case and/or from determining their relevance to the legal problem. However, due to its emphasis on the normative perspective, this chapter will not address this here. See: Moreno Cruz (2012), at 170–173.

20 Tobin, above n. 10 at 25–28.

21 Bell, above n. 17 at 19.

22 Balasco (2013) at 202.

"A bridge to be formed between what a blackletter application of any one of the legal regimes might require and the difficulty of 'fitting' each regime to transitional justice dilemmas."[23] Therefore, building "Bell's bridge" necessitates an approach to adjudication and legal argumentation that goes beyond "a blackletter legal analysis" and demands deeper contemplation of the political, social and economic complexities of transitional justice adjudication.

2.1.2. Political and Socio-Economic Complexities of Adjudication[24]

While the legal analysis of adjudication in transition relies on the logic of a "system of rules", a political analysis would find it important to take into account "premises about power, interest, prudence, and strategic interaction in light of expected outcome".[25] For instance, during transitions from authoritarian regimes to democracies, it is relevant to consider how any decision is going to impact the balance of power between political actors of the "old regime" and the reformers and "new" political actors of the transition period.[26] Likewise, with transitions in "conflicted democracies", institutional identities are often delicate, because it is difficult to challenge their legitimacy, while in transitions from war to peace, armed actors may look to win political "victories".[27] Therefore, the outcome of any ruling should be based on considerations regarding this context, in order to overcome political obstacles that might otherwise prevent outcomes of the transition or make its measures inefficient.

However, such an analysis cannot omit socio-economic contexts and their complexities during transition.[28] According to Mani, from a social perspective, a model of adjudication must address at least three sets of issues: (i) social injustice, inequality; (ii) marginalization and discrimination; and (iii) post-transition social violence or the possible contribution of the transitional adjudicative mechanism to new conflicts.[29] Likewise, one must consider what causal role economics had in the violent past. As Miller has argued, the inclusion of an economic perspective in implementing transitional justice mechanisms

---

23 Bell, above n. 17 at 19.

24 It is important to clarify that this section does not purport to encompass all of the political and socio-economic complexities of adjudications in transition contexts because they can vary from case-to-case. Instead, it highlights some of the characteristics of these complexities to illustrate their relevance in the process of transitional justice adjudication.

25 Vinjamuri and Snyder (2015) at 305.

26 Teitel, above n. 3 at 310.

27 Ni Aolain and Campbell (2005) at 207.

28 Evans criticizes the absence of a socio-economic perspective in the implementation of transitional justice mechanisms and the omission to consider socio-economic rights violations alongside the civil and political ones. See: Evans (2015).

29 Mani (2008) at 253–254.

will assist to (i) evaluate the economic causes and consequences of the violent past; (ii) note whatever economic changes are required during the transition; and (iii) establish the basis for future socio-economic development.[30] Thus, in order for an adjudicative process to be able to overcome the structural inequalities of the past, it should incorporate an analysis of the economic roots of the violent past to allow for an effective evaluation of possible consequences of decisions in terms of short- and long-term social expectations.[31]

2.2. THE DYNAMIC APPROACH TO THE RULE OF LAW IN TRANSITIONS

So far, it is evident that the complexities inherent in transitional justice may require a new approach to the Rule of Law.[32] Teitel has asserted that such an understanding must be "dynamic" because while in ordinary contexts the Rule of Law is prospective, in transitions the Rule of Law instead has to be both backward- and forward-looking as it deals with the past and reclaims the future.[33] This means that the Rule of Law ordinarily implies an adherence to settled and to written law, while in transitional times things must be more flexible because the law is a channel of change.[34] Therefore, as Teitel argues, it seems that "the juxtaposition is always between the Rule of Law as settled norms versus the Rule of Law as transformative".[35] This means that legality is socially and politically constructed, and somehow judge-made.[36] In transitions, therefore, the judge has a law-making role that allows and requires him to set aside conventional understandings of adjudication, such as strict adherence to the principle of legality or the equal and consistent application of the law, in order to reach the needs of justice and peace.[37] In consequence, transitional justice adjudication requires reasoning in which decisions preserve "a threshold level of formal continuity" at the same time that they pursue "transformative discontinuity".[38]

This "dynamic" understanding of the Rule of Law has inspired scholars analyzing transitions in Argentina and Nigeria respectively to argue for a

30 Miller (2008) at 267.
31 Ibid. 280–284.
32 This approach would vary depending on each context. In societies with a restrictive formalistic approach to the Rule of Law, the variation would be greater than in societies in which the substantive elements of the Rule of Law are conventionally accepted.
33 Teitel, above n. 3 at 7.
34 Ibid. 11–12.
35 Ibid. 17.
36 Ibid. 25.
37 Ibid. 215.
38 Ibid. 220.

purposive model of adjudication.[39] González, for instance, has argued that in Argentina judges have had to depart from the formalist and positivist legal culture in order to realize the claims of justice and truth in society.[40] He describes a legal culture in which the "dominant hermeneutic" of the judiciary was an insistence on the supremacy of the domestic written law resting on the longstanding hegemony of a positivist approach to law, and argues that this culture was a major obstacle in the fight against impunity. Contrary to such a highly positivist culture, Gonzalez argues that judges needed to remove amnesty provisions and other written norms that might imply limitations to the investigation, prosecution and punishment of gross human rights violations.[41] By this logic, the transitional judge may need to adopt less formal methods of reasoning, even if that involves giving lesser weight to values such as the principle of legality or the equal application of the law.

Likewise, Yusuf has defended a "purposive judicial interpretational approach" as the most suitable method of argumentation in transitional justice adjudication. This method is particularly necessary in those contexts in which the traditional legal culture is attached to formalistic and positivistic understandings of the Rule of Law.[42] To support this argument, Yusuf analyses two decisions of the Nigerian Supreme Court of Justice during transitional periods. In order to reject what he labels "plain-fact jurisprudence", Yusuf disputes the ruling of the Court in the "*Oputa Panel Case*" where it rejected the establishment of the Human Rights Violations Investigations Commission for being inconsistent with written law.[43] According to Yusuf, judges in this case opted for a "legalist" approach to the Rule of Law by favoring domestic written law over the international legal obligations of the state, the social context, and the pursuit of truth regarding human rights violations.[44] In contrast, Yusuf analyses the "purposive judicial interpretational approach" employed by the ruling of the Court in the "*ICPC Case*".[45] In this case, the Court upheld the legality of the Independent Corrupt Practices Commission (ICPC), even though there was written law that supported the opposite conclusion.

39 This approach, therefore, would prioritize the later elements of Tamanaha's scheme, i.e. preferring substantive justice over formal justice. See: Tamanaha above n. 4.

40 González Ocantos (2014) at 481.

41 Ibid. 483.

42 Yusuf, above n. 5 at 32–33.

43 Ibid. 3–5.

44 Ibid. 12.

45 Yusuf based this approach on Aharon Barak's theory of legal interpretation. In this theory, Barak establishes that the main purpose of the interpretational activity is to find the "intention" that the law pursues. Thus, Yusuf supports this theory to the extent that it allows the judge to go beyond the written law in order to achieve the goals of the transition. However, as is explained below, this theory is not suitable to provide the theoretical foundation of transitional justice adjudication. Regarding Barak's theory see: Barak (2005).

According to Yusuf, the judgment was based on the grounds of "peace, order and good government of the Federation".[46] In this approach the Court, by being consistent with the aims of transitional justice, "clearly made a policy decision to reject the black letter of the law".[47]

In light of these arguments, it is convincing that a "dynamic" understanding of the Rule of Law in transitions is suitable to face the complexities of transitional contexts. Such a model facilitates judicial activity by allowing the use of political or social grounds in judicial reasoning over the written law. Through a "purposive, interpretational approach", a judge would be able to identify the final purpose of a law and adjudicate in ways that would achieve the goals of the transition. However, this "dynamic" understanding of the Rule of Law has raised concerns that even Teitel has recognized as being risky because the "arguments for limiting conventional legality are often pretextual."[48]

2.3. THE RISKS OF THE DYNAMIC APPROACH

Defending the "dynamic" approach to the Rule of Law implies three general risks. Firstly, this approach assumes a strong and well-structured judicial system. However, if transition involves the transformation of institutions that were involved in the violent past, this poses a problem, as it would be likely that judiciaries were part of those institutions. Thus, it may be problematic to grant a high degree of discretion to bodies that may lack sufficient capacity to assume the transformative challenge and to succeed with it.[49] Furthermore, the political flux of the transition can also impact the composition of judiciaries. Different political forces with diverse purposes can affect how these bodies are established.[50] Furthermore, they may have to co-exist with new transitional justice mechanisms that might seek to pursue opposing ends.[51]

Secondly, this dynamic approach may overemphasize the importance of the uniqueness of transitional adjudication, thereby giving it too great a scope for flexibility, discretion and arbitrary decision-making, and may be resistant to counter-arguments or criticism.[52] Indeed, if a judiciary is given a broad scope

46 Yusuf, above n. 5 at 26–30.

47 Ibid. 33.

48 Teitel, above n. 3 at 224.

49 Krygier (2001) at 29.

50 David Dyzenhaus argues that in transitions judges can serve either the interests of the political actors of a repressive regime or those of the new transition politicians. This, according to him, is risky because this political orientation can undermine the independence that is required of any judicial body. See: Dyzenhaus (2003) at 347.

51 Regarding this argument Loyle and Davenport study Rwanda's case and conclude that the Government has used justice mechanisms to pursue alternative ends. See: Loyle and Davenport (2016).

52 Krygier, above n. 49 at 31.

of discretion that is justified by the achievement of certain transition goals, then the system as a whole will be characterized by the means being justified by the ends. This poses a risk that fighting the arbitrariness of the past may promote arbitrariness in the future.

Thirdly, this paradoxical effect of the "dynamic" approach can also contradict one of the aims of transition, which is precisely the (re)-establishment of the Rule of Law in the long-run.[53] In fact, as McAuliffe has noted, in the UN Secretary-General's report *Rule of Law and Transitional Justice* of 2004,[54] the Rule of Law and transitional justice concepts are inseparably linked and mutually reinforcing.[55] Likewise, Pablo de Greiff has highlighted this relationship in his 2012 *Report on the Promotion of Truth, Justice, Reparation and Guarantees of Non-Recurrence*, where he asserts that strengthening the Rule of Law is one of the main goals of transitional justice mechanisms.[56]

McAuliffe seems to understand this paradox. While it is true that transitional justice adjudication requires a flexible understanding of the Rule of Law in order to achieve its goals of peace, justice, restoration, and reconciliation, it is also true that one of the aims of transitional justice mechanisms is to (re)-establish the Rule of Law in its conventional meaning. As McAuliffe argues:

> [T]he great danger in applying even the most ephemeral of realist and idealist deviations from the Rule of Law is that their perceived success in mediating transitions from repressions or war to democratic rule risks undermining or delegitimizing the Rule of Law values of coherence, enforcement, equal application etc., in the years after the transition.[57]

3. PAVING THE WAY FOR A TRANSITIONAL JUSTICE ADJUDICATION MODEL

Let's return to the scene of the notional judge in section 2. The judge is still studying the case. He has identified the context in which his decision will take place, and he is aware that he needs a model of adjudication with which he can solve the problem before him, or at least decrease the tension between the short-term goals of transition the long-term aim to (re)-establish the Rule of Law. Such a model should be capable of (i) guaranteeing that the adjudicatory process triggers desirable consequences in the light of both the aims of transition and the values of the Rule of Law; (ii) providing methods of argumentation

53 Andersen argues that this is precisely the purpose of any transition because without the establishment of the Rule of Law the other purposes would fail. See: ANDERSEN (2015) at 312.
54 UNGA, above n. 2.
55 McAuliffe, above n. 6 at 128.
56 UNHRC (2012) UN Doc. A/HRC/21/46, at 13–14.
57 McAuliffe, above n. 6 at 150.

to adjudicate "hard cases"; and (iii) evaluating whether these methods are compatible with the dual-purpose of transitional justice adjudication.

3.1. JUDGING BY CONSEQUENCES IN TRANSITIONS

The first requirement of a model of transitional justice adjudication is a theoretical foundation that guarantees that the adjudicatory process produces desirable consequences in light of both the aims of transition (i.e. overcoming the violent past, and restoring and transforming victims' realities) and the ideals of the Rule of Law. Neil MacCormick's legal argumentation theory seems to fulfil this requirement with its cardinal feature of "judging by consequences".[58] MacCormick's justificatory scheme requires that a ruling "must make sense both in its own legal system and in the outside world".[59] To do so, it should be based on two criteria: (i) to be consistent and coherent in the light of the legal system; and (ii) to produce juridical consequences that make sense in reality.[60]

MacCormick's notion is grounded on two assumptions. First, it assumes that the process of adjudication involves two orders of justification. The first order takes place when a judge can structure his decision through the judicial syllogism "whenever OF (operative fact) then NC (normative consequence)".[61] However, because disputes can arise in relation to premises such as facts, classification, interpretation or relevance, a second order of justification is required.[62] In this way, the adjudication of "hard cases" or "problem cases" involves a process of justification that is not based on deductivism but instead on practical reasoning. Here, argumentation enters the realm of "the better-or-worse, the arguable, the preferable, the more or less persuasive".[63] As a consequence, justification is persuasive rather than demonstrative.[64] As Peczenik has argued, in this order there are no definitive and exclusive ways to reach a correct legal answer.[65]

However, this does not imply that in this stage of practical reasoning any kind of arguments are compatible and acceptable from a legal perspective. Indeed, as a special case of general practical reasoning, arguments and counter-arguments are contemplated in order to find better or preferable

58 Del Mar (2015) at 438.
59 Bertea (2008) at 7.
60 Ibid.
61 Eveline Feteris and Harm Kloosterhuis have stated that MacCormick recognizes that there are cases in which, due to the clarity of both premises, judges can resolve cases through "deductive justification". See: Feteris and Kloosterhuis (2009) at 315.
62 MacCormick (2005) at 43.
63 Ibid. at 77.
64 Ibid. at 1–2.
65 Peczenik (2009) at 37.

legal solutions. As such, there cannot be assertions without reasons and those reasons should allow for challenges or revisions in the future. In addition, this second-order justification also involves arguments that are based on sound legal reasoning that are necessary in order to reach a level of acceptability that can persuade a legal audience.[66]

In order to imbue arguments with this sound legal reasoning, MacCormick affirms that "they have to be subsumable under a relevant principle of action universally stated, even if the universal is acknowledged to be defeasible".[67] This idea of "universalizability" can be understood as a backward- and forward-looking concept in which a decision is grounded in reasons that are capable of being adopted in future cases, as well as in reasoning from prior cases and/or the established law.[68] Thus, a judge must draft a normative "premise" in universal terms in order make it applicable to similar scenarios and then structure his or her decision through the judicial syllogism of the first-order of justification.[69]

However, as MacCormick notices, it is necessary to evaluate the choice of the universal proposition because there can be different ways to solve a case and because the acceptability of such universalization can be challenged.[70] In this evaluation it is necessary: (i) to consider the universal statement in light of its consistency and coherence with the legal system; and (ii) to evaluate this choice in view of its consequences in the outside world.[71] Consequently, two kinds of arguments or reasons can be found in the second-order justification: (a) arguments about consistency and coherence, or "rightness-reasons"; and (b) consequentialist arguments, or "goal-reasons".[72] It is important to note that these criteria do not imply a hierarchy but rather a confluence between them within the process of practical reasoning, since they arise from the same source: the principles and values of the law.[73]

66 MacCormick follows Robert Alexy in the definition of legal reasoning as a special case of general practical reasoning. See: MacCormick, above n. 62 at 17.

67 Ibid. at 99.

68 Spaak (2006) at 122.

69 MacCormick illustrates this idea of universalization through the analysis of Solomon's well-known decision regarding the mother of the disputed child. According to MacCormick, even though the decision was specific to a case, Solomon's justification was based on the universal provision that every child must be under the custody of his or her real mother. Thus, as soon as Solomon knew who the real mother was, he could decide who should have custody over it. See MacCormick, above n. 62 at 78–89.

70 Ibid. 100.

71 Del Mar, above n. 58 at 440.

72 Spaak uses this division without establishing a parallel with "rightness-reasons" or "goal-reasons"; however, in this chapter's interpretation of MacCormick's theory, "rightness-reasons" are mainly about consistency and coherence with the legal system while goal-reasons relate to consequences regarding the legal system and the "external" world. See Spaak, above n. 68 at 122.

73 MacCormick, above n. 62 at 255.

In sum, the notion of "judging by consequences" goes beyond evaluating the immediate impact of a decision on the parties to a case, even though that may play an important role in the decision.[74] It also differs from the idea of "purposive interpretation" because, as Spaak has asserted, whereas consequentialist reasoning requires a logic in which a decision yields the best consequences on the whole (within the legal system and in reality), teleological reasoning requires a decision that yields the best consequences in light of the purpose of the legislation in question.[75] Thus, this approach emphasizes the legal implications of the decision in terms of both its possible impact in the material world and its normative status within the legal order.[76] Therefore, the consequentialist argumentation can be understood as forward-looking reasoning in which the judge is evaluating his ruling through values such as reasonability, self-discipline, or substantive justice, etc.[77] The examination of a decision's consequences, in contrast, is mainly an examination from the perspective of the values of the law, whose rightness-reasons and goal-reasons are, as MacCormick states, "two sides of the same coin".[78]

In the light of this "cardinal" feature, MacCormick's theory seems to be suitable for transitional justice adjudication. Through the criteria of judging by consequences, a decision can be tested to ensure that it creates desirable consequences regarding the purpose of the adjudicative mechanism – such as restoration, reconciliation or justice – and that these consequences do not severely contradict the legal system within which it is based.[79] It allows the judge to analyse whether the legal consequences of his decision will satisfy transitional legality and the goals of the measure. It will reveal whether or not they are contrary to the internal legal framework or to the purpose of the mechanism, and whether the reasoning will produce an outcome inconsistent with the aims of transitional legislation and the (re)-establishment of the Rule of Law.[80]

However, this does not mean that through this model a judge can reach an unimpeachable decision. Indeed, it is possible to identify different methods of argumentation and to choose those that would be more likely to be imbued with sound legal reasoning. Such arguments would have to be somehow

---

74 Ibid. 103.

75 Spaak, above n. 68 at 133.

76 Neil MacCormick, above n. 62 at 110.

77 As Del Mar explains, reasonability can be understood as being reasonable from a practical view, self-disciplinarity implies that the judge is not guided by its bias, and the search of substantive justice relies on the avoiding of substantive injustice in the future. See Del Mar, above n. 58 at 438.

78 MacCormick, above n. 62 at 120.

79 Dyzenhaus, above n. 50 at 357.

80 Ibid.

persuasive and, conclusive at the same time, even if whatever certainty is reached is defeasible.[81] By these rational standards, it is possible to undermine a degree of uncertainty about the justification of judicial decisions and to guarantee an absence of arbitrariness as one of the essential values of the Rule of Law.[82] In other words, MacCormick's thesis is based on the idea that it is through good legal reasoning that the values of the Rule of Law are not just respected but even enhanced.[83]

3.2. METHODS OF ARGUMENTATION IN "HARD CASES"

MacCormick develops three main methods of argumentation that are useful to solve "hard cases" that can be evaluated in light of the "judging by consequences" criteria as far as they usually involve rightness-reasons and goal-reasons. These methods are: (i) interpretative argumentation; (ii) using precedents; and (iii) analogies. Regarding methods of interpretation, MacCormick establishes three general categories: (i) linguistic arguments; (ii) systematic arguments; and (iii) teleological-evaluative arguments.[84] The two first categories are linked with rightness-reasons because they aim for consistent and coherent consequences within the legal system.[85] On the other hand, teleological-evaluative arguments are linked with goal-reasons because they evaluate whether an interpretation would produce desirable consequences vis-à-vis the purposes of the statute that is being interpreted.[86]

By the same token, arguing with precedents[87] and analogies in light of principles involves the double-standard test of judging by consequences. Indeed, in reasoning that uses precedents, as Soriano has noticed, two factors are relevant: (i) the backward-looking notion that requires a judge to take into account the coherence and consistency of the reasoning that prior decisions used to solve similar legal problems; and (ii) the forward-looking notion in which a judge must consider and assess the juridical consequences of his decision in future similar cases.[88]

Likewise, arguing by analogy in order to fill legal gaps requires principled reasoning in which a judge identifies a prevailing legal principle in another

81 MacCormick, above n. 62 at 28.
82 Ibid.
83 Veitch (2006) at 493.
84 MacCormick, above n. 62 at Chapter 7.
85 Ibid. 132.
86 Ibid.
87 It is not the purpose of this section to explore the scope of argument by precedent in continental law. Thus, the inputs regarding this method are applicable in those jurisdictions in which precedent is binding or plays a relevant role in the argumentation process.
88 Moral Soriano (2008) at 35.

relevant and similar provision. In doing so, the judge achieves coherence by making sense of the legal system by applying a principle that governs similar situations.[89] However, the identification of a suitable principle involves pursuing a legal value in a way that encompasses not just evaluating its coherence with the legal system but also evaluating its consequences for substantive justice.[90] In this way, this method implies using the concept of "judging by consequences" to make decisions through which a transitional judge can test the suitability of a solution given the dual-purpose of the mechanism.

3.3. BUILDING SCHEMES TO ADJUDICATE BY CONSEQUENCES IN TRANSITIONS

So far, judging by consequences seems to provide a suitable theoretical foundation to pursue the dual-purpose of transitional justice adjudication. Correspondingly, three methods of argumentation in hard cases have been identified and explained in the light of this model of adjudication. Now, it is necessary to construct schemes in which it is possible to structure a decision and/or evaluate it in order to verify the suitability of the model. In doing this, it is necessary to conceive of three different schemes for cases of (i) indeterminacy; (ii) normative conflicts; and (iii) legal gaps that are likely to occur during transitions. The schemes are based on the "the rational reconstruction of argumentation of judicial decision justified by referring to the consequences in relation to the purpose of the rule" proposed by Feteris.[91] This is applicable to the first scheme of indeterminacy, with no changes or adjustments needed because it allows for an assessment of hermeneutical arguments in transition as will be shown in section 3.3.1 below. The two other schemes that deal with normative conflicts and legal gaps are built upon Feteris' model and will also tested later in sections 3.3.2 and 3.3.3.

3.3.1. *Scheme of Cases of Indeterminacy in Transitions*

According to Feteris, general indeterminacy in legal cases arises due to the possibility of different interpretations of a rule. In order to decide which interpretation should prevail, a judge must follow this first step:

> (1) If the application of rule X in interpretation X' leads to Y', and Y' is desirable, and if the application of rule X in interpretation X" leads to Y" and Y" is undesirable,

89 MacCormick, above n. 62 at 207.
90 Ibid. 203–204.
91 Feteris (2005) 459.

> then the application of rule X in interpretation X' is desirable, and the application of the rule X in interpretation X" is undesirable.[92]

The second step requires proving that (i) a chosen interpretation (rule X as X") actually leads to the desirable result (Y') and that the result (Y') is actually desirable from the perspective of the legal system as well as compatible with the purpose/goal of the legislation (P) that was intended by the historical legislator or that is the rational purpose prescribed by the valid legal order.[93] This scheme entails the following:

> (2) Consequence Y' is desirable from the perspective of the legal system and consequence Y' is compatible with the purpose or goal P. Purpose P is intended by the historical legislator, where purpose P is a rational purpose objectively prescribed by the valid legal order. Purpose P can be found in the following documents ... and purpose P is underlying the following rules, principles and values of the valid legal order.[94]

In this way, the global structure of the scheme would combine step one and step two, thereby operating to equally (re-)build the previously dismissed interpretation.

3.3.2. *Scheme of Cases of Normative Conflicts in Transitions*

For a transitional case (C1), two rules are applicable. Rule X' [transitional rule] and rule X" [ordinary rule]. The application of rule X' leads to solution Y' but affects the purpose P" of rule X". The application of rule X" leads to solution Y" but affects the purpose P' of rule X'. Both solutions Y' and Y" are desirable from the perspective of P' and P" respectively. The consequences of Y' are compatible both with the values, principles and goals of the Ordinary Law (OL) and the Transitional Mechanism (TM). Y" consequences are incompatible either with the values, principles and goals of OL and/or TM, and therefore the consequences of the choosing rule X' (over rule X") are preferable to the consequences of the choosing rule X".

> (1) If the application of rule X' (over X") leads to Y', and Y' is desirable from the perspective of P' and the consequences of Y' are compatible both with the values, principles and goals of OL and TM, then rule X' shall prevail over rule X", the consequences of which, if applied, would undermine the purposes, goals, and principles of OL and/or TM; or

92 Ibid. 463.
93 Ibid.
94 Ibid. 464.

(2) If the application of rule X" (over X') leads to Y", and Y" is desirable from the perspective of P', and the consequences of Y" are compatible both with the values, principles and goals of OL and TM, then rule X" shall prevail over rule X', the consequences of which, if applicable, would undermine the purposes, goals, and principles of OL and/or TM.

3.3.3. *Scheme for Filling Legal Gaps in Transitional Laws*

A legal question in a transitional case (C1) does not have an applicable provision in the transitional law (TL). However, ordinary rule X' solves a similar legal problem. The application, by analogy, of rule X' leads to Y', and Y' is desirable from the perspective of P' [purposes of TL]. If the consequences of Y' are compatible in the light of the goals, principles, values of TM, then, the application of rule X' to fill the legal gap of TL is suitable.

(1) If the application by analogy of rule X' to fill the legal gap of TL leads to Y', and Y' is desirable from the perspective of P', and if the consequences of Y' in light of P' are compatible with the goals, principles and values of TM, then the analogic implementation of X' is suitable to fill the legal gap of TL; or
(2) If the application by analogy of rule X' to fill the legal gap of (TL) leads to Y', and Y' is undesirable from the perspective of P' of TL, and if the consequences of Y' undermine the goals, principles and values of TM, then the analogic implementation of X' is not suitable to fill the legal gap of TL.

4. TESTING THE MODEL IN PRACTICE: "COLOMBIA'S LAND RESTITUTION PROCESS"

Our notional transitional judge now needs to test the model proposed in the prior section in order to verify its suitability for the land restitution process in Colombia. This restitution process was created by Law 1448 of 2011 or the "Victims and Land Restitution Law",[95] and attempts to restore one of the main consequences of the Colombian armed conflict, namely land seizure and forced abandonment.[96] In the judicial stage of this mechanism, as developed below, land restitution judges and tribunals have faced a tension between Rule of Law values – such as consistency, equal applicability of the law, due process

95 Congreso de la República de Colombia, Ley de Víctimas y Restitución de Tierras (Ley 1448) 2011 [Diario Oficial 48096], (Hereinafter 'Law 1448').
96 Unidad de Restitución de Tierras, *La Restitución De Tierras En Colombia: Del Sueño A La Realidad* (Presidencia de la República de Colombia, 2015), http://wp.presidencia.gov.co/sitios/especiales/Documents/20150513-especial-restitucion-tierras/docs/restitucion-tierras-caolombia-sueno-a-realidad.pdf.

or adherence to the principle of legality – and the overall aims of the land restitution process.[97] These tensions generally result from: the convergence of different legal regimes applicable to the procedures, indeterminacy, normative conflicts, and legal gaps.[98] Furthermore, the process has to deal with a complex reality in which political and socio-economic issues surround the adjudication of land restitution claims.[99] As such, the judicial practice in this process seems to be an appropriate test of the model posed in Section 3. This section does so by analysing a series of land restitution rulings that resolved "hard cases" by assessing the argumentation methods used and by verifying whether the solution chosen was adequate from the perspective of the posed model.

4.1. LEGAL ARGUMENTATION IN LAND RESTITUTION CASES

This section analyses a sequence of rulings in which the tension between the dual purpose of transitional justice adjudication has arisen. Each of the sequences relates to at least one of the categories of "hard cases" developed before, and each is surrounded by the political and socio-economic complexities of the process. The first, the "secondary occupants case", analyses a case of

---

97 According to Articles 76 and 91 of Law 1448, Colombia's land restitution process encompasses two stages, one administrative (before the Special Administrative Unit for the Restitution of Dispossessed and Forcibly Abandoned Land (URT)), and the other judicial (before land restitution judges and tribunals). Once the administrative process is finished, judges have 4 months to issue a decision.

98 Law 1448, which contains the main provisions upon which the land restitution process is based, is characterized by notably indeterminate language that leaves considerable scope for judicial discretion. Likewise, although the land restitution process is based on international law standards, one of the central issues that the land restitution legal action tries to resolve is a matter of private and agrarian law, since it relates to the regulation of property, contracts or inheritance, and access to land, among other things. Therefore, judges and tribunals have faced several issues of normative hierarchy, suitability, and conflicts. This situation has also given rise to tensions between longstanding understandings of private and agrarian law concepts and the purposes of Law 1448.

99 In fact, the dispute for natural resources and the control of land is one of the roots of the Colombian armed conflict. Thus, the resolution of land disputes can be imagined as having a direct impact upon the contrary interests of diverse actors in the conflict. Likewise, land restitution adjudication is being implemented in a complicated socio-economic contextual reality. Forced displacement and land seizures have impacted directly upon the inequality of land ownership concentration in Colombia. See: Centro Nacional de Memoria Histórica, *¡Basta Ya! Colombia: memorias de guerra y dignidad* (Centro Nacional de Memoria Histórica, 2013), http://www.centrodememoriahistorica.gov.co/descargas/informes 2013/bastaYa/basta-ya-colombia-memorias-de-guerra-y-dignidad-2016.pdf.; and Ana María Ibáñez and Juan Carlos Muñoz, "The Persistence of Land Concentration in Colombia: What Happened Between 2000 and 2009?" in *Distributive Justice in Transitions* (Torkel Opsahl Academic ePublisher, 2010), https://www.fichl.org/fileadmin/fichl/documents/FICHL_6_web.pdf.

indeterminacy in which the consequences of the ordinary understanding of a provision impacted negatively upon the aims of the process and the involved actors. The second, the "agrarian law vs. land restitution law case", analyses a case of normative conflict in which two provisions are potentially applicable to solve the same legal problem but with contrary outcomes. Finally, the third case involves a legal gap in which the use of analogical reasoning could have generated problematic outcomes vis-à-vis the nature of the process. Each analysis will present a description of the legal problem followed by the reconstruction of the argumentation that has solved it through the use of the schemes posed in section 3. Finally, the ultimate solutions the legal problems each faced is assessed in light of the proposed model of adjudication.

4.1.1. *The "Secondary Occupants" Case*

4.1.1.1. The Problem

One of the cases that perhaps best illustrates the complexities of adjudication in Colombia's land restitution process is the case of "secondary occupants". According to the "Pinheiro Principles", states have the duty to protect those persons who are occupying, living on or owning seized or abandoned land. Such protection should ensure them the right to due process, legal remedies and legal redress, if applicable, without prejudice to the rights of legitimate claimants of the land. In particular, states must take positive steps to protect those who are in a vulnerable situation and do not have the means to access adequate alternative housing.[100] However, Law 1448 does not include the concept of "secondary occupants". Instead, it merely established the concept of "opponents" to label all persons who oppose a victim's land claim. The law establishes that such opponents have two main forms of defense. First, they can prove that (i) the claimant is not a victim; (ii) the claimant has no legal relationship with the land; or (iii) there is no link between the armed conflict and the loss of the land.[101] Second, if the opposition fails to prove any of these, they can nevertheless seek compensation if they succeed in demonstrating that they acquired the land in "good faith with no fault" (*buena fe exenta de culpa*).[102] However, Law 1448 does not incorporate a definition of "good faith with no fault". This indeterminacy of the criterion, as will be illustrated below, has created serious consequences for the rights of opponents facing

100 UNECOSOC, "Principles on Housing and Property Restitution for Refugees and Displaced Persons" (28 June 2005) UN Doc. E/CN.4/Sub.2/2005/17, at Principle 17.

101 This chapter follows Céspedes' translation and explanation of this feature of the process. See: Céspedes-Baéz (2016) at 8.

102 Ibid. Céspedes' translation.

transitional justice land claims, especially those who could otherwise be classified as "secondary occupants" of the land.

4.1.1.2. Giving Meaning to the Criterion

On 11 September 2014, the Bogotá Land Restitution Tribunal adjudicated the case of *Ana María Montoya and Juan Gabriel Montoya v. Inversiones Futuro Verde S.A.*[103] In deciding whether the commercial opponent had acquired the plot in "good faith with no fault", the Tribunal asserted that the "good faith with no fault" criterion of Law 1448 of 2011 means the following: "the unequivocally conscious acts undertaken with loyalty, honesty, and transparency, and a certainty that the acts taken are absolutely legal without defects or fraud".[104] In its analysis of this definition, the Tribunal stated that "good faith with no fault" involved two elements: (i) a subjective element that requires that the person truly believes that the action is legal; and (ii) an objective element that requires that the person has taken positive steps to verify that the action is actually legal.[105] Based on this understanding, the Tribunal dismissed the opponent's right to compensation because although the company had consciously acted to legally purchase the land, it had not taken further steps to verify this legality and, therefore, failed in proving the objective element of the criterion.

Likewise, in a prior case of 13 August 2013, the Cartagena Land Restitution Tribunal used the same understanding of the criterion of "good faith with no fault" when it adjudicated the case of *Lucio Torres and Andrés Torres v. Custodio Abad.*[106] In this case, the opponent, who was a victim of displacement, acquired the land by legal means and had not participated directly or indirectly in the claimants' loss of the land. Nevertheless, the Tribunal dismissed any kind of compensation, again because the opponent was unable to prove the objective element of the mentioned criterion since he had not taken positive steps to verify whether his behavior was legal and he had not carefully verified the legal status of the land.[107]

Both Tribunals, therefore, used the same means of interpretation. First, they implemented a conceptual argument to seek out a suitable doctrinal definition of the relevant criterion.[108] Secondly, they used an argument from analogy to use this concept as a test both in the private law and constitutional

---

103 *Ana María Montoya and Juan Gabriel Montoya v. Inversiones Futuro Verde S.A.*, 20130003000 (Tribunal Superior de Bogotá – Sala Civil Especializada en Restitución de Tierras 2014).

104 Ibid. 47. Author's translation.

105 Ibid. 48.

106 *Lucio Torres and Andrés Torres v. Custodio Abad*, 201200010600 (Tribunal Superior de Cartagena – Sala Civil Especializada en Restitución de Tierras 2013).

107 Ibid. 43–44.

108 For instance, in the *Ana María Montoya and Juan Gabriel Montoya* case, the Bogotá Tribunal quoted the work of Arturo Valencia Zea, *Derecho Civil. Tomo I Parte General y Personas* of

jurisdiction.[109] Due to the consistency of the definitions both in doctrine and in jurisprudence, they concluded that the criterion of "good faith with no fault" had the above-mentioned meaning. Their arguments, therefore, can be reconstructed as follows:

> (1) If the application of rule X [good faith with no fault] in Law 1448 with interpretation X' [which means the conscious to act properly before the law (subjective element) and the verification that the conduct is actually legal (objective element)], is consistent and coherent with the doctrinal and jurisprudential understanding of the criterion, and the consistency and coherence are relevant legal values, then X with interpretation X' is applicable to the case.

In consequence, in both cases the criterion of "good faith with no fault" was interpreted similarly regardless of the type of opponent (a company in the former case, a peasant victim of the conflict in the latter). This interpretation of the criterion can be justified by certain principles of the Rule of Law, such as equal enforcement of the law, certainty (due to consistency) and legal security, due process, and the avoidance of arbitrariness. Furthermore, one can argue that this interpretation was also compatible with the purposes of Law 1448. As Céspedes notices, the land restitution process is founded on two main assumptions: (i) claimants' good faith and defenselessness; and (ii) opponents' correlative bad faith and incapacity to successfully rebut claimants' allegations in the process.[110] Therefore, this interpretation fulfills the high standards of evidence that are required of the opponents of the claims.

4.1.1.3. Switching the Interpretation

However, such an interpretation of the criterion, although seemingly adequate, has negatively impacted upon the rights of "secondary occupants". Indeed, during the 2012–2014 period, in 91.44 per cent of opposed cases throughout the country, tribunals did not compensate opponents because they did not achieve the objective standard of the criterion.[111] This invoked a strong criticism of the process, especially because opponents who had "secondary occupants" status were being evicted from lands without any legal redress.[112]

1981; likewise in *Lucio Torres and Andrés Torres v. Custodio Abad* used the work of Jorge Parra Benitez regarding the "Study of Good Faith" (*Estudio sobre la buena fe*). See: *Ana María Montoya and Juan Gabriel Montoya* above n. 103 at 47 and *Lucio Torres and Andrés Torres v. Custodio Abad* above n. 106 at 32, respectively.

109 Likewise, in both cases the Tribunals quoted several rulings of the Civil Chamber of the Supreme Court of Justice and the Constitutional Court.

110 See: Céspedes above n. 101 at 10.

111 Moncada Roa and Buitrago Palacios (2014) at 21.

112 For instance, an Association of Victims of the Land Restitution Process was created and protested against the process in different regions of the country. See: Ortiz Franco (2016),

In response, the Government started to create new strategies to support them in such cases.[113] Likewise, some tribunals and judges became aware of the consequences of this kind of interpretation and adjusted it according to the specific conditions of each opponent, irrespective of whatever problems might then arise regarding the equal application of the law, consistency and legal certainty.

For instance, in the case of *Segundo Domínguez v. César Martelo*[114] that was adjudicated on 16 December 2014 by the Cartagena Land Restitution Tribunal, the opponent Martelo was also a victim of forced displacement, which was why he ended up on the disputed plot to begin with. In this case, the Tribunal established that "good faith with no fault" required a differential interpretation even though Law 1448 established the same treatment for all opponents regarding their right to be compensated. The Tribunal noticed that an equal application of the criterion of "good faith with no fault" could create disproportional consequences for vulnerable opponents such as Martelo. Hence, it was decided that the mentioned criterion could not be applicable to the behavior of an opponent that was not in a vulnerable position compared to the behavior of one that *was*, because the latter had also suffered from forcible displacement due the armed conflict.[115] Consequently, the Tribunal concluded:

> In order to be granted compensation ... it is necessary that the opponent prove "good faith with no fault"; however, this requirement would produce disproportionate results in this case and would be contrary to the constitutional duty to adopt affirmative actions to protect internally displaced persons. Consequently, with the aim to avoid collisions between two constitutional purposes, the Constitution permits the application of a different treatment when the opponent is subject of special constitutional protection and when the application of the general rule ["good faith with no fault"] causes highly disproportionate results for them ...[116]

By this understanding, the Tribunal ultimately granted compensation to Martelo notwithstanding that he was unable to prove the objective element of

---

http://www.vice.com/es_co/read/hablamos-con-los-defensores-del-no-a-la-restitucin-de-tierras-en-la-marcha-del-uribismo.

113 Due to criticisms about the access to adequate defense of some opponents, the Unit of Land Restitution has issued resolutions that order measures of legal assistance to "secondary occupants". See among others: Unidad Administrativa Especial de Gestión de Restitución de Tierras Despojadas, Acuerdo 21 de 2015 [Diario Oficial No. 49.617].

114 *Segundo Domínguez v. César Martelo*, 20130002200 (Tribunal Superior de Cartagena – Sala Civil Especializada en Restitución de Tierras 2014).

115 Ibid. 26.

116 Ibid. 27. Author's translation.

the "good faith with no fault" criterion. The argumentation in this decision can be reconstructed as follows:

(1) If the application of rule X [good faith with no fault] with interpretation X' (meaning that the standard is adjustable to the condition of the opponent) leads to Y' [upholding Martelo's right of compensation], and Y' is desirable, and if application of rule X with interpretation X" (which means the high good faith standard) leads to Y" [the rejection of Martelo's right of compensation] and Y" is undesirable, then application of rule X with interpretation X' is desirable, and application of the rule X with interpretation X" is undesirable.

(2) Consequence Y' is desirable (from the perspective of the legal system) because Martelo (i) acted in good faith [subjective element], (ii) is also a victim of forced displacement, (iii) did not directly or indirectly participate in the loss of the land, and (iv) is himself in a vulnerable situation; and consequence Y' is compatible with the purpose P' [protect vulnerable population and victims of the armed conflict and offer redress to those who are occupying the claimed lands]. P' is a rational purpose objectively prescribed by the valid legal order [constitutional] and international standards [Pinheiro Principles], and P' underlies the valid legal norms and/or values: [the constitutional duty to adopt affirmative actions to protect the IDPs; Principle 17 of the Pinheiro Principles].

4.1.1.4. Assessing the "Secondary Occupants" Case

This sequence of rulings demonstrates the suitability of the proposed model of transitional justice adjudication for three reasons. First, it shows that the formalistic approach in which consistency, coherence and equal application of the law prevail can present problems when those principles produce undesirable consequences in light of the general context of transition. Indeed, this interpretation resulted in a massive rejection by the courts of compensation in cases that took no heed of the character of the opponents and negatively affected those who were themselves victims of the conflict and in vulnerable situations. Secondly, it also shows the dangers of the purposive approach. Certainly, the interpretation used in the two first rulings was coherent from the perspective of the assumptions of the legislator (defenseless victims and the opponent's correlative capacity to succeed in the process). However, this analysis proved to be misleading and undesirable. Thirdly, in the third ruling, the evaluation from the perspective of the *consequences* of interpretation provided a better argument in the light of the principles of the transition and in light of the values of the Rule of Law due to its consistency with the constitutional system and with international legal standards. Furthermore, it also seemed appropriately adjustable to the political and socio-economic complexities surrounding the case because it was sensitive to the reality of the victims and the problems that could arise if a great number of "secondary occupants" were not compensated in terms of social stability and reconciliation.

4.1.2. *"Agrarian Law vs. Land Restitution Law" Case*

4.1.2.1. The Problem

The legal action for land restitution proceeds when a claimant has or had a legal relationship with a given plot of land. One of these legal relationships that is recognized by Law 1448 is occupation. In this mode of acquisition, ownership is granted as a result of the occupation of "wasteland" (*baldío*) and the fulfillment of specific legal requirements.[117] However, these requirements are not stipulated in Law 1448 but rather, generally, by Law 160 of 1994,[118] which establishes that in order to acquire ownership of land through occupation the following requirements need to be met: (i) exploitation of the land for at least five years; (ii) the occupant cannot own other rural properties; (iii) the occupant's net worth cannot exceed 1000 times the minimum wage in Colombia; (vi) the land shall be adaptable for agricultural exploitation; and (v) the size of the plot cannot exceed that of the "Family Agricultural Unit" (*Unidad Agrícola Familiar*).[119]

Thus, when adjudicating cases of occupation, land restitution judges and tribunals have to verify that a claimant fulfills the requirements of both Law 1448 and Law 160. However, some of the requirements of the latter can result in the rejection of the restitution, even though claimants might be victims of forced abandonment or land seizure, may lack housing, and/or are not able to overcome their vulnerable situation by other means. This rejection, therefore, may imply a contradiction with the provisions and aims of Law 1448 that establish that the legal relationship with the land should be assessed as it was before the loss of the land, and/or in keeping with the purpose of offering redress to IDPs. Nevertheless, by not fulfilling the requirements of Law 160, one may ultimately violate the Rule of Law's principles of legality, equal application of the law, legal certainty and legal security. The next

---

117 The acquisition of property by occupation is a complex legal issue in the Colombian legal system. The definition of "wasteland" (where a plot of land was not owned before), among other issues, is highly technical. In addition, a diverse set of rules may be applicable to different issues related to the occupation. For the purpose of this chapter, it will just highlight the general requirements of the acquisition of the ownership of wasteland and, specifically, those which have generated tensions with the land restitution process. This chapter uses the translation "wasteland" as it was used by Céspedes and others in an article which explores the complexity of the origins of private property in Colombia and the intricacies of the occupation as a mode of acquisition of the land. See: CÉSPEDES-BÁEZ ET AL. (2015).

118 Congreso de la República de Colombia, Ley 160 1994 [Diario Oficial No. 41.479]. (Hereinafter Law 160)

119 The Family Agricultural Unit has a range of area that the granted plot cannot exceed. This range varies according to the region in which the plot is located.

two sequences of rulings illustrate this normative conflict and how it has been resolved.

4.1.2.2. The Prevalence of Agrarian Law

On 24 October 2013 the Bogotá Land Restitution Tribunal[120] reviewed a decision of the Ibagué First Judge of Land Restitution in which the restitution claim of Orlando Ramírez and Ana Morales was rejected.[121] The Tribunal upheld the rejection of the restitution on the following grounds: (i) the claimants were requesting the restitution of wasteland that was being occupied; (ii) the claimants were already owners of another rural plot that they had obtained via restitution; (iii) Law 160 prohibits the restitution of wasteland to persons who own other rural plots; (iv) Law 160 aims to prevent land concentration; and (v) Law 1448 prohibits double reparation.[122]

In the revised decision, the Tribunal established that there was a normative conflict between the agrarian law and land restitution law. This conflict, in the Tribunal's words, arose between (i) Law 1448's [TM] provision that establishes the right to obtain the restitution of the property of wasteland when the requirements to acquire it via occupation were fulfilled at the moment of the seizure or forced abandonment (Rule X'),[123] and (ii) the prohibition of Law 160 [OL] on acquiring by occupation the ownership of wasteland when the occupant owns another agricultural plot (Rule X").[124]

In resolving the conflict between Law 1448 and Law 160, the Tribunal asserted that the application of either Rule X' or Rule X" would undermine the purpose of the TM to restore seized and/or forcibly abandoned land (P'), or the purpose of OL to prevent land concentration (P"). However, it nevertheless upheld the decision of the First Judge because the consequences of rejecting the restitution were compatible with the principles of the TM since the rejection did not undermine the principle of reparation, as the claimants had been awarded a prior restitution of land earlier. Likewise, the

---

120 *Orlando Ramírez Molano y Ana Fidelbia Morales Prada*, 20120012101 (Tribunal Superior de Bogotá – Sala Civil Especializada en Restitución de Tierras 2013).

121 Law 1448 encompasses two different judicial scenarios. When there is no opposition to the claim, the case is resolved by single judges. When there is opposition, the case is adjudicated by Tribunals. In addition, Law 1448 establishes that "judicial decisions are not subject to appeal" in either scenario. However, in the case that a single judge rejects the restitution it automatically goes to judicial review before the Tribunal. See: Céspedes, above n. 101 at 10.

122 *Orlando Ramírez Molano y Ana Fidelbia Morales Prada*, above n. 120 at 3.

123 The claimants fulfilled the requirements of occupation at the moment of losing the land rather than at the moment of the judicial decision.

124 *Orlando Ramírez Molano y Ana Fidelbia Morales Prada*, above n. 120 at 17.

rejection was consistent with the principle of OL since the prevention of land concentration furthered the democratic access to property.[125] The reasoning of the Tribunal can be reconstructed as follows:

(1) If application of Rule X" (over Rule X') leads to Y" [rejection of the restitution], and Y" is desirable from the perspective of P" [to prevent land concentration] and the consequences of Y" are compatible both with the values, principles and goals of OL [guaranteeing democratic access to the land] and TM [by not undermining the principle of reparation since the claimants had already received restitution with a better plot as well as redress for damage suffered], then rule X" shall prevail over rule X', the consequences of which, if applied, would undermine the purposes, goals, and principles of OL and/or TM [the principle of democratic access to land and the prohibition of double-reparation].

4.1.2.3. Prevalence of Land Restitution Laws

On 16 June 2014 the Bogotá Land Restitution Tribunal reviewed the case of Rafaél Merchán,[126] which presented the same normative conflict. Merchán claimed restitution of four wasteland plots that he had had to abandon due to the armed conflict. However, the First and Second Land Restitution Judges of Ibagué rejected the restitution of two and one of the plots, respectively.[127] The reasoning of these rulings was based on the prohibition against acquiring ownership of wastelands when an occupant already owns rural property. Thus, the normative conflict again arose between Rule X' and Rule X". However, on this occasion the Tribunal reversed the decision of the Judges and granted Merchán's restitution right over all four plots. The reasoning of the Tribunal was based on four arguments: (i) the four plots were barely enough to guarantee Merchán and his family subsistence and effective enjoyment of rights; (ii) Merchán had not been compensated in any way for the forcible abandonment of the plots that he had been working for around 50 years; (iii) Merchán and his family were living on one of the plots that the restitution process had rejected, directly affecting their right to housing; and (iv) the aims of Law 160 included a guarantee for vulnerable populations to access land and subsist on it through its exploitation, and thereby fulfill the constitutional

---

125 Ibid.

126 *Rafael Merchán*, 20130016601 (Tribunal Superior de Bogotá – Sala Civil Especializada en Restitución de Tierras 2014).

127 Article 95 of Law 1448 establishes the judge's duty to accumulate in one process different land restitution legal actions when, *inter alia*, they are submitted by the same claimant. In this case, however, the Ibagué Land Restitution Judges omitted this provision and adjudicated the cases in different decisions. The fourth claim was accumulated by the Tribunal in its review of the other decisions, ultimately ruling on all four plots.

provision regarding the social function of the land.[128] The reasoning of the Tribunal can be reconstructed as follows:

> (1) If application of Rule X' (over Rule X") leads to Y' [restitution of the plots], and Y' is desirable from the perspective of P' [effective redress to victims of land seizure and forced abandonment], and the consequences of Y' [Merchán and his family enjoying the right to housing and the right to produce for their subsistence] are compatible with the values, principles and goals of both OL [to ensure access to land for peasants, to guarantee the improvement of the quality of life of vulnerable persons, and to ensure the social function of property] and TM [to provide corrective measures regarding the loss of land due to the armed conflict and to ensure the effective enjoyment of rights of the displaced population], then rule X' shall prevail over rule X", the consequences of which, if applied, would undermine the purposes, goals, and principles of OL and/or TM [access to land, improvement in the quality of life of a vulnerable population, the social function of the property, and the right to obtain reparations and the effective enjoyment of rights].

4.1.2.4. Assessing the "Agrarian Law vs. Land Restitution Law" Case

These two cases demonstrate the importance of judging by consequences rather than by limiting the argumentative process to formalistic or purposive approaches. In both cases the formalistic approach to the rule in Law 1448 or the rule in Law 160 would imply the violation of the principle of legality. Likewise, if the Tribunal had upheld in both cases the purposive interpretation of Law 1448, i.e. to offer redress to IDPs, the juridical consequence of such approach would have undermined Law 160's goal of guaranteeing democratic access to land in the country in future cases. This could be a dangerous outcome, taking into account the high degree of land concentration in Colombia and its relationship with the armed conflict. The same logic would operate with the purposive approach of the rule in Law 160, which would undermine both the corrective and distributive goals of Law 1448 in cases in which claimants' socio-economic situation was precarious and where neither access to land nor the right of reparation had been granted to them. The juridical consequences of such reasoning would be dangerous in future cases involving occupation of wastelands.

Thus, the Tribunal's approach seems to be preferable because it based its reasoning not in the purposes or the letter of the law, but in seeking out the rightness-reasons and goal-reasons that could sustain the outcome. In the first case, the rightness-reasons involved adhering to principles such as the democratic access to the land and the prohibition of double-reparation, while the goal-reasons relied on the idea that the claimant was already enjoying the right of restitution

[128] *Rafael Merchán*, above n. 126 at 29.

and the possibility to cultivate the land. In the second case, the reasoning was based on the idea that the consequences of applying Law 160's rule would be contrary both to legislative principles and to the reality of Merchán's circumstances when considered in light of the law's goals.

4.1.3. "Claimants' Withdrawal" Case

4.1.3.1. The Problem

Law 1448 did not legislate for all of the procedural issues of the land restitution legal process. Legal gaps have arisen regarding, among other things, rules of gathering of evidence, rights of the parties in judicial hearings and claimants' right to withdraw their claims. While the Colombian General Procedural Code applies to civil, commercial, family and agrarian law procedures, it also applies to all other judicial procedures that lack specific procedural regulations.[129] Thus, land restitution judges and tribunals have usually applied by analogy the procedural rules of the aforementioned Code to resolve procedural legal gaps. Nevertheless, the application of some of these provisions can create tensions with the aims of this transitional justice mechanism or can severely affect the nature of its judicial procedure. The next sequence of rulings illustrates this problem.

4.1.3.2. Ordinary Law's Solution

In 2012, the Colombian Supreme Court of Justice resolved on appeal a writ to protect fundamental rights (*acción de tutela*) issued by María and Mario Robledo against the Montería Land Restitution's First Judge on the basis of his rejection of a withdrawal application presented by the restitution claimant.[130] In the original case, the claimant had filed for withdrawal, arguing that he had not been properly informed about the rationale of the process and that he had erroneously given consent to file the legal action because of that misunderstanding. However, in reality he had sold his land around 12 years prior and he did not want to pursue the restitution. Nevertheless, the Montería Land Restitution's First Judge had rejected the withdrawal based on an interpretation of a prior decision which established that this action was not allowable within this procedural framework.[131]

---

129 Congreso de la República de Colombia, Código General del Proceso (Ley 1564) 2012 [Diario Oficial No. 48.489]. (Hereinafter General Procedural Code) art. 1.

130 *María Elena Robledo y Mario Francisco Robledo v. Juzgado Primero Civil del Circuito Especializado en Restitución de Tierras de Montería*, 20150008601 (Sala de Casación Civil – Corte Suprema de Justicia 2015).

131 Ibid. 3.

The opponents in the case, María and Mario Robledo, argued that the judge's decision violated their right to due process, was based on a misunderstanding of the law (Law 1448 did not expressly prohibit the withdrawal), and had failed to apply Article 314 of the General Procedural Code that grants the right of claimants to withdraw their legal actions.[132] Nevertheless, the Antioquia Land Restitution Tribunal upheld the judge's decision on the grounds that the opponents lacked *locus standi* to issue such a constitutional action (*acción de tutela*). Thus, the Tribunal determined that the rejection of the withdrawal was not a violation of the fundamental rights of the opponents.[133]

On appeal, the Civil Chamber of the Supreme Court of Justice, dismissed the Tribunal's arguments and found that the Judge's decision lacked sufficient legal reasoning. According to the Supreme Court, the judge's rationale was not valid because the prior decision did not establish the impossibility of withdrawing the land restitution legal action. Instead, it decided that the possibility of withdrawal depended on the specific circumstances of each case.[134] Furthermore, the Supreme Court asserted that the withdrawal would be valid as long as the claimant's consent was given without error, fraud, or duress. In conclusion, the Court ordered a review of the original case and the application of the correct legal considerations.[135] Although the Supreme Court's decision did not expressly uphold the possibility of withdrawal in the context of a land restitution action, it is inferable that in the Court's opinion the rule of withdrawal established by the General Procedural Code was applicable by analogy as long as the claimant's consent was valid. Furthermore, the Supreme Court asserted that the Judge's decision omitted to reflect the principles of efficiency and procedural economy that must govern judicial actions.[136]

4.1.3.3. Defeasibility of the Analogy

The decision of the Supreme Court was selected for review by the Constitutional Court.[137] In its decision, the Constitutional Court rejected the Supreme Court's reasoning and upheld the original judge's decision based on three

132 Ibid. 4.
133 Ibid. 6.
134 Ibid. 10.
135 Ibid. 11.
136 Ibid.
137 *María Elena Robledo y Mario Francisco Robledo v. Juzgado Primero Civil del Circuito Especializado en Restitución de Tierras de Montería*, T244/16. (Corte Constitucional de Colombia 2016).

main arguments: (i) although the provisions of the General Procedural Code generally applied by analogy to procedures that lacked specific norms, this residual character was not absolute, particularly in extraordinary procedures, such as those of land restitution processes; (ii) the land restitution process was different than other related private law processes because it pursued purposes such as the effective reparation of the victims that was an international duty of the state; (iii) due to the opposition of armed groups to the process and the victims' vulnerability, an analogical application of the withdrawal rule would incentivize pressures against victims, thereby undermining their rights; and (iv) the analogical implementation of the provision of the General Procedural Code undermined Law 1448's goals such as the achievement of peace and reconciliation, the establishment of the truth, justice, reparations, and non-recurrence guarantees that were of public interest.[138]

Thus, the reasoning of the Constitutional Court was based on a consequentialist argumentation that can be reconstructed as follows: application by analogy of rule X' [claimants' right of withdrawal] to fill the legal gap of Transitional Law (TL) [Law 1448 lacks provision regarding claimants' withdrawal] leads to Y' [the end of the land restitution process before the decision]; if Y' is undesirable from the perspective of the purposes P' [reparation for harm to victims] of TL; and if the consequences of the Y' [risk of incentivizing the opponents of the process to pressure victims to withdraw their claims] undermine the goals of the TM [achievement of peace and reconciliation, and the establishment of the truth, justice, reparations, and non-recurrence guarantees], then the analogic implementation of X' is not suitable to fill the legal gap of TL.

4.1.3.4. Assessing the "Claimants' Withdrawal Case"

This case illustrates that the use of the analogical argument in transitional contexts requires an analysis that goes beyond the similarity between two legal problems and the way in which a provision resolves it in one of them. A formalistic approach, in which the adherence to written law prevails (in this case the General Procedural Code that established its applicability to all unregulated judicial procedures) prevails, can affect the nature of the process wherein an analogous provision is implemented. Likewise, the purposive approach can be misleading because the right of withdrawal may nevertheless pursue the purpose of judicial effectiveness and procedural economy, which are clearly general principles that should guide judicial activity. However,

[138] Ibid. paras. 50–57.

these analyses would ignore the consequences both in the context of the legal process and in that of the circumstances of typical land restitution claims

5. CONCLUSION

Returning to our notional judge, who is still at his desk. He is willing to finally decide the case. In his perspective, he has paved the way for a model of transitional justice adjudication in which he can justify his decision without severely compromising either the aims of transformation or the values of the Rule of Law, and has found new arguments that he can use to persuade the peasant before him that there is a new law for him. The judge started with a question about how to decide a case based on that new law about which the peasant was doubtful. He understood that the answer to that question required a model of adjudication that was capable of triggering two effects in the peasant's reality: (i) transforming and restoring his reality by the restitution of his land and thereby repairing the harms that he suffered from past atrocities; and (ii) ensuring that this land is going to be subject to the Rule of Law.

MacCormick's approach to the theory of legal argumentation offered our judge such a ground. MacCormick's goal of reconciling the arguable nature of law and the values of the Rule of Law seems compatible with the context of adjudication in transitional contexts. In particular, the concept of "judging by consequences" offered the judge a tool to contemplate both rightness-reasons and goal-reasons, and to build a bridge with which the restorative and transformative aims of the transitional mechanisms and the values of Rule of Law can be united and enhanced. Such an approach can decrease the risks, paradoxes, or obstacles of formalistic or dynamic understandings of the Rule of Law and the adjudicative process. Furthermore, the notion of "judging by consequences" can allow the judge to construct his reasoning and also allow others to evaluate it in the light of the dual-purpose of transitional justice adjudication.

Colombia's land restitution process illustrates the complexity of adjudicative practices in transitions as well as the tensions that can arise between the goals of the mechanism and the values of the Rule of Law. Such tensions were depicted in certain "hard cases" and analyzed via a series of rulings in which the model was tested. This also illustrated the importance of imbuing the decisions with sound legal reasoning. Naturally, the decisions are neither definitive nor demonstrative, but they are persuasive in the light of the proposed model.

It may be that judges will intuitively synthesize all of these relevant considerations and achieve a just outcome without resorting to this prescriptive model of adjudication; they may instead propose a model through which one can achieve greater transparency and accountability. Thus, promoting the underlying aims of transitional justice and ensuring the peasant's realization that the new law may finally have paved a genuine path by which he can return to his land requires new arguments. These arguments are not necessarily contrary to or located outside of the values of the Rule of Law. They are a part of its very nature. By using them in his adjudication, our judge hopefully can persuade the peasant that he can return to his restored land: a land of new arguments, a land of new law.

References

Case Law

Ana María Montoya and Juan Gabriel Montoya v. Inversiones Futuro Verde S.A., 20130003000 (Tribunal Superior de Bogotá – Sala Civil Especializada en Restitución de Tierras 2014).

Lucio Torres and Andrés Torres v. Custiodio Abad, 201200010600 (Tribunal Superior de Cartagena – Sala Civil Especializada en Restitución de Tierras 2013).

María Elena Robledo y Mario Francisco Robledo v. Juzgado Primero Civil del Circuito Especializado en Restitución de Tierras de Montería, 20150008601 (Sala de Casación Civil-Corte Suprema de Justicia 2015).

María Elena Robledo y Mario Francisco Robledo v. Juzgado Primero Civil del Circuito Especializado en Restitución de Tierras de Montería, T244/16 (Corte Constitucional de Colombia 2016).

Orlando Ramírez Molano y Ana Fidelbia Morales Prada, 20120012101 (Tribunal Superior de Bogotá – Sala Civil Especializada en Restitución de Tierras 2013).

Rafael Merchán, 20130016601 (Tribunal Superior de Bogotá – Sala Civil Especializada en Restitución de Tierras 2014).

Segundo Domínguez v. César Martelo, 20130002200 (Tribunal Superior de Cartagena – Sala Civil Especializada en Restitución de Tierras 2014).

Legislation

Congreso de la República de Colombia, Ley 160 1994 [Diario Oficial No. 41.479].

—— Ley de Víctimas y Restitución de Tierras (Ley 1448) 2011 [Diario Oficial 48096].

—— Código General del Proceso (Ley 1564) 2012 [Diario Oficial No. 48.489].

Unidad Administrativa Especial de Gestión de Restitución de Tierras Despojadas, Acuerdo 21 de 2015 2015 [Diario Oficial No. 49.617].

Bibliography

Andersen, E. (2015) "Transitional Justice and The Rule of Law: Lessons From the Field." *Case Western Reserve Journal of International Law* 47, no. 1: 305–342.

Balasco, L.M. (2013) "The Transitions of Transitional Justice: Mapping the Waves From Promise to Practice" *Journal of Human Rights* 12, no. 2: 198–216.

Barak, A. (2005) *Purposive Interpretation in Law*. Princeton N.J.: Princeton University Press.

Bell, Ch. (2008) "Transitional Justice, Interdisciplinarity and the State of the 'Field' or 'Non-Field'". *International Journal Of Transitional Justice* 3, no. 1: 5–27.

Bertea, S. (2008) "Law and Legal Reasoning". *Northern Ireland Legal Quarterly* 59, no. 1: 5–20.

Centro Nacional de Memoria Histórica (2013) *¡Basta Ya! Colombia: memorias de guerra y dignidad*. Centro Nacional de Memoria Histórica, http://www.centrodememoriahistorica.gov.co/descargas/informes2013/bastaYa/basta-ya-colombia-memorias-de-guerra-y-dignidad-2016.pdf.

Céspedes-Báez, L.M., Del Pilar Peña-Huertas, R., Cabana-González, D.S. and Zuleta-Ríos, S. (2015) "Who Owns the Land? Litigants, Justices, Colonos, and Titleholders' Struggle to Define the Origins of Private Property in Colombia". *Global Jurist* 15, no. 3: 329–459.

Céspedes-Baéz, L.M. (2016) *Women in Conflict, Women in Litigation: Problems and Inconsistencies in the Protection of Women in the Colombian Land Restitution Process*. DPhil thesis, Temple University.

Del Mar, M. (2015) "The Forward-Looking Requirement of Formal Justice: Neil MacCormick on Consequential Reasoning". *Jurisprudence: An International Journal of Legal and Political Thought* **6**, no. 3: 429–450.

Dyzenhaus, D. (2003) "Judicial Independence, Transitional Justice and the Rule of Law". *Otago Law Review* **10**, no 3: 345–369.

Evans, M. (2015) "Structural Violence, Socioeconomic Rights, and Transformative Justice". *Journal of Human Rights* **15**, no. 1: 1–20.

Feteris, E.T. (2005) "The Rational Reconstruction of Argumentation Referring to Consequences and Purposes in the Application of Legal Rules: A Pragma-Dialectical Perspective". *Argumentation* 19, no. 4: 459–470.

Feteris, E.T. and Kloosterhuis, H. (2009) "The Analysis and Evaluation of Legal Argumentation: Approaches From Legal Theory and Argumentation Theory". *Studies in Logic, Grammar and Rhetoric* **16**: 307–331.

González Ocantos, E. (2014) "Persuade Them or Oust Them: Crafting Judicial Change and Transitional Justice in Argentina". *Comparative Politics* **46**, no. 4: 479–498.

Ibáñez, A.M. and Muñoz, J.C. (2010) "The Persistence of Land Concentration in Colombia: What Happened Between 2000 and 2009?" in *Distributive Justice in Transitions*. Torkel Opsahl Academic ePublisher. https://www.fichl.org/fileadmin/fichl/documents/FICHL_6_web.pdf.

Krygier, M. (2001) "Transitional Questions About the Rule of Law: Why? What? and How?". *East Central Europe* **28**, no. 1: 1–34.

Loyle, C.E. and Davenport, C. (2016), "Transitional Injustice: Subverting Justice in Transition and Postconflict Societies" *Journal of Human Rights* **15**, no. 1: 126–149.

MacCormick, N. (2005) *Rhetoric and the Rule of Law: A Theory of Legal Reasoning*. Oxford: Oxford University Press.

Mani, R. (2008) "Dilemmas of Expanding Transitional Justice, or Forging the Nexus Between Transitional Justice and Development". *International Journal of Transitional Justice* 2, no. 3: 253–265.

McAuliffe, P. (2010) "Transitional Justice and the Rule of Law: The Perfect Couple or Awkward Bedfellows?". *Hague Journal on the Rule of Law* 2, no. 2: 127–154.

Miller, Z. (2008) "Effects of Invisibility: In Search of the 'Economic' in Transitional Justice". *International Journal of Transitional Justice* 2, no. 3: 266–291.

Moncada Roa, P. and Buitrago Palacios, N. (2014) "Los opositores en el proceso de restitución de tierras: Análisis cuantitativo de la jurisprudencia, 2012–2014". *Revista de Derecho Público*, no. 33: 1–34.

Moral Soriano, L. (2008) "Precedents: Reasoning by Rules and Reasoning by Principles". *Northern Ireland Legal Quarterly* 59, no. 1: 33–42.

Moreno Cruz, R. (2012) "Argumentación juridica, por qué y para qué?" *Boletín Mexicano de Derecho Comparado* no. 133: 165–192.

Ní Aoaláin, F., Campbell, C. and Bell, Ch. (2004) "Justice Discourses in Transition". *Social & Legal Studies* 13, no. 3: 305–328.

Ni Aolain, F. and Campbell, C. (2005) "The Paradox of Transition in Conflicted Democracies". *Human Rights Quarterly* 27, no. 1: 172–213.

Ortiz Franco, J.D. (2016) "Hablamos Con Los Defensores Del 'No A La Restitución De Tierras' en la Marcha del uribismo", *VICE* (Colombia): http://www.vice.com/es_co/read/hablamos-con-los-defensores-del-no-a-la-restitucin-de-tierras-en-la-marcha-del-uribismo.

Peczenik, A. (2009) *On Law and Reason*. 2nd edn. New York/Berlin: Springer.

Rincón Covelli, T. (2012) "La Justicia Transicional: una concepción de la justicia que se hace cargo de las atrocidades del pasado" in T. Rincon Covelli and J. Rodriguez Zepeda (eds.) *La Justicia y las Atrocidades del Pasado. Teoria y analisis de la justicia.* México D.F.: Universidad Autónoma Metropolitana (UAM).

Sartor, G. (2008) "Syllogism and Defeasibilty: A Comment on Neil MacCormick's 'Rhetoric and the Rule of Law'". *Northern Ireland Legal Quarterly* 59, no. 1: 21–32.

Spaak, T. (2006) "Deduction, Legal Reasoning and the Rule of Law" *Constitutional Commentary* 23, no. 1: 121–137.

Tamanaha, B.Z. (2004) *On the Rule of Law: History, Politics, Theory*, 3rd edn. Cambridge: Cambridge University Press.

Teitel, R.G. (2000) *Transitional Justice*. New York: Oxford University Press.

—— (2003) "Transitional Justice Genealogy". *Harvard Human Rights Journal* 16: 69–94.

Tobin, J. (2010) "Seeking to Persuade: A Constructive Approach to Human Rights Treaty Interpretation". *Harvard Human Rights Journal* 23, no. 1: 1–50.

UNECOSOC (2005) "Principles on Housing and Property Restitution for Refugees and Displaced Persons" (28 June 2005) UN Doc. E/CN.4/Sub.2/2005/17.

UNGA (2004) "Report of the Secretary General on the Rule of Law and Transitional Justice in Conflict and Post-Conflict Societies" UN Doc. S/2004/616.

UNHRC (2012) "Report of the Special Rapporteur on the Promotion of Truth, Justice, Reparation and Guarantees of Non-Recurrence" UN Doc. A/HRC/21/46, at 13–14.

Unidad de Restitución de Tierras (2015) *La Restitución de Tierras en Colombia: Del Sueño a la Realidad*. Presidencia de la República de Colombia. http://wp.presidencia.gov.co/sitios/especiales/Documents/20150513-especial-restitucion-tierras/docs/restitucion-tierras-caolombia-sueno-a-realidad.pdf.

Veitch, S. (2006) “Rhetoric and the Rule of Law: A Theory of Legal Reasoning”. *Journal of Law and Society* 33, no. 3: 492–495.

Vinjamuri, L. and Snyder, J. (2015) “Law and Politics in Transitional Justice”. *Annual Review of Political Science* 18, no. 1: 303–327.

Yusuf, H.O. (2007) “The Judiciary and Constitutionalism in Transitions: A Critique”. *Global Jurist* 7, no. 3: 1–47.

Zajac Sannerholm, R. (2012) *Rule of Law After War and Crisis: Ideologies, Norms and Methods*. Cambridge/Antwerpen /Portland O.R.: Intersentia.

CHAPTER 12

THE INTERPLAY BETWEEN HISTORY, TRADITION AND LOCAL AGENCY IN SHAPING RWANDA'S FUTURE

Beyond Gacaca

Felix Mukwiza NDAHINDA

"A people without the knowledge of their past history, origin and culture is like a tree without roots."

Marcus Garvey (1887–1940).

1. INTRODUCTION

Rwanda has inspired an ever-growing literature documenting the 1994 genocide against the Tutsi and its aftermath. The colonial manipulations and antagonisation of identities, the power struggle that accompanied the decolonisation process, the ethnicisation of the post-colonial state, the dynamics of the genocide and post-genocide responses, are all widely covered in academic and non-academic literature.[1] In the field of transitional justice, examinations of post-genocide processes in Rwanda have largely focused on the *Gacaca* courts that were instituted to try the overwhelming caseload of the 1994 genocide. The *Gacaca* mechanism is generally examined in terms of its compliance with human rights norms or its possible contribution to peace, social cohesion, healing and reconciliation. Often overlooked in dominant analyses is the fact that the *Gacaca* courts fit into wider socio-political narratives and processes in the post-genocide reconstruction landscape, and also how they fit into a post-genocide governmental ambition to re-create an ethnicity-free Rwandan society based on locally held values drawn mainly from the country's pre-colonial past.

Over the last decade, a number of government-sponsored initiatives appealing to tradition and presented as home-grown responses to the country's socio-political and economic challenges have been revived or reinvented. These include: *Ubudehe* (local collective action/ mutual assistance), *Abunzi* (mediation committees), *Ingando* (solidarity camps), *Itorero ry' igihugu* (civil education programme), *Urugerero* (national service), *Girinka* (one cow per family in poverty), *Umuganura* (harvest day), *Umuganda* (community work), *Imihigo* (performance contracts), *Ndi Umunyarwanda* (Rwandan-ness/I am Rwandan) and *abarinzi b'igihango* (guardians of the Covenant).[2]

These initiatives are increasingly imagined as foundational pillars of the country's economic development and poverty reduction strategy,[3] as well as essential tools for building social cohesion among Rwandans.[4] The embracing of these initiatives is accompanied by a rewriting of the country's history, both literally and figuratively, and by the emergence of official narratives memorialising the near and distant past. Just like many other aspects of post-genocide policies, the adoption and implementation of what are locally labelled as home-grown initiatives sponsored by post-genocide Rwandan authorities are subject to highly polarised debates within political and academic spheres.[5] They are frequently denounced, especially in various academic or

---

1 For some relevant sources, see: Prunier (1995); Chrétien et al. (1995); Chrétien (1997); Gourevitch (1998); Des Forges (1999); Mamdani (2001); Dallaire (2004); Straus (2006).

2 For some relevant literature, see: Ntakirutimana (2011); Rwanda Governance Board (RGB) (2014); Corry/Institute of Policy Analysis and Research (IPAR) 2012.

3 Republic of Rwanda (RoR), *Economic Development and Poverty Reduction Strategy II 2013–2018: Shaping Our Development*, p. 13, at: http://www.minecofin.gov.rw/fileadmin/templates/documents/NDPR/EDPRS_2.pdf.

4 Corry/IPAR, above n. 2.

5 For an analysis on the polarisation of scholarship on Rwanda, see: Fisher (2015).

journalistic publications in the global West for lacking democratic legitimacy, not being inclusive enough, or being unlikely to lead to lasting peace.[6] A clear understanding of these institutions or practices is essential for any attempt to capture the contours of the socio-political landscape of post-genocide governance in Rwanda. The polarisation of debates about the most appropriate path for post-genocide Rwanda's reconstruction signals the difficult quest for governance approaches that transcend antagonistic ethnic identities. In essence, opposing views on the reconstruction path reflect a struggle for the very soul of the country in the post-genocide era.

The concepts of "memory" and "restoration" that undergird the various contributions to this volume are used in this chapter to refer to contextual dynamics that, at their core, step outside the predictable frames of transitional justice mechanisms. In essence, the chapter proposes a holistic reading of post-conflict dynamics in Rwanda as a form of restoration. In line with the understanding provided in the introduction to the volume: "restoring trust engages memory in the sense of retrospection and regeneration". Retrospection in context entails that memory covers different processes and temporalities: it encompasses ritualised remembrances of atrocities committed in a relatively recent past (the genocide era) as well as reconnecting with an idealised and romanticised distant past of societal harmony (pre-colonial era). Regeneration is the cornerstone in the reconstruction project, and supposes the mending of a broken bridge to that pre-colonial past through a revival of traditional norms and institutions.

An in-depth examination of the contours of each one of these tradition-inspired institutions and programmes certainly requires more than just a single book chapter. The present inquiry is therefore intended to introduce these initiatives and to critically examine the linkages between them in attempts to (re)create social cohesion and transcend the country's toxic history of institutionalised and antagonised ethnic identities. This analysis will revolve around frequently raised questions of agency and legitimacy in endeavours that aim at reshaping Rwanda's future, based on reconstructions of the country's pre-colonial, colonial, post-colonial and post-genocide historical trajectories.

2. IDENTITY, AGENCY AND LEGITIMACY IN POST-COLONIAL GOVERNANCE

Post-colonial literature has extensively explored the tensions between colonially inherited structures and the complex realities of colonised countries in terms

[6] For relevant literature, see: Straus and Waldorf (2011); Reyntjens (2011); Melvin (2010).

of how these can best be reconciled to build stable societies.[7] In the words of Ivison, post-colonial writings are focused on "forms of agency, subjectivity and modes of sociality governed by colonial and imperialist institutions, as well as the historiography and political theory that accompanied them".[8] Negotiating statehood within contexts of tensions between ethnic and state institutions; the inability of many decolonised states to project power to the peripheries of central administrative structures; and uses of the past as a socio-political commodity remain salient themes in studies of several post-colonial societies in Africa and beyond.[9] In such contexts, "political identity, both individual and collective, is inherently contestable; constituted as much by relations of power, culture and history as it is by ideals of autonomy and authenticity".[10]

Several countries, including African states, that emerged from the decolonisation movements of the mid-twentieth century have indeed wrestled with multifaceted challenges in their attempts to build stable nations out of diverse ethno-cultural identities lumped together by the territorial demarcating of colonial possessions by European imperial powers.[11] In most contexts, nation-building dilemmas consist of striking a difficult balance between, on the one hand, aspirations for unity and, on the other hand, recognition and the celebration of ethno-cultural diversity. Most post-colonial states were erected on dominantly liberal pillars of state-building that they inherited from former colonial powers. Hence, bridging the divide between competing allegiance to ethno-cultural communities and a unified state has generally raised questions about the legitimacy and accountability of the actors involved, particularly state actors, whenever they try to stray away from the socio-political trajectory designed by the characteristically coercive colonial state.[12]

Strategies deployed to accommodate multi-layered identities and tensions between tradition and modernity in state-building involve a constant balancing act between competing demands. In some cases, compromises take the shape of the continued recognition of colonially instituted traditional authorities (chieftaincies) as parallel or integral parts of the administrative structures of the state.[13] In these and many other contexts, new traditions aimed at cementing a sense of shared nationhood are constantly being invented, with strong appeals made to traditional features or values of (mainly dominant) African ethno-cultural communities.[14] In essence, appeals to pre-colonial values,

---

7 On this, see: Mbembe (2001); Young (2001); Loomba (2005).
8 Ivison (2002), 108.
9 See: Boone (2003); Lund (2008).
10 Ibid, p. 41.
11 See for instance: Herbst (2000); Mamdani (1996); Berman (1998).
12 Ivison (2002), above n. 8, pp. 14 *et seq.*
13 See: Herbst (2000), above n. 11, pp. 173–197.
14 Ranger (1993).

practices and institutions in the construction of the modern African state are intended to inject an element of authenticity into what are otherwise artificial structures of governance inherited from the colonial order. Post-genocide governance in Rwanda is the archetypical example of the deployment of reinvented traditional institutions, practices and customs in an attempt to mend a society fractured by several decades of political antagonisation between the Hutu, Tutsi and Twa social categories.

3. *U RWANDA RUSHYA*:[15] THE POLITICS OF POST-GENOCIDE RECONSTRUCTION IN RWANDA

In July 1994, Rwanda was a country in ruins. People were killed simply because they were born Tutsi while others were targeted because they were political opponents to the genocidal authorities or simply because they opposed the killings. The country not only lost around one million lives in one of the most efficiently undertaken genocides in recorded human history, but also much of its already limited infrastructure was devastated by nearly four years of civil war, the end of which saw Rwanda's already scarce resources ransacked by the defeated forces as they fled the country. Those who were targeted but survived the atrocities were left with incurable scars of personal victimisation and/or the loss of loved ones.[16] In the chaos that accompanied the genocide, property belonging to Tutsi and other targeted opponents was either damaged or confiscated. With only very few exceptions, both perpetrators and victims were Rwandans.

The civil war and genocide against the Tutsi ended with the military victory of the Rwandan Patriotic Front/Army (RPF/A). The RPF had taken up arms against the government of Rwanda in October 1990, publicly advocating for the return of refugees who had fled Rwanda from the late 1950s, and for a more inclusive society.[17] Composed mainly, but not exclusively, of former Tutsi refugees who had been in exile for more than three decades, the RPF built its strength on a network of support across the region and beyond.[18] As defeat became inevitable, the strategy adopted by Rwandan authorities and militias was to drag the Hutu population into exile, thereby ensuring not only that the country would become ungovernable for the new authorities, but also

---

15 Literally, "A New Rwanda"; a leitmotiv in official discourses in reference to post-genocide governance aspirations.

16 Reference to a documentary produced 10 years after the genocide capturing the lasting impact of victimisation: P. Freedman, *Time Machine: Rwanda – Do Scars Ever Fade?* Bill Brummel Productions Inc., 2004.

17 See: Prunier (1993).

18 Ibid. See also: Watson (1991).

to better prepare for a future comeback. Around two million people fled to neighbouring countries, namely Zaire (now Democratic Republic of Congo/DRC), Tanzania, Burundi and Uganda.[19] The refugee crisis this spawned tremendously destabilised those neighbouring countries, particularly the DRC. Even today, persistent insecurity in the region is partly linked to the presence of Rwandan armed groups, most notably the Democratic Forces for the Liberation of Rwanda/FDLR, which is a source of insecurity in the Congolese territories where they operate as well as in Rwanda itself where they have made several random attacks over the years.[20]

On the security front, the war did not fully end with the capture of the Capital, Kigali. The RPF did not gain full control of the country until August when French troops of Operation Turquoise pulled out.[21] Even then, insecurity continued. The threat posed by the reorganisation of the defeated forces was used as a pretext by Rwanda, together with Congolese and Ugandan actors, to intervene in the DRC, then Zaire. After the fall of the Zairian/DRC President Mobutu, infiltration back into Rwanda by members of the defeated forces also posed a real threat, especially in the Northern provinces between 1997 and 1998, resulting in a robust military intervention, of which there are many allegations of abusive conduct.[22] Since the early 2000s, internal security has been somewhat restored even if armed Rwandan groups operating mainly in the DRC have persisted.

By the time that the RPF seized power in 1994 with the capture of Kigali, Rwanda was synonymous with death, destruction, and desolation. The country had very limited prospects of ever recovering from such an unprecedented tragedy. In a country known as the land of a thousand hills, the road to recovery and healing has been quite steep and bumpy. Throughout the country, survivors who were personally victimised or lost their relatives in the genocide had to live in the same neighbourhoods as people who took part in the same atrocities. Exposure to some of the most atrocious crimes and humiliations left many genocide survivors, perpetrators, soldiers, and even returnees very traumatised. Descendants of Rwandan refugees who fled as far back as the 1950s were returning to the country and needed land and access to other vital resources. The wounds and scars of the genocide as well as a history marked by conflict were, and to a great extent are still, quite visible within Rwandan society. Reconstruction efforts have been made even more challenging by the fact that the country's educated elite had either largely been killed or had participated in the genocide and subsequently went into exile.

---

19 On this, see: Mamdani (2001), above n. 1, pp. 234 et seq.
20 See generally: Prunier (2008); Lemarchand (2009).
21 Prunier (1995), above n. 1, 281.
22 Jackson (2004); African Rights (1996).

Rebuilding a country in ruins and mending a fragmented and highly traumatised society has been a very complex task for the new authorities. A mix of ideological and pragmatic considerations dictated the course of the reconstruction process. The new authorities faced almost impossible odds in their efforts to restore security, the rule of law and a functioning socio-economic environment. They relied heavily on international financial, technical and humanitarian assistance in efforts to rebuild the country. Several factors justified the important global mobilisation of assistance to Rwanda's reconstruction process after the genocide against the Tutsi. In the wake of the Holocaust, one of the early undertakings of the newly created United Nations after the Second World War was its adoption of a 1948 Convention dedicated to the prevention and punishment of the crime of genocide. Ratified by an overwhelming majority of the member states of the United Nations, the Genocide Convention carried the promise that the global community of states would take action to prevent future genocides anywhere in the world. In 1993, however, instead of taking action as the crime was unfolding in Rwanda, the United Nations decided to pull out most of the international troops deployed in the country to observe compliance with a peace agreement signed between the warring parties.[23]

The nature of the crime and the failure of most powerful global actors to intervene in Rwanda to save lives during the genocide created a sense of moral responsibility that spurred the international community to assist the country in its recovery process. Global actors keenly got involved in Rwanda not only because of their appreciation of its compelling humanitarian needs and the almost-unsolvable challenges that its reconstruction process faced, but also because several of those actors had a sense of guilt for not intervening earlier to save the lives of those who were slain.[24] Some overcame their initial resistance to collaborate with the former rebels, who now hold the reins of power, largely because they felt morally compelled to address the consequences of the genocide – sometimes labelled the "crime of crimes" – since their lack of action likely exacerbated its disastrous consequences for Rwanda and the wider region.[25] Several foreign benefactors of Rwanda attached conditions to their funding, though. They wanted to have a say on how and in which sectors their funds were to be spent.[26] As the saying goes, "He who pays the piper calls the tune". In such a context, the coordination of reconstruction and recovery activities undertaken by local and foreign (governmental, intergovernmental

23 See for instance: Melvern (2000); Grünfeld and Huijboom (2007).

24 For a critical elaboration in international guilt, see: Reyntjens (2011); Ansoms and Rostagno (2012).

25 For more on this, see references in n. 20 above.

26 See for instance: Brown (2013); Paris (2002).

and non-governmental) actors with different agendas proved to be quite challenging for the new Rwandan authorities.[27]

Against all odds, though, Rwanda managed to make very significant strides in its recovery process in various sectors. First, for the new authorities, the main priority was to secure control over the territory and address both internal and external military and other threats. By building a very strong security apparatus, they managed to achieve relative stability after several episodes of unrest, most notably an insurrection from the DRC between 1997 and 1998 (known as the *abacengezi* or infiltrators' war).[28] This context of insecurity in the years immediately following the genocide had tragic consequences in terms of human casualties, not only in Rwanda but also the wider region, particularly the DRC. The coalescence of domestic socio-political and economic crises with the spill over of the Rwandan conflict has sparked wars in the Congo since the mid-1990s, with contemporary ramifications in terms of instability, human suffering and lawlessness.[29]

In the socio-economic sphere, Rwanda's reconstruction has scored indisputable successes in sectors such as education, health care, gender justice, infrastructural development and more broadly, poverty reduction.[30] In the political domain, the post-genocide Rwandan authorities, leaning on a strong security apparatus, have engaged in a process of erecting strong state institutions of accountability (justice sector, ombudsman), and promoting policies that are geared towards socio-economic development, not only for citizens' empowerment but also as a means of burying the so-called ethnic cleavages of the past.[31] A cornerstone of colonial and post-colonial governance until 1994, ethnicity was officially banned and replaced by a public discourse that promotes a national unity model erected on a perceived imperative to revisit positive values drawn from a shared precolonial past.[32]

The radical nature of changes undertaken by Rwandan authorities and the processes by which they have been implemented have received numerous criticisms. Questions are frequently raised on whether peace and stability in the country are either just, sustainable or simply a mirage.[33] The dominant line of criticism relates particularly to the human rights record of the post-genocide

---

27 For instance, Kumar et al. (1996), 7 suggests that more than 130 NGOs were operating in the country one year after the end of the genocide, leading authorities to expel 38 of them in December 1995 while suspending 18 others pending further negotiations.

28 On an elaboration on this, see: African Rights (1998).

29 On this, see: Prunier (2008), above n. 20; Lemarchand (2009), above n. 20.

30 See more generally: Clark and Kaufman (2008); Stys (2012).

31 For a relevant critical analyses thereon, see the various chapters in: Campioni and Noack (2012); Straus and Waldorf (2011), above n. 6.

32 On this, see: Vandeginste (2014); Ingelaere (2010).

33 For some relevant debates, see: Clark and Kaufman (2008); Straus and Waldorf (2011).

Rwandan authorities, mostly in terms of socio-political freedoms, but also because of land tenure reforms and an agricultural policy that is perceived as not always being in the best interests of ordinary farmers.[34] Moreover, Rwandan authorities have widely been criticised for intervening in neighbouring DRC since 1996, and for the destabilising effects that those interventions have generated in terms of regional security and the predatory exploitation of resources.[35] In response to the latter criticism, Rwandan authorities have frequently denounced what they consider to be double standards by western counties in international relations, most notably in matters relating to prosecutions and use of force, particularly with regard to humanitarian interventions.[36]

In several transitional societies that are ravaged by conflict, one of the factors that complicate the recovery process is the inability of local actors, especially public authorities, to take ownership of the transitional trajectory and set the agenda for the future.[37] In countries such as the DRC, international actors such as the United Nations, but also influential non-governmental organisations (including human rights organisations), wield considerable power that, at times, challenges or fills the void left by local or even national leadership.[38] From the outset, post-genocide Rwandan authorities strongly insisted on determining the agenda, even as they had to rely on funds from external partners in order to implement it. On several occasions, this put them on collision courses with international actors, most pointedly NGOs, leading to some of them being expelled from the country.[39] The determination of the authorities to recreate Rwandan society was informed by a particular RPF-reading of Rwandan history and politics that can be traced back to the organisation's inception, as will be explained in sections below.

4. *UBUTABERA*[40] OR JUSTICE IN THE POST-GENOCIDE LANDSCAPE

The civil war and genocide left Rwandan judicial institutions in ruins. Several of the already few magistrates with proper legal training that the country had prior to the genocide were killed, and others fled the country as the RPF defeated

34 See for instance: Straus and Waldorf (2011); Musahara (2005); Ansoms (2009).
35 See for instance Prunier (2008); Reyntjens (2009).
36 Fisher (2015); Rhoads (2016).
37 See: Donai (2009); Vinck and Pham (2008).
38 On this, see: Hellmüller (2012); Autesserre (2010).
39 See: Cavalieri et al (1996); Reyntjens (2004) at 197 fn. 74.
40 *Ubutabera* is a concept used to mean "Justice" as an idea/ideal and as an institution. However, the literal meaning translates as *impartiality*.

governmental forces.[41] Next to many other socio-political emergency actions that the new authorities had to take, rebuilding the justice infrastructure was among their most urgent priorities. In different sectors, laws were revised or new ones adopted to suit the imperatives of, among other things, reconstruction, unity and reconciliation policies, or to secure land/property and inheritance rights. Some of these laws are examined in sections below. Yet, in view of the magnitude of the atrocities that were committed, the reactivation of the criminal justice apparatus was, arguably, the most pressing imperative in this particular domain. The authorities considered the administration of criminal justice to be a crucial component of the reconstruction process for a number of reasons. First, since the decolonisation era, perpetrators of heinous crimes were rarely punished but often instead rewarded whenever such crimes were committed by supporters of governing authorities.[42] The Rwandan leadership argued, perhaps too optimistically, that there was a need to put an end to impunity by prosecuting persons suspected of playing a role in the preparation and execution of the genocide. Moreover, it was simply unimaginable for survivors of the genocide to live peacefully alongside those who had decimated their families and relatives without some form of accountability. For anyone who fully grasps the dynamics and magnitude of the crimes committed – for instance how neighbours turned against neighbours, in some cases wiping out entire families – it was simply hard to envisage peaceful co-existence and, even less, reconciliation without some form of (criminal) accountability.[43] Finally, besides survivors' demands and a governmental determination to prosecute genocide suspects, there were also some practical considerations that rendered the revival of the justice sector an urgent imperative. Just after the genocide, several suspects were imprisoned without trial and many of them spent years in prison without a hearing. It is generally estimated that by the end of the 1990s, "more than 100,000 waited in detention for trials to begin, a source of great social tension and an enormous burden on one of the poorest countries in the world".[44]

Rwanda was struggling with a quest for the appropriate judicial response to the genocide caseload at the time when post-Apartheid South Africa was in the process of instituting its much-acclaimed Truth and Reconciliation Commission. Some argued that given the magnitude of the task at hand, the South African path of dealing with atrocities committed during Apartheid would be more fitting for the Rwandan case.[45] However, based on the

41 National Service of the Gacaca Courts (NSGC), *Gacaca Courts in Rwanda*, Report, June 2012, at 15–16.

42 On this, see: Des Forges (1999), above n. 1, pp. 47–48.

43 This is captured by: Schabas (1996).

44 Schabas (2005).

45 On this, see: Sarkin (1999).

rawness of emotions in the immediate aftermath of the genocide, survivors and Rwandan authorities were uncomfortable with the idea of disregarding criminal accountability for persons responsible for the killing of roughly one million people.[46] What followed in practice was a series of experiments with different forms of criminal accountability mechanisms in response to the committed crimes.

A law was adopted in August 1996 by the Transitional National Assembly that provided for the prosecution of genocide suspects by Specialised Chambers established within the existing ordinary courts.[47] Twelve Chambers were established within the Tribunals of First Instance to handle genocide cases, with the possibility for appeal before one of the four Appeals Courts nationwide. The law encouraged suspects to confess their crimes, which potentially carried a reduction of sentence. But soon after it came into force and proceedings started, the pace of investigations and trials combined with the huge number of suspects awaiting trial led authorities to realise that the chosen path was simply unrealistic. It was clear that if it continued, several detainees would spend a lifetime in jail without a hearing. Following relatively long debates, the creation of the *Gacaca* courts in early 2001 was an acknowledgement that the classical courts were incapable of delivering justice in this particular context.

The genesis, functioning and evaluations of the *Gacaca* courts have been the subject of an extensive and ever-expanding literature.[48] During the one decade that the *Gacaca* courts functioned, starting with the pilot phases in 2002 and ending with the closing of activities in 2012, successive amendments to the laws governing them were adopted to address identified shortcomings of a mechanism that remained essentially experimental until the end.[49] Despite the numerous amendments that aimed at improving the mechanism,

---

46 Ibid.

47 Organic Law N°. 08/96 of 30 August 1996 on the *Organization of Prosecutions for Offences constituting the Crime of Genocide or Crimes against Humanity committed since October 1, 1990*, OGRR, Year 35, No. 17, September 1996 (The 1996 Organic Law).

48 For a critical review of *Gacaca* scholarship, see: Ndahinda and Muleefu (2012). See also: Clark (2007); Ingelaere (2008).

49 For the initial and successive amendments of the Gacaca Law, see: Organic Law N° 40/2000 of 26 January 2001 setting up "Gacaca Jurisdictions" and Organizing Prosecutions for Offences Constituting the Crime of Genocide or Crimes against Humanity Committed between October 1, 1990 and December 31, 1994, OGRR No. 6 of 15 March 2000. Organic Law N° 16/2004 of 16 June 2004 Establishing the Organization, Competence and Functioning of Gacaca Courts Charged with Prosecuting and Trying the Perpetrators of the Crime of Genocide and other Crimes against Humanity, Committed between October 1, 1990 and December 31, 1994, Official Gazette, N°. Special of 19 June 2004; N° 28/2006 of 27/06/2006; Organic Law modifying and complementing Organic Law N° 16/2004 of 19/06/2004 Establishing the Organization, Competence and Functioning of Gacaca Courts Charged with Prosecuting and Trying the Perpetrators of the Crime of Genocide and other Crimes against Humanity, committed between October 1, 1990 and December 31, 1994; Organic Law N° 10/2007 of 1 March 2007 Modifying and completing Organic Law N° 16/2004

the central features of post-genocide justice mechanisms introduced by the 1996 Organic Law remained in place. These included the categorisation of committed crimes and the encouragement of confessions and guilty pleas accompanied by potential reductions of sentences. Moreover, amendments of *Gacaca* laws resulted in a clarification of the mandate of the courts and, of the initially vague semantics that were used to classify the crimes that were to be prosecuted. In the end, official data showed that between 10 March 2005 and the official closure of the activities on 18 June 2012, the *Gacaca* courts handled some 1,958,634 cases resulting in 1,681,648 convictions and 277,066 acquittals.[50]

The *Kinyarwanda* language did not have a word for genocide at the time when the country witnessed this human tragedy in 1994. In official statements and the initial legislation that was promulgated thereafter, the concept came to be captured under two neologisms namely "*itsembabwoko n'itsembatsemba*": literally, "elimination of an 'ethno-cultural'/social category and massacre".[51] The use of the notion of massacre combined with a reference to the imprescriptibility of crimes against humanity and war crimes in the preamble of both the Organic Law of 1996 and the initial Gacaca Law of 2001, suggested that these legal frameworks covered not only the crime of genocide but also crimes against humanity and war crimes committed between October 1990 and December 1994. However, the 2004 amendment to the Gacaca Law replaced mentions of "*itsembabwoko n'intsembatsemba*" with a single, "Rwandanised" word: *jenoside*. Subsequently, in a bid to counter a rising wave of publications and other dynamics that challenged the official narrative on the historiography of the genocide, especially since the mid-2000s,[52] Rwandan authorities and survivors' organisations initiated a push for the use of the terminology: *jenocide yakorewe Abatutsi* meaning "genocide against the Tutsi".

The significance, impact, legacy and shortcomings of the *Gacaca* courts are still subject to ever-growing academic scrutiny.[53] Examined against their stated objectives, the *Gacaca* courts clearly handled the legal caseload of

of 16 June 2004 establishing the Organization, Competence and Functioning of Gacaca Courts Charged with Prosecuting and Trying the Perpetrators of the Crime of Genocide and other Crimes against Humanity, Committed between October 1, 1990 and December 31, 1994, OGRR N° 5 of 1 March 2007. Organic Law N° 13/2008 of 19 May 2008 Modifying and completing Organic Law N° 16/2004 of 16 June 2004 establishing the Organization, Competence and Functioning of Gacaca Courts Charged with Prosecuting and Trying the Perpetrators of the Crime of Genocide and other Crimes against Humanity, Committed between October 1, 1990 and December 31, 1994, OGRR N° 11 of 1 June 2008.

50 NSGC, above n. 41, 261.

51 As in the titles of the 1996, and 2001 Organic Laws. For an elaboration on the use of concepts, but with mistranslations, see: Burnet (2012), 20–21.

52 See: Péan (2005); Philpot (2004); Lemarchand (1998).

53 Any simple search of academic articles and books examining *Gacaca* courts generates hundreds of materials.

the genocide expeditiously. The process also led to the gathering of a lot of information that allowed survivors to know more about the fate and/or whereabouts of the remains of loved ones.[54] Proceedings also shed more light on the dynamics of genocide in particular geographies.

From its very inception, the idea of instituting courts modelled on traditional *Gacaca* jurisdictions to try genocide cases was criticised for not conforming to dominant liberal norms governing criminal justice, particularly due process guarantees.[55] The mechanism has also been frequently denounced as essentially a political tool used by the ruling RPF to exert power and control over the country by subjugating the Hutu masses.[56] Since the archives of the *Gacaca* courts are not yet fully available for examination (they are still undergoing a process of digitisation and indexation as we write) and as more evaluative studies are conducted across Rwanda to examine how survivors, convicts, the acquitted, or other generations of Rwandans not necessarily fitting these categories live and co-exist in the same hills, the jury is still out on whether the *Gacaca* courts ultimately achieved their stated goals of revealing *the* truth and contributing to national reconciliation.

5. *KWIBUKA*[57] OR MEMORIALISATION OF GENOCIDE VICTIMS

Gisozi, Murambi, Nyamata, Ntarama, Nyarubuye, Bisesero are some of the most known shrines of memory harbouring the remains of thousands of slain victims of the genocide. Most of these places were theatres of some of the most atrocious mass killings during the 1994 genocide, and, therefore, are not only resting places for victims but are also intended to offer to world the most poignant, at times graphic, images of the horrendous nature of the committed atrocities.[58] The Kigali Genocide Memorial alone is said to host the remains of more than 250,000 victims of the genocide.[59] Beyond these most known and visited memorials, the Rwandan National Commission for the Fight against Genocide has listed 207 memorials and 159 graves across the 30 Districts of Rwanda.[60]

54 NSGC, above n. 41, p. 270.

55 This is discussed elsewhere in: Ndahinda and Muleefu (2012). See also among many others: Des Forges and Longman (2004); Ingelaere (2009).

56 For a review of the relevant literature thereon, see: Clark (2014).

57 Literally: remembering. The Kinyarwanda word/verb *kwibuka* is increasingly used in Rwanda and beyond for the memorialisation events in April each year.

58 On this, see for instance: Jessee (2017b), at 45 et seq.

59 See: http://www.kgm.rw/; http://cnlg.gov.rw/genocide/memorial-sites/ (visited on 22 February 2018).

60 See: National Commission for the Fight against Genocide, *Ishusho Rusange Y'inzibutso* (A General Overview of Memorials), Unpublished Report (with the Author).

From the early days after the genocide, several steps were taken to keep the memory of the slaughtered victims of the genocide alive. Since the post-genocide authorities were faced with numerous, competing imperatives in rebuilding a country in ruins, memorialisation in the immediate aftermath of the tragedy was mostly undertaken by the surviving victims. Soon enough, however, the government became involved in shaping a public, official form of memorialisation.[61] Victims had often been killed and thrown in mass graves or even latrines, so over the years, their remains were dug out and reburied in dignity, mostly during this commemorative period.[62] In some cases, it was possible for survivors to identify the remains of loved ones, but in many others, it was simply not possible as the bodies had decomposed. Progressively, memorials of different sizes and shapes were erected across the country as both decent burial sites for victims and spaces for reflection about humanity's commitment to atrocity prevention.[63]

Yearly remembrance ceremonies for victims of the genocide are held across the country. During the period between April and July each year, these commemorative events, which include remembrance rituals, re-burials of remains of victims and public seminars, are organised at the national, local, and/or family levels.[64] Memorialisation activities are officially coordinated by a National Commission for the Fight against Genocide established in 2007 and commonly known under the French acronym: CNLG.[65] CNLG works in close collaboration with the ministry "in charge of genocide memory",[66] and organisations working "in defence of interests of Genocide survivors".[67] Its mandate covers research and documentation on, and prevention of, genocide, but also advocacy for genocide survivors.[68]

As stated in the previous section, studies conducted on the history, dynamics of conflicts, civil war and genocide in Rwanda, particularly over the last decade, have generated an increasing body of literature that questions different aspects of the dominant, official narratives and policies.[69] In the particular field of memory, concepts such as "chosen amnesia" have been used to capture what is considered to be the partial or selective memory of both the immediate and

61 On this, see: Dumas and Korman (2011).

62 Ibreck (2010).

63 On this, see for instance: Yusin (2016), 345.

64 Ibreck (2010).

65 Law N° 09/2007 of 16 February 2007on the attributions, organisation and functioning of the National Commission for the Fight against Genocide, OGRR, N° Special Issue of 19 March 2007 (CNLG Law of 2007).

66 Article 2 of the CNLG law of 2007. Currently the Ministry of Sports and Culture (MINISPOC)

67 Article 5 of Law No 15/2016 of 2 May 2016 governing ceremonies to commemorate the Genocide against the Tutsi and organization and management of memorial sites for the Genocide against the Tutsi, OGRR, N° 22 of 30 May 2016.

68 Article 4 of the CNLG law of 2007.

69 See for instance: Jessee (2017a). See also the various sources in n. 5 above.

distant history that shaped the genocide.[70] Just as the *Gacaca* process focused on the crime of genocide, studies have criticised a limited acknowledgment of the pain and suffering of Hutu and Twa who lost loved ones during the civil war and the genocide period, either as accidental casualties of war or victims of revenge and other killings by members of the RPF/A.[71] Moreover, memorialisation in Rwanda is also associated with the country's policy to fight against "genocide ideology", "divisionism", or what the CNLG Law refers to as "revisionism, negationism and trivialisation" of the genocide.[72] The content and application of laws relating to these concepts have been frequently denounced for their vagueness, which has made it difficult to determine the precise boundaries of what is or is not criminalised.[73]

In spite of these contentious aspects in the construction of memory in post-genocide Rwanda, the determination of the country's authorities to erect a new Rwanda from the ashes of a destructive civil war and genocide has led them to adopt more or less inclusive policies that seek to heal the wounds of the past.[74] The section below on radical policies adopted in attempts to reshape Rwanda shows how authorities have used unorthodox paths to address some of most contentious aspects of Rwanda's past in shaping the future.

6. PLURALITY OF TRANSITIONAL PROCESSES IN SHAPING A "NEW RWANDA"

6.1. *AMOKO* AND *ABAZUNGU*: NARRATIVES ON ETHNICISATION AND ANTAGONISATION OF SOCIETY

Dominant literature about Rwanda from the last few decades refers to the Hutu, Tutsi and (often omitted) Twa as ethnic groups. At the time of the colonial encounter in the 1890s and until the 1930s, the three groups were described as distinct races, with different origins and distinctive characteristics ascribed to them.[75] The first European explorers who came in contact with the Rwandan Kingdom formulated and popularised theories about the separate origins and distinctive attributes of these groups without subjecting such theories to rigorous examination. Oscar Baumann and Count Gustav von Götzen framed the earliest recorded hypotheses that shaped colonial narratives over the Hutu, Tutsi or Twa identities in Rwanda and the wider

70 Buckley-Zistel (2006).
71 See: Ibreck (2010), 330–332. See also: Lemarchand (2006–2007).
72 Article 4(7) of the CNLG Law of 2007.
73 Ibreck (2010), 330; Lemarchand (2006–2007), 25.
74 RoR (2016).
75 See for instance: Pagès (1933). The book extensively refers to the races of Rwanda.

Great Lakes sub-region.[76] Baumann theorised about the "White Negroes" inhabiting Rwanda before he even reached the country, while von Götzen made an elaborate differentiation in terms of physical appearance, origin and social position between the "races" inhabiting the kingdom of Rwanda, despite spending only a few weeks in the country.[77] Others followed in their footsteps.[78] What was initially formulated as mere hypothesis was progressively crafted into scientific knowledge through the work of colonial historiographers and anthropologists who popularised their racial/ethnic theories using questionable methodologies and measurements to determine who fitted into which racial/ethnic group. Documents from colonial Rwanda portray images of measurements of facial features or sizes of noses to determine who was Hutu, Tutsi or Twa.[79] The climax of the socio-political institutionalisation of "racial" or "ethnic" differences in the colonial era was the issuance by Belgian colonial authorities in the 1930s of identity cards mentioning the holder's ethnic affiliation. In a country whose population shared the same language, this racialisation, ethnicisation, and antagonisation of Rwanda's social identities created a new reality that became the cornerstone of domestic politics for the first three decades after the country's independence.[80]

The decolonisation process occurred within this poisoned socio-political climate. Belgian colonial authorities and catholic religious leaders, who had initially favoured the Tutsi ruling elite, over time reversed their alliance from the 1940s and mostly the 1950s by siding with the "oppressed" Hutu masses.[81] The appropriation of colonially-shaped identity narratives by early post-colonial authorities perpetuated the rift that had been created between Rwanda's social groups. As Rwanda acquired its independence in a bloodbath, where thousands of Tutsi were forced into exile from 1959 to 1962, one of the pillars of the newly independent Rwandan republic was the appeal to ethnic majoritarian legitimacy. In this context, rule by an ethnic majority (Hutu) was construed as synonymous with democratic rule. Symptomatic of early post-independence ethnocratic conceptions of governance – inspired by the colonial ethnicisation of the Hutu, Tutsi and Twa categories – is the very name of the party that took the reins of power upon independence: *Parmehutu* (*Parti du Mouvement de l'Emancipation Hutu* or Party of the Hutu

---

76 For a list of early stereotypical references to various ethnicities in Rwanda, see: Muzungu (2011).

77 For a discussion thereon, see: Ndahinda (2011), 220–224.

78 For an elaboration thereon, see: Muzungu (2011).

79 Such images are reproduced in Pagès (1933), PL.I–PL. XXIX.

80 A reality acknowledged by the United Nations' International Criminal Tribunal for Rwanda in *The Prosecutor v. Jean Paul Akayesu*, Case No. ICTR-96-4-T, Trial Chamber 1, Judgment, 2 September 1998, §§. 112–172.

81 Prunier (1995), 41–54.

Emancipation Movement).[82] The framing of the political debates in the wake of independence, the crises and early genocidal killings that accompanied the decolonisation process (1959–1962),[83] the early armed uprisings of the 1960s (dubbed *Inyenzi* rebellion), the civil war and, the genocide in the 1990s were a culmination of politically engineered tensions between the Hutu, Tutsi and, to a lesser extent, Twa social categories.

The above reading of the country's encounter with the *Abazungu*[84] colonial politics of divide and rule has shaped current fixations on pre-colonial realities as a source of inspiration for contemporary post-genocide politics. Post-genocide Rwandan authorities have attempted to "rewrite" history by reshaping perceptions and narratives on Hutu, Tutsi and Twa identities. In the reconstructed narrative on socio-political realities of pre-colonial Rwandan society, it is contended that there are hardly any records of collective "ethnic" violence depicting the Hutu against the Tutsi or the Twa.[85] Contrary to stereotypical representations of killings in Rwanda and Burundi (and Africa in general) as part of "ancient tribal hatreds",[86] *Abazungu* (in the Rwandan case the Germans and mostly the Belgians) are, henceforth considered to be the ideological godfathers of ethnic divisions that have escalated into destructive violence since the 1950 and 1960s, to reach its peak with the 1994 genocide.[87] The role of *Abazungu* in dividing Rwandans was already a prominent theme in RPF's narrative since the launch of its armed struggle in 1990.[88] The antagonisation of the Hutu and the Tutsi came to be interpreted as a transposition by Belgian colonial authorities of their own Flemish vs. Walloons conflict to the Ruanda-Urundi colony.[89] With this background and narrative in mind, Rwandan authorities have geared their post-genocide politics towards reshaping these colonially antagonised identities through inclusive policies that are anchored in a restorative rediscovery of a (real or imagined) shared and more harmonious past.

---

82 I elaborated on "Ethnicities in Rwanda: The Mythical Foundations of a Contemporary Reality" in a piece on *Love Radio. Episodes of Love and Hate*: http://www.loveradio-rwanda.org/episode/2/info/essay.

83 For references on the genocidal nature of the killings in 1959.

84 *Abazungu* (singular *Umuzungu*) is the word used in several central African languages, including Kinyarwanda, for Whites. It is important to note that unlike in several western languages (e.g. English, French, German, Dutch …) where "racial" categories refer to colours, *abazungu* does not refer to a colour in Kinyarwanda and related languages. Different words are, for instance, used to refer to "white" as a colour (*umweru*) and as a "racial" category (*umuzungu*).

85 Byanafashe and Rutayisire (2016), 163.

86 For a relevant analysis of semantics, see: Bancel and Riot (2008).

87 A document commissioned by the Office of the President of Rwanda in 1999 on the "Unity of Rwandans: Before the whites, during colonization and during the First Republic" makes this point: RoR (1999), 10–22.

88 Chemouni and Mugiraneza 2018.

89 RoR (1999), 50.

6.2. *UBUMWE* AND *UBUNYARWANDA*:[90] NARRATIVES ON UNITY AND RECONCILIATION

National Unity was a central feature in the Protocol of Agreement between the Government of the Republic of Rwanda and the Rwandese Patriotic Front on the Rule of Law, signed in Arusha on 18 August 1992. The document proclaimed the creed that the RPF had pushed forward during the negotiation process that "the Rwandese people, as constituent elements of the Rwandese nation, are one and indivisible",[91] and expressed the necessity "to fight all obstacles to national unity, notably, ethnicism, regionalism, integrism and intolerance which subordinate the national interest to ethnic, regional, religious and personal interest".[92] The commitment of the RPF to abide by the spirit of the Arusha Accords after securing a military victory over governmental forces and halting the genocide meant that a quest for unity among Rwandans remained a key priority for the new government.

The first concrete steps in fostering that unity were taken in July 1994 with the establishment of a unity and reconciliation government comprising members of different political parties who had not actively participated in the genocide. Since the victorious RPF drove the agenda, the inclusion of different political forces within the country's governance was not always successful, as some actors could not find common ground on the orientation of national policies.[93] However, this idea of inclusive politics has remained a constant feature of national post-genocide politics and was enshrined in the national Constitution in 2003.[94]

A National Unity and Reconciliation Commission (NURC) was established by Presidential Decree in 1997[95] and then formally instituted through an act of parliament in 1999.[96] The mandate of the NURC was not modelled on the contemporaneous Truth and Reconciliation Commission of South Africa (TRC) as an institutional legal body tasked with addressing the committed

---

90 Kinyarwanda for unity/togetherness and "Rwandanness" respectively. For a critical analysis on Ubumwe, see: Purdeková (2015).

91 Article 2 of the *Protocol of Agreement between the Government of the Republic of Rwanda and the Rwandese Patriotic Front on the Rule of Law*, signed in Arusha on 18 August 1992.

92 Ibid.

93 The first post-genocide Prime Minister, Faustin Twagiramungu, resigned not very long after and became a strong critic of RPF governance.

94 For instance, Article 116 of the Constitution of 4 June 2003 (currently Article 62 of the 2003 Constitution amended in 2015) provide for the appointment of cabinet ministers from different political organisations and prohibit any political organisation from occupying more than 50% of cabinet positions.

95 Presidential Order N° 5/01 of 1997, *Establishing the Rwanda National Unity, and Reconciliation Commission*, 1 November 1997, available at: http://www.refworld.org/docid/3ae6b51a0.html.

96 Law No. 03/99 12 March 1999 *establishing the National Unity and Reconciliation Commission*, available at: http://www.refworld.org/docid/3ae6b59a18.html.

mass atrocities. Instead, it was entrusted with a mandate to undertake different activities that aimed at promoting unity, fighting division, educating the public on and sensitising them to peace and unity among Rwandans.[97] Identity cards showing the ethnicity of the bearer were abolished and policies were pursued that put an emphasis on a shared Rwandan identity by downplaying the Hutu, Tutsi and Twa "ethnic differences", eventually generating the concept of "*ndi umunyarwanda*" (I am a Rwandan).[98] The NURC presents *ndi umunyarwanda* as a programme erected on three pillars: (1) patriotism, or as the document puts it, "Rwandan spirit"; (2) a commitment to uphold Rwandan values; and (3) shying away from taboos under Rwandan culture.[99] The *ndi umunyarwanda* programme and narrative is one in a succession of state-sponsored socio-political and legal programmes or institutions construed as home-grown solutions designed to meet the challenges facing Rwandan society in the post-genocide era. Since 2015, the concept of *Abarinzi b'Ingihango* (guardians of the Covenant) has been coined and appended to the *ndi umunyarwanda* programme to celebrate unparalleled deeds (*ibikorwa by'indashyikirwa*) by Rwandans or foreigners that foster(ed) positive values promoted under the *ndi umurwandanda* or national unity project.[100] Under *abarinzi b'igihango*, rescuers (also known as the righteous) during the 1994 genocide in Rwanda have been recognised and celebrated.[101]

6.3. *KWIGIRA*:[102] TRADITION-INSPIRED PROGRAMMES OR "HOME GROWN INITIATIVES-SOLUTIONS"

In the course of more than two decades of post-genocide politics in Rwanda, the RFP-led administration has adopted numerous initiatives with the expressed aim of fostering national unity and reconciliation. The common denominator between these initiatives is an attempt to (re)invent a Rwandan nationalism that transcends the country's colonially-shaped referents by drawing inspiration

---

97 For a critical analysis of Rwanda's reconciliation approach, see: Clark 2010.

98 NURC, *Ndi Umunyarwanda Isobanurampamvu Kuri Gahunda Ya "Ndi Umunyarwanda"* (I am Rwandan: A Background on the "I am Rwandan" Programme), http://www.nurc.gov.rw/fileadmin/templates/nurc/documents/NDI_UMUNYARWANDA.pdf.

99 Ibid. pp. 2–3.

100 See: NURC, *Abarinzi b'Igihango bashimwe ku mugaragaro na Nyakubahwa Perezida wa Repubulika mu ihuriro rya 8 ry'umuryango Unity Club Intwararumuri* [His Eminence/excellency. the President of the Republic publicly recognises Abarinzi b'Igihango during the 8th meeting of Unity Club Intwararumuri], N° 018 *Igorora Magazine* [NURC], November 2015–February 2016.

101 On this, see: NURC, *Abarinzi b'Igihango*, Report, at 12–13, at: http://www.nurc.gov.rw/index.php?id=70.

102 Translates as a complex idea of "being resourceful, self-reliant", self-empowering, self-valuing (self-worth).

from pre-colonial socio-political institutions and practices considered by sponsors as authentically Rwandan. A close examination of these initiatives suggests that they are inspired by the same ideological quest for locally-designed mechanisms aimed at addressing societal challenges. The timeline of the creation, institutionalisation, and frequent readjustments of the programmes or initiatives suggest that they are also pragmatic responses to the imperatives of the moment. However, they are increasingly imagined as fitting into a coherent restorative project.

Ingando solidarity camps represent one of the earliest post-genocide mechanisms inspired by Rwandan tradition and sponsored by the new Rwandan authorities attempting to rebuild the socio-political fabric of the country. It is claimed that within traditional Rwandan society, *ingando* referred to a retreat during which elders, leaders or young people left their homes to stay in a place where they shared ideas on how to solve societal problems.[103] From 1994, but more formally from 1996 onward,[104] *ingando* were (re-)instituted as platforms that brought together a variety of actors for training with the stated aim of instilling values of peaceful cohabitation. They were imagined as platforms whose major goal was to

> enable Rwandans to come to terms with the past by facing history, forging a common vision for a united future, and creating a forum for trust building and critical analysis of national challenges with a view to searching for solutions to address them.[105]

Initially organised by the Ministry of Youth, *ingando* were subsequently brought within the purview of the NURC after the latter was established. Over the decade between 1996 and 2006, *ingando* sessions were organised for more than 100,000 participants including demobilised soldiers, returning refugees, students (mostly those completing high school education[106]), youth, civil servants and many other sectors of society.[107] Participants in *ingando* were subjected to various physical and mental exercises, including lectures and debates on a variety of topics with societal relevance. The environment combined military-style discipline with a friendly atmosphere that encouraged bonding with strangers.[108]

103 NURC, *Ingando: Impact Assessment on Unity and Reconciliation of Rwandans*, Kigali (2007), p. 7.

104 Ibid., at15; NURC/ Sentama (2016), 101.

105 NURC/Sentama (2016), 104.

106 The present author participated in the first *Ingando* organised for university students enrolled in the National University of Rwanda in 1998.

107 NURC, above n. 103, at 17–18.

108 Personal experience/participant observation by the author in 1998.

The establishment of *Itorero ry'igihugu* (Civic Education Programme) in 2007 brought certain activities of the *ingando* under the purview of *itorero*. Another institution that appealed to tradition, the historical *itorero* has been described as, "a civic education channel or school through which the nation could convey the messages to the people regarding national culture in different areas such as language, patriotism, social relations, sports, dance, songs and the defense of the nation".[109] The *Intore* dancers that are the emblematic embodiment of Rwandan cultural entertainment heritage were historically, and still are, affiliated with *amatorero* (plural of *itorero*).

The new *itorero* is tasked with a similar mission of shaping a Rwandan patriotic citizenry characterised by compliance with culturally held values and taboos.[110] An emphasis was put on values such as patriotism, unity, selflessness, integrity, responsibility, volunteerism and humility.[111] The institution targets "all categories of Rwandans and is intending to design different curricula to suit different sections of the population including children – seven years and above".[112] One particular dimension of *itorero*, known as *urugerero* or National Service, is compulsory for youth completing secondary (higher) education and targets the 18–35 year-old demographic.[113] With a particular emphasis on fostering patriotism and the spirit of volunteerism, *urugerero* is also open to other sections of the Rwandan population, the Rwandan diaspora and, in principle, to foreigners willing to participate.[114]

Post-genocide reforms of the Rwandan justice sector have also dug into the well of tradition in a quest for the most effective conflict settlement mechanisms, particularly for family and neighbourhood disputes. The re-invention of the *Gacaca* dispute resolution mechanism to deal with the caseload of the genocide was the first step in the Rwandan authorities' move towards involving ordinary Rwandan citizenry in delivering justice. Following the initial steps that operationalised the *Gacaca* courts, *Abunzi*[115] Mediation Committees were instituted to serve as a local dispute resolution mechanism for specified cases that had previously fallen under the jurisdiction of ordinary courts. The move was intended to relieve pressure on the overburdened ordinary courts, but also to "promote the spirit of dialogue and reconciliation among Rwandans as well as to reinforce the unity of the Rwandan community".[116] Contemplated under

109 NURC/Sentama, above n. 104, at 107. See also: Riot (2008).

110 Article 2 of Law n° 41/2013 of 16 June 2013, establishing the National *Itorero* Commission and determining its mission, organisation and functioning.

111 RoR (2011), 11.

112 Ibid., p. 12.

113 Ibid.

114 Ibid.

115 *Abunzi* (plural of *Umwunzi*) derives from the verb *kunga* which carries the idea of both mediating and uniting.

116 RCN-Justice & Démocratie (2015), 26.

the first Rwandan post-genocide Constitution of 2003, the *Abunzi* Mediation Committees, composed of persons of integrity recognised for their mediation skills, were formally set up in 2004 and empowered to handle listed civil and criminal disputes.[117] Successive amendments to the law that established the *Abunzi* Mediation Committees have reflected the persistent debate within Rwanda over their jurisdictional reach. Despite institutional and operational challenges, assessments of the work of the *Abunzi* Committees have generally been rather positive.[118]

In the socio-economic sphere, poverty reduction strategies adopted by Rwandan authorities in recent years have also borne imprints of tradition. *Ubudehe* and *Girinka* are two government-sponsored programmes that appeal to traditional Rwandan practices and values of socio-economic solidarity. Rwandans have a tradition of mutual assistance in performing certain tasks, like cultivating, planting crops, harvesting or building houses, that could either inherently or more efficiently be performed through collective action.[119] This practice is known as *Ubudehe*, and was taken up and refined by Rwandan authorities around 2001 as a poverty alleviation framework. Based on their living conditions (income), Rwandan households have since been categorised into, initially six, and later four, socio-economic categories ranging from extremely poor to wealthy.[120] The categorisation system is then used as a basis for determining who should benefit from what and to what extent, in specific governmental programmes such as the Mutual Health Insurance [widely known as *mutuelle (de Santé)*], education sponsorships from the Student Financing Agency for Rwanda (SFAR), direct financial support through Vision 2020 Umurenge Programme (VUP), the *girinka* programme, etc.[121]

The latter programme, *girinka* (one cow per poor family),[122] draws from a deep-rooted Rwandan tradition of bestowing cattle to someone as a sign of appreciation or friendship. A cow is also the quintessential property that is transferred by the family of a prospective groom to the family of the bride as a dowry, a tradition that is meant to seal an alliance between the two families. In 2006, the Rwandan government drew inspiration from this cultural practice when it institutionalised a cow distribution scheme that came to be known as *girinka*. Its stated objectives were to fight malnutrition by

---

117 See also: Article 7–8 of Organic Law No. 17/2004 of 20 June 2004 determining the organisation, competence and functioning of the mediation committee, OGRR N°. special of 8 July 2004.

118 RCN, above, n. 116; Mutisi (2012).

119 NURC/Sentama (2016), 96–97.

120 See: Rwanda Governance Board (RGB) (2014), 15; see also: http://www.minaloc.gov.rw/index.php?id=469&tx_ttnews%5Btt_news%5D=461.

121 RGB (2014), 16–21.

122 Literally, *girinka* translates as "have/own a cow!" something that was traditionally part of Rwandan greetings, expressed in the form of a positive wish.

making milk available to as many households as possible, increasing farming productivity through the use of manure to fertilise soil, increasing household income through the sale of milk, and promoting social cohesion by revitalising this cultural practice.[123] Cattle have historically been associated with the Tutsi ethnicity/social category, while farming and, hunting and gathering have been described as the traditional livelihood activities of the Hutu and Twa respectively. By using poverty levels as the guiding criteria for selecting beneficiaries of the *girinka*, the programme is aligned with stated governmental policies of breaking down the pillars upon which the ethnicisation of Rwandan society was erected. The cow distribution scheme does not factor in ethnicity. Instead, it uses a need-based approach and the ability to rear livestock to determine who should ultimately benefit from the programme.

Next to the revival and institutionalisation of the cattle transfer culture through the *girinka* programme, the Rwandan traditional feast of *umuganura*, or "first fruits" festival, has been revalued in relatively recent years. According to Alexis Kagame, traditional *umuganura* consisted of rituals whereby the Rwandan King and, after him elders in their respective families, ate the first fruits of crops such as sorghum before the start of the harvest season.[124] In the words of Newbury, the festivity was "central to the restatement – and renewal – of kingship in Rwanda".[125] Vansina states that the *umuganura* ritual "unified the whole population around the king through participation of many people from all over the country".[126] The Rwandan government has revived the celebration of *umuganura* since 2011 by elevating it to a public holiday celebrated on the first Friday of the month of August.[127] On this domestic variant of the American *Thanksgiving*, the population is expected to join in celebrations for the good things that have occurred during the past year, while also setting even more ambitious goals for the year to come.[128]

One of the traditional practices that have survived the various changes in the Rwandan socio-political landscape is *umuganda*, or community work.[129] Similarly to *ubudehe*, *umuganda* was, it is claimed, a practice within pre-colonial Rwandan society consisting of joining forces to perform certain tasks that benefit community members and, as such, the community as a whole.[130]

123 Ibid., pp. 46–47.
124 Kagame (1954), 07-208.
125 Newbury (2001), 292.
126 Vansina (2004), 39.
127 Ministeri ya Siporo N'umuco, *Inyandiko Ngenderwaho: Kwizihiza Umuganura Na FESPAD 2016 Insanganyamatsiko: "Twubakire ku Muco Twiteze Imbere"* [Ministry of Sport and Culture, *Concept Note: Celebration of Umuganura and FESPAD 2016*], Kigali, 2016, p. 2 http://ralc.gov.rw/fileadmin/user_upload/Final_Concept__UMUGANURA-FESPAD_2016_02.pdf.
128 Ibid.
129 RGB, above n. 2, pp. 69–84.
130 Ibid.

The practice was reportedly co-opted by colonial administrations through use of *umuganda* for the performance of public work or work that benefited the colonial administration.[131] Post-independence administrations kept the practice of community work but its meaning became tarnished by the use of the concept to mobilise the masses to participate in the genocide killings.[132] Post-genocide authorities have reclaimed *umuganda*, however, as a useful and needed concept and practice in mobilising Rwandans to actively participate in the reconstruction process. Performed as a matter of policy since 1998, *umuganda* was formalised through the adoption of a law regulating it in 2007.[133] In their neighbourhoods or communities, citizens, residents and even visitors come together on the last Saturday of every month for a couple of hours to perform certain activities of public interest. Such activities include: cleaning up neighbourhoods; infrastructural development or maintenance (for instance roads); and construction of bridges, heath centres, classrooms or houses for vulnerable people.[134] *Umuganda* activities are generally concluded with meetings that are intended to cement social cohesion by conveying official discourses within neighbourhoods: local or national socio-political matters are discussed in a typical "palaver tree" format.[135]

The above list of the so-called home-grown initiatives is far from exhaustive. In the framework of *umuganura*, but also beyond, Rwandan leaders and, increasingly, also members of the general population are either mandated or encouraged to set goals or *imihigo* on things they undertake to achieve within a period of time, usually a year.[136] Moreover, once a year, a national gathering known as the *Umushyikirano* Council brings together citizens' representatives, including some from the diaspora, and the country's top leadership, including the President, to debate "issues relating to the state of the Nation and national unity";[137] with the ultimate goal of improving institutional service delivery to the population.[138] *Akagoroba k'ababyeyi* (parents'/mothers' evening) is another platform that has been established for parents, mainly mothers, living in specific neighbourhoods to meet and exchange views on various issues of particular interest to them regarding the family, parenting, reproductive

131 Ibid.
132 See for instance: WILLAME (1995), 100–104; 142–143.
133 Organic Law n° 53/2007 of 17 November 2007 Governing Community Works, OGRR, n° 2 of 15 January 2008.
134 RGB (2014), 69.
135 The author regularly attended such meetings in Kigali, Kimironko between May 2016 and December 2017.
136 RoR, *Inyandiko Ngenderwaho [Guiding Document] Umuganura* 2015, Ministry of Sports and Culture, at 4.
137 Article 140 of the Constitution of the Republic of Rwanda of 2003 Revised in 2015, OGRR, n° Special of 24 December 2015.
138 Ibid.

health and, more broadly, socio-economic domains.[139] All these and other initiatives are increasingly framed as Rwanda's tradition-anchored and yet innovative approach to governance, peace-building and path to socio-economic prosperity. For a country whose population bears the heavy legacy and negative reputation arising from the history of conflict and genocidal killings, these processes are presented as embodying *Agaciro*: a new-found sense of pride and re-valuation of the self and of the shared Rwandan identity and heritage.[140]

7. MANAGING THE PAST, SHAPING THE FUTURE: AN APPRAISAL

The civil war and genocide in Rwanda marked a turning point in the country's socio-political history. Looking back at the utter chaos and devastation in the country in July 1994 when the RPF seized power, it was hard to imagine what life would look like in the near or distant future. After securing control over the country, the RPF pushed for an agenda of rebuilding the country through a radical form of social engineering. In an era when truth and reconciliation commissions, rather than trials, were fashionable for dealing with mass atrocities, the authorities' determination to try persons suspected of involvement in the genocide led to a reinvention of the traditional *Gacaca* dispute resolution mechanism to do so. The relative success of the mechanism from the authorities' point of view inspired them to institute other tradition-inspired restorative mechanisms to bolster post-genocide governance. Since the mid-2000s, and in a few cases even before, several tradition-inspired initiatives were formally instituted to shape Rwanda's post-genocide governance and politics. The re-discovery, re-invention and idealisation of Rwandan historical traditions, values and institutions are premised on a perceived need to uproot the seeds of discord sowed by divisive colonial politics. Romanticisation of a harmonious pre-colonial Rwanda where Hutu, Tutsi and Twa co-existed peacefully acts as an inspiration for this perceived imperative to rediscover the essence of authentic Rwandan-ness.

The institution of mechanisms appealing to traditional values invokes Mobutu's Zaire of the end of the 1970s and 1980s, where a professed "*recours à l'authenticité*", a rediscovery of authenticity, generated the country's governing ideology of "Zairianisation", which resulted in, among many other things, the semantic "de-Belgianisation" of places, things and people's names, including, in the latter case, abandoning "western" first (so-called Christian) names.[141]

---

139 See: NURC/Sentama (2016), 127–128.

140 On *Agaciro*, see: Rutazibwa (2014).

141 On this, see: Mussia (1983); Ndaywel è Nziem (1998).

A rediscovery of Rwandan ancient traditions through "home-grown initiatives" was the outcome of governmental determination to shape Rwanda's future with limited outside (particularly Western) influence. Interestingly, this involved revisiting pre-colonial Rwandan society in search for the building blocks upon which a future, economically prosperous, and modernised Rwandan society should be erected. Socio-economic modernisation is not seen as being antithetical to initiatives that appeal to pre-colonial traditional values and practices. On the contrary, the past is re-appropriated as a means to shape a future anchored in values presented as authentically Rwandan. Deconstructing the *abazungu* negative legacy of an ethnicised and antagonised society is presented as necessitating this radical shift.

The adopted course is not without its critics. Several references quoted in this analysis showed that nearly every aspect of post-genocide governance in Rwanda is subject to contestation, both from within and without. Questions have been and are still raised on issues such as how just was the justice that was delivered through the Gacaca courts, or on the healing power and inclusiveness of memorialisation of processes, or on the legitimacy and genuine authenticity of the various "home grown initiatives" adopted in post-genocide Rwanda. Yet, while many achievements have been made possible through global partnerships, including heavy donor investment in the reconstruction process, post-genocide Rwandan authorities have displayed a determination to drive a reconstruction agenda that seeks to radically shape Rwanda's future through a multiplicity of processes that are inspired by a distant and romanticised pre-colonial past. A politically reconstructed past is henceforth given a central place in shaping the future.

References

African Rights (1996) *Rwanda Killing the Evidence: Murder, Attacks, Arrests and Intimidation of Survivors and Witnesses*, Report, April 1996.

Ansoms A. and Rostagno, D. (2012) "Rwanda's Vision 2020 Halfway through: What the Eye Does Not See" in *Review of African Political Economy* **39**, no. 133: 427–450.

Ansoms, A. (2009) "Re-Engineering Rural Society: The Visions and Ambitions of the Rwandan Elite" in *African Affairs* **108**, no. 431: 289–309.

Autesserre, S. (2010) *The Trouble with the Congo: Local Violence and the Failure of International Peacebuilding*. Cambridge: Cambridge University Press.

Bancel N. and Riot, T. (2008) "Génocide ou 'guerre tribale': les mémoires controversées du génocide rwandais" in *Hermès, La Revue* **52**, no. 3: 139–146.

Berman, B.J. (1998) "Ethnicity, Patronage and the African State: The Politics of Uncivil Nationalism" in *African Affairs* **97**, no. 388: 305–341.

Boone, C. (2003) *Political Topographies of the African State: Territorial Authority and Institutional Choice*. Cambridge: Cambridge University Press.

Brown, W. (2013) "Sovereignty matters: Africa, donors, and the aid relationship" in *African Affairs* **112**, no. 447: 262–282.

Buckley-Zistel, S. (2006) "Remembering to Forget: Chosen Amnesia as A Strategy for Local Coexistence in Post-Genocide Rwanda" in *Africa* **76**, no. 2: 131–150.

Burnet, J.E. (2012) *Genocide Lives in Us: Women, Memory, and Silence in Rwanda*, Madison W.I.: University of Wisconsin Press.

Byanafashe, D. and Rutayisire, P. (eds) (2016) *History of Rwanda: From the Beginning to the End of the Twentieth Century*. Kigali: National Unity and Reconciliation Commission.

Campioni, M. and Noack, P. (2012) *Rwanda Fast Forward. Social, Economic, Military and Reconciliation Prospects*. Basingstoke: Palgrave Macmillan.

Cavalieri, G. et al. (1996) *Rwanda: United Nations Situation Report* for December 1995, January 1996.

Chemouni, B. and Mugiraneza, A. (2018) *Singing the Struggle: The Rwandan Patriotic Front's ideology through its songs of liberation*. Kigali, Aegis Trust WP N° 11, November 2018.

Chrétien, J.-P. (1997) *Le défi de l'ethnisme. Rwanda et Burundi: 1990–1996*. Paris: Karthala.

Chrétien, J.-P. et al. (1995) *Rwanda: les médias du génocide*. Paris: Karthala.

Clark, P. (2007) "Hybridity, Holism, and Traditional Justice: The Case of the Gacaca Courts in Post-Genocide Rwanda" in *George Washington International Law Review* **39**, no 4: 765–838.

—— (2014) "Bringing the Peasants Back In, Again: State Power and Local Agency in Rwanda's Gacaca Courts" in *Journal of Eastern African Studies* **8**, no 2: 193–213.

Clark, P. and Kaufman, Z.D. (2008) *After Genocide: transitional justice, post-conflict reconstruction and reconciliation in Rwanda and beyond*. London: Hurst & Company.

Corry B. /Institute of Policy Analysis and Research (IPAR), (2012) *Policy Framework for Social Cohesion*. Report, July 2012.

Dallaire, R. (2004) *Shake Hands with the Devil: The Failure of Humanity in Rwanda*. New York: Carroll & Graf Publishers.

Des Forges, A. (1999 *Leave None to Tell the Story: Genocide in Rwanda*, New York: Human Rights Watch.

Des Forges, A. and T. Longman (2004) "Legal responses to genocide in Rwanda" in E. Stover and H.M. Weinstein *My Neighbor, My Enemy: Justice and Community in the Aftermath of Mass Atrocity*. Cambridge: Cambridge University Press, 49–68.

Donais, T. (2009) "Empowerment or Imposition? Dilemmas of Local Ownership in Post-Conflict Peacebuilding Processes" in *Peace and Change* **34**, no. 1: 3–26.

Dumas H. and R. Korman (2011) "Memorial Spaces for the Tutsi Genocide in Rwanda" in *Afrique contemporaine* **238**, no. 2: 11–27.

Fisher, J. (2015) "Writing about Rwanda since the Genocide: Knowledge, Power and 'Truth'" in *Journal of Intervention and Statebuilding* **9**, no. 1, 134–145.

Gourevitch, P. (1998) *We Wish to Inform You That Tomorrow We Will Be Killed With Our Families: Stories From Rwanda*. New York: Farrar, Straus & Giroux Publishers.

Grünfeld F. and A. Huijboom (2007) *The Failure to Prevent Genocide in Rwanda: The Role of Bystanders*. Leiden: Martinus Nijhoff.

Hellmüller, S. (2012) "The Ambiguities of Local Ownership: Evidence from the Democratic Republic of Congo" in *Africa Security* **5**, no. 3–4: 236–254.

Herbst, J. (2000) *States and Power in Africa: Comparative Lessons in Authority and Control*. Princeton N.J.: Princeton University Press.

Ibreck, R. (2010) "The politics of mourning: Survivor contributions to memorials in post-genocide Rwanda" in *Memory Studies* **3**, no. 4: 330–343.

Ingelaere, B. (2008) "The Gacaca Courts in Rwanda" in L. Huyse and M. Salter (eds.), *Traditional Justice and Reconciliation after Violent Conflict: Learning from African Experiences*. Stockholm: IDEA, 25–59.

—— (2009) "Does the Truth Pass across the Fire without Burning? Locating the Short Circuit in Rwanda's Gacaca Courts" in *Journal of Modern African Studies* **47**, no 4: 507–528.

—— (2010) "Peasants, power and ethnicity: A bottom-up perspective on Rwanda's political transition" in *African Affairs*, 109, no. 435: 273–293.

Ivison, D. (2002) *Postcolonial Liberalism*. Cambridge: Cambridge University Press.

Jackson, P. (2004) "Legacy of Bitterness: Insurgency in North West Rwanda" in *Small Wars & Insurgencies* **15**, no. 1: 19–37.

Jessee, E. (2017a) "The danger of a single story: Iconic stories in the aftermath of the 1994 Rwandan genocide" in *Memory Studies* **10**, no. 2: 144–163.

—— (2017b) *Negotiating Genocide in Rwanda: The Politics of History*. New York N.Y.: Palgrave Macmillan.

Kagame, A. (1954) *Les organisations socio-familiales de l'ancien Rwanda*. Bruxelles: Institut Royal Colonial Belge.

Kumar, K. et al. (1996) *Rebuilding Postwar Rwanda: The Role of the International Community*, USAID Evaluation Special Study No. 76, July 1996. Washington D.C.: USAID.

Lemarchand, R. (1998) "Genocide in the Great Lakes: Which Genocide? Whose Genocide?" in *African Studies Review* **41**, no. 1: 3–16.

—— (2006–2007) "Genocide, Memory and Ethnic Reconciliation in Rwanda" in S. Marysse, F. Reyntjens, and S. Vandeginste (eds.) *L'Afrique des Grands Lacs. Annuaire*. Paris 2007: 21–30.

—— (2009) *The Dynamics of Violence in Central Africa*. Philadelphia P.A.: University of Pennsylvania Press.

Loomba, A. (2005) *Colonialism/Postcolonialism*, 2nd edn. London/New York: Routledge.

Lund, Ch. (2008) *Local Politics and the Dynamics of Property in Africa*. Cambridge: Cambridge University Press.

Mamdani, M. (1996) *Citizen and Subject: Contemporary Africa and the Legacy of Late Colonialism*. Princeton N.J.: Princeton University Press.

—— (2001) *When Victims become Killers: Colonialism, Nativism and Genocide in Rwanda*. Princeton N.J.: Princeton University Press.

Mbembe, A. (2001) *On the Postcolony. Studies on the history of society and culture*. Berkeley: University of California Press.

Melvern, L. (2000) *A People Betrayed. The Role of the West in Rwanda's Genocid*. London: Zed Books.

Melvin, J. (2010) "Reconstructing Rwanda: balancing human rights and the promotion of national reconciliation" in *International Journal of Human Rights* **14**, no. 6: 932–951.

Musahara, H. (2005) "Land reform, land scarcity and post-conflict reconstruction: A case study of Rwanda" in Ch. Huggins and J. Clover (eds), *From the Ground Up. Land*

Rights, Conflict and Peace in Sub-Saharan Africa, Nairobi/Pretoria African Centre for Technology Studies and Institute for Security Studies, 269–346.

Mussia. K. (1983) "Authenticité, un système lexical dans le discours politique au Zaïre" in *Mots* **6**: 31–58.

Mutisi, M. (2012) "Local conflict resolution in Rwanda: The case of abunzi mediators" in Martha Mutisi and Kwesi Sansculotte-Greenidge, *Integrating Traditional and Modern Conflict Resolution: Experiences from selected cases in Eastern and the Horn of Africa* (Africa Dialogue Monograph Series No. 2). Umhlanga Rocks (South Africa): Accord, 41–74.

Muzungu, B. (2011) "A qui profite encore la zizanie entre les rwandais". Kigali: Cahiers Lumière et Société.

National Service of the Gacaca Courts (NSGC), (2012) *Gacaca Courts in Rwanda* (Report June 2012). Kigali.

National Unity and Reconciliation Commission (NURC) / Ezechiel Sentama, (2016) *Unity and Reconciliation Process in Rwanda*, Kigali: NURC.

Ndahinda, F.M. (2011) *Indigenousness in Africa: A Contested Legal Framework for Empowerment of "Marginalized" Communities*. The Hague/Berlin: Asser Press/Springer.

Ndahinda F.M. and Muleefu, A. (2012) "Revisiting the Legal and Socio-Political Foundations and (Western) Criticisms of Gacaca Courts" in T. Bennett, E. Brems, G. Corradi, L. Nijzink, and M. Schotsmans (eds.), *African Perspectives on Tradition and Justice*. Cambridge/Antwerp/Portland: Intersentia, 149–173.

Ndaywel è Nziem, I. (1998) "De l'Authenticité à la Libération: Se prénommer en République Démocratique du Congo" in *Politique Africaine*, no. 72: 98–109.

Newbury, D. (2001) "Precolonial Burundi and Rwanda: Local Loyalties, Regional Royalties" in *International Journal of African Historical Studies* **34**, no. 2: 255–314.

Ntakirutimana, E. (2011) *Le Rwanda et la politique du saumon: Un retour à la source pour un développement durable intégré*. Butare: Editions de l'Universite Nationale du Rwanda.

Pagès, A. (1933) *Au Ruanda sur les bords du lac Kivu, Congo Belge: Un royaume hamite au centre de l'Afrique*. Bruxelles: G van Campenhout.

Paris, R. (2002) "International peacebuilding and the 'mission civilisatrice'" in *Review of International Studies* **28**, no. 4: 627–656.

Péan, P. (2005) *Noires fureurs, blancs menteurs: Rwanda 1990–1994*. Paris: Mille et Une Nuits.

Philpot, R. (2004) *Ça ne s'est pas passé comme ça à Kigali*. Paris: Editions Duboiris.

Prunier, G. (1993) "Eléments pour une Histoire du Front Patriote Rwandais" in *Politique africaine*, no 51: 121–138.

—— (1995) *The Rwanda Crisis: History of a Genocide*. New York: Columbia University Press.

—— (2008) *Africa's World War: Congo, the Rwandan Genocide, and the Making of a Continental Catastrophe*. Oxford: Oxford University Press.

Purdeková, A. (2015) *Making Ubumwe: Power, State and Camps in Rwanda's Unity-Building Project*. Oxford: Berghahn Books.

Ranger, T. (1993) "The Invention of Tradition Revisited: The Case of Colonial Africa" in T. Ranger and O. Vaughan (eds.), *Legitimacy and the State in Twentieth Century Africa*. London: Palgrave Macmillan, 94–101.

RCN Justice & Démocratie (2015) *Proximity Justice in Rwanda – Mediation in Rwanda: Conceptions and Realities of Abunzi Justice* (2011–2014), 3 RCN Report.

Reyntjens, F. (2004) "Rwanda, Ten Years On: From Genocide to Dictatorship" in *African Affairs* **103**, no. 411: 177–210.

—— (2009) *The Great African War. Congo and Regional Geopolitics, 1996–2006*. Cambridge: Cambridge University Press.

—— (2011) "Constructing the truth, dealing with dissent, domesticating the world: Governance in post-genocide Rwanda" in *African Affairs* **110**, no. 438: 1–35.

Rhoads, E.P. (2016) *Taking Sides in Peacekeeping: Impartiality and the Future of the United Nations*. Cambridge: Cambridge University Press.

Riot, T. (2008) "Pratiques du corps, ethnicité et métissages culturels dans le Rwanda colonial (1945–1952)" in *Cahiers d'Études Africaines* **48**, no. 192: 815–833.

RoR (Republic of Rwanda) *Economic Development and Poverty Reduction Strategy 2013–2018: Shaping Our Development*, 13, at: http://www.minecofin.gov.rw/fileadmin/General/EDPRS_2/EDPRS_2_FINAL1.pdf.

—— (1999) *Ubumwe bw'abanyarwanda: Mbere y'abazungu n'igihe cy'ubukoloni, mu gihe cya repubulika ya mbere*. Kigali: Presidency of the Republic.

—— (2011) *National Itorero Commission* (Strategy), November 2011.

—— (2016) *Unity and Reconciliation Process in Rwanda*. Kigali: National Unity and Reconciliation Commission, 38–132.

Rutazibwa, O.U. (2014) "Studying Agaciro: Moving beyond Wilsonian Interventionist Knowledge Production on Rwanda" in *Journal of Intervention and Statebuilding* **8**, no. 4: 291–301.

Rwanda Governance Board (RGB) (2014) "The Assessment of the Impact of Home Grown Initiatives" in IV *Rwanda Governance Review*.

Sarkin, J. (1999) "The Necessity and Challenges of Establishing a Truth and Reconciliation Commission in Rwanda" in *Human Rights Quarterly* **21**, no. 3: 767–823.

Schabas, W.A. (2005) "Genocide Trials and Gacaca Courts" *Journal of International Criminal Justice* **3**, no 4: 879–895.

—— (1996) "Justice, Democracy, and Impunity in Post-Genocide Rwanda: Searching for Solutions to Impossible Problems" in *Criminal Law Forum* 7, no. 3: 523–560.

Straus S. and Waldorf, L. (eds.), (2011) *Remaking Rwanda: State Building and Human Rights after Mass Violence*. Madison, University of Wisconsin Press.

Straus, S. (2006) *The Order of Genocide: Race, Power, and War in Rwanda*. Ithaca N.Y.: Cornell University Press.

Stys, P. (2012) "Revisiting Rwanda", *Journal of Modern African Studies* **50**, no. 4: 707–720.

Vandeginste, S. (2014) "Governing ethnicity after genocide: ethnic amnesia in Rwanda versus ethnic power-sharing in Burundi" in *Journal of Eastern African Studies* **8**, no. 2: 263–277.

Vansina, J. (2004) *Antecedents to modern Rwanda: The Nyiginya Kingdom*. Madison.W.I.: University of Wisconsin Press.

Vinck P. and Pham, Ph. (2008) "Ownership and Participation in Transitional Justice Mechanisms: A Sustainable Human Development Perspective from Eastern DRC" in *International Journal of Transitional Justice* **2**, no. 3, 398–411.

Watson, C. (1991) *Exile from Rwanda: background to an invasion*. Washington D.C.: US Committee for Refugees.

Willame, J.-C. (1995) *Aux Sources de L'Hécatombe Rwandaise*. Paris: L'Harmattan.

Young, R.J.C. (2001) *Postcolonialism: An Historical Introduction*, Oxford/Malden: Blackwell Press.

Yusin, J. (2016) "The Itinerary of Commemoration in the Kigali Memorial Centre: On Trauma, Time and Difference" in *Culture, Theory and Critique* 57 no. 3: 338–356.

CHAPTER 13

UNCONVENTIONAL RESTORATIVE JUSTICE AND THE DIPLOMACY OF CLOSURE

The Israeli Policy on the Armenian Genocide and the Geopolitics of Memory

Eldad BEN AHARON*

* An earlier version of this chapter was originally published as E. BEN AHARON, "Between Ankara and Jerusalem: the Armenian Genocide as a Zero-Sum Game in Israel's Foreign Policy (1980's–2010's)" in *Journal of Balkan and Near Eastern Studies*, **20**, no. 5, 2018: 459–476.

1. INTRODUCTION

This chapter examines the degree to which the absence of "restorative justice" between Armenians and Turks has become a factor in international relations, especially since the late 1970s and early 1980s. It is argued that for more than three decades (1980s–2010s) Israel has chosen to reinforce the Turkish account of the events of 1915 for its own diplomatic ends. After a long period of silence, during the late 1970s the differing Armenian and Turkish interpretations of the 1915 genocide became increasingly, and somewhat violently, entrenched. This chapter explores the particular role that Israel played with respect to the "diplomacy of closure" between Armenians and Turks, and argues that for more than three decades (1980s–2010s) Israel consciously has chosen to reinforce the Turkish narrative for its own selfish diplomatic and political ends. The Israeli parliament's failure to recognise the Armenian genocide has made it easier for successive Israeli governments to reinforce the Turkish account of the events of the 1915 genocide, making Israel's economic, military and arms deals with Turkey and, in recent years, with Azerbaijan, much smoother. In these respects, the chapter explores the paradox of Israel, a country born in large part out of a post-World War II sense of restorative justice for the Holocaust and the commemoration of its own genocide as "unique" colluding in the denial of recognition of the Armenian genocide. As this chapter will show – especially during the 1980s but also throughout the 1990s and 2000s – Israel took advantage of the consequences of a lack of conventional restorative justice for the Armenian genocide, such as Armenian terrorism and pressure on Turkey in international forums, as diplomatic leverage to restore Israeli–Turkish relations.

2. CONCEPTUAL FRAMEWORK AND METHODOLOGY

The Nuremberg trials of prominent Nazis after the end of World War II and the growing awareness of international human rights have boosted the emergence of what we now identify as the field of Transitional Justice (TJ),[1] an umbrella term covering measures undertaken by societies that seek to transition to the

[1] For an excellent analysis of the Nuremberg trails see among many others: Marrus (1998), 5–41; and Bloxham (2001).

rule of law after episodes of mass violence.[2] This chapter examines the question of those TJ mechanisms that have been labelled as "restorative justice" in the context of Israeli–Turkish and Israeli–Azerbaijani relations. The chapter aims to question how the absence of conventional restorative justice mechanisms between perpetrators and victims' groups regarding the 1915 Armenian genocide has generated contested memories and how these memories have influenced Israeli–Turkish relations.

To demonstrate the argument that Israel has reinforced the Turkish account of events for its own ends, the chapter proposes that the Israeli policy on the 1915 genocide has been mainly dependent on a low degree of domestic pressure on successive Israeli governments to recognise the genocide of 1915, namely in the form of a lack of substantial parliamentary pressure by opposition parties. The chapter seeks to offer a systematic analysis of the symbiotic relationship between Israel's foreign policy and its domestic political and cultural arenas by characterising it as a zero-sum game.

A short methodological note is needed about the approach undertaken in this chapter. Due to meticulous censorship regulations governing the Israeli State Archive (ISA), many of the archival documents regarding Israel's policy on the Armenian genocide (specifically, from late 1989 onwards) are inaccessible to historians, since such archival records remain classified for a minimum of 25 years.[3] To circumvent this lack of data, the author, especially in the second and third parts of this chapter, makes use of oral historical accounts from former Israeli diplomats and Parliament Members (PMs), specifically diplomats and politicians, in order to provide first-hand insights into Israel's policy with respect to the Armenian genocide.[4] Furthermore, the chapter applies Robert Putnam's momentous (1988) work *Diplomacy and Domestic Politics: The Logic of Two-Level Games* as a theoretical framework to understand the relationship between domestic political pressure and foreign policy.[5] Putnam theorises "the paradoxical fact that institutional arrangements which strengthen decision-makers at home may weaken their international bargaining position and vice versa."[6] According to Putnam's model, an essential factor in the two-level game is the existence of *pressure* from domestic interest groups such

---

2 Among the extensive literature that this field has to offer, and among many other recent works, see a good global overview of TJ: Teitel (2014).

3 These shadows are deepened by rigorous Israeli state censorship regulations governing the Mossad (national intelligence agency) archives, as well as those of other state security institutions that prevent scholars from engaging with records like these. See [in Hebrew] the law in full and its history: www.main.knesset.gov.il/activity/aegislation/laws/pages/2000178.

4 For more on the author's elite oral history project see: E. Ben Aharon (2020a), and Ben Aharon (2020b).

5 See Putnam (1988), 427–460.

6 Ibid., 460.

as social activists and political parties on the Israeli government eager to secure their support. Putnam's hypothesis offers a compelling model with which to analyse Israel's policy on the Armenian genocide as a two-level game.[7]

The main argument is developed across three main sections: the first part outlines the late Cold War period (1982–1988). During this period, Israel's Ministry of Foreign Affairs (MFA) had to engage for the first time with the contested memories of the Armenian genocide, as they were sporadically mentioned in Israel's domestic political arena. This period is characterised by the relatively very low pressure exerted in Israel's domestic political arena to recognise the Armenian genocide. The second part focuses on the early post-Cold War period (1989–2000), what is here called the interim period, and considers the growth in domestic pressure for recognition, demonstrated by resolutions proposed in the Knesset to commemorate the 1915 Armenian genocide on 24 April of each calendar year, although to date these have never been passed. The interim period ends with the significant speech by Yossi Sarid, the (then) Minister of Education, who, on his own personal initiative, recognised the 1915 genocide and was determined to include it in Israeli history textbooks and curricula. These events unfolded into the third period (2001–2016) examined in this chapter, when more significant domestic political pressure for recognition emerged, culminating in resolutions made by the Education Committee in 2011 and 2016.

3. THE DIPLOMACY OF CLOSURE

3.1. THE HOLOCAUST, ISRAEL AND WEST GERMANY

With respect to restorative justice in the context of the Holocaust, the key event in the immediate post-war period for both Germanies was the "1952 Luxembourg Reparations Agreement", which committed West Germany to compensating individual Jews for loss of property during the war as well as Israel for resettling Jews from Europe. A second key event was Israel's development of a Holocaust memory culture from the early 1960s onward. This has been based upon an understanding that the Holocaust was a "unique" event in human history, an approach initially developed by Holocaust survivor/scholars such as Meir (Mark) Dworzeck, Israel Gutman, Shalom Cholawsky and Aharon Weiss, who together shaped the Israeli realm of memory and set the initial research priorities for and the establishment of Yad Vashem.[8] A third key event was the

---

7 For a successful application of Putnam's model on other case studies, see for example, among others: Mo (1994); Milne (2011).

8 The World Holocaust Remembrance Centre (Yad Vashem).Yosef Michman (director of Yad Vashem, 1957 to 1960), Israel Gutman, Dov Kulka, Shalom Cholawsky and Zvi Bachrach,

Eichmann trial in 1961 that re-triggered Israeli awareness of the suffering of the European Jews and catapulted the suffering of its victims into mainstream cultural and political arenas. Fourthly, and even more importantly, was the 1967 Six-Day War. As noted in the works of Yehuda Bauer, David Engel, Peter Novick, Tom Segev, Idith Zertal and others, the war was perceived as a triumph that prevented "another Holocaust" and provided a sense of legitimacy for Israeli territorial expansion and the occupation of the Palestinian territories. The notion of Israel being a "country under blockade" explains why and how the concept of the "uniqueness of the Holocaust" was leveraged to support Israeli territorial expansion and for its associated political, cultural, military and diplomatic ends.[9] In this context, even though Yad Vashem aims to act as a centre for the global memory of the Holocaust in the twenty-first century, the museum still functions as the dominant agent in Israel that shapes the memory, culture and politics of the country, all of which regard the Holocaust as being a "unique" event. As Amos Goldberg noted, Yad Vashem encourages visitors to identify with Jewish victims and blocks any other more complex understanding of the events.[10] In a restorative context, if the Holocaust can be considered to be a global symbol of dehumanisation and abuse of human rights, then it also had to be realised in an international arena that included states like Turkey and Azerbaijan, which also repudiate the Armenian genocide.[11]

This chapter, therefore, offers a systematic cross-cutting account of Israel's policy with respect to the Armenian genocide in the context of the Israeli-Turkish and Israeli–Azerbaijani relations. As already noted, even though Israel has applied restorative justice mechanisms, such as the "1952 Luxembourg Reparations Agreement", or the Eichmann trial of 1963, its course of action with respect to the Armenians possibly led to the denial of their opportunity for restorative justice. As the chapter will demonstrate, Israel's narrow strategic interests are shown to have overridden what might have been considered its natural affinity with the Armenian desire for recognition and restorative justice for the genocide of 1915.

With respect to restorative justice, the Armenian genocide of 1915 is still a highly politicised and disputed historical event. Although in recent years there has been a shift in academic discussions, with a series of conferences launched by leading Armenian, American, Turkish and Kurdish scholars,[12] this has not

---

among others, established Holocaust research in Israel. For the survivor scholars' literature see, for example, Cohen (2015); Cholawsky (1973); Gutman (1976), 90.

9 See Bauer (2001); Novick (1999); Zartel (2005); Rothberg (2009); Engel (2010), to mention a few.

10 For an excellent analysis on this, see Goldberg (2012).

11 For a short discussion on this, see Ben Aharon (2019d).

12 The WATS workshop (Workshop on Armenian/Turkish Scholarship) was first launched in 2000 to bring together Armenian, Kurdish and Turkish scholars in a number of workshops

led to any mutually agreed factual baseline for how the Republic of Armenia and the Republic of Turkey should remember or commemorate it. In fact, far from attempts to attain closure with respect to the 1915 genocide – which would have provided a basis from which to develop a restorative justice programme for the Armenians – there has been a significant deterioration since the 1970s in victim–perpetrator relations. This deterioration has had consequences in the international arena and has led to a parallel victim/perpetrator campaign that has, at times, included further rounds of violence. Between the years of 1973–1985, militant Armenian terrorism emerged in the Middle East, ultimately taking the lives of about 50 Turkish diplomats and their family members around the world, mainly in an attempt to force the Turkish Republic to acknowledge the genocide of 1915.[13]

3.2. THE 1915 GENOCIDE: ARMENIAN SILENCE AND TURKISH DENIAL (1965–1982)

To understand the early years of the international campaign to acknowledge the 1915 genocide, we need to go back to the mid-1960s at the height of the Cold War. The polarisation of the Cold War greatly contributed to silence on the topic. During the first years following the 1915 genocide, the Armenian survivors and their offspring spread around the globe. These Armenian communities settled and put down new roots in the interwar years, but in the period after the Second World War they faced a new reality that shaped their priorities differently in terms of how the 1915 genocide should be commemorated. Specifically, during the Cold War the Armenians lived under many different regimes that had different interpretations of what the role of law, human rights and freedom of speech should be. These interpretations greatly affected the Armenian diaspora's ability to create a substantial dialogue and to construct a coherent and shared position with respect to claims for restorative justice from Turkey.[14]

During the Cold War, the Communist Bloc, but especially the Soviet Union, ignored the Armenian genocide, mainly because the Kremlin delegitimised human rights protection as part of Communist ideology. Even though Armenia was an integrated part of the Soviet Union, the Armenian genocide was by and large not recognised by the Kremlin at all. Nonetheless, on 24 April 1965, on the fiftieth anniversary of the 1915 genocide, the Armenian communities in the

---

in Chicago and Michigan to study the faith of the Ottoman Empire and the role of ethnic minorities in the declining Empire and the Republic of Turkey. See for example Suny, et al. (2011).

13 See for example among many others: Bloxham (2005), 219 and Gocek (2015).

14 See Sanjian (2018).

Communist Bloc were granted a low-profile commemoration rally in Yerevan, in what in Armenian historiography has been recalled as the "turning point". As noted in the work of Razmik Panossian:

> An official but relatively low-profile event was organised in the Opera building, attended only by the political leadership and prominent intellectuals. However, this one event was the catalyst that set loose the forces of nationalism in Soviet Armenia. While the official ceremony was taking place, 100,000 to 200,000 people spontaneously gathered outside, chanting "Our Lands! Our Lands!" (i.e. western Armenia) and "Justice! Justice!" (i.e. Genocide recognition).[15]

Turkey, meanwhile, was busy developing a different narrative that denied the Armenian genocide at home. Inherent to the legacy of Atatürk was a policy to assimilate all ethnic minorities under the Turkish culture and language ("Turkification"). A substantial part of this Turkification process and its consequent efforts at social engineering during the interwar period entailed the silencing of the social memory of the Armenian genocide. Although many direct eyewitnesses to the genocide were still alive, and the traumatic memories of it were an important component of Turkified Armenians' identity and collective memory, the official, sanitised, state narrative was continually reinforced as part of the national narrative via history textbooks and school curricula, but also by the systematic destruction and removal of physical traces of Armenian culture in Turkey, such as Armenian architecture. Moreover, a state law was promulgated that stipulated that labelling the "Armenian question" as a genocide constituted an insult to the Turkish Republic, the country's institutions and to Turkish-ness.[16]

3.3. UNCONVENTIONAL RESTORATIVE JUSTICE: ARMENIAN TERRORISM

This Turkish campaign, however, was undertaken with almost no direct engagement with Israel. This was because from 1948, the year of Israel's establishment, until the 1967 Six-Day War the Israeli government did not have to address the claims of the Armenians of the Old City of Jerusalem to recognise their genocide, since East Jerusalem only came under the full control of the Israeli authorities after the June 1967 Six-Day War.[17] In contrast to

15 Among others, see Panossian (2006), 320; Dadrian (1977).

16 For example, see UNGOR (2014); UNGOR (2013); Ekmekcioglu (2016). Article 159 of the former Turkish Penal Code of 1926 was transformed into Article 301 of the Turkish Republic Criminal Code in 2004 as a necessary revision to Turkey's renewed application to the EU for membership.

17 For more on this see Azarya (1984).

the Armenians in the Eastern Bloc, the Armenian diaspora communities in Western Europe, North America and the Middle East largely kept silent and suppressed memories of the 1915 genocide, and did not launch any local campaigns in their host countries.[18]

The absence of restorative justice measures between a perpetrator and victims' groups, supplemented by the fact that the Armenians were polarised under the Iron Curtain during the Cold War further impeded the emergence of a common Armenian commemorative strategy.[19] From 1973 to 1985, therefore, the international campaign for recognition took a violent turn, and split into two discrete campaigns. One involved Middle Eastern Armenian terrorists based out of Beirut who were affiliated with the Soviets and Eastern Bloc, while the other was a subnational diplomatic campaign led by the Armenian diaspora in Western Europe and North America.[20] Although Armenian terrorism would warrant a focused and separate study of its own, some of the main features of this violence should be noted briefly here in order to understand how the absence of a shared narrative, and thus any possibility of restorative justice, has affected the relationship between victims and perpetrator.[21] The Marxist-Leninist (and pro-Soviet) Armenian Secret Army for Liberation of Armenia (ASALA) and, by contrast, the national-socialist (and anti-Soviet), Justice Commandos Against Armenian genocide (JCAG), affiliated with the Dashnak party, later known as the Armenian Revolutionary Federation (ARF),[22] both carried out a series of assassinations of Turkish diplomats in Western Europe, North America and Australia in an effort to provoke a global discussion of the Armenian genocide in international forums and to force the Republic of Turkey to recognise the genocide perpetrated against their forebears.[23] Even though the terrorist attacks utterly failed to create any sympathy in Western countries, both discrete campaigns did succeed in bringing the events of 1915 onto the agenda of both the US Congress and the European Parliament in the form of resolutions describing the Armenian catastrophe as genocide.[24]

---

18 Walker (1980), 380–381.

19 For an excellent short discussion on this see: Bloxham (2005); Walker (1980).

20 For further discussion and study regarding the subnational commemorative campaign led by the Armenian diaspora in Western Europe and North America see for example: Ben Aharon (2019c).

21 For more on this perspective, specifically regarding how the Armenian terror was leveraged by Israeli diplomats in the context of the First Lebanon War, and vis-à-vis Palestinian terror, and for reconciliation means in the Israeli-Turkish relations crisis (1980–1985), see Ben Aharon (2019b).

22 See for example Wilkinson (1983); Hyland (1991); Hoffman (2006), 72.

23 For a detailed account on this, see Totolyan (1992); Kurz and Merari (1985).

24 For an excellent survey of the American Armenians bringing the 1915 genocide into the US public arena, see for example Zarifian (2014).

The terrorist attacks had an opposite effect, however, on Turkish attitudes towards the events of 1915, instead provoking a "narrative boom" of Turkish historiography and public and international advocacy on those events.[25] The Turks were very much aware that the events of 1915 had become a focus of the world's attention because of the Armenian terrorist campaign. In response, they developed a counter-narrative,[26] written by veteran Turkish diplomats,[27] that was accompanied by vigorous public and international advocacy that strongly indicated that any discussion of those events in terms of a genocide among Turkey's Western allies, especially other NATO members, would be offensive to the Turks and liable to provoke diplomatic repercussions, even a Cold War crisis.[28] At the same time, Turkey's Western allies, such as Israel, France, West Germany, and the United States, were subjected to severe pressure to not allow the topic to arise for debate in their political and cultural arenas.

4. EARLY YEARS OF ISRAEL'S ARMENIAN GENOCIDE POLICY (1983–1988)

4.1. THE 1915 GENOCIDE REMEMBRANCE DAY, 24 APRIL 1983

It should be stressed that during this period, Israeli–Turkish relations were particularly tense, with a perceived looming danger of a complete severing of relations, something that has been explored in detail by other scholars.[29] A document dated 11 April 1983 that was sent from the Turkish embassy in Tel-Aviv to the Israeli MFA in Jerusalem reveals the degree to which Turkey was concerned about Armenian demonstrations and terror threats:

> the [Turkish] MFA wishes to draw the kind attention of the Israeli authorities, especially during the month of April, that the Armenian communities in Jerusalem and Haifa had organised demonstrations as part of Armenian propaganda that is an

[25] See Gocek (2011), 49; Dixon (2010); Gurpina (2016).

[26] For further reading on this issue, see Bloxham and Gocek (2008), 344; Also, more recently, Gurpinar (2016).

[27] Among them, see for instance: Gurun (1985); URAS (1988).

[28] Ben Aharon (2019c).

[29] Among the approaches dealing with Turkey's decision to downgrade relations with Israel to a Second Secretary, the dominant view is that it was part of the Islamist trend to integrate Turkey into the Palestinian and the Arab world. Another important factor was the energy crisis of 1978–79 that impinged upon Turkey and compelled it to develop a pro-Arab foreign policy in order to obtain greater access to oil, and consequently to downgrade its relations with Israel. Another factor was the reaction to the 1980 Jerusalem Law that united Jewish West Jerusalem with that part of Jordanian East Jerusalem that was captured during the Six-Day War of 1967. See, for example, just mention a few: Liel (2001); Aykan (1993).

intensive defamation campaign against Turkey and intersected with the Armenian terrorist movements against Turkey.[30]

The Turkish MFA, thus, argued that pro-Armenian advocacy within the Israeli community in recent years could have been motivated by the Armenian terrorists' campaign against Turkish diplomats. This paragraph of the document reveals that the Turks viewed the Armenian diaspora as a unified and focused community with a single mind striving to gain recognition of the 1915 genocide. Moreover, the Turks were speculating about the Armenian diaspora and possible ties between the communities in Israel and Lebanon, of which the latter was harbouring both ASALA and JCAG terrorists. As appears from the document, the Turks turned their attention to Israel's responsibility with respect to the actions of Israeli Armenians: "Unfortunately enough, these demonstrations, which encourage Armenian terrorism, were also covered by the Israeli radio and television".[31] Such statements demonstrate how Turkey's MFA sought to pressure Israel to take a clear stance regarding the disputed past in the contest of Turkish and Armenian memories about the 1915 genocide.

4.2. ISRAELI DEFENSE FORCE RADIO BROADCAST, MAY 1983

In late April 1983, Ankara again voiced alarm over commemorative activities to mark the 1915 genocide. Furthermore, Ankara expressed its outrage to Jerusalem concerning the incompetence of Israeli executive forces for failing to halt a radio broadcast on the "alleged genocide" aired over the Israeli Defense Force (IDF) radio channel. In what follows, one can observe the dilemma facing Israel's executive forces in confronting the Armenian genocide commemoration campaign. Alon Liel, the *chargé d'affaires* of the Israeli embassy in Ankara between 1981 and 1983, recounted in an oral interview:

> In a meeting held with Erdam Erner, Turkey's MFA executive, he expressed his grave concern regarding a looming problem for Turkey's MFA. I instantly telephoned Ron Ben-Yishai, chief commander of IDF radio and told him, "Ron, Israel will be in deep trouble about that broadcast; please remove it from the broadcast agenda." Ron replied that the broadcast was already scheduled and we could not remove it from the agenda. I told Ron that Ankara will be deeply outraged by this. Erner told me,

30 The Turkish embassy in Tel Aviv to Israel's MFA in Jerusalem: "confidential", 11 April 1983, 969/17–83, ISA/MFA/0003679.

31 Ibid.

> "Do not give [me] such an answer"; this is the IDF radio station. We tried to prevent the broadcast, however, in a restrained way. All in all, Israel is a democracy.[32]

Following that meeting, Liel telegrammed Israel's MFA saying that Erner was angered by the IDF broadcast and that they did not prevent the discussion about the "alleged genocide" despite it being a station supervised by the Israeli authorities. Liel replied to Erner's complaint and wrote to Jerusalem that "Israel made our best efforts to prevent the discussion; however, we flunked this mission."[33] In the telegram, Liel reported telling Erner that Israel acknowledged "that the [radio] discussion about this topic was unnecessary and highlighted to Erner that the broadcast did not represent Israel's official stance on the matter".[34] Thereafter, Liel attempted to demonstrate to Erner that the Israeli executive did not control the Israeli media, noting that,

> occasionally Israel's MFA read anti-Israeli propaganda and incitement in the Turkish newspapers and television broadcasts but Israel's MFA do not find it requires filing a formal complaint because we acknowledge that [the Turkish executive] are not able to fully monitor the Turkish media.[35]

Despite Liel's explanations, Erner was not pleased, expressing further outrage at Israeli historian Yehuda Bauer, who had discussed the similarity between the killing methods used by the Nazis and the Ottomans. Liel further informed Jerusalem in the telegram of how he had reminded Erner of extensive pressure by Israel's MFA to block the Armenian scholars from presenting the Armenian narrative at a 1982 workshop on Holocaust and Genocide Studies in Israel.[36] Liel had asked Erner to accept this as valid proof of Israel's official stance on the issue.

4.3. 1915 GENOCIDE RESOLUTION IN THE EUROPEAN PARLIAMENT 1987

Four years later, following a decline in Armenian terrorist attacks after 1985, Armenian diaspora communities focused more on political and commemorative activities, particularly pursuing efforts to enact resolutions in the American

32 Oral interview with A. Liel, 3 September 2015, Jerusalem, Israel.
33 *Chargé d'affaires* in Ankara to Jerusalem, Re: "Alon Liel's Conversation with Erdam Erner", secret incoming telegram, 28 April 1983, ISA/MFA/0003679, 1.
34 Ibid.
35 *Chargé d'affaires* in Ankara to Jerusalem, ISA/MFA/0003679, 1.
36 Ibid., 2.

Congress and the European Parliament to formally label the 1915 events as a genocide. Focusing on the European Parliament resolution, on 20 February 1987, the Israeli *chargé d'affaires* in Ankara, Yehuda Milo, wrote to the MFA in Jerusalem. In this previously secret, but now declassified, ISA document, Milo transmitted the following message to Jerusalem:

> The Turks are conducting a losing battle against the decision to hold the Turks responsible as perpetrators of genocide. The Chairperson of the Turkish Homeland Party is conducting a battle with the European Parliament members regarding the upcoming vote on February 24th.[37]

After this very brief introduction, Milo further notes that

> although we [Israelis] were not approached [by the Turks], can we help them somehow? In the Turkish advocacy materials provided to members of the Parliament, the Turks emphasised their tolerant and sympathetic attitude to the Jews in Turkey, and prior to that, their role in opening the borders of the Ottoman Empire and later the Turkish Republic to Jewish refugees (i.e. during the Spanish inquisition (1492) and subsequently from Middle Eastern countries).[38]

In the final paragraph, Milo enquires about possible practical help from Israeli PMs: "can we [Israel] use the services of Shevah Weiss, Sarah Doron and others?[39] Please follow through and make sure that the Turkish representatives in Paris will be notified of these efforts."[40] Further, in an oral interview, the general director of the Middle East Department at the time, Yitzhak Lior (1983–1987) recalls the characteristics of this period:

> [O]ur priority with the Turks was helping them with European Parliament and American Congress members. If one of these American or European members were asking us what is currently going on in the Middle East, we needed to underline that Turkey contributed as a mediator to the Middle East peace process, and thereby helping to improve Turkey's reputation. We did that with a complete lack of conscience to the miserable Armenians. It was done as a result of constraints. Specifically, I remember the controversy with the Israeli academics, who we admired a great deal and appreciated their opinion.[41]

---

37 Ankara to Jerusalem: "The Armenian Decision in the European Parliament", 27 February 1987, ISA/MFA/000A4GN, 1.

38 Ibid. For in-depth assessment on this topic, see Bali (2012).

39 Shevah Weiss was a Knesset member from Israeli Labour party (1981–1999) and later was appointed to be the Knesset Chairman. Sarah Doron was a Knesset member from the Likud (1977–1992).

40 Ankara to Jerusalem, ISA/MFA/000A4GN.

41 Oral Interview with Y. Lior, 26 June 2016, Ramat Gan, Israel.

Summing up the first period and contextualising it into Putnam's two-level game, such documents demonstrate that concerted efforts were made with respect to reinforcing Turkey's denial narrative, mainly, but not exclusively, by the Israeli MFA. This was mainly due to a lack of any countervailing pressure from within Israel's domestic arena, other than the radio broadcast and the Armenian demonstration on 24 April 1983. An early pattern emerges, therefore, in which it appears that diverse diplomatic tools of the Israeli MFA were used to support Turkey's narrative. Specifically, Israel employed its PMs and diplomats to support the Turkish position in the European Parliament and the US Congress. The absence of restorative justice mechanisms between Armenians and Turks, supplemented by the relative lack of pressure to recognise the 1915 genocide domestically, gave Israel more diplomatic negotiating room, and thus improved the chances of restoring relations with Ankara during the 1980s.

5. POST-COLD WAR: INTERIM PERIOD (1989–2000)

5.1. BACKGROUND TO THE KNESSET'S 1915 GENOCIDE RESOLUTIONS

An examination of Knesset resolutions concerning the 1915 genocide reveals a sustained period of increasing yet fragmented pressure building to recognise it. One can identify a sporadic movement towards an Armenian genocide resolution that from time to time surfaces at certain periods. Thus, a brief historical survey of the period is needed. The first unsuccessful endeavour to pass an Armenian genocide resolution in the Israeli Parliament occurred in 1989, almost seven years after the 1982 Holocaust and Genocide conference in Tel Aviv at which the Armenian genocide issue was first raised.[42] This first Knesset resolution was initiated by Yair Tzaban, a *Mapam* party member.[43] In his first-hand account, Alon Liel observes that

> the Armenian-Israeli community is relatively small in numbers with a weak lobby. Furthermore, the Armenian community never had an Israeli parliament member of Armenian origin who was able to put forth a significant [parliamentary] campaign for acknowledging of the 1915 genocide.[44]

Liel's observation casts light on the relative weakness of the Armenian lobby, specifically in terms of its (in)competence in building political pressure to recognise the Armenian genocide. In the Knesset's early discussions regarding

42 See Ben Aharon (2015).

43 Mapam was the United Israeli Workers Party which promoted a left-wing socialist ideology.

44 Interview with Liel, 3 September 2015.

1915 genocide resolutions, another party was supportive of the Armenian cause. *Meretz*, driven by left-wing socialist ideology and since its establishment in 1992 for the most part an opposition party, became a great supporter of Armenian resolutions in the Knesset. The Chairperson of *Meretz*, PM Zehava Galon (2012–2017), proposed in an oral interview that

> The elite of the Armenian-Israeli community, which play a significant part in this campaign, live in the Armenian quarter of East Jerusalem. Clearly, from the Israeli government's perspective, the Armenians of East Jerusalem are Palestinian-Israelis and the current Israeli government dislikes Palestinians – an understatement.[45]

It should be noted that Galon's account represents the far-left of the Israeli political landscape, and that her perspective was in line with *Meretz*'s doctrine of equality for non-Jewish ethnic-minorities, such as Palestinian Israelis, among whom Galon includes the Armenians of East Jerusalem. Each of Galon's and Liel's oral histories sheds light on how the local Armenian community conducted its 1915 genocide commemoration campaign and how difficult it was to apply pressure on the Knesset to acknowledge it from such a relatively low position in the Israeli political arena.

Moreover, in a first-hand account, a former elite member of the Israeli MFA, speaking anonymously, has uncovered the process of removing the 1915 genocide issue from the Knesset agenda altogether during the 1990s in order to allow the Israeli executive to leverage it in their diplomatic negotiations with Ankara. The anonymous official reports that the MFA's efforts to remove the Armenian issue from the Knesset discussions were extensive, arguing that

> MFA always had the right people on their side: Chairmen of the Foreign Affairs and Defence Committees such as Dan Meridor, Yitzhak Mordechai, Tzachi Hanegbi, and Shaul Mofaz. They would let the discussion go on for a while but then they would smoothly proceed to the next issue and remove it from that meeting's agenda.[46]

In another first-hand account, Dan Meridor, who acted as a Chairman of the committee (1999–2001) recounts the path that the discussions on the Armenian genocide took:

> As chairman of the committee I used to meticulously follow the government guidelines; i.e., I acknowledged that we could not discuss the topic very openly; however, I demonstrated a great deal of sensitivity. However, putting forward a distinctive, moral pro-Armenian announcement was something that would really get

---

45 Oral Interview with Z. Galon, 1 February 2016, Jerusalem, Israel.

46 Oral Interview with a former Israeli MFA high-ranking official who agreed to speak anonymously.

> the whole world standing on its feet and could have harmed Israel's interests. I had to be extremely careful.[47]

Such oral accounts throw new light upon the reasons behind the absence of any solid political pressure from the Knesset on the Armenian resolution. Despite the Armenian genocide being brought up for discussion in the Knesset for the first time in 1989 and arguably there being some possible chance to achieve an Armenian genocide resolution, the Israeli executive closely monitored and suppressed communication about the resolution in the Knesset in order to leverage it for smooth diplomatic consensus with Ankara, thereby lending support to Turkey's denial narrative.

5.2. BREAKING RANKS: YOSSI SARID'S SPEECH, 24 APRIL 2000

This segment examines the first subnational occurrence of domestic pressure and how immediately it affected the diplomatic arena. As demonstrated above, during the 1990s resolutions in the Knesset were monitored and suppressed by successive Israeli governments acting to maintain their diplomatic strategies. It is quite surprising, however, that the then Minister of Education, Yossi Sarid, Chairperson of *Meretz* (1996–2003), was nevertheless adamant that the 1915 genocide be included in Israeli history textbooks and curricula. During the 1980s and 1990s Sarid had been an active supporter of the Armenian community's campaign for acknowledgment of the 1915 genocide. During a 1989 meeting of the Foreign Affairs and Defence Committee, for instance, Sarid spoke out against the Israeli MFA's stance on the 1915 Armenian genocide resolution in the US Congress. Subsequently, on 24 April 2000, as a minister in the Israeli government, Sarid caused a diplomatic embarrassment when he delivered a speech at the eighty-fifth 1915 genocide Remembrance Day at the Armenian quarter in Eastern Jerusalem. Sarid undoubtedly broke ranks with the government's guidelines in his speech when he declared:

> I join you, members of the Armenian community on your Memorial Day as you mark the eighty-fifth anniversary of your genocide. I am here with you as a human being, as a Jew, as an Israeli, and as Minister of Education of the State of Israel.[48]

Three days later, Ankara demanded that Jerusalem clarify its official stance on the Armenian issue. Uri Bar-Ner, the Israeli ambassador to Turkey, drafted an

---

47 Oral Interview with D. Meridor, 2 September 2015, Jerusalem, Israel.

48 The speech made by the Israeli Minister of Education, Yossi Sarid, 24 April 2000; see: www.armeniangenocide.org/current_category.172/. For a full detailed account of this scandal, see Auron (2003).

official statement clarifying that Sarid's speech was an example of Israeli freedom of expression that did not reflect in any way Israel's policy on the Armenian issue. Alon Liel, Director General of Israel's MFA (2000–2001), recalls: "Sarid's words were very harmful to our relations with Ankara. The Turks considered themselves 'stabbed in the back' … even Turkey's senior army generals who were very supportive of Israel, were disappointed by Sarid's speech."[49] After this embarrassment, Ankara–Jerusalem relations deteriorated dramatically, undermining what was considered at that time to be the Israeli MFA's most substantial achievement in the region. Liel proceeds with his first-hand account:

> Ankara understand that they granted us something that was super important to Israel's position in the region. That said, when the Education Minister announces, "I will teach Franz Werfel in Israeli high schools"[50] … it was a shock to Ankara. We immediately denied that this is Israel's official stance on the issue.[51]

In a later oral interview, Yossi Sarid elaborated on his political agenda behind this notable speech:

> [F]requently, when Israel has been following a pragmatic realpolitik agenda, as with Turkey, people wish to frame me as a naive and righteous individual; however, I have come to the general conclusion that a moral foreign policy defines human beings as human beings and thus it is the better foreign policy in the mid and long run.[52]

From the government's perspective, however, as Liel notes in his first-hand account, "when Sarid was asked by Prime Minister Ehud Barak (1999–2001) for an explanation, Sarid replied: 'What do you want from me? I am not the foreign minister. My mission is to educate the children of Israel.'"[53] As Liel recalls, the Prime Minister did not accept Sarid's explanation and chastised him: "a minister is a minister":[54] In other words, in Barak's eyes, each minister, even if not a member of Barak's party, had pledged him or herself to stand behind each government policy without exception. Nevertheless, one should highlight that despite Sarid's speech provoking a major diplomatic embarrassment for Israel's government, the fact that Sarid was not fired immediately after

49 Oral Interview with A. Liel, 12 July 2013, Mevasseret Zion, Israel.
50 Ibid. Franz Werfel, an Austrian Jewish author wrote the novel *Die Vierzig Tage des Musa Dagh* (*The Forty Days of Musa Dagh*), published in 1933, detailing the massacre, mass murder and expulsion of Armenians from eastern Anatolia in 1915.
51 Ibid.
52 Oral interview with Y. Sarid, 24 July 2013, Tel Aviv, Israel.
53 Liel, 12 July 2013.
54 Ibid.

the speech illustrates to some degree that there were limits to how far Israeli authorities were willing to go to appease Ankara's denial narrative. Liel concludes,

> Ehud Barak's government worked very hard for a few months to mellow the impact of Sarid's speech. However, to repair the overall damage took years after that, specifically with Turkey's army leadership who had persuaded the Turkish government to accept the alliance with Israel as strategically important for Turkey in the Middle East.[55]

Sarid's speech should be seen as the first serious kind of pressure exerted in order to decrease the government's diplomatic negotiating room with Turkey and limited the opportunity to strike agreements, in a way that compellingly demonstrates Putnam's premise concerning the relationship between domestic political pressure and foreign policy being a zero-sum game. This increased pressure came from a somewhat unexpected direction, though, since Sarid was a member of the government, as Liel explained. Specifically, Sarid's promise to the Armenians that they would include Franz Werfel in school textbooks should be regarded as the first shift in the dynamics between Israel's domestic and diplomatic arenas with respect to a possible Knesset resolution on the 1915 Armenian genocide. After the dust of Sarid's speech had begun to settle, however, the agenda he had proposed was not in fact integrated into history textbooks and the curriculum has never actually been settled, mainly due to pedagogical bureaucracy at the Israeli Ministry of Education and ideological disputes regarding the singularity of the Holocaust.[56] The topic was returned to the remit of the Foreign Affairs and Defence Committee and remained relatively low profile for a number of years. Sarid's intervention, therefore, should be seen as an indication of the *potential* for the domestic dynamics to bring about change regarding recognition of the genocide but not yet a sign of that change itself.

6. FROM THE MILLENNIUM ONWARDS: THIRD PERIOD (2001–2016)

After a silence of about a decade, however, two significant changes occurred in the Middle Eastern environment and the question of a Knesset resolution on the 1915 Armenian genocide. The first was the Israeli raid on the Gaza Freedom flotilla. The *Mavi Marmara* was a Turkish vessel that was boarded by the IDF in 2010. Turkish activists on the boat violently resisted the IDF, and

---

55 Ibid.

56 Auron (2003), 197.

nine Turks were killed. This raid caused a severe rupture between Israel and Turkey, and diplomatic relations between them sunk to their worst point in the two countries' history. The second issue was Israel's increasingly warm relations with Azerbaijan, a new player in the oil-rich Caspian basin that was embroiled in an ongoing dispute with Armenia over the province of Nagorno-Karabakh. These two regional developments arguably changed the status of the Armenian genocide resolution in the Knesset.

6.1. EDUCATION COMMITTEE, DECEMBER 2011

With respect to the *Mavi Marmara* crisis, discussions in December 2011 revolved around including the Armenian genocide in the history curricula and textbooks in Israel, as they had in in 2000 with Sarid's speech (see previous section), and pressure increased on the government to recognise the genocide because of the current crisis with Turkey. Clearly, although relations with Turkey in 2000 had been good, Israel had wanted to maintain relations and not upset the Turks with the genocidal label. However, from 2003 onwards, relations had deteriorated to a great extent, pushed farther by growing anti-Israeli sentiments in Turkey promoted by Recep Tayyip Erdoğan.[57] For some in Israel, the time was right to "punish" Turkey by recognising the Armenian genocide. In his oral account, Liel further explains this rationale in terms of the Knesset committees involved. The government wanted to return the discussion [under censorship regulations] to the Foreign Affairs and Defence Committee. The "groomsmen of the resolution" [such as PMs Zehava Galon and Aria Eldad] supported the Education Committee because of the *Mavi Marmara* incident.[58]

In an oral account, Efraim Sneh, a former PM and member of the Israeli Labour Party in the Knesset and one of the initiators of Israel's relation-building with Azerbaijan, attempted to explain the motivation of Knesset members to include the Armenian issue in the agenda:

> Excluding one or two Knesset members, such as Haim Auron, who brought up the Armenian genocide for discussion, Knesset members are politicians after all and [the issue of] historic justice is just not in their veins. They are only [interested in] producing headlines. Putting forward the controversial Armenian issue for a parliamentary debate clearly generated headlines for those Knesset members.[59]

---

57 Erdoğan has repeatedly taken a pro-Palestinian and anti-Israeli stance in the Israeli-Palestinian conflict.

58 Interview with Liel, 3 September 2015.

59 Oral Interview with E. Sneh, 9 September, 2015, Herzlia, Israel.

These two accounts by Liel and Sneh outline how Israel's opposition parties re-evaluated their ability to pressure the government domestically to recognise the genocide after the *Mavi Marmara* crisis of 2010. The crisis was seen by some Israeli politicians and parties as a turning point in Israeli–Turkish relations, a crisis that was significant enough to alter the domestic consensus with respect to recognising the Armenian genocide. The combination of the anti-Israeli and pro-Palestinian stance taken by the Turkish President, Recep Tayyip Erdoğan, Israel's peace agreement with Egypt and Jordan, and the rise of new regional actors such as Azerbaijan, together devalued the image of Turkey as a regional power in the eyes of Israeli politicians and the Israeli government.

In an oral interview, Aria Eldad, former PM and Chairman of the right wing *HaIhud HaLeumi* party, agrees with Sneh's assessment:

> Although I am confident that my own personal position in this issue does not reflect my voters' stand or even that of some of my party members who think that Armenians are not too sympathetic towards Israel, the Armenian genocide is an important issue that needs clarification.[60]

Elaborating with a comparative perspective, Eldad further notes

> [G]enocide was perpetrated in Cambodia, Rwanda and Darfur. Israel recognised all of them. There was also the 1915 genocide, and it is no different from any of the others mentioned. The Jews have the Shoah that is in a distinguished category.[61]

PM Zehava Galon, along with Eldad, initiated the Armenian genocide resolution in the 2011 Knesset and further clarified some of Eldad's arguments and offered insights into the dynamics of the Knesset debate. Although usually we see right-wing Israeli Knesset members making use of the uniqueness of the Holocaust in order to present Jews as the ultimate victims, in this case even right-wingers such as Aria Eldad, Ruvi Rivlin, Ze'ev Elkin and Benny Begin were initiators of the resolution. From their point of view, the Jewish "never again" lesson should apply to the Armenians.[62]

With respect to Putnam's premise concerning the relationship between domestic political pressure and foreign policy, formatted as a zero-sum game, this brief discussion outlining Israeli PMs' accounts about a renewed opportunity to pass a Armenian genocide resolution demonstrates how increasing domestic pressure could drive the government towards supporting, or at least acceding to, such a resolution. Particularly important here is Liel's account of the change of committees that occurred in the context of that

60 Oral Interview with A. Eldad, 7 July 2013, Jerusalem, Israel.
61 Ibid.
62 Interview, Galon, 1 February, 2016.

domestic pressure, evidence that the top levels of government were now less concerned about offending Turkey and prepared to let the domestic momentum take its course.

6.2. DOMESTIC PRESSURE? THE ARMENIAN LOBBY AND ISRAELI ACADEMIA

The debate in the Education Committee on 26 December 2011 demonstrates that nothing had actually much changed with respect to an Israeli acknowledgement of the 1915 genocide. Knesset members from across the whole Israeli political landscape, as well as Israeli academics like Yehuda Bauer and Israel Charny, attended these discussions. Furthermore, some elite members of the local Armenian community were also present, such as the Armenian Archbishop, Aris Shirvanian; Tzolag Momjian; the Armenian consul in Israel, George Hintlian; and the Armenian historian and activist, Georgette Avakian. Among these various participants, this brief section highlights, in particular, accounts of Avakian, Bauer and of Irit Lilian, the Israeli MFA representative at the meeting.

When the Education Committee chairman, Alex Miller, granted Avakian the right to speak, the latter took the opportunity to criticise the official Israeli stance on the Armenian genocide:

> If Israel had acknowledged the 1915 genocide during a period of good relations with Ankara, the alliance would have survived; Ankara would have respected this position, and the Armenian genocide would have stopped being the elephant in the room.[63]

Avakian's words demonstrate the somewhat naive approach taken by the Armenian–Israeli lobby towards Israel's policy on the 1915 genocide. Avakian may have been attempting to solicit sympathy from the members of the Education Committee by putting forward a reasonable argument, but, clearly, as the previous section featuring Sarid's speech illustrated, even during a period of good Israeli–Turkish relations a possible acknowledgment of the Armenian genocide by Jerusalem was not something Turkey would simply respect or accept. After Avakian's account, it was Irit Lilian from the Israeli MFA who countered:

> While we all agree that this discussion should focus on ethical decisions, the moral dimension has become a political dispute … again, MFA will not go into details

---

[63] Protocol 520 of the Education, Culture and Sport Committee. The Israeli 18th Knesset, 26 December 2011. Also available at: www.knesset.gov.il/protocols/data/rtf/chinuch/2011-12-26-02.rtf, 9.

> because this discussion in the Education Committee is taking place in public, by contrast to the closed sessions at the Foreign Affairs and Defence Committee. The request to address the Armenian issue as a discrete factor separate from our relationship with Ankara is clearly highly problematic because it is not about what Israel wants, but about the possible Turkish reaction as a result of acknowledgment of the Armenian genocide by Israel.[64]

Lilian's words clarify the degree to which the relationship with Ankara was as problematic in 2011 as it had been for most of the 1980s, meaning that allowing domestic pressure to emerge might critically risk any chances of normalising relations with Turkey in the future. In what follows, Yehuda Bauer received the right to speak:

> I advise the committee to approach the Ministry of Education to warmly recommend that the 1915 genocide be taught across the Israeli schools including universities. Moreover, I want to propose that on 24 April, the Knesset should pass the resolution to recognise of the Armenian genocide.[65]

Turning to the domestic pressure analysis, Avakian's and Bauer's words, on the one hand, clearly illustrate that there was increasing pressure from the civil and academic spheres to acknowledge the Armenian genocide in order to benefit Israeli domestic interest groups. By contrast, Lilian's words represent the MFA's position on why it should not be recognised. Even though Lilian accepts that, morally speaking, what happened in 1915 should not be ignored, she maintains that it is important for Israel's international interests to stay neutral, as it has done in the preceding decades.

6.3. COUNTER PRESSURE: THE AZERBAIJAN DIMENSION

As a short foreword to this section on the Azerbaijan dimension, the significance of the violent armed conflict in the Nagorno-Karabakh region of Azerbaijan, as it played out in the Israeli context, should be underlined. The disintegration of the Soviet Union at the end of the Cold War greatly impacted this region, populated by an Armenian majority and an Azeri minority, and in time it descended into an ethnic war in the early 1990s. According to Edmund Herzig's research, 200,000 Armenians fled Azerbaijan to Nagorno-Karabakh and Armenia, while 185,000 Azeris from Armenia and 45,000 Azeris from Nagorno-Karabakh sought refuge in Azerbaijan, with each group making accusations of ethnic cleansing against the other.[66]

---

[64] Protocol 520, at 14–15.

[65] Ibid, at 16–17.

[66] Harzig (1999), 66.

Israeli involvement in Nagorno-Karabakh can be assessed in two discrete dimensions. Firstly, Israel was the only state to conduct arms trading with Azerbaijan. From 2012 until 2015 an estimated US$4 billion in arms were sold to the Azeris.[67] Secondly, the Azerbaijan–Israel International Association (*AzIz*) commenced its activities around the same time, financed by the Azerbaijan government and representing the country's national interests in Israel.[68] According to Arye Gut, executive member of *AzIz*, the 20,000 Jewish residents of Azerbaijan as of 2013, benefited from a great deal of religious freedom and complete autonomy.[69] Galia Lindenstrauss's work assesses that Azerbaijan's relations with the Israeli–Azerbaijan lobby are generally driven by a narrative "that there has never been any anti-Semitism in Azerbaijan."[70]

Evidence of counter-pressure by the Azerbaijani lobby can be found in the 2011 failure to pass an Armenian genocide resolution in the Knesset. One of the invited guests mentioned above who attended this public debate was the *AzIz's* representative, Arye Gut. His words underline the main features of Israel–Turkish–Azerbaijan relations:

> Firstly, if the Israeli parliament decides to accept the 1915 genocide resolution, it will further harm and thereafter disconnect Israel's relationship with Turkey. Indeed, I am aware that some individuals would argue that the Israeli-Turkish relations have been deteriorating. I acknowledge that fact. … do not forget the Ottoman Sultan saved the Spanish Jews who fled from Spain in 1492; and do not forget that during Nazi occupation, while Jews in Europe went through the Shoah, Turkey protected its Jewish community … Turkey is a dominant voice in the Arab and Muslim world these days and Israel still has a chance for political dialogue. In parallel to our state with Turkey, if we put forward the 1915 genocide resolution, we will clearly harm our relations with Azerbaijan.[71]

Gut turned to highlight Israel's financial affairs in Azerbaijan and some Jewish concerns: "these days Azerbaijan is a regional force in the South Caucasus, a secular Muslim nation that shares a border with Iran. For many years Israel has been enjoying excellent relations with Azerbaijan."[72]

The arms trade and a shared concern over a nuclear Iran were obviously important features of this ever-closer relationship between Jerusalem and Baku. Furthermore, Israel, as in cases of other Jewish communities in the Muslim world, has sought to protect the interests of the Azerbaijan

---

67 Murinson (2014), 22–24 and Opall-Rome (2014). For further debate on this see Goksa (2015); Lindenstrauss (2015).

68 Murinson (2014), 15–16.

69 Gut (2013).

70 Lindenstrauss (2015), 73.

71 Protocol 520, 17.

72 Ibid.

Jewish community. Therefore, one can see why in light of the substantial financial and Jewish interests in Azerbaijan, the Israeli government chose not to reinforce the Armenian version of the violent conflict in Nagorno-Karabakh or their account of the 1915 genocide.

6.4. ACKNOWLEDGEMENT?

After a 90 minute discussion, Miller, the committee chairman, decided to end the debate, saying:

> We have generally discussed the "tragedy" of the Armenians. Hopefully, at the next meeting, we will be able to discuss the concerns raised today in more depth ... we need to end the meeting. We shall have another meeting sometime in the future. Thank you all very much.[73]

Arguably, Miller's decision to end the debate was premeditated, especially in light of the oral history account of the anonymous Israeli MFA official quoted above,[74] which clearly indicates the degree to which these discussions were being monitored by successive Israeli governments. As Zhava Galon notes in an oral interview, Miller is a member of the *Israel Beiteno* party, which in 2011 was an integral coalition member. Furthermore, the party Chairman Avigdor Lieberman, Israel's Foreign Minister between 2009 and 2015, had carefully guided Miller on how to structure the discussion and monitor it, making sure that it terminated in a dead-end.[75] Subsequently, on 18 February 2016, a further accusation was directed at Lieberman by Galon claiming that *Israel Beiteno* party members were operating a secret plot to include Azerbaijan's national oil and gas company in an Israeli gas exploration project in the Mediterranean Sea, with the Azeri company set to receive five per cent of the contract.[76] Whether Galon's accusations were true or not, arguably Lieberman and his party members also had another hidden motivation to ensure that the Knesset discussion was curtailed in the way that Miller managed.

A substantial step towards acknowledging the 1915 genocide in the Knesset took place on 1 August 2016, when the Education Committee resumed its debate on the 1915 genocide resolution. One should emphasise, however, that this discussion resulted in a somewhat surprising declaration. PM and the chairman of the Committee, Ya'acov Margi (*Shas* party), stated at the end of this discussion:

---

73 Ibid, 19.

74 See n. 46 above.

75 Interview with Galon, 1 February, 2016.

76 Available at: www.haaretz.co.il/news/politi/1.2855304 [in Hebrew].

> [A]s the state of the Jewish people, morally, we should have acknowledged the 1915 genocide a long time ago. I am saying it now and will say it in the future; some people [Turkey] even during 2016, are not ashamed to try to rewrite history.[77]

After one hour of discussion, Margi declared,

> Ladies and gentlemen, I would like to conclude this discussion. The Committee wishes to thank the guests that attended this meeting. Unfortunately, the Knesset did not acknowledge the 1915 genocide in 2016 either. Until then, if the Knesset does not acknowledge the genocide, then the Education Committee is declaring that Israel recognises the 1915 genocide.[78]

Even though this was a private declaration made by Margi, it was clearly made in order to pressure the Knesset chairman and the government into acknowledging the Armenian genocide. Arguably, however, this shift might be explained in the future by analysis of domestic pressure, according to which an Armenian genocide resolution in the Knesset Education Committee and thereby in the full house of the Knesset would impact on Israel's foreign policy and the alliance with Turkey and Azerbaijan. To recap, the contested memories of the 1915 genocide, and the absence of restorative justice between Armenians and Turks, as well as between Armenians and Azerbaijanis, have affected international relations, while the latter's absence has continued to fuel the very contestation of the genocide narrative. The outcome is that perpetrators' narratives have been reinforced by Israel in the diplomatic and domestic political arenas, while the Armenian narrative is left behind.

7. CONCLUSION: THE TWO-LEVEL GAME AND THE DIPLOMACY OF CLOSURE

To conclude, Putnam's two-level game theory helps to shed new light on Israel's Armenian genocide resolution in contemporary history. This chapter has examined the degree to which the lack of a shared understanding of the events of 1915 between Turks and Armenians, and the associated absence of a shared basis for "restorative justice" for the Armenians, has affected the geopolitics of memory. As this chapter has shown – especially during the 1980s but also

---

77 Protocol 260 of the Education, Culture and Sport Committee. The Israeli 18th Knesset, 1 August 2016. Also available at: www.oknesset.org/meetings/2/0/2006553.html.

78 Ibid.

throughout the 1990s and 2000s – Israel took advantage of the consequences of a lack of conventional restorative justice for the Armenian genocide, such as Armenian terrorism and pressure on Turkey in international forums, as diplomatic leverage to restore Israeli–Turkish relations. Exploring the case study of Israel, the chapter argued that for more than three decades (1980–2010) Israel chose to reinforce the Turkish narrative for its own diplomatic ends. It demonstrates that Israeli policy on the Armenian genocide has only been possible in practice due to a lack of domestic pressure, more specifically a lack of significant parliamentary pressure by opposition parties on successive Israeli governments to recognise the genocide. The failure of the Israeli parliament to recognise the Armenian genocide has made it easier for successive Israeli governments to support the Turkish position, thus making Israel's economic, military and arms deals with Turkey and, in recent years, with Azerbaijan much easier.

Testing Putnam's premise, the most tangible developments in the context of Israel's domestic pressure occurred between the years 2000–2016: (1) 24 April 2000 – Yossi Sarid's speech; (2) the 2010 *Mavi Marmara* incident, which motivated Israel's political spectrum to join the academic and Armenian lobbyists and domestically push for Armenian genocide resolution; and thereby (3), the recognition provided by Ya'acov Margi (*Shas* party) on 1 August 2016. The Sarid and Margi initiatives are definitely milestones in the domestic campaign towards recognising the genocide. Following this line of argument, if such extensive domestic pressure continues to grow rapidly in the future, arguably there is a better chance that the 1915 genocide will eventually be recognised by the Israeli parliament. Nevertheless, the domestic campaign clearly is facing some serious challenges, as noted in the first-hand accounts of Galon, Sneh and Liel.

Finally, this historical yet topical analysis of the symbiotic relations between domestic politics and diplomacy regarding the 1915 genocide supplements an understanding of the question of "restorative justice" between Turks and the Armenians regarding the 1915 genocide. By showing how this question has been leveraging Israeli–Turkish and Israeli-Azerbaijan relations, this chapter has argued that restorative justice is not just a matter of domestic politics but that it may be also embedded in an international context of ever-changing alliances and disputes between nation states. It should offer some further stimulating research directions, not just in respect of Israel, but also in the wider context of the question of "restorative justice" and the Armenian genocide, namely, how other Turkish allies such as France and the United States, who are also home to a number of well-established Armenian communities, addressed the contested memories of the Armenian genocide and balanced their domestic debates on genocide recognition with their diplomatic relations with Turkey.

References

Auron, Y. (2003) *The Banality of Denial: Israel and the Armenian Genocide* New Brunswick N.J.: Transaction Publishers, 185–199.

Aykan, M.B. (1993) "The Palestinian Question in Turkish Foreign Policy from the 1950s to the 1990s" in *International Journal of Middle East Studies*, **25**, no. 1, 91–110.

Azarya, V. (1984) *The Armenian Quarter of Jerusalem*. Berkeley C.A.: University of California Press.

Bali, R. (2012) *Model Citizens of State: The Jews of Turkey during the Multi-Party Period*. Madison W.I.: Dickinson University Press.

Bauer, Y. (2001) *Rethinking the Holocaust*. New Haven C.T.: Yale University Press.

Ben Aharon, E. (2015) "A Unique Denial: Israel's Foreign Policy and the Armenian Genocide" in *British Journal of Middle Eastern Studies* **42**, no. 4, 638–654.

—— (2020a) "Doing Oral History with the Israeli Elite and the Question of Methodology in International Relations Research" in *Oral History Review, 47:1, 3–25.*

(2020b) Author Interview: "Eldad Ben Aharon on the Use of Oral History in the Study of International Relations", *American Oral History Association*, 14 February 2020.

—— (2019a) "Superpower by Invitation: late Cold War Diplomacy and Leveraging Armenian Terrorism as a Means to Rapprochement in Israeli–Turkish Relations (1980–1987)" in *Cold War History* **19**, no. 2, 275–293.

—— (2019b) *The Geopolitics of Genocide in the Middle East and the Second Cold War: Israeli-Turkish-American Relations and the Contested Memories of the Armenian Genocide (1978–1988)*. Royal Holloway, University of London. (Ph.D. diss).

—— (2019c) "Recognition of the Armenian Genocide Means Acknowledgement of the Universal Lesson of the Holocaust", *Mekomit* (1 May), [in Hebrew].

Bloxham, D. (2001) *Genocide on Trial War Crimes Trials and the Formation of Holocaust History and Memory*. Oxford: Oxford University Press.

—— (2005) *The Great Game of Genocide: Imperialism, Nationalism, and the Destruction of the Ottoman Armenians*. Oxford: Oxford University Press.

Bloxham, D. and Gocek, F.M. (2008) "The Armenian Genocide" in D. Stone (ed), *The Historiography of Genocide*. New York: Palgrave Macmillan.

Cholawsky, S. (1973) *City and Forest under Siege*. Tel-Aviv, Jerusalem.

Cohen, B. (2015) "Dr Meir (Mark) Dworzecki: the Historical Mission of a Survivor Historian" in *Holocaust Studies* **21**, no. 1–2, 24–37.

Dadrian, V.N. (1977) "Nationalism in Soviet Armenia A Case Study of Ethnocentrism" in G.W. Simmonds (ed.), *Nationalism in the USSR and Eastern Europe in the Era of Brezhnev and Kosygin*. Detroit M.I.: University of Detroit Press.

Dixon, J.M. (2010) "Defending the Nation? Maintaining Turkey's Narrative of the Armenian Genocide" in *South European Society and Politics,* **15**, no. 3, 467–485.

Ekmekcioglu, L. (2016) *Surviving the New Turkey: Armenians in Post-Ottoman Istanbul*. Stanford C.A.: Stanford University Press.

Engel, D. (2010) *Historians of the Jews and the Holocaust*. Stanford: Stanford University Press.

Gocek, F.M. (2011) "Reading Genocide: Turkish Historiography on 1915" in R. Suny et al. (eds.), *A Question of Genocide Armenians and Turks at the End of the Ottoman Empire*. Oxford: Oxford University Press.

—— (2015) *Denial of Violence: Ottoman Past, Turkish Present, and Collective Violence against the Armenians 1789–2009*. New York: Oxford University Press.

Goksal, O. (2015) "Beyond Countering Iran: A Political Economy of Azerbaijan–Israel Relations" in *British Journal of Middle Eastern Studies*, **42**, no. 4: 655–675.

Goldberg, A. (2012) "'The 'Jewish Narrative' in the Yad Vashem Global Holocaust Museum" in *Journal of Genocide Research* **14**, no. 2, 87–213.

Gurpina, D. (2016) "The Manufacturing of Denial: The Making of the Turkish 'Official Thesis' on the Armenian Genocide Between 1974 and 1990" in *Journal of Balkan and Near Eastern Studies* **18**, no. 3, 217–240.

Gurun, K. (1985) *The Armenian File: The Myth of Innocence Exposed*. London: Rustem.

Gut, A. (2013) "There Has Never Been Anti-Semitism in Azerbaijan" in *News-Az*, 12 November 2013. Available at: www.news.az/articles/commentary/84165.

Gutman, I. (1976) *Warsaw: Ghetto Uprising* Jerusalem, Tel-Aviv: Lochamei Ha'ghettaot.

Harzig, E. (1999) *The New Caucasus: Armenia, Azerbaijan and Georgia*. Royal Institute for International Affairs.

Hoffman, B. (2006) *Inside Terrorism* New York: Columbia University Press.

Hyland, F.P. (1991) *Armenian Terrorism: The Past, the Present, the Prospects* Boulder C.O.: Westview Press.

Kurz, A. and Merari, A. (1985) *ASALA: Irrational Terror or Political Tool*. Boulder C.O.: Westview.

Liel, A. (2001) *Turkey in the Middle East: Oil, Islam and Politics*. Boulder C.O.: Lynne Rienner Publishers.

Lindenstrauss, G. (2015) "Israel-Azerbaijan: Despite the Constraints, A Special Relationship" in *Strategic Assessment*, **17**, no. 4: 69–79.

Marrus, M.R. (1998) "The Holocaust at Nuremberg" in *Yad Vashem Studies*, **26**, 5–41.

Milne, D. (2011) "The 1968 Paris Peace Negotiations: A Two-Level Game?", *Review of International Studies*, **37**, no. 2, 577–599.

Mo, J. (1994), "The Logic of Two-Level Games with Endogenous Domestic Coalitions." *Journal of Conflict Resolution*, **38**, no. 3, at 402–422.

Murinson, A. (2014) *The Ties Between Israel and Azerbaijan*. Bar Ilan University: The Begin-Sadat Center for Strategic Studies, 22–24.

Novick, P. (1999) *The Holocaust in American Life* Boston M.A.: Houghton Mifflin.

Opall-Rome, B. (2014) "Israel Bolsters Strategic Ties with Azerbaijan" in *Defense News*, 10 September 2014.

Panossian, R. (2006) *The Armenians from Kings and Priests to Merchants and Commissars*. New York: Columbia University Press.

Putnam, R. (1988) "Diplomacy and Domestic Politics: The Logic of Two-Level Games" in *International Organization*, **42**, no. 3, 427–460.

Rothberg, M. (2009) *Multidirectional Memory: Remembering the Holocaust in the Age of Decolonization*. Stanford C.A.: Stanford University Press.

Sanjian, A. (2018) "Armenians and the Global Cold War: History, Memory and Legacies", lecture organised by the Programme of Armenian Studies, London, 24 May (in English).

Suny, R. et al. (2011) *A Question of Genocide: Armenians and Turks at the End of the Ottoman Empire*. New York: Oxford University Press.

Teitel, R.G. (2014) *Globalizing Transitional Justice: Contemporary Essays* New York: Oxford University Press.

Totolyan, K. (1992) "Terrorism in Modern Armenian Political Culture" in *Terrorism and Political Violence*, **4**, no. 2, 8–22.

Ungor, U.Ü. (2013) "Creative Destruction: Shaping a High-Modernist City in Interwar Turkey" in *Journal of Urban History* **39**, no. 2, 297–314.

Uras, E. (1988) *The Armenians in History and the Armenian Question.* Istanbul: Documentary Publications.

Walker, C. (1980) *Armenia: The Survival of a Nation.* London: Routledge.

Wilkinson, P. (1983) "Armenian Terrorism" in *The World Today*, **39**, no. 9, 344–350.

Zarifian, J. (2014) "The Armenian-American Lobby and Its Impact on U.S. Foreign Policy" in *Society* **51**, no. 5, 503–512.

Zartel, I. (2005) *Israel's Holocaust and the Politics of Nationhood.* Cambridge: Cambridge University Press.

INDEX

www.ingramcontent.com/pod-product-compliance
Ingram Content Group UK Ltd.
Pitfield, Milton Keynes, MK11 3LW, UK
UKHW051043120926
8556IPUK00031B/864

9 781780 689081